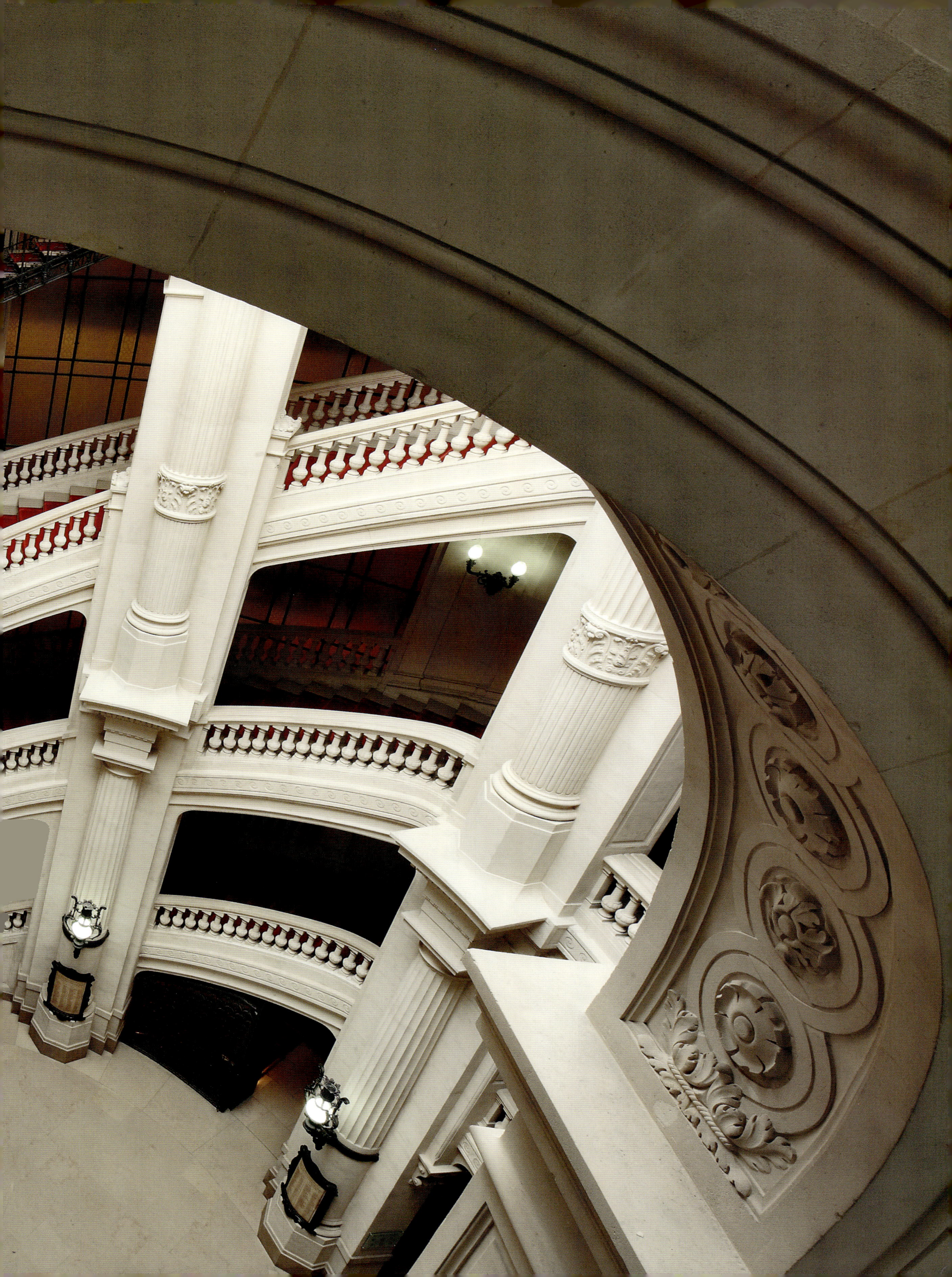

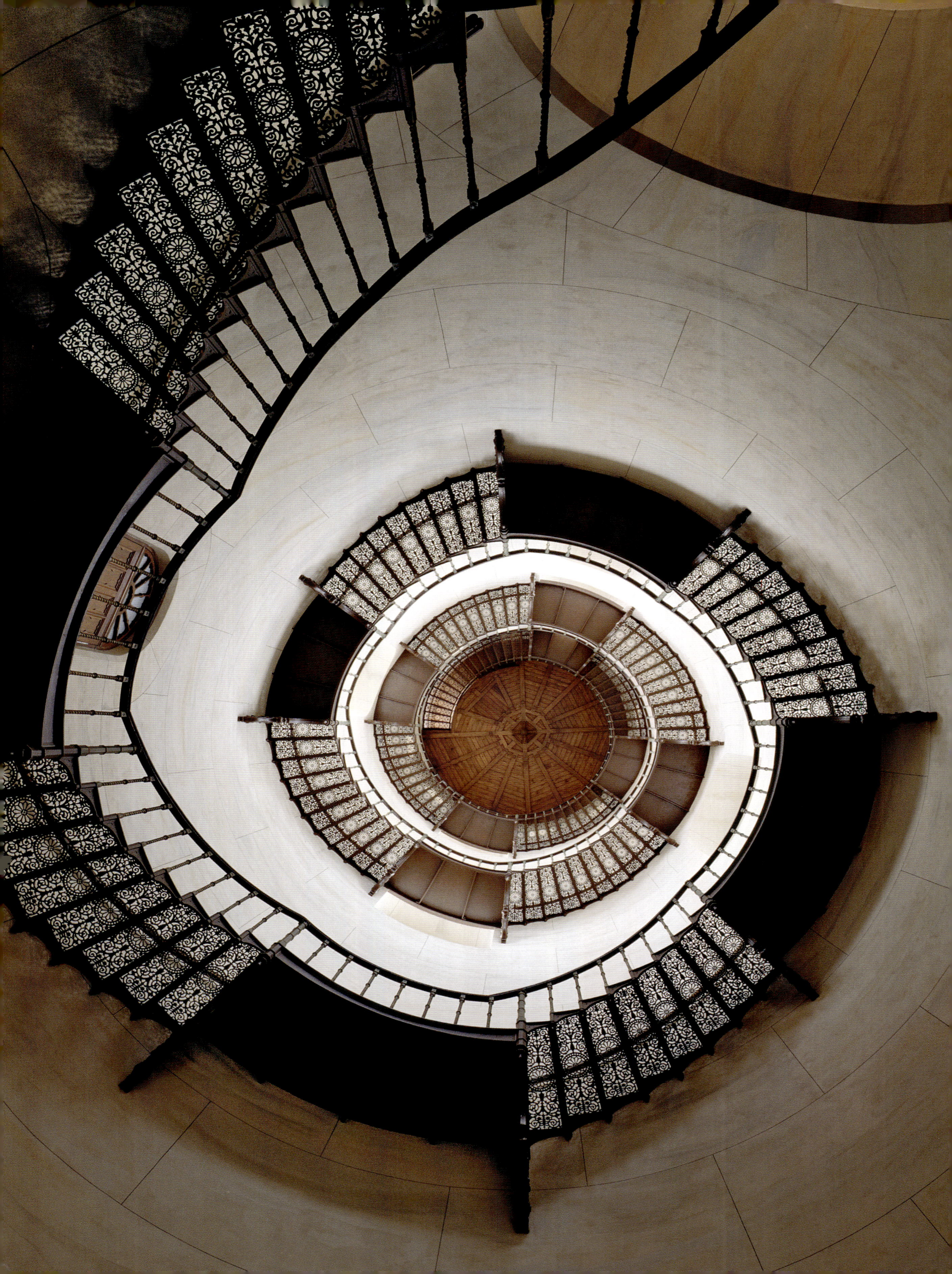

Oscar Tusquets Blanca
Martine Diot
Adelaïde de Savray
Jérôme Coignard
Jean Dethier

of Ascent

The Architecture

The Staircase

With 324 illustrations, 288 in colour

Thames & Hudson

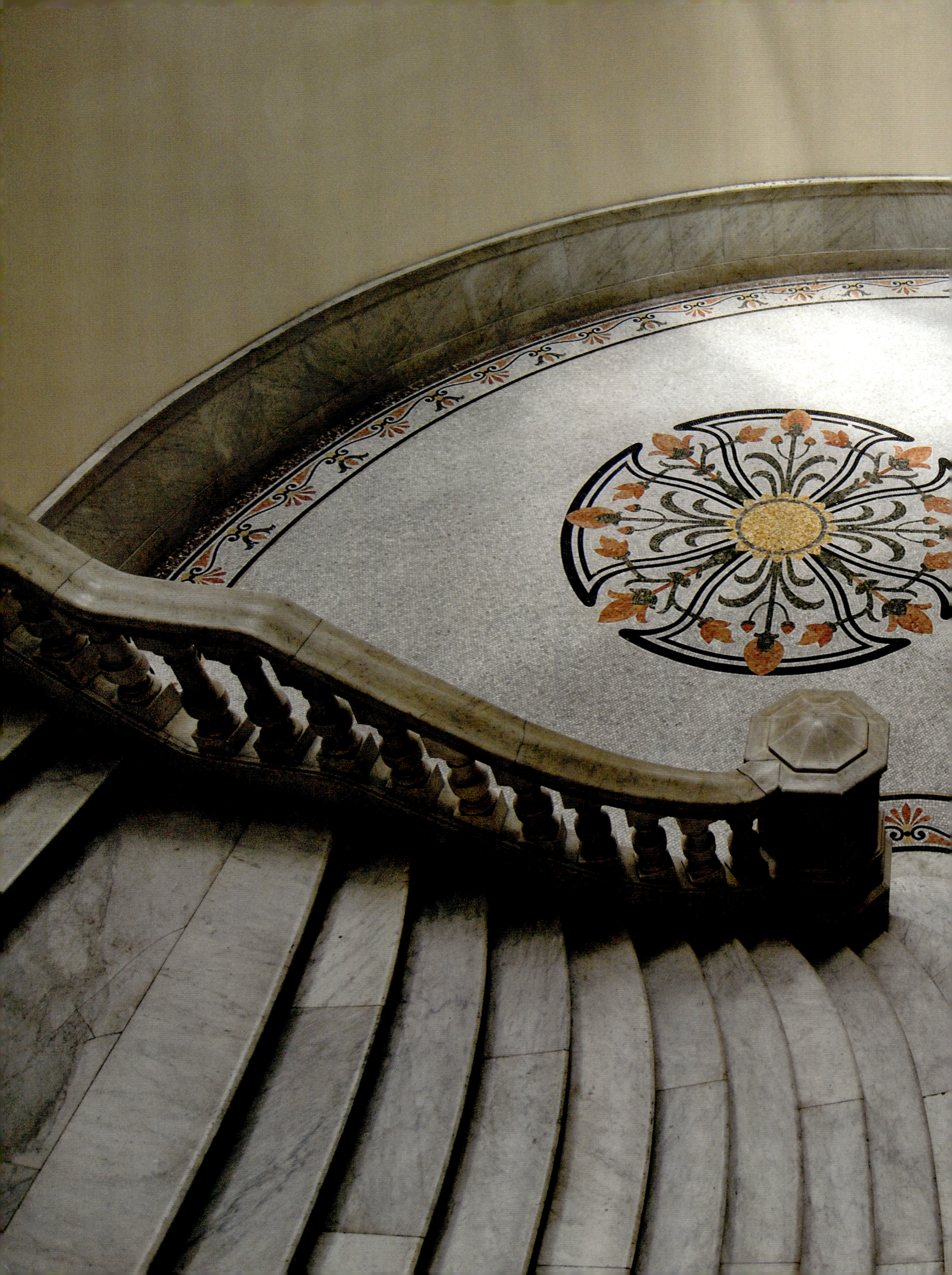

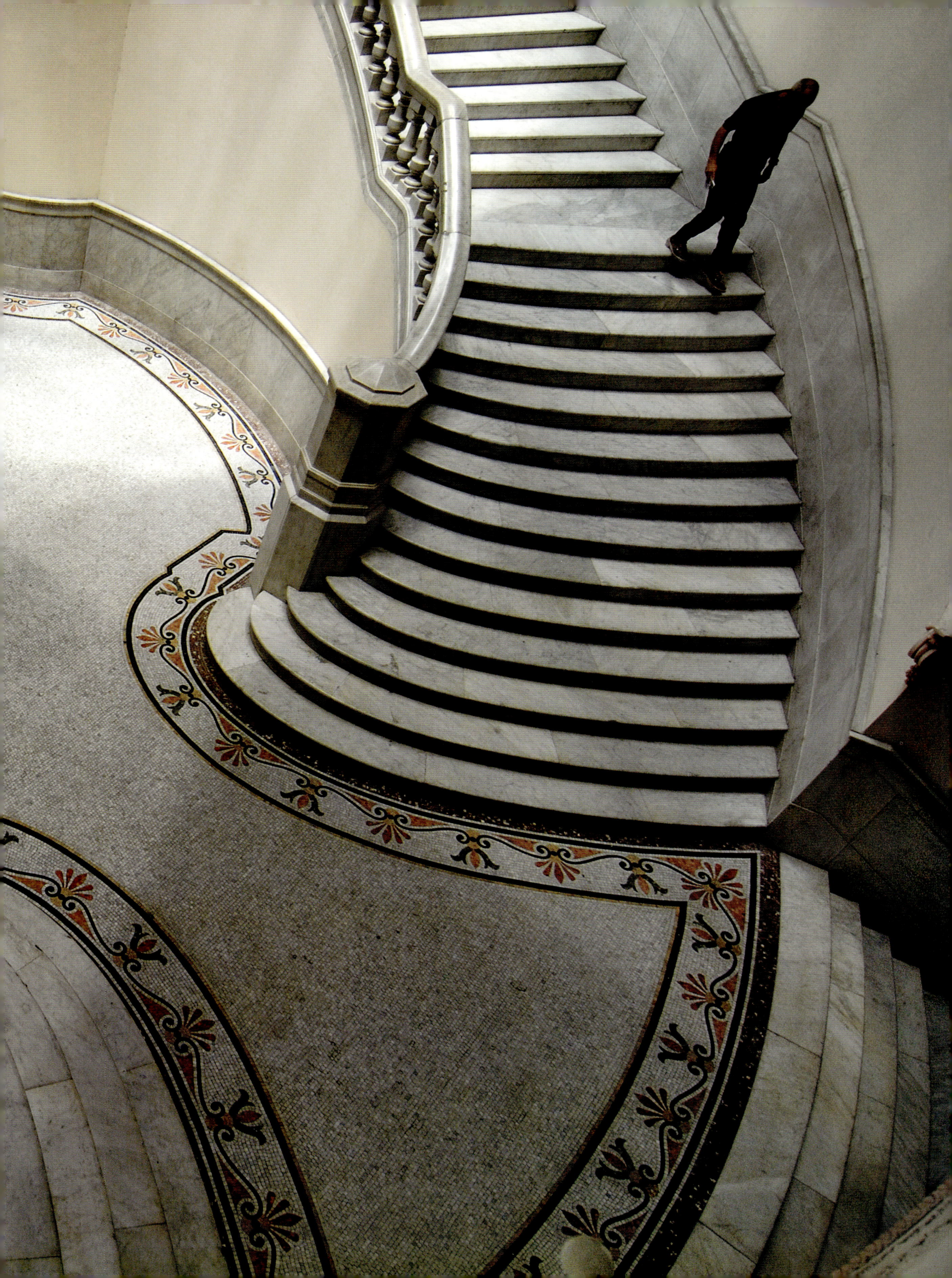

Conceived and produced by Marc Walter and Sabine Arqué

Translated from the French *L'escalier* by Barbara Mellor

First published in the United Kingdom in 2013 by
Thames & Hudson Ltd, 181A High Holborn,
London WC1V 7QX

Original edition © 2012 Éditio-Éditions Citadelles & Mazenod
This edition © 2013 Thames & Hudson Ltd, London

All Rights Reserved. No part of this publication may be
reproduced or transmitted in any form or by any means,
electronic or mechanical, including photocopy, recording or
any other information storage and retrieval system, without
prior permission in writing from the publisher.

British Library Cataloguing-in-Publication Data
A catalogue record for this book is available from
the British Library

ISBN: 978-0-500-51709-3

Printed and bound in China

To find out about all our publications, please visit
www.thamesandhudson.com. There you can subscribe
to our e-newsletter, browse or download our current
catalogue, and buy any titles that are in print.

Contents

10   Requiem for the Staircase
      INTRODUCTION   Oscar Tusquets Blanca

38   A Lesson in Architecture
      1100–1600   Martine Diot

78   A Theatre of Power
      1600–1800   Adelaïde de Savray

128   The Apotheosis of Ornament
      1800–1900   Jérôme Coignard

182   From Art Nouveau to the Present Day
      1900–NOW   Jean Dethier

238   Further Reading
239   Picture Credits and Acknowledgments
240   Index

PAGE 1
The staircase of the Opéra at Versailles, made entirely of stone to avoid the risk of fire. It was built between 1763 and 1770 by Ange-Jacques Gabriel.

PAGES 2–3
The grand staircase at the head offices of Crédit Lyonnais, Paris, built by William Bouwens van der Boijen (1876–82).

PAGE 4
A spiral staircase in the central tower of the hunting lodge at Granitz, Germany, by Karl Friedrich Schinkel (1837–46).

PAGE 5
Handrail (detail), Bauhaus School, Dessau, Germany (1925).

PAGES 6–7
The staircase of the Grand Theatre at Havana, Cuba, built in 1838 and refurbished in 1908–14 in a neo-Baroque style.

OPPOSITE
One of a pair of symmetrical staircases in the town hall of Boulogne-Billancourt, Paris, by the architect Tony Garnier (1934).

THIS PAGE
The staircase of the Deutsche Kinemathek in Berlin, by Hans Dieter Schall (2001).

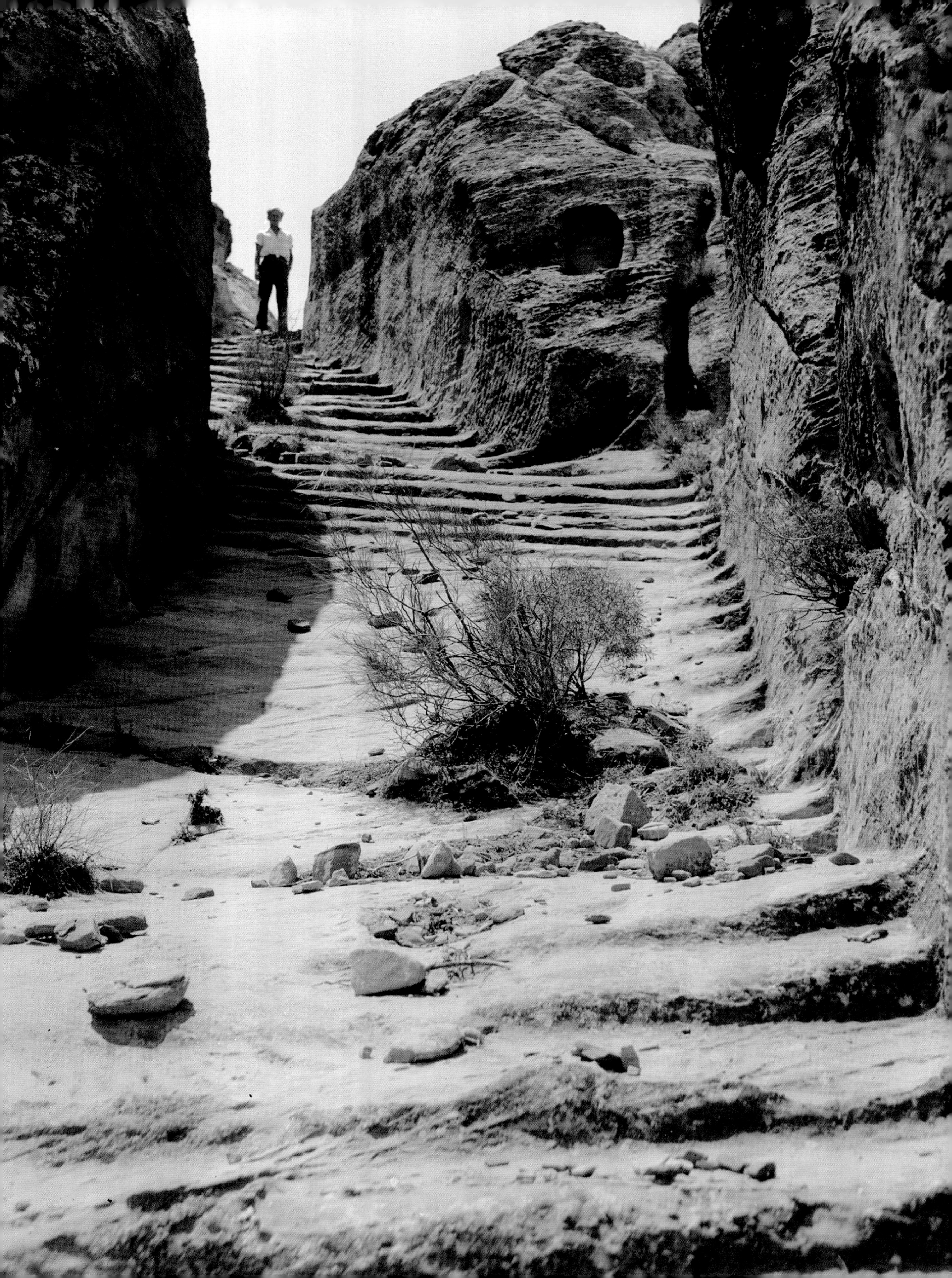

Requiem for the Staircase

That day's lecture by Josep Maria Sostres, the Catalan architect who taught us architecture, was astounding: an utter revelation.

Sostres was very unusual, both as an architect and as an individual. In the first year of our degree course he provided us with a complete survey of the history of art, which he followed in our second year with an equally comprehensive account of the history of architecture. The breadth of learning and professionalism to which he treated us in those two years were equalled only by the unremittingly conventional nature of his approach. Then, towards the end of our second year, he delivered a series of lectures that were slightly less dull, on a subject more to his taste: modern architecture. And one day, to our great amazement, he gave us a lesson that was simply masterly. He started to outline the significance, both for the history of architecture and for humankind, of the discovery and implementation of horizontal planes. He taught us how the use of the horizontal plane was the product of human creativity, since – except for the surface of still water (not easy to walk on outside holy scripture) – such a thing does not exist in nature. He showed how human beings, now that they were able to walk freely without fear of tripping up, could begin to reflect as they walked; this facilitated the development of abstract rational thought, exemplified by the philosophical explorations of the School of Athens. Sostres made us understand that, if the construction of level planes to facilitate horizontal movement had required a degree of creativity, then imagining a succession of horizontal planes on different levels so as to allow movement in three dimensions – or, in other words, the concept of steps – was a cultural and architectural development of fundamental importance. So astonishing was this revelation that, when Sostres had stopped speaking, we broke into spontaneous, thunderous applause.

Sostres was right: steps were an extraordinary invention. A few steps hacked into the ground, on a path that one would otherwise struggle to climb, are indisputably useful. But steps and staircases are not merely functional: in architecture they are also imbued with meaning. That is what makes a book such as this so important. Delighted as I am to write the introduction, readers should be aware that I am neither a theorist nor a historian of art; rather, my contribution is that of a designer intrigued by a subject of universal significance, and of an architect who has so often struggled with, and taken pleasure in, the process of devising staircases.

Designing a staircase is a fascinating business, but it is also a difficult one: first you have to resolve the geometrical conflict between the diagonal of the pitch and the floor, and then you must consider the delicate and complex question of the handrail, turns and landings. You also have to work out how to finish both the upper level and the base – that point where the steps leave the ground and take off,

Steps carved into the rock lead up to a mountain top – a sacred sacrificial site – in the ancient city of Petra, Jordan.

soaring upwards. These are the challenges that have entertained, engaged and often frustrated architects throughout history.

While the pitch of a staircase is a reinterpretation of nature, the staircase itself is pure invention, albeit one found in every culture around the globe. Since the time of the first Egyptian monuments, and even before, it has remained a perfect construction, a universal principle unsurpassed throughout millennia. And, what is more, the staircase is charged with symbolic force, representing power, hierarchy, mysticism (the powerful concept of a staircase leading up to heaven or down to hell exists in virtually every culture) and even eroticism. Generally recognized as a phallic symbol, the staircase makes an ideal setting for erotically charged scenes in film: I particularly remember Claudia Cardinale's lingering descent of the stairs in the 1961 film *The Girl with a Suitcase* (in black and white, just like in a dream).

In my book *Todo es comparable* (*Everything Is Comparable*; 1994), I devoted a chapter to staircases, expressing for the first time my admiration for this architectural feature, and lamenting the fact that it was becoming an endangered species. A few months later, Josep Ramoneda, a former director of the Barcelona Centre of Contemporary Culture, invited me to curate an exhibition on this theme. *Requiem por la escalera* (*Requiem for the Staircase*), which opened in late 2001, brought together original drawings (including Michelangelo's design for the staircase of the Biblioteca Laurenziana, Florence), paintings, sculpture, maquettes, photographs, film projections and real staircases that visitors to the exhibition could walk up and down.

When it came to design the exhibition, I decided to abandon the usual chronological and geographical approaches and opted instead for a structure based around typology. Grouping staircases by genre allowed me to juxtapose examples from different cultures that were far removed from each other not only in time, but also in space. It was startling to discover that a staircase carved from a tree trunk in Mali was virtually indistinguishable from another made in Denmark, or Japan, or Norway; or that steps clinging to a wall in Mexico had virtual twins in Jordan or Switzerland.

OPPOSITE
The initiation well in the gardens of the Quinta da Regaleira, Sintra – an estate bought by the Portuguese-born Brazilian millionaire Antonio Carvalho Monteiro in 1892. Monteiro commissioned the Italian architect Luigi Manini to build him a 'philosophical residence'.

LEFT
Rembrandt's Philosopher in Meditation *(1632); Musée du Louvre, Paris.*

OVERLEAF
Models by Oscar Tusquets Blanca for the exhibition Requiem for the Staircase *at the Barcelona Centre of Contemporary Culture, 2001–2.*

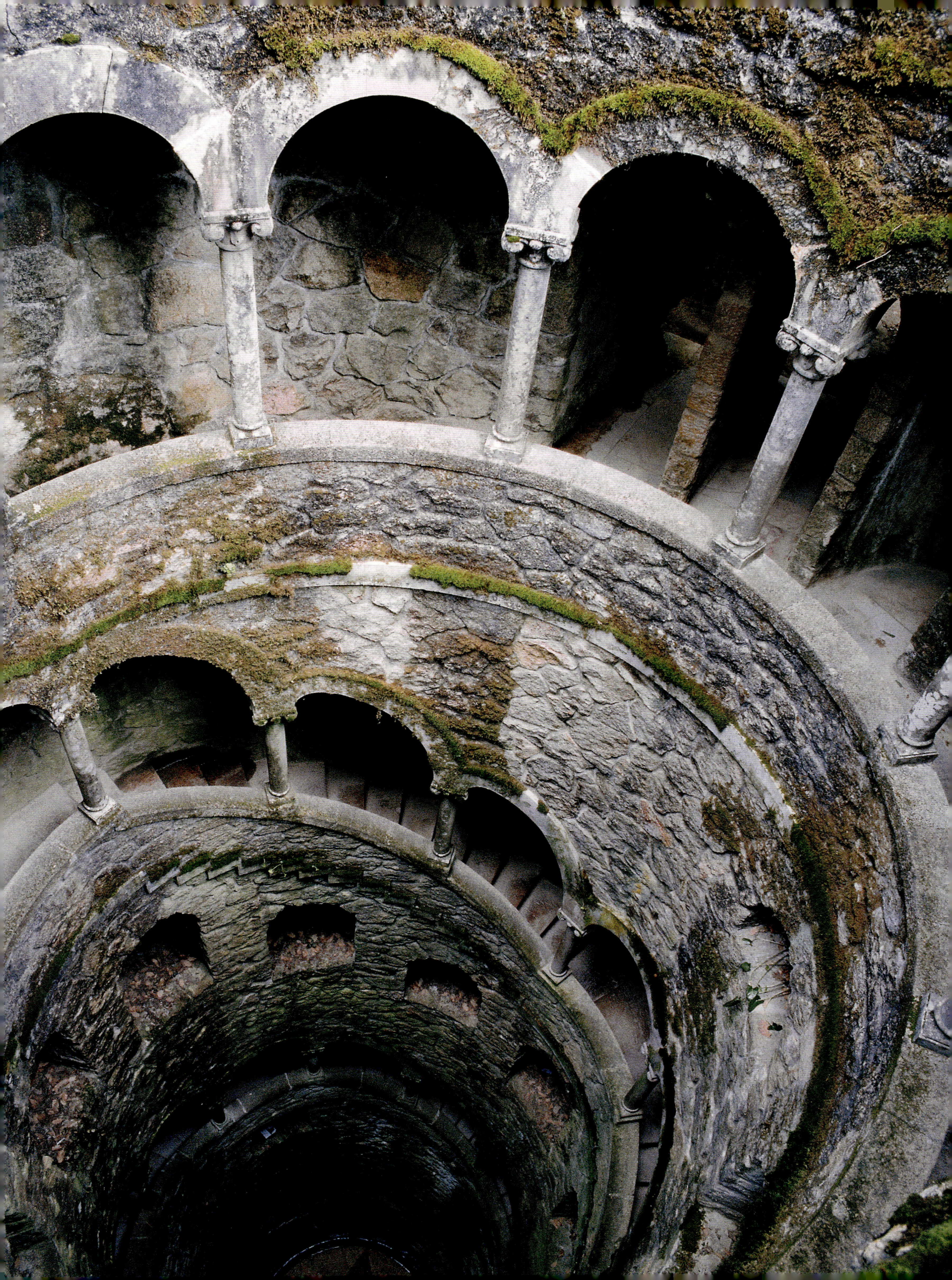

STRAIGHT-FLIGHT STAIR

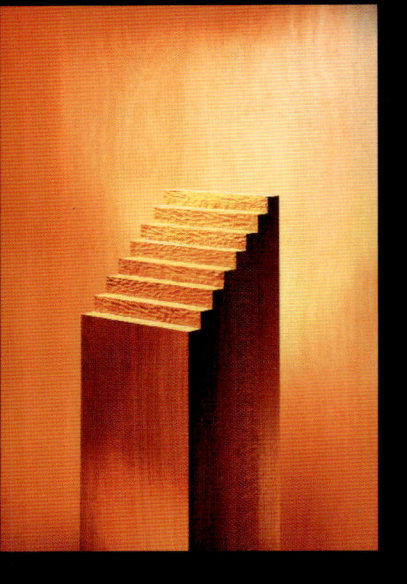

WALL-MOUNTED STAIR

CURVED STAIR

IMPOSSIBLE STAIR

SAMBA STAIR

FLOATING STAIR

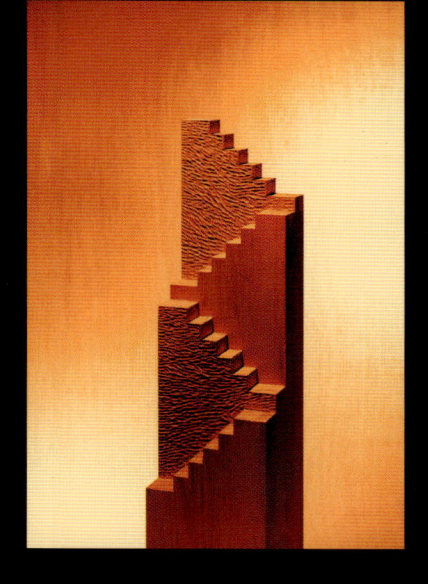

PARALLEL STAIR

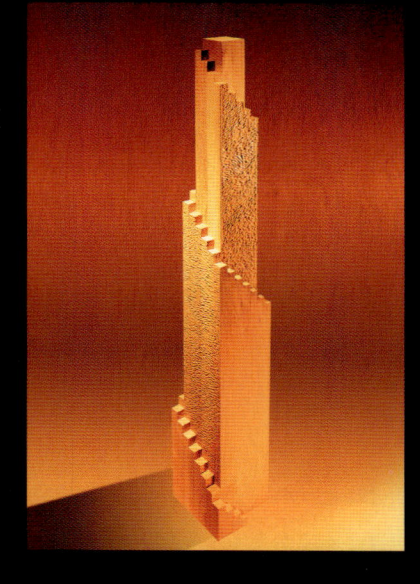

UNPROTECTED STAIR

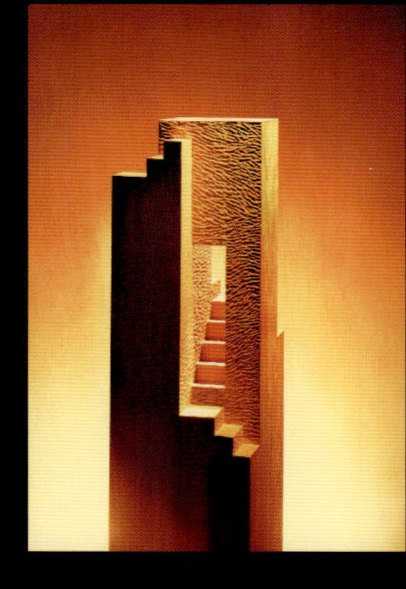

MULTI-BRANCHED STAIR

RANDOM STAIR

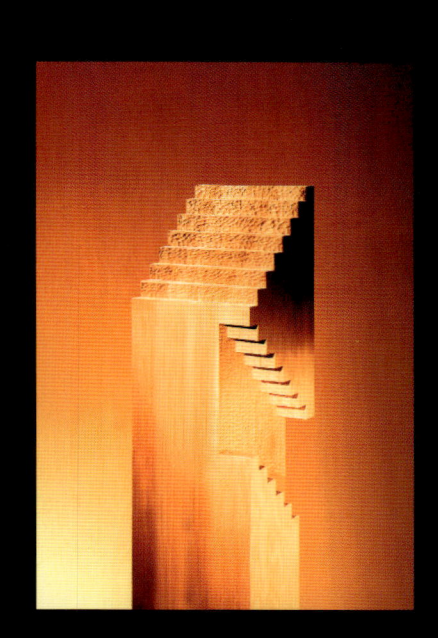

STAIRWAY TO HEAVEN
OR HELL

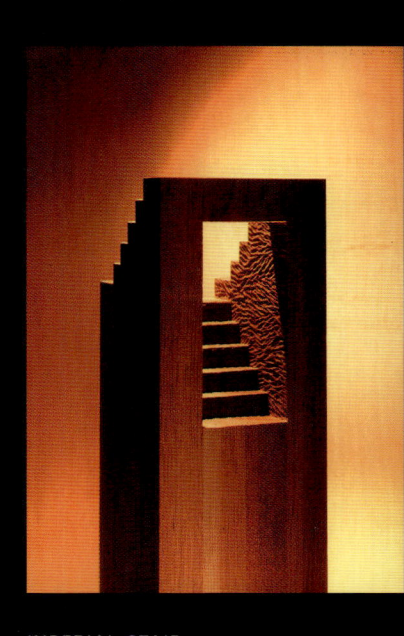

IMPERIAL STAIR

LEFT
Hopi girls photographed by Edward Curtis at Walpi village, Navajo County, Arizona, 1907.

RAMPS, LADDERS AND ESCALATORS There are several close relations to the staircase, such as ramps and gradients, but in no way can they be confused with true staircases, and they do not feature often in this book. There are staggered or stepped ramps or gradients, as in the streets of Perugia, and there are staircases with shallow steps, as in the double helical staircase in the Vatican Museums. Ramps may be used to interesting architectural effect, as demonstrated with conviction by Le Corbusier, Richard Meier and Zaha Hadid. And then there are ladders. From the rope ladders on old sailing ships to library steps, they are intriguing in their design, but since they are scaled using both feet and hands they belong to a different family. Finally, there are mechanical staircases, or escalators. An escalator consists of a series of horizontal planes that transport people up and down without them moving their feet. In appearance they are like staircases, but in function they are closer to lifts. Furthermore, when an escalator breaks down (not a rare occurrence) you are reminded that using one as a classic staircase is tiring in the extreme. There is a formula, $2R+T = 63$ cm, that governs the proportions of steps, in which R is the height of the step, or riser, and T its depth, or tread. It does not, however, apply to escalators. When this relationship is not respected, and above all if one step is different from the others, stairs become a veritable form of torture. Somebody – possibly Borges, thinking of Dante – imagined hell as a Piranesian ruin filled with uneven staircases. For very steep steps in gardens and outside spaces, the formula's total will sometimes exceed 63 cm, or 24¾ inches, but the riser should never be higher than 17 cm, or 6¾ inches.

Below is a series of staircase types, in which examples are grouped by family. Occasionally the logic governing their inclusion in one category or another is a little elastic. In his 1942 essay 'The Analytical Language of John Wilkins', Borges includes a fictitious taxonomy of animals that he claims to have found in an ancient Chinese encyclopedia. It divides beasts into fourteen categories: those that belong to the emperor; those that are embalmed; suckling pigs; mermaids or sirens; stray dogs; those drawn with a very fine camel-hair brush; those that have just broken a flower vase; those that, at a distance, resemble flies – and several other whimsical types. Though it might not be as evocative, I fear my list may be just as arbitrary.

OPPOSITE
The steps of the Toltec–Maya pyramid at Chichén Itzá, Mexico, 9th–12th centuries CE.

THE STRAIGHT-FLIGHT STAIRCASE The ancestor of all staircases, this is the simplest and certainly the most ancient of all. At its smallest, it might consist of three steps and measure a couple of hands in width. At its most monumental, it might lead up to a Roman temple, a great museum or law courts, and it might be lofty in height and consist of several flights of steps. In an artist's imagination it may appear infinite, like the Odessa Steps in Eisenstein's film *Battleship Potemkin* (p. 18) or the steps in Orson Welles's *The Trial*. This is the type of staircase that symbolizes ascent to heaven. It was also down a straight flight of steps that the great stars of the music hall made their majestic descent. The straight flight is to be found on the pyramids of the Maya, in Darius's great meeting hall in Persepolis, in front of the basilica of Santa Maria in Aracoeli, Rome, and at the Villa Malaparte, Capri (p. 19). No one knows for certain who designed this villa, but the owner, the journalist Curzio Malaparte, almost certainly drew inspiration from the steps of the church of the Annunziata on Lipari, which he had discovered during his exile on the island.

The ideal staircase – the most basic and geometrically clear, like most of those cited here – consists of a single flight. Yet contemporary architects are obliged to introduce landings at every seventeenth step. While prudent and necessary, this safety measure nonetheless detracts from the power of the image, and makes the design of handrails and banisters even more complicated. Having reached a certain age myself, I understand the need to avoid potential vertiginous tumbles, but at the same time

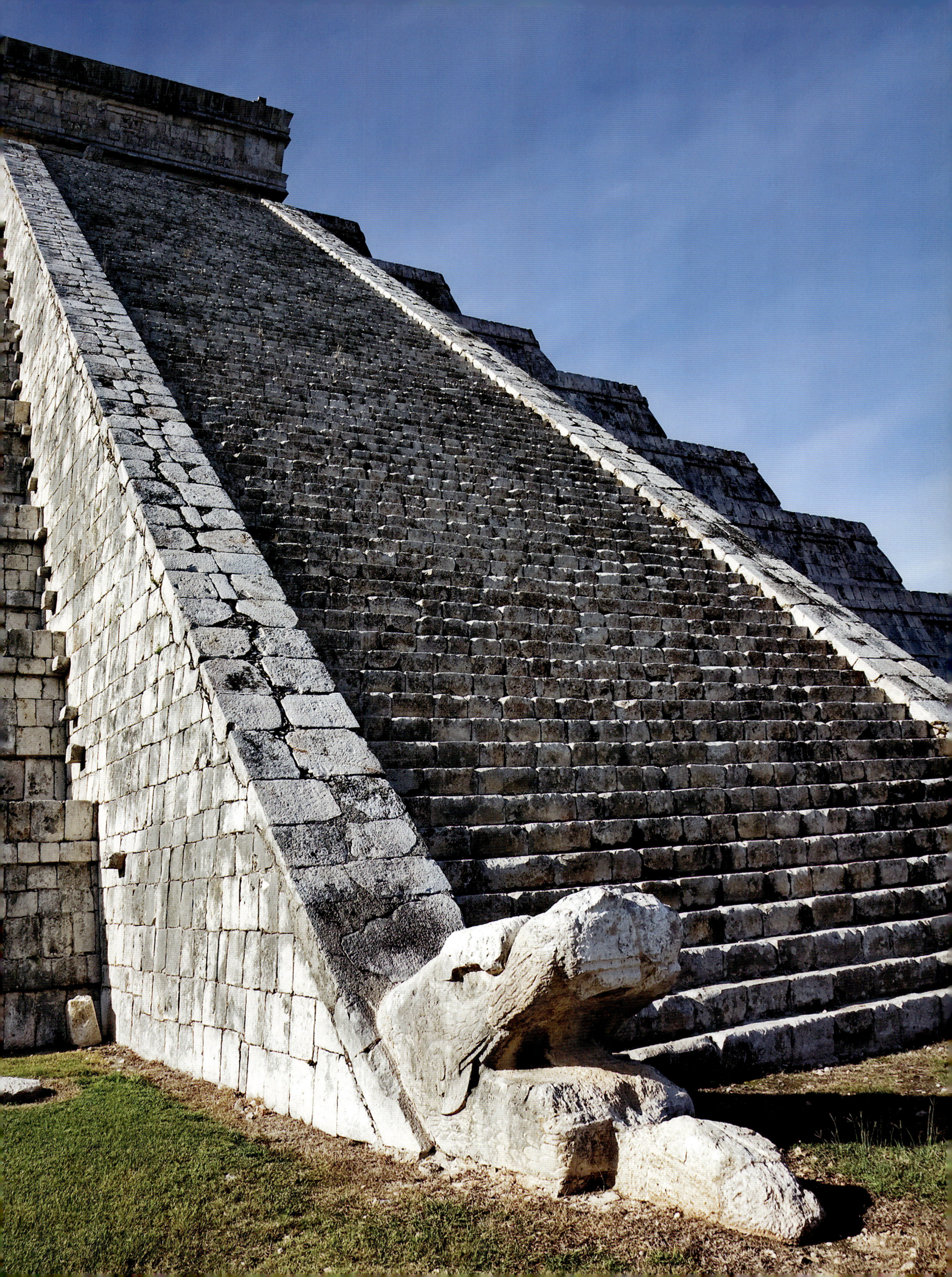

18 | REQUIEM FOR THE STAIRCASE

the great staircase of the Villa Malaparte, to choose an example, would lose much of its majesty if it had landings, while the steps leading up to the Grande Arche de la Défense in Paris would be greatly improved if its landings were not there.

THE WALL-MOUNTED STAIRCASE This type is constructed either by excavating into a wall or by fixing steps to the wall and leaving them exposed. These staircases may be very simple – as in the terraced gardens and vineyards of Cadaques or Capri, where steps are incorporated into the walls' thickness – or extremely high tech, with metal or glass steps rising boldly and independently, one by

LEFT
The Odessa Steps in Odessa, Russia; photochrome from 1898.

BELOW LEFT
Scene from Sergei Eisenstein's film Battleship Potemkin *(1925) showing the 1905 massacre on the Odessa Steps.*

OPPOSITE
Brigitte Bardot and Michel Piccoli on the steps at the Villa Malaparte, Capri, in a scene from Jean-Luc Godard's Le Mépris, *1963.*

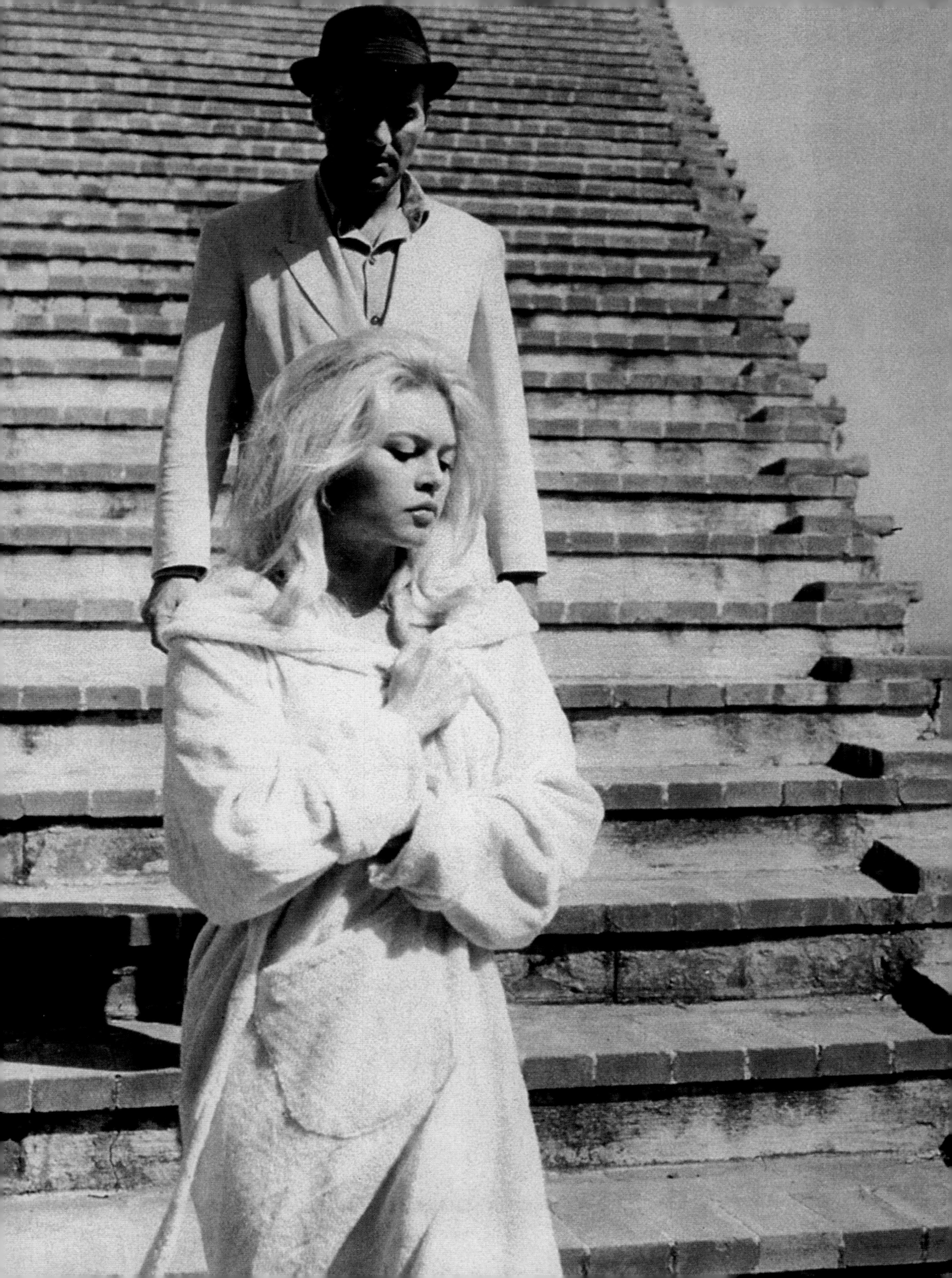

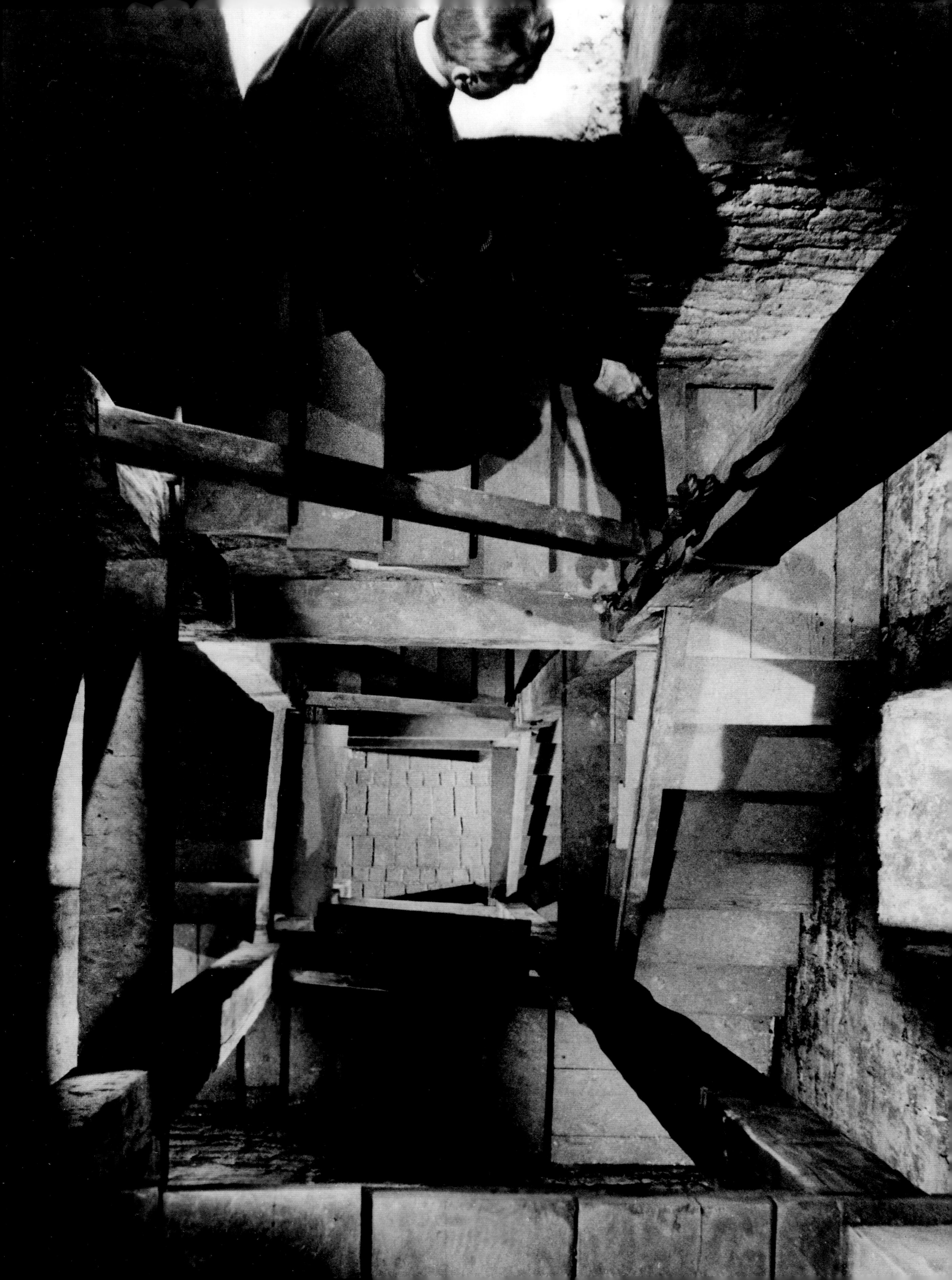

OPPOSITE
James Stewart in Alfred Hitchcock's Vertigo, *1958.*

RIGHT
Vernacular steps in the Ksar of Medenine, Tunisia.

one. In both cases the delicate problem of how to create the point of departure is resolved, whether the steps are set deep into the wall or merely attached to it.

THE PARALLEL-FLIGHT STAIRCASE This is the most common type of staircase, the standard form that takes up the least room and is easiest to build and prefabricate. These are the stairs found in modern houses, that every architect has designed innumerable times, that are used for emergency exits in enclosed spaces (but not externally), that readers of this book will almost certainly walk up and down several times a day. And yet, in the hands of a talented artist, it is also a form that offers a great deal of aesthetic potential. This is the type we turn to when space is limited, or when there is a pronounced external gradient and any other type of staircase would be too steep to climb. This is the solution adopted, for example, in the extraordinary steps leading up to the sanctuary of Bom Jesus do Monte in Braga, Portugal (p. 95).

THE WINDER STAIRCASE Generally speaking, straight staircases turn, and their steps continue to mount, because there is a lack of space or a need to fit the requirements of a specific site. In this type at least two steps will be supported by the short, 'end' wall. The winder staircase, which has a central well (sometimes occupied by a lift) and large landings giving access to several apartments, is widely found in well-to-do residential buildings constructed before the introduction of new safety regulations. It is the form of staircase usually found in the Parisian *hôtel particulier* and is familiar from countless films. The steep stairs in Hitchcock's *Vertigo* are a quarter-landing variant of the winder staircase. On rare occasions, when an architect has a generous amount of space with which to work, the flights may stand completely free of the walls, like a large sculpture in the middle of the room. Such freestanding structures can be reminiscent of the Tower of Babel, having a polygonal plan and myriad angled flights visible from their exterior.

THE MULTI-BRANCHED STAIRCASE Staircases may branch off, multiply and divide to form a complex ensemble suggesting a variety of different routes by which they might be negotiated. There are staircases that start at one point and finish at another, as at the church of the Trinità dei Monti, Rome (known as the Spanish Steps), or that start at several points and meet at the summit, as in Michelangelo's design for the Biblioteca Laurenziana (pp. 74–75). Some lead to a variety of places – as in Ricardo Bofill's Muralla Roja, near Alicante (p. 225), or the fortifications of Santiago de Cuba – while others lead nowhere and are imprisoned within themselves, like those found in the works of Piranesi.

THE IMPERIAL STAIRCASE The dignity and imposing nature of the imperial staircase derive from its absolute symmetry. The staircases with several flights described above are symmetrical in plan, but not in three dimensions. If, in a building laid out on a central axis, an architect places the first of two flights on this axis, it follows that the second flight will be to one side, and will therefore not be on axis when it reaches the upper floor – a frustrating anomaly for architects of the Baroque period, obsessed as they were with absolute symmetry. However, a solution had been found in the sixteenth century: the *escalera imperial*, which was to be Spain's most important contribution to the universal history of architecture. The first flight of the imperial staircase was divided in two symmetrical sections at a first half-landing, where it also turned through an angle varying from 90 to 180 degrees. This device was given an enthusiastic welcome and was adopted for Baroque palaces and, later, for many other monumental buildings. It is impossible to imagine the Paris Opéra without its imperial staircase. The same is true of the Würzburg Residenz (p. 112), the masterpiece of the architect Johann Balthasar Neumann, whose stairs ascend beneath a ceiling of unrivalled scale and beauty painted by Giambattista Tiepolo. In his great fresco – a composition of surprising clarity – Tiepolo contrived to depict Apollo and the other Olympian gods; clouds of angels and cupids thronging the sky; personifications of the four classical continents; countless allegorical and exotic figures; a horse, a camel, two elephants, two stags, a monkey, a parrot, a cayman, a crocodile, an ostrich and a disturbing grass snake; the prince-bishop himself; and a portrait of Balthasar Neumann, accompanied by his son and his dog.

THE 'SAMBA' STAIRCASE Behind this ingenious and very ancient solution to the problem of getting up and down stairs in a tight space is the idea that, since you place only one foot on each step at a time, the width of the step can be divided in half. The 'samba' staircase (so named after the swaying, dance-like gait the staggered construction produces in its users) enables you to climb through an angle of 45 degrees, but only on condition that you start off on the right foot. In his *Dictionary of Architecture*, Eugène Viollet-le-Duc expresses an interest in this unusual design, used in backstairs for servants, on cathedral roofs and in medieval fortifications. For many years this curious form of staircase was held in scant esteem, but over time twentieth-century architects – such as Edwin Lutyens in his ultra-modern, ultra-medieval Castle Drogo, or Carlo Scarpa in several of his works – restored its reputation.

THE FLOATING STAIRCASE Throughout history, artists have imagined staircases floating miraculously in a void. A stairway to heaven should ideally be suspended, and if possible consist of a straight flight of steps stretching to infinity. To come close to realizing this dream, architects and engineers have striven to defy the laws of gravity by using materials that enable them to create sections of increasing subtlety. Reinforced concrete, steel and glass (capable of absorbing the forces of tension and compression in equal measure) have made it possible for contemporary designers to turn the dreams of past centuries into reality. This type of staircase does not lend itself easily to the addition of a handrail, a subject to which we shall return.

LEFT
The Drawbridge *by Giovanni Battista Piranesi, plate 7 of the* Carceri *series (1760–61).*

OPPOSITE
The ceremonial stair par excellence: the gilded staircase of Burgos Cathedral in Spain, by Diego de Siloé (1516).

LEFT
'Samba stairs' at Castle Drogo, Devon, by Edwin Lutyens (1910–30).

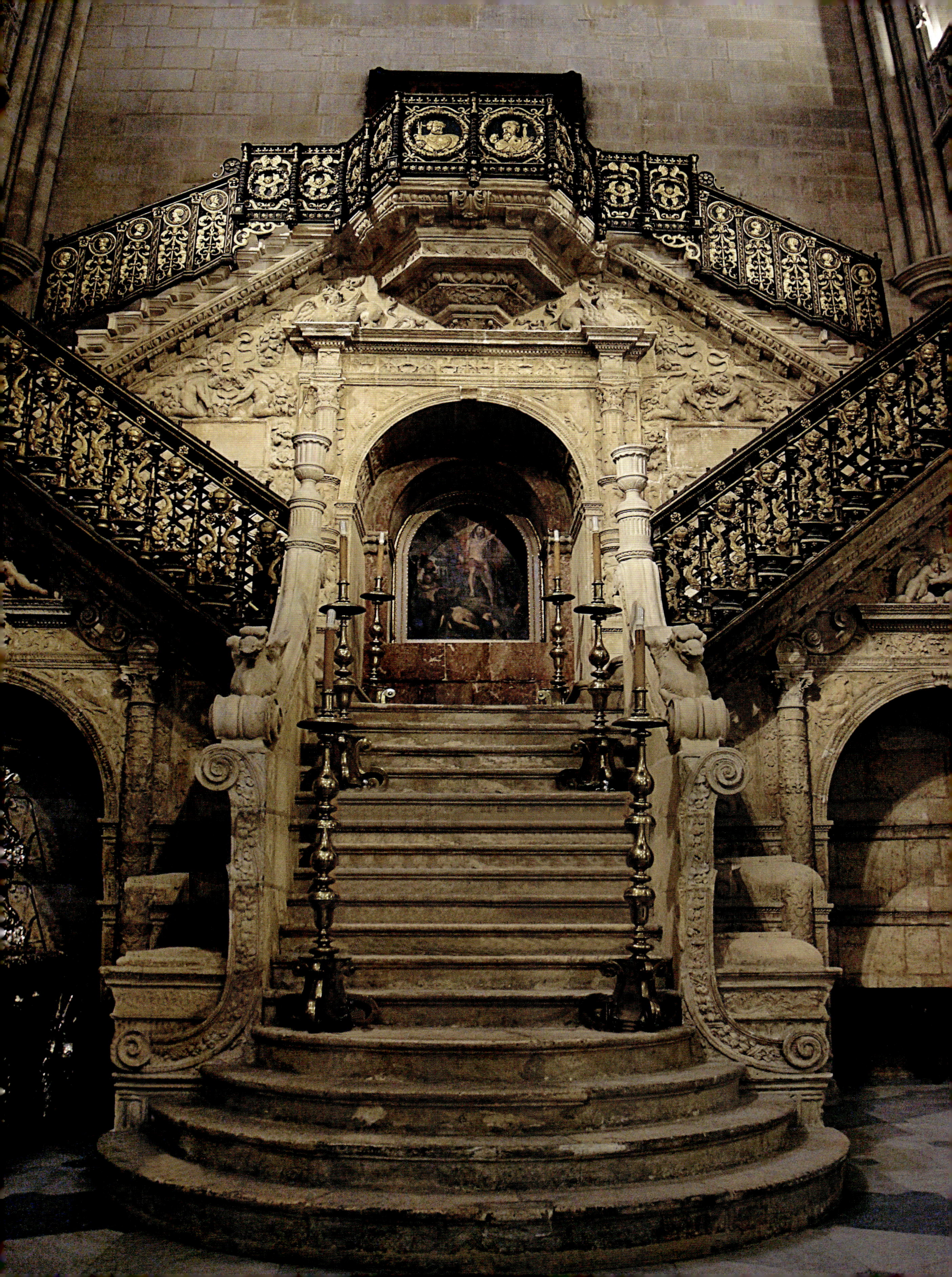

THE RANDOM STAIRCASE This type of staircase usually results from the difficult topography of a particular site, but may also be a response to the designer's desire to move away from a strictly geometrical approach, in order to work with forms that are freer and more organic. In the ruins of Machu Picchu or the remarkable pathways woven around the Acropolis by Dimitris Pikionis, it is clear that the designs have been adapted to suit the terrain. But no mere topographical considerations can account for the apogee of non-Euclidean geometry: the astonishing Chapter House steps in Wells Cathedral, Somerset.

LEFT
The external staircase of Frank Lloyd Wright's Fallingwater, Pennsylvania (1936–39).

THE CURVED STAIRCASE From stairways with gently sweeping lines to those that coil round themselves in spirals, curved staircases have for centuries represented one of architecture's greatest challenges, as well as one of its most spectacular successes. They may display the undulating beauty of the entrance staircase at the château of Fontainebleau (p. 99), or of the steps built by Josep Maria Jujol – the finest architect of Catalan modernism after Gaudí – at Torre de la Creu. They may ascend in helical curves, as in the Llotja de la Seda in Valencia, I. M. Pei's staircase at the Louvre (p. 217) or Rembrandt's *Philosopher in Meditation* (p. 12). They may be double, with two spirals mirroring each other in perfect symmetry, as at Graz Castle (p. 57), or consist of two spirals superimposed, as in the double staircase at

LEFT
'A Sea of Steps': Frederick H. Evans's photograph, taken in 1903, of the steps leading up to the Chapter House of Wells Cathedral, Somerset.

OPPOSITE
Steps climbing up to the ancient rock fortress of Sigiriya in Sri Lanka.

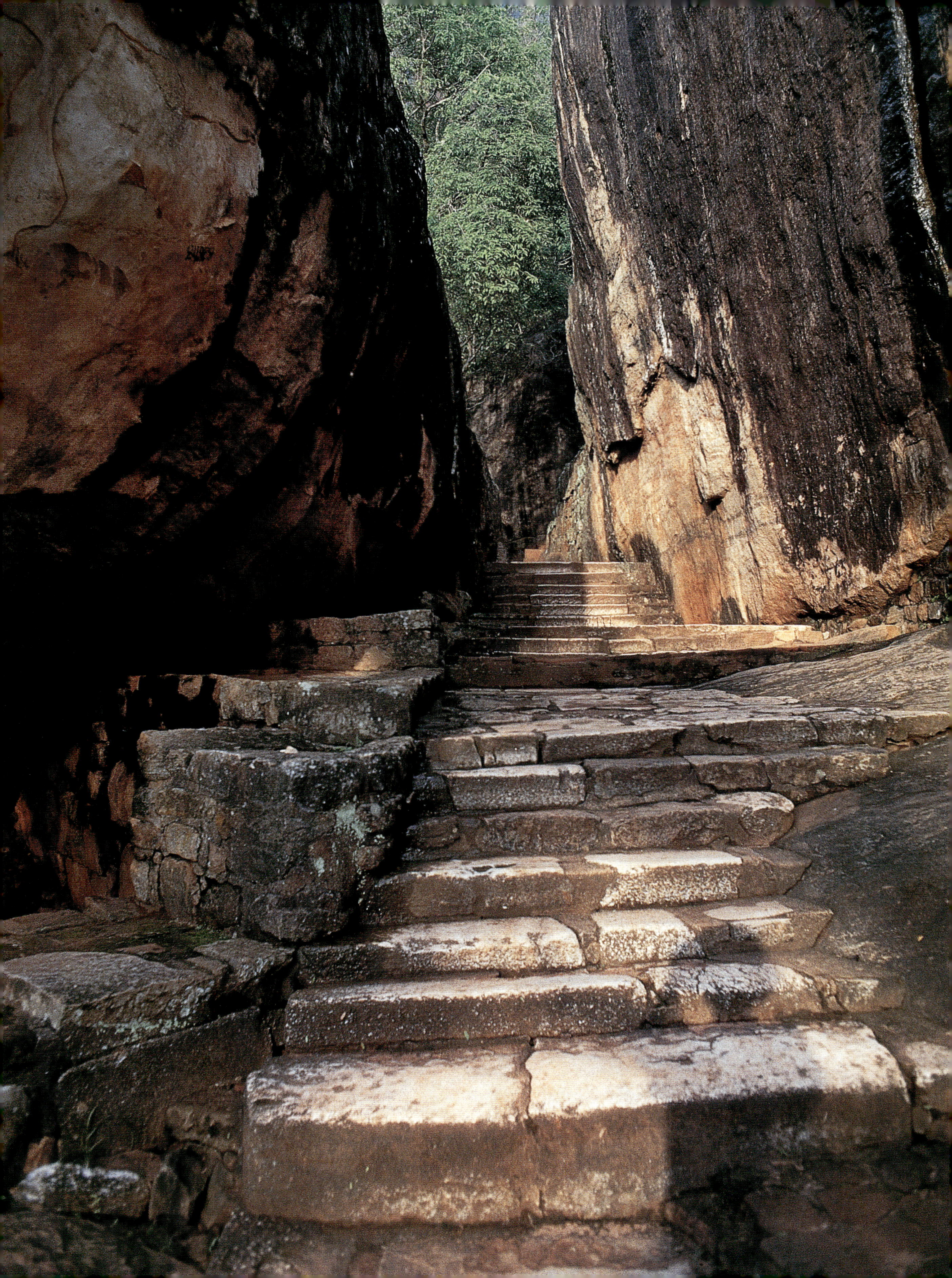

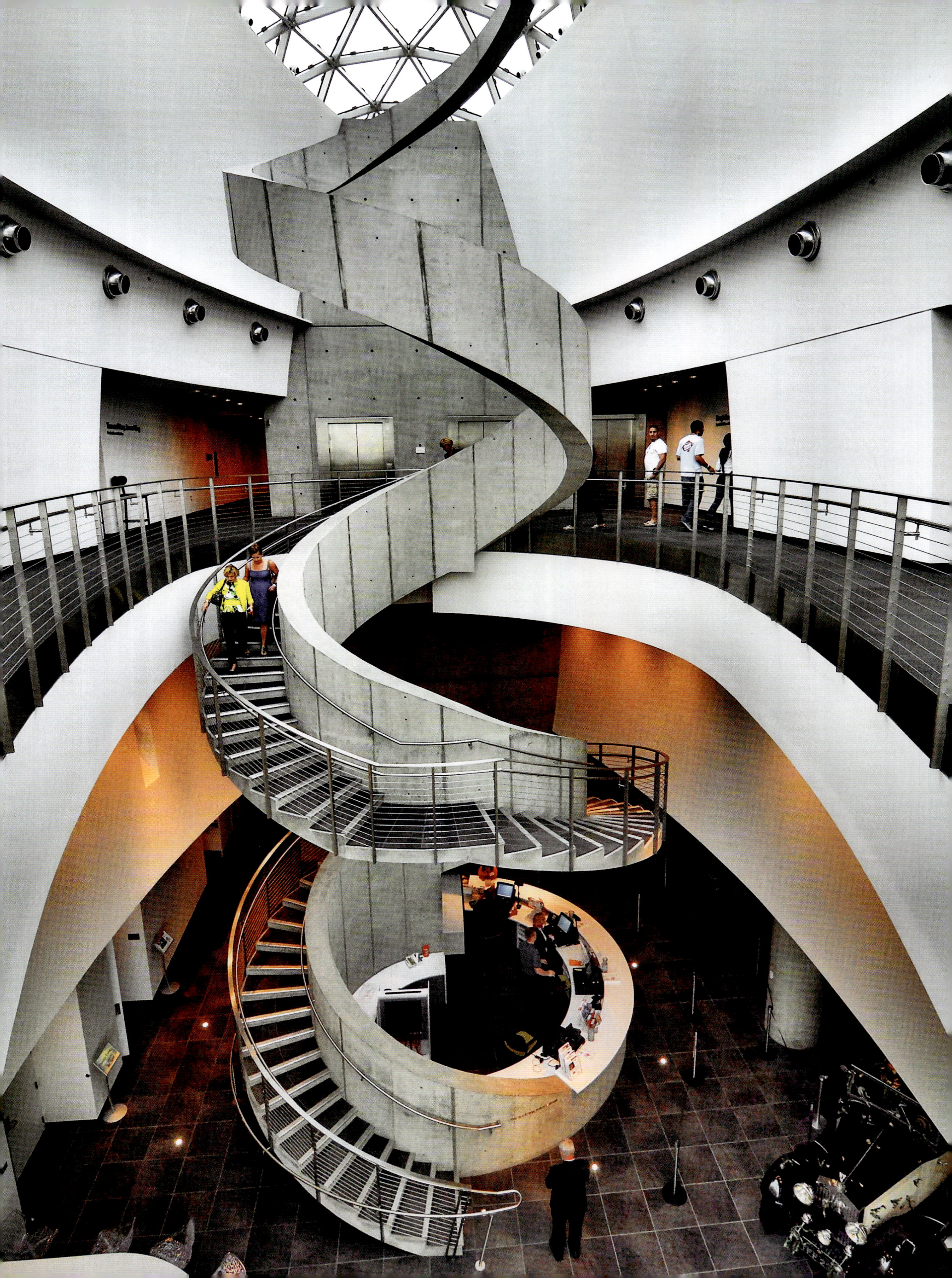

OPPOSITE
The helical staircase of the Salvador Dalí Museum in St Petersburg, Florida, designed by the architect Yann Weymouth for HOK (2011).

RIGHT
Spiral staircase designed by Frank Gehry for the Art Gallery of Ontario in his native Toronto (2008).

the château of Chambord (pp. 62–63). In the hands of Andrea Palladio, they even combine four superimposed spirals. Some also branch out only to come back together again, as in the series of maquettes by Frank Gehry presented at the competition for Berlin's Museum Island. Curved staircases, whose charm derives from the fact that our field of vision changes constantly as we go up or down, are sadly destined to disappear – from public buildings at least, for reasons that will be explained later.

THE STAIRWAY TO HEAVEN – OR HELL Flights of stairs symbolizing an ascent into heaven are a recurring theme, familiar from biblical imagery and still current today. From traditional depictions of the Tower of Babel, to the pyramids of Mexico and the *Stairway of Heaven* by land artist Hannsjörg Voth (p. 28), and from the minaret at the mosque of Samarra, Iraq (p. 28), to the startling astronomical observatory of Jaipur (p. 29), the human desire to ascend heavenwards has always existed, and is often expressed in works of art and architecture.

Steps that lead down towards death, and quite possibly damnation, have also given rise to striking images: a baby in a perambulator hurtling down the Odessa Steps in *Battleship Potemkin* (p. 18);

LEFT
Stairway to Heaven, a symbolic sculpture conceived by the German artist Hannsjörg Voth in 1987 and installed in the desert landscape of Plaine de Marha, Morocco.

an invalid in a wheelchair pushed from the top of a staircase in *Whatever Happened to Baby Jane?*; a stabbed man falling backwards down the stairs in Hitchcock's *Psycho*; the dizzying staircase in *Vertigo* (p. 20). These are only a few of the stair-related deaths that litter the history of cinema. Noteworthy in an altogether different vein, meanwhile, are two sites in Catalonia: an impressive memorial to Walter Benjamin by the Israeli artist Dani Karavan, which plunges down to the sea at Portbou, and the steps designed by Carme Pinós and Enric Miralles that lead down into the cemetery at Igualada.

THE IMPOSSIBLE STAIRCASE Some seemingly impossible constructions have inspired modern interpretations, such as the entrance to Kisho Kurokawa's Roppongi Prince Hotel, Tokyo, or Ezra Orion's monumental sculpture in Jerusalem known as 'Jacob's Ladder'. On the whole, however, these fantasies remain too disconcerting even to attempt. These are structures that can exist only as designs or images: they are staircases as drawn by Escher, that can be neither built nor explained by Euclidean geometry. They exist only in our dreams.

FAR LEFT
The Tower of Babel, from Athanasius Kircher's Turris Babel *(1679).*

LEFT
The spiral-shaped minaret of the Great Mosque of Samarra, Iraq, built c. 845–50 in the ancient capital of the Islamic world.

OPPOSITE
The Jantar Mantar astronomical observatory in Jaipur, India (first half of the eighteenth century).

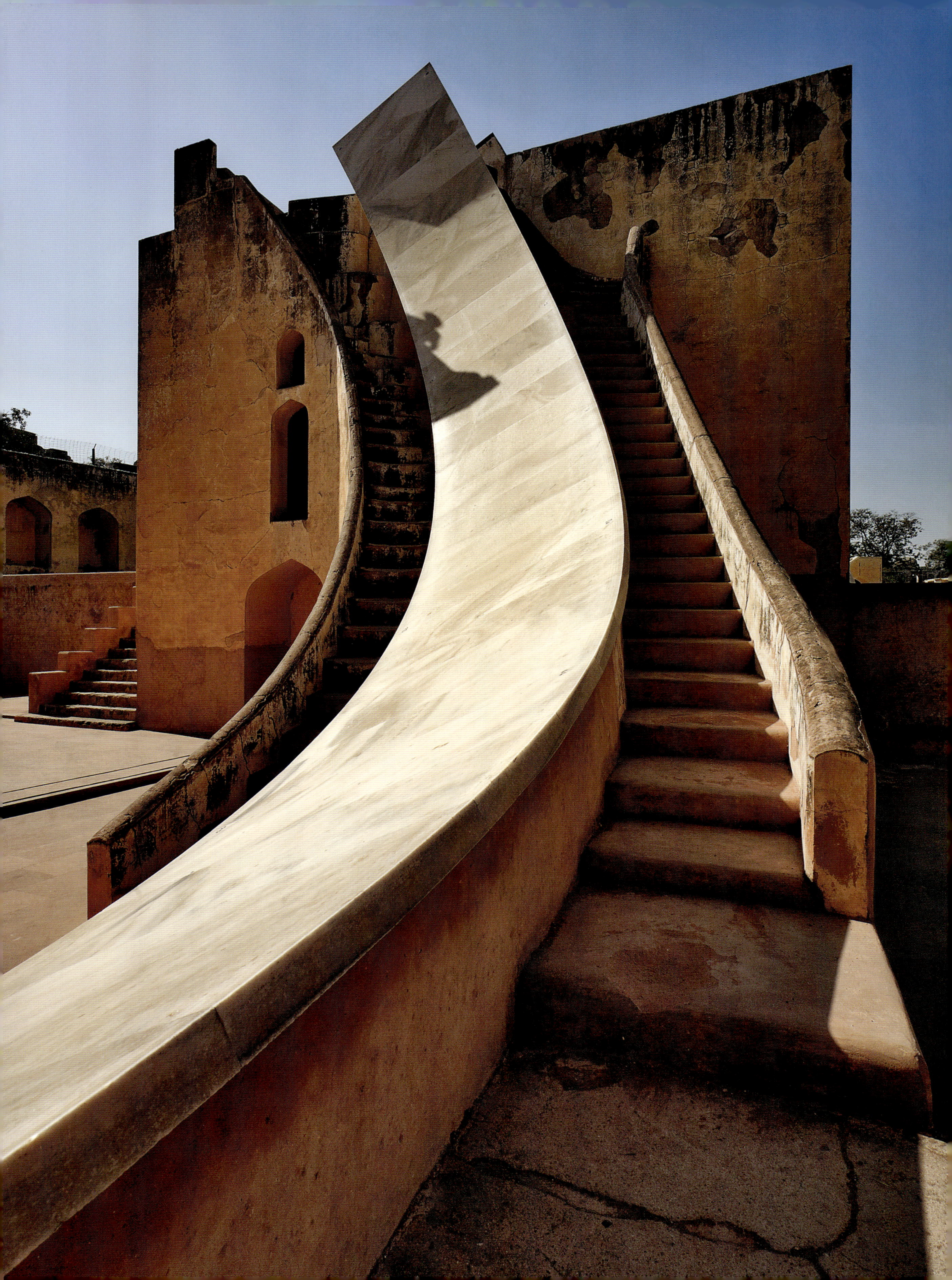

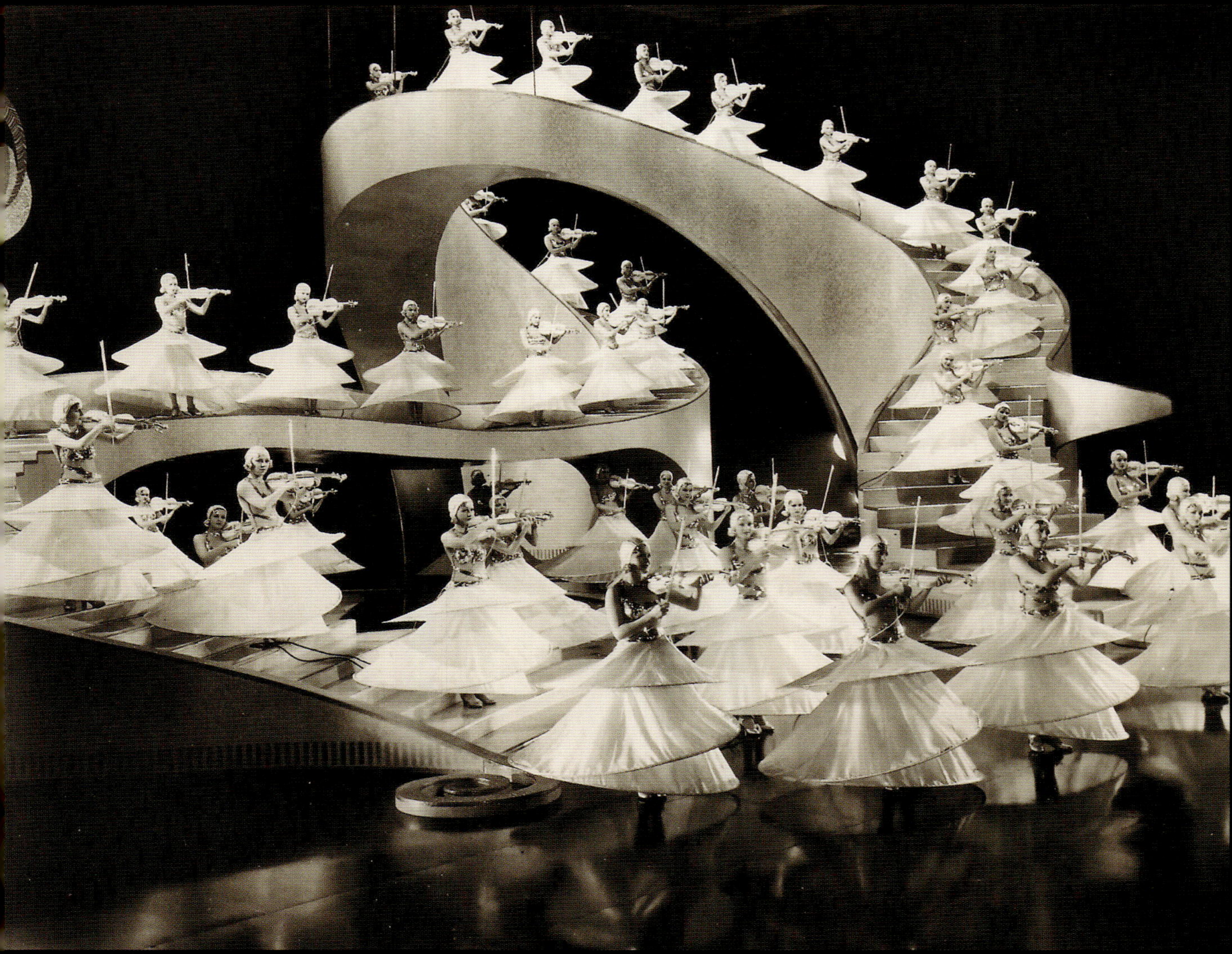

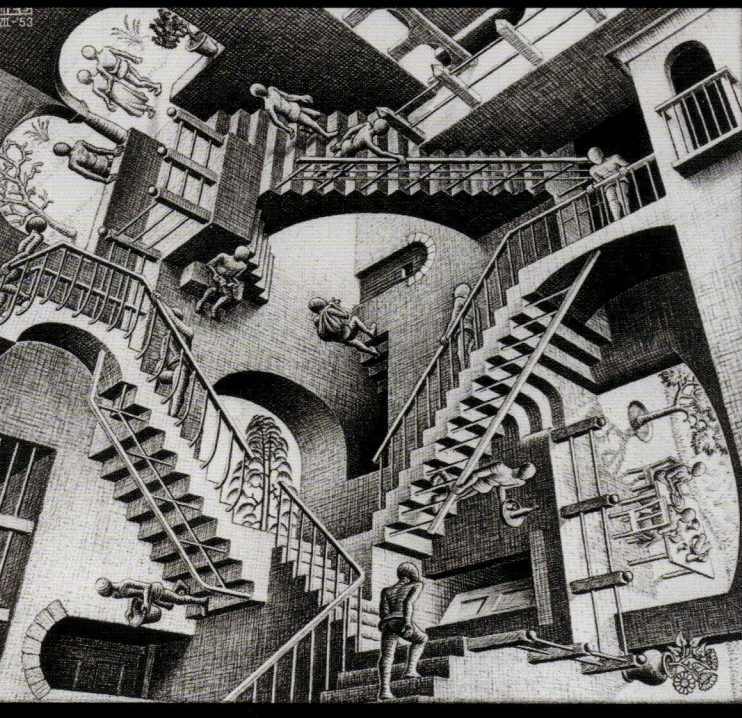

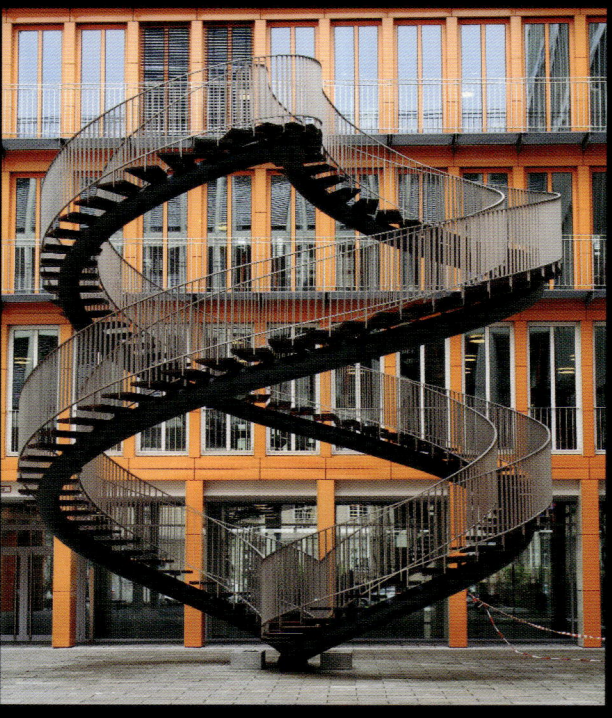

OPPOSITE
Set piece from Mervyn LeRoy's film Gold Diggers of 1933, *choreographed by Busby Berkeley.*

OPPOSITE, BELOW LEFT
Relativity, *lithograph by M. C. Escher (1953).*

OPPOSITE, BELOW RIGHT
Rewriting Stairs, *a sculpture by the Danish artist Olafur Eliasson for the accountancy firm KPMG, Munich (2004).*

BALUSTRADES AND HANDRAILS All (or almost all) staircases, irrespective of type, will have two features in common.

These are the twin horrors of handrails and balustrades. Artists ignore them in their drawings and paintings, film-makers add them only when a scene demands it, and architects design them solely when their presence is demanded by the unavoidable necessities of daily use. Artists and designers have always preferred their stairs to be free of either feature, abandoning the tedious, sloping line of the handrail and leaving steps fully exposed, in all their beauty, nakedness and purity. Even in the face of the risks and inconvenience their absence poses for users, designers are as determined as ever to find a way around this stumbling block.

Among drawn or painted staircases, ranging from the etchings of Piranesi and Escher to Leonardo's *Adoration of the Magi* and Duchamp's *Nude Descending a Staircase* (p. 33), the absence of a handrail is the general rule. More or less the same is true in cinematic works. How many musketeers' duels have been fought out on stairs with handrails? How many staircases with handrails are to be found in German Expressionist films, or in the films of Busby Berkeley or Robert Leonard?

In reality, as this book clearly shows, most historical staircases had no handrail. It is beyond dispute that a handrail detracts from the gravity of a monumental staircase. Despite the spreading dictatorship of health and safety standards, contemporary architects have either done their utmost to simply omit the handrail altogether – the approach taken by Le Corbusier, Luis Barragán, Miguel Fisac and Anthony Hoete – or they have invented a subterfuge of some kind, such as Oscar Niemeyer's innovative balustrades at Brasília. But there is no avoiding the fact that these projects were daring swansongs, for contemporary architecture is now subject to diktats, regulations, standards, insurance policies, court cases and lawyers, and we are no longer at liberty to embark on such adventures.

RIGHT
Staircase in the Olivetti showroom on the Piazza San Marco, Venice, by Carlo Scarpa (1957–58).

LEFT
Set design from the film Mary Shelley's Frankenstein, *directed by Kenneth Branagh (1994).*

OPPOSITE
Nude Descending a Staircase (No. 1), *by Marcel Duchamp (1911).*

When, for reasons of safety, prudence or legal obligation, an architect is forced to include a handrail, he or she will use a variety of tricks to make it less noticeable. The staircases of many Gothic buildings have imposing stone balustrades, but the steps can be seen between the balusters and are visible from the outside. In many cases – from the palace of Knossos on Crete to Carlo Scarpa's staircase for Olivetti (p. 31) – the handrail refuses to follow the diagonal pitch of the stairs, instead forming a sequence of staggered horizontal planes. It is this exasperating diagonal that is at odds aesthetically with the staircase's perpendicular geometry. That is why a balustrade is never a problem on a ramp, but becomes a real headache when you are designing a staircase.

The relatively recent appearance of toughened and laminated glass has provided a way of making the balustrade disappear. So engrossed are we with this concern for concealment that sometimes architects eliminate the handrail, despite the fact that it is a legal requirement and an indispensable aid to people of a certain age.

With or without a handrail, the glass balustrade is the preferred choice for today's staircases: it is the easiest type to design, and the least problematic on the legal front. Its minimalism is clearly no rival for the beautiful forms achieved in antique stone or iron, but it makes our job much easier. That said, we are also aware that glass is transparent only when it is spotlessly clean and viewed against the light; when the light is behind you and the glass is set against a dark background, it becomes as opaque as stone, as reflective as polished black granite.

THE 'ILLEGAL' STAIRCASE All the staircases described under this heading have one characteristic in common: they would all be illegal under the legislation now in force in 'developed' countries. Laws governing disabled access and fire regulations would render them inconceivable today.

Clearly, the legislators who draw up such measures do not share the same passion for staircases that architects feel. It is undeniably true that, in the case of fire, a stairwell may act as a chimney, enabling smoke and flames to spread to the upper floors and making it unusable as an emergency exit. But this fact has led to the bluntest of legislation. Standardized and cheapened, staircases can no longer open onto any living space, but must be totally independent, isolated from any fire risk and accessible only through self-closing doors – which require herculean efforts to use, and which are therefore routinely propped open (in strict contravention of the law). The doors, usually double, open onto lonely and

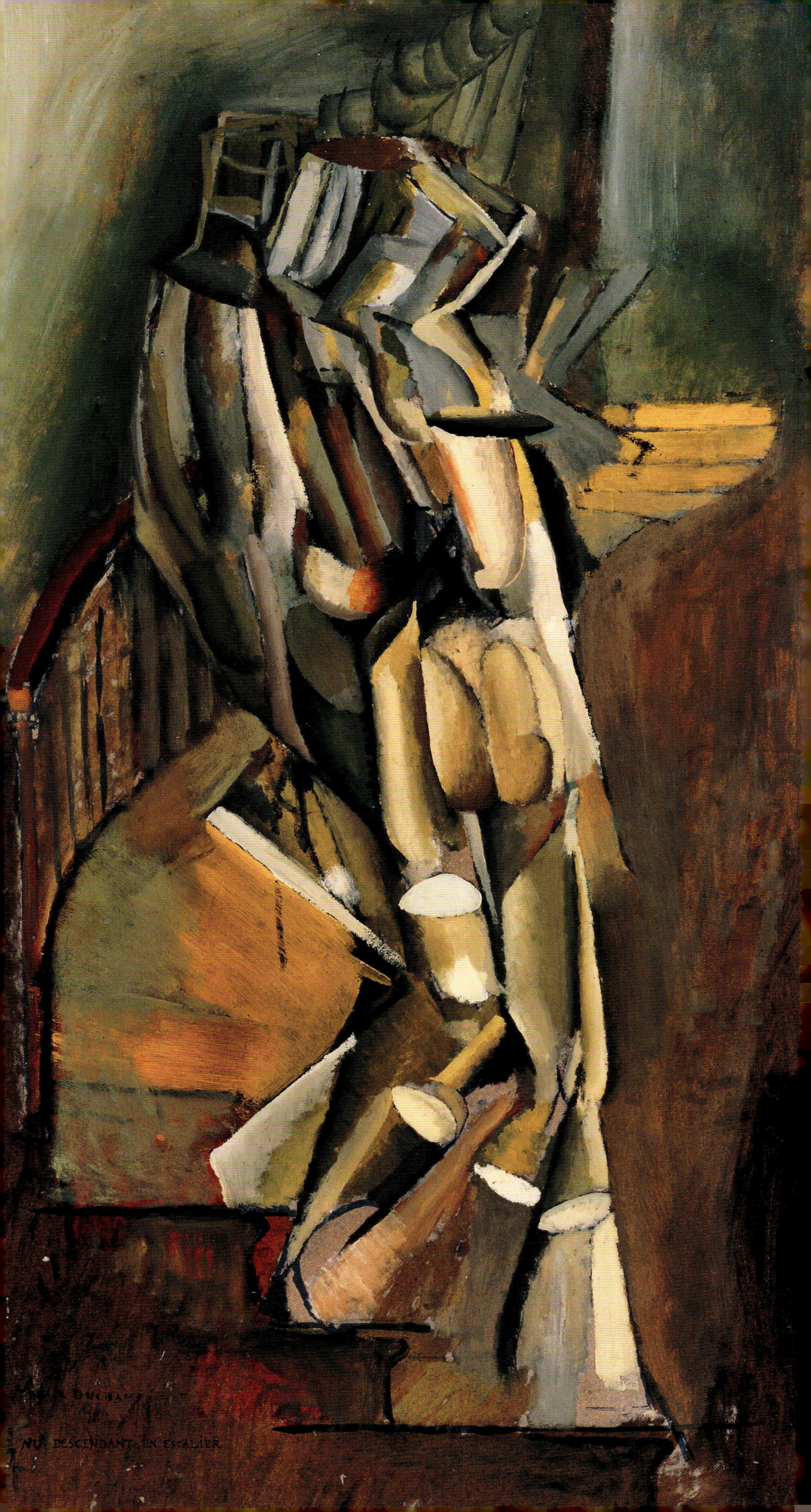
DUCHAMP
NU DESCENDANT UN ESCALIER

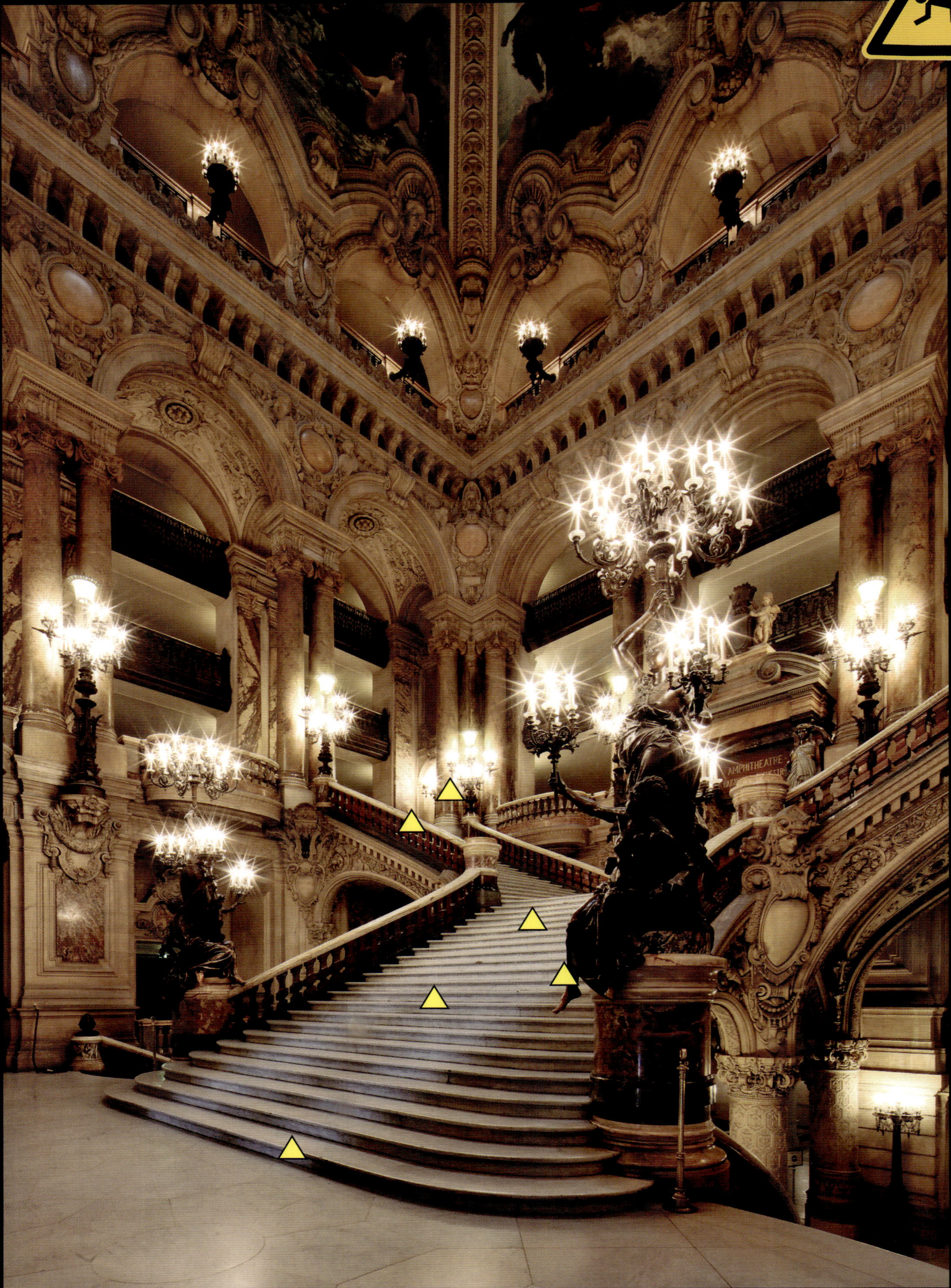
AMPHITHEATRE

OPPOSITE
Illegal features of the grand staircase at the Paris Opéra: handrail not at the regulation height; no emergency exit; no emergency lighting; no landing after the eighteenth step; no disabled access; no central handrail; no hall to provide independent access; balustrade contains hazardous features; steps not at regulation height (17–18.5 cm).

RIGHT
Original poster by Saul Bass for West Side Story *(Robert Wise, 1961).*

depressing spaces such as halls and lobbies. Other features of staircase design that have fallen foul of current legislation include curves, steps of gradually increasing (or decreasing) dimensions, and bullnose entry steps: all have been banned outright.

If the legislation were rigorously applied, the grand staircase of the Paris Opéra would fall short on almost all counts. Having examined it, we identified seven major infringements of the law, but a health and safety specialist would undoubtedly find more. According to current building standards it is therefore highly dangerous, and in a case of emergency would give rise to numerous tragic falls. The number of deaths caused by this manifest danger to the public in its 150 years of existence has yet to be ascertained with any degree of certainty.

No one should be surprised, therefore, if architects, faced with increasing constraints of this kind and worn out by a futile struggle to champion alternative projects, become demoralized and turn to solutions that deserve every blessing without incurring any legal risks. What is left to us except the enclosed staircase, small in scale, rectilinear in outline, with steps that are equal and perpendicular; the hackneyed, standard, universal staircase, the same in Barcelona as it is in Seoul, economical and safe, but also banal and mundane? When we design a staircase as though it were a machine room, we no longer think of it as the heart of a building. If today we wanted to build a staircase that was as interesting and as beautiful as those in this book, it could be done; but the law would not consider it a proper emergency exit, and we would have to convince the client to commission and finance it as a piece of decorative sculpture instead, separate from and in addition to the obligatory law-abiding version.

These are the reasons why I fear that the staircase, which has played a major role in great architecture from every era, is a vanishing species. It no longer offers architects an opportunity to display their bravura, but instead has become a mere service facility, functional, marginal, isolated. In addition, the growing popularity of lifts, and the increasingly widespread use of ramps as an alternative, pose further threats to its survival.

FROM LIFT TO ACCESS RAMP The lift is a great invention. Without it, the first skyscrapers in Chicago would never have seen the light of day, and we need only toil up the narrow stairs, laden with heavy bags, to an attic room in Paris where a bohemian friend has invited us to stay to be convinced of its positive effect on our daily lives. But the apparent convenience of the lift has relegated stairs to an emergency role only, to be used strictly in case of mechanical breakdown or accident. Today, stairs are so marginalized and lacking in appeal that we neglect them even if we are going down only a couple of floors. In any hospital or administrative building you can see workers waiting for several minutes for the lift, only to get out at the next floor or the one after. Medical science tells us that walking up and down stairs is one of the healthiest forms of exercise and highly beneficial for the circulatory system. Despite this evidence, their potential is increasingly overlooked, even though using a handsome staircase can amount to nothing less than an aesthetically satisfying experience in three dimensions.

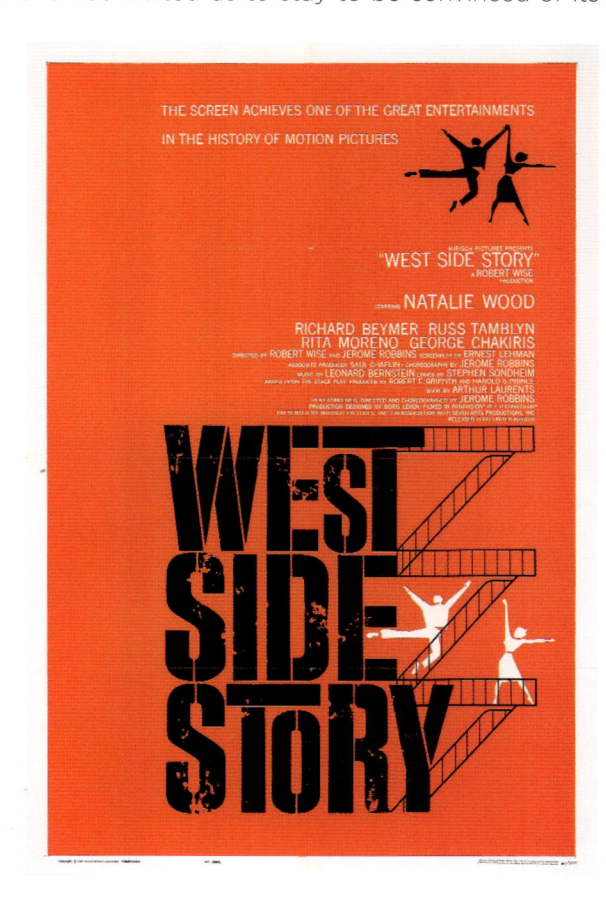

Nobody today wants to take the stairs. This is why, in dispiriting gyms around the world, a machine has appeared alongside all the other elaborate instruments of torture that enables city-dwellers to replicate precisely the movements involved in climbing the stairs. They go up to the gym – which is often on the top floor, naturally – in the lift, and once there set about climbing virtual stairs with the aid of a machine. You have to admire the business skills at work here.

There remains the question of the access ramp. In the architecture of the ancient world, ramps rarely stood in for stairs. There are long external ramps, such as those leading up to the Egyptian mortuary temples at Deir el-Bahari; internal ramps of multiple flights, as in the Giralda in Seville; helical ramps for horsemen, as in the Bramante Staircase in the Vatican; or the ingenious double helical ramp built by Antonio da Sangallo in Orvieto so that draught animals drawing water from the San Patrizio well would not pass people on their way down. Internal access ramps were the exception, and as an architectural theme ramps in general are exceedingly difficult to master. Whatever the site, they invariably give rise to geometrical conflicts: even bridge designers are wary of them.

Yet in contemporary architecture ramps have multiplied. This vogue is doubtless the result of a fascination with forms associated with speed and traffic, as fostered by avant-garde movements such as

LEFT
The staircase in the central bell tower of Frombork Cathedral in Poland, restored after the Second World War.

RIGHT
Stairwell with lift at the Pera Palace Hotel in Istanbul, Turkey.

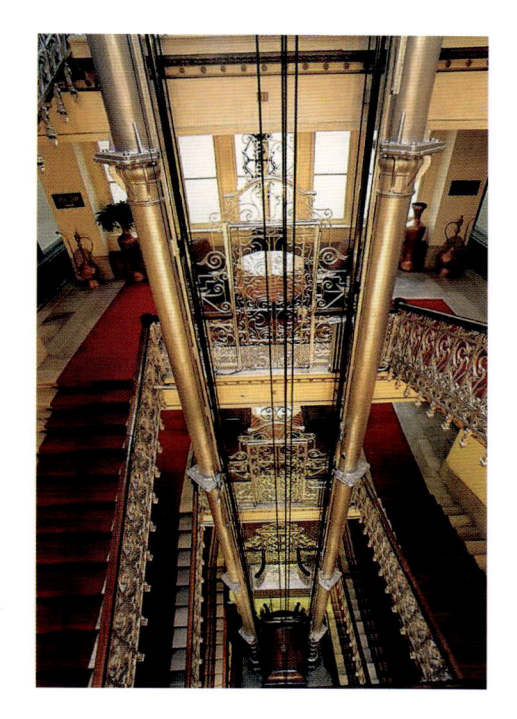

RIGHT
Demon Tumbling Down Stairs, a three-dimensional work created by Erica Van Horn (1988) from five books, their spines painted to produce a trompe-l'oeil *effect.*

Russian Constructivism, Futurism in Italy or Rationalism in Central Europe. Even though such forms could be integrated relatively naturally into a car factory in Turin, a penguin pool in London or a museum interior in New York without causing any great problems, their introduction into domestic and everyday spaces has always seemed forced and gratuitous. Is it really necessary for people to make a detour and take an access ramp that swallows up half of a dwelling's usable surface area? Can we not take a *promenade architecturale*, in Le Corbusier's phrase, by going up the stairs? Does it make sense that in Richard Meier's Museum of Contemporary Art in Barcelona a large part of the space – the part with the most natural light, as it happens – should be given over exclusively to an arrangement of broad ramps that conduct the visitor to the upper floors in an endless slalom? One might argue that access ramps allow us to dispense of the architectural barrier represented by the staircase, but the examples mentioned here are too long or too steep to be used by anyone of limited mobility. Building standards require that they should be short and tight, that they should replace short flights of steps, but ramps should never be used as an alternative to a staircase several metres in height. The most appropriate solution would be a lift large enough to accommodate wheelchairs.

This situation makes me pessimistic about the future of the staircase. It saddens me, since throughout my career I have been happy to design some staircases, and throughout my life I have been happy to go up and down many more. It is with sincere regret that I have written this requiem to a once noble feature of architecture.

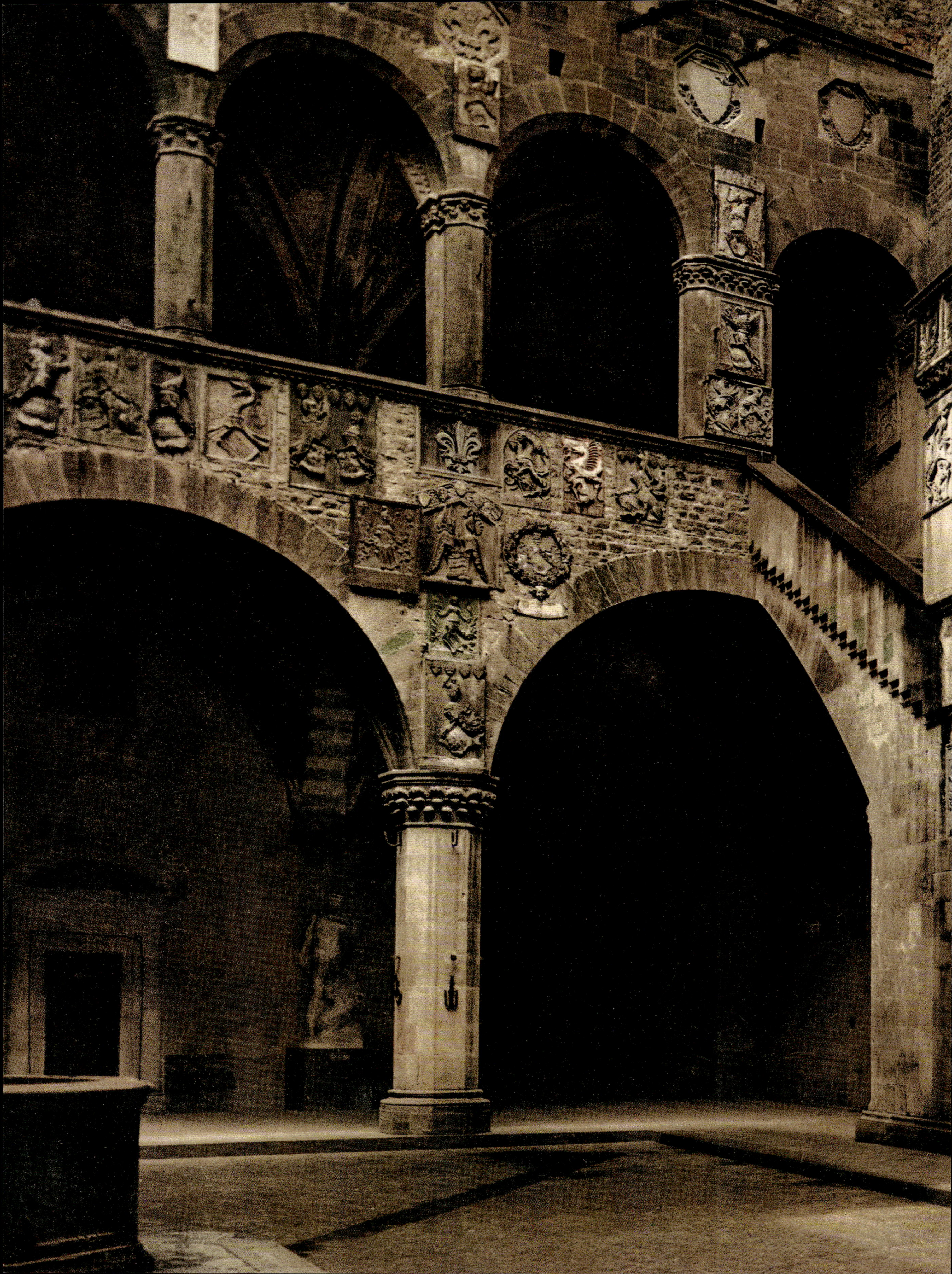

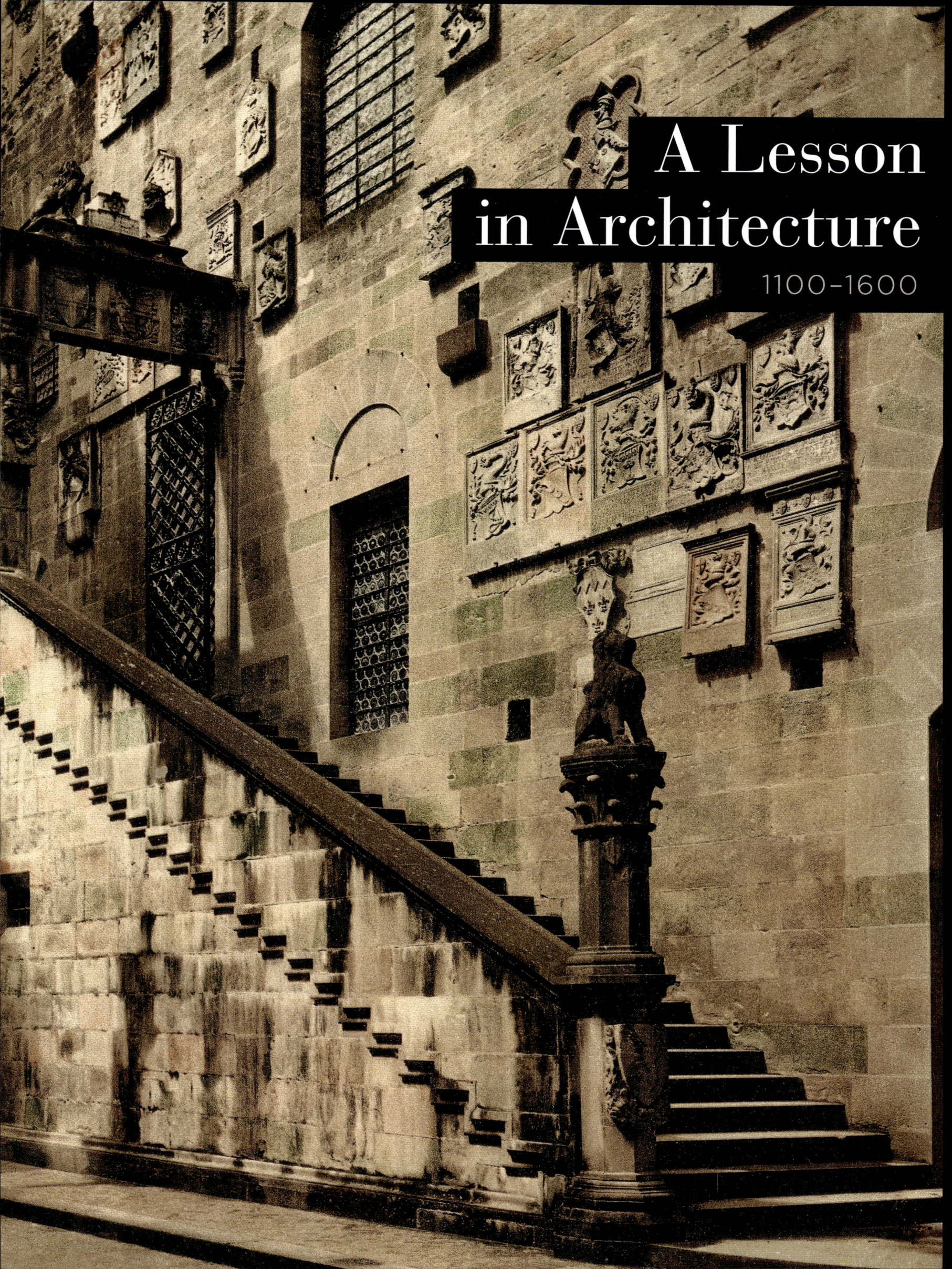

A Lesson in Architecture
1100–1600

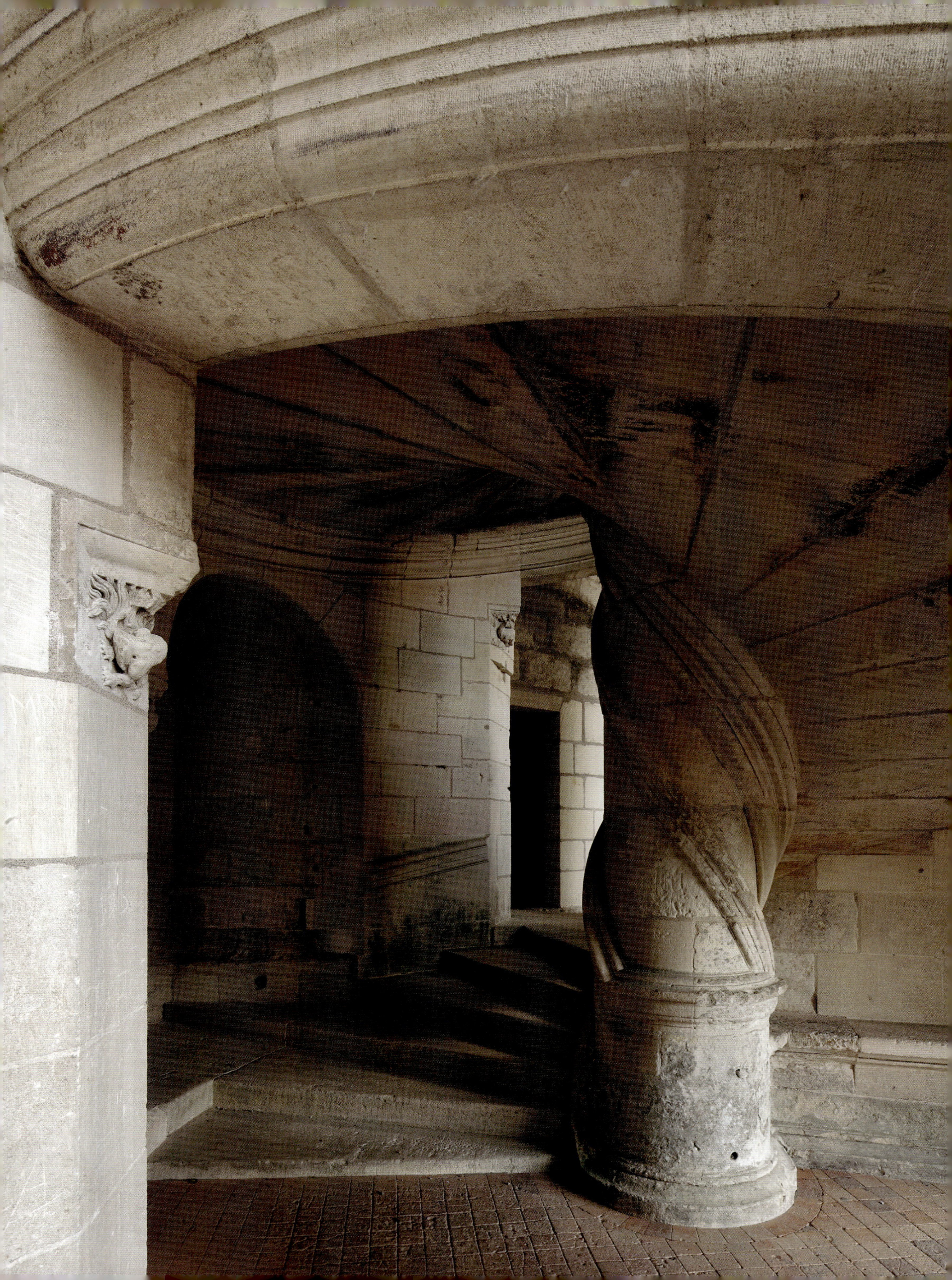

PREVIOUS PAGES
The staircase of the Bargello, Florence. Neri di Fiorivanti built this grand stair in 1367, during refurbishment of the existing twelfth-century structure, to give access to the first-floor gallery.

OVERLEAF
Built in Renaissance style by Antonio Rizzio between 1484 and 1501, the Giants' Staircase in the Palazzo Ducale, Venice, takes its name from its colossal statues of Mars and Neptune, carved by Jacopo Sansovino in 1554 and installed in 1566.

OPPOSITE
The spiral staircase in the chapel wing of the château at Chambord. Set in an octagonal tower attached to the façade, it is reached from the courtyard. Decorative mouldings on the broad newel, built of courses of dressed stone, lead the eye upwards.

According to Alberti, there were two types of *scala*, or stair: one enabled the user to climb by means of an inclined ramp, the other by means of steps. As the idea of moving from one level to another appeared, so did the notion of steps or stairs (the word *scala* is believed to derive from the Latin verb *scandere*, 'to ascend'). Ramps and stairs were governed by the same principle, by which the course to be followed was lengthened in order to produce an acceptable pitch. They could be used for either ascent or descent. But the staircase served not only to link the different levels within a structure: it also provided a passage from the outside to the inside. Its primary function in domestic buildings was utilitarian. Until the twelfth century, arrangements for vertical movement were modest. Circulation was permitted primarily by means of wooden stairs or ladders, which could be likened to the early moveable steps that were used to give access from one floor to another in fortresses without compromising their defences.

From the last third of the eleventh century, advances in building techniques resulted in the appearance of stone staircases in castles and monasteries. At the same time the spread of vaulting through the upper floors meant that architects were obliged to take a general overview of circulation when positioning the stair. Henceforward, stairs formed an integral part of the construction process.

Initially contained within the thickness of a wall, the stair was narrow, straight or curved, and led in one direction only. Straight flights, often serving only one floor, were the simplest and most widespread form, as they took up little space and were easily accessible. The starting and finishing points were different; and the steps, which were parallel and of identical size, were embedded between two blank walls.

THE GRAND STAIRCASE From the mid-thirteenth century on, stone architecture was no longer more or less exclusively religious. Civil and secular buildings, both private and public, were now springing up on all sides. In the design of palaces, the grand staircase became an important symbolic feature of great prestige. This was a stair without a well, either set against the building's facade or completely independent, unlike the perron staircase, which led up to an entrance door. In Viollet-le-Duc's view the great staircase was highly convenient 'because it did not interfere with internal arrangements, nor did it slice through the building from top to bottom, so interrupting the main routes of communication'. Essentially it served the great hall, which was often situated on the first floor. The bottom of the stair was positioned so as to create the most impressive effect, either on axis with the entrance or to form an extension to the entrance drive. Thus the grand staircase of the Palais de la Cité, built by Philippe le Bel in 1298, rose up opposite the courtyard gates.

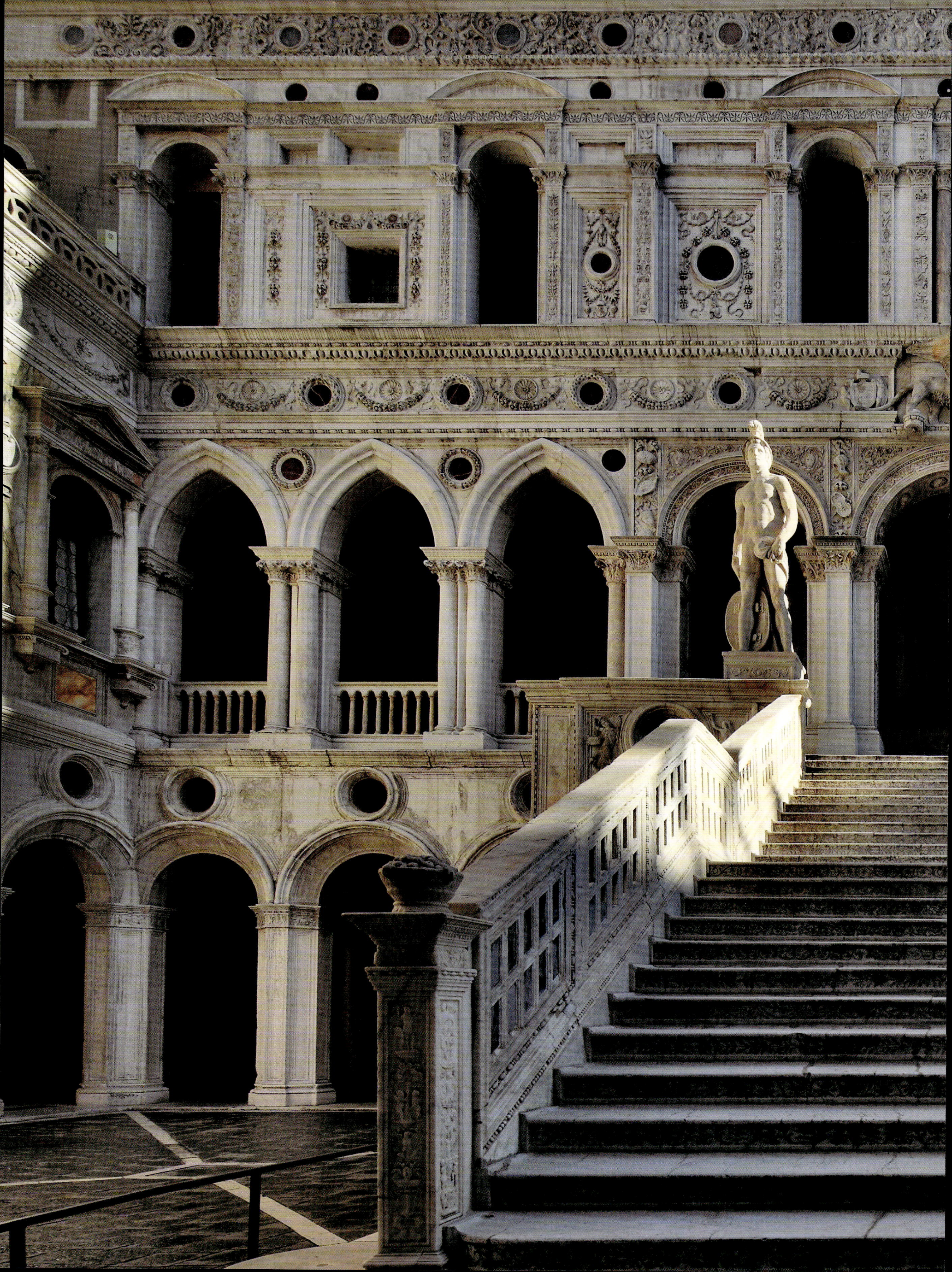

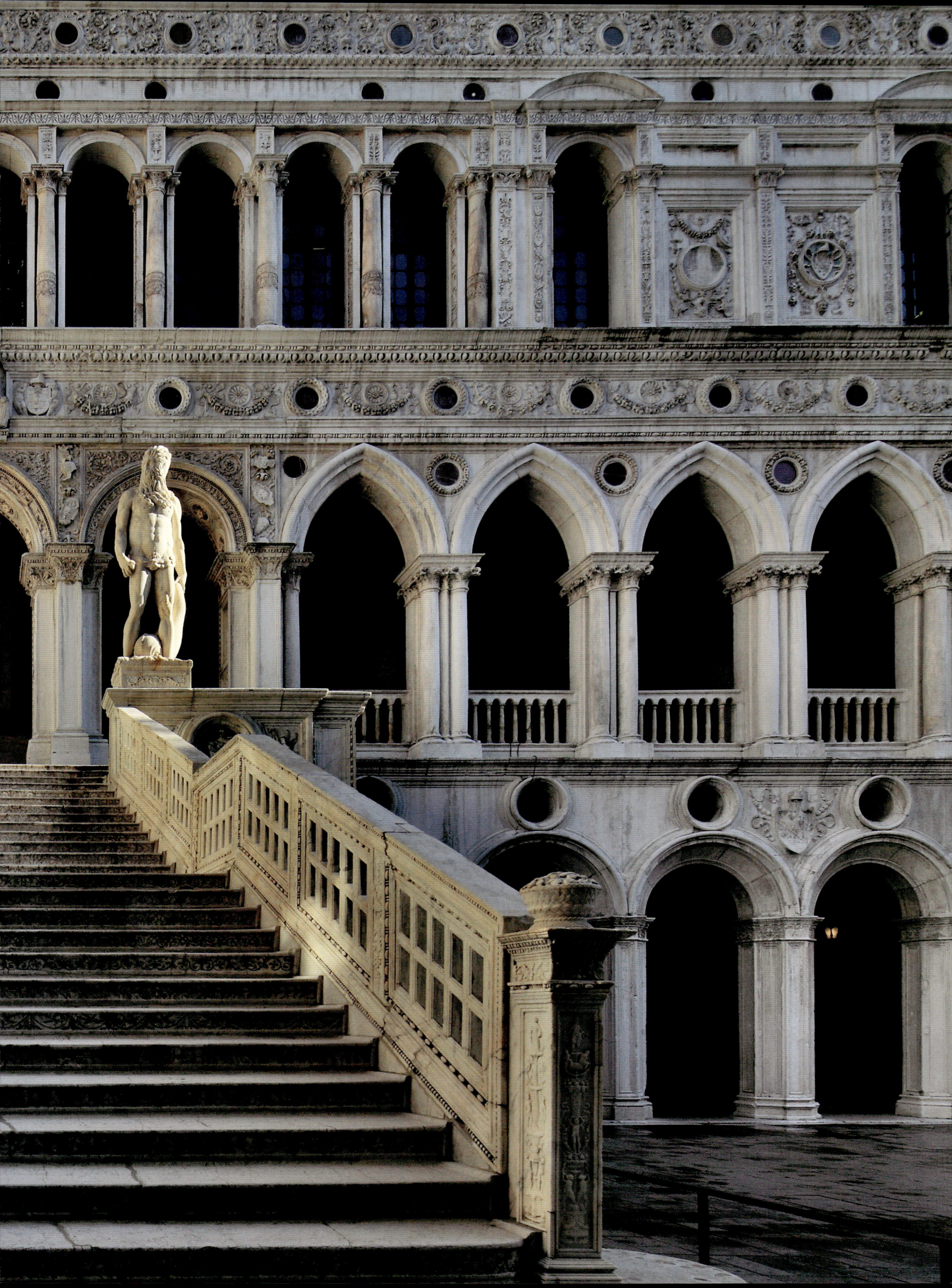

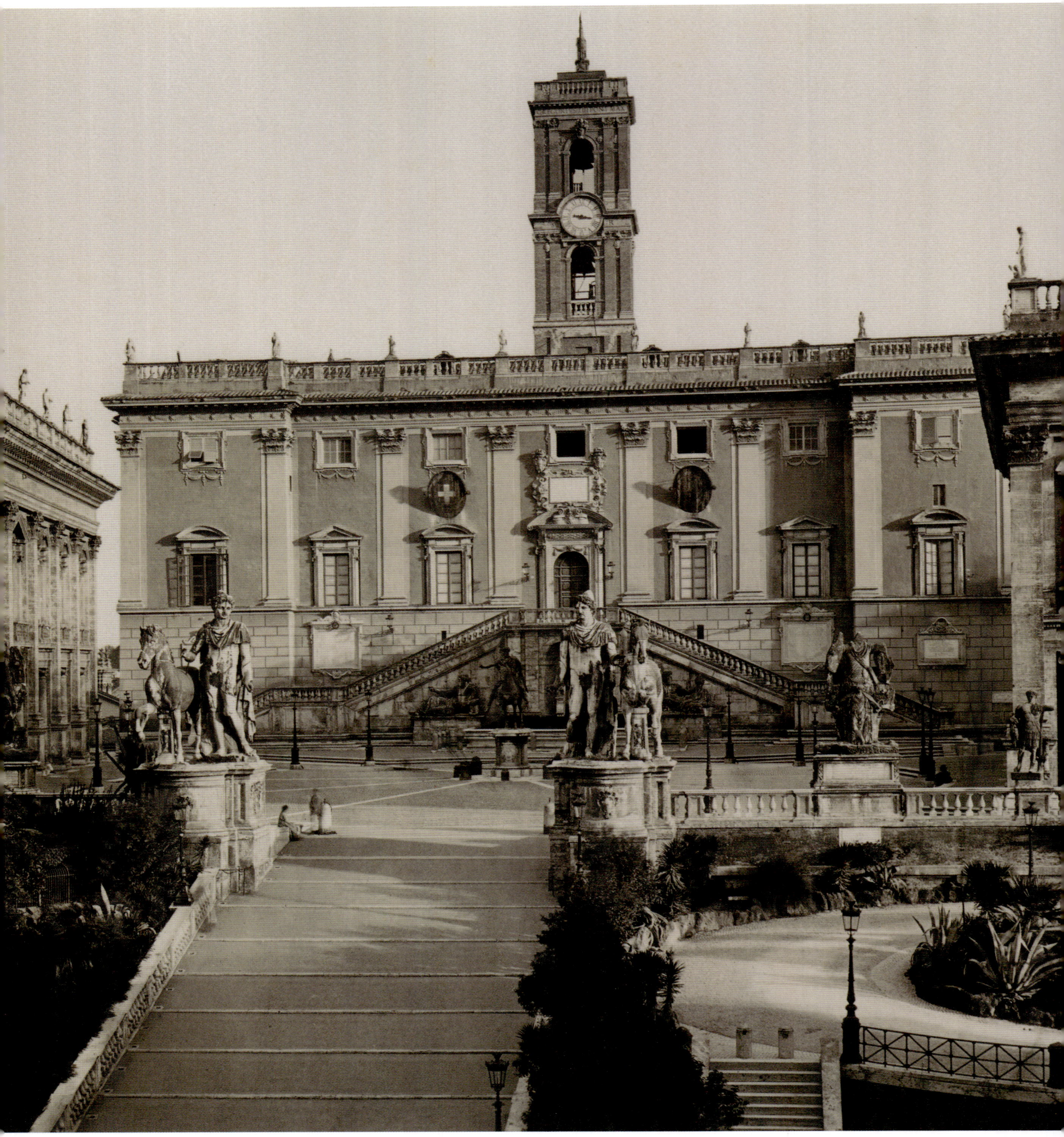

OPPOSITE
Piazza del Campidoglio, Rome, photographed c. 1880. The monumental staircase, with its pair of convergent flights, was added to the existing façade of the Palazzo dei Senatori between 1546 and 1552. The design was by Michelangelo.

RIGHT
Aerial view of the Piazza del Campodoglio. The Palazzo dei Senatori and its staircase are enhanced by the refurbishment of the square, carried out by Michelangelo from 1538.

This type of external stair was very widespread throughout medieval Europe, especially around the Mediterranean, where it was associated with the loggia, a ceremonial space with vault or ceiling that formed a covered and arcaded extension to the courtyard.

The Italian *palazzo* was designed primarily to house city councils and institutions. It was a public building par excellence, the seat of political life. In Florence, the classical plan of a palazzo consisted of the original core building, often fortified, with an arcaded courtyard and a staircase in one corner giving access to the first floor. The city's Palazzo Pretorio was built on this plan for the *capitano del popolo* in 1255; according to Vasari, it was the work of Lapo Tedesco, the father of Arnolfo di Cambio. This fortress, with its symbolic Volognana Tower, consisted of a courtyard surrounded by an arcaded portico on the ground floor and an audience chamber on the first floor, as was the convention in Italian public palazzos. When it was enlarged at the end of the century for the *podestà*, or chief magistrate, an external courtyard stair was added, leading up to the great hall. In the sixteenth century the palazzo housed the police chief and became known as the Bargello (pp. 38–39).

In Venice, the courtyard of the Palazzo Ducale was completely refurbished in the 1480s following a fire that ravaged the building's east wing. The architect Antonio Rizzo designed the courtyard façade and the new Giants' Staircase in the Renaissance style. Built between 1484 and 1501, this thirty-step staircase rises opposite the entrance; and since 1566 it has been watched over by two colossal statues by Jacopo Sansovino representing Mars and Neptune, gods of commerce and the sea, and symbols of the commercial and maritime power of the Venetian Republic. From the top of these steps, each newly elected doge would thank the members of the Great Council for his appointment. In Rome in 1538, Pope Paul III commissioned Michelangelo to draw up a plan for rebuilding all the buildings lining the Piazza del Campidoglio. For the Palazzo dei Senatori, the side pavilions and the rusticated plinth of the old building were reused in order to allow the construction of a monumental staircase with two converging flights. They also served as a plinth for the façade's colossal orders (1546–52). The construction of the rest of the palazzo, begun in 1573, was completed in 1612.

THE INTERNAL STAIRCASE AND THE TOWER HOUSE From the fourteenth and especially the fifteenth centuries, the level of luxury that formerly had been reserved for religious buildings found expression throughout Europe in secular architecture. For reasons of defence or on account of urban density, dwellings of any ambition – châteaux, palaces and mansions – were effectively vertical buildings in which the upper floors were at least as important as the ground floor. A twofold concern to increase both convenience and prestige of appearance led to the development of the internal staircase. This feature was to become one of the major themes of architecture, to which each country would bring its own solution.

Renouncing the external staircase on one side of the courtyard, Italy opted for the staircase with parallel flights beneath a more elaborately decorated barrel-vaulted roof. This development led to broader flights and shallower steps, in order to enhance the solemn dignity of the ascent from the palazzo entrance to the open galleries overlooking the courtyard. The grand staircase – a sign of distinction during this period, in which fortified dwellings became aristocratic mansions – was indissolubly linked with the *piano nobile*. In dwellings with a traditional vertical arrangement, the bottom floor was reserved for storage, shops or warehouses, the first floor for ceremonial and reception rooms, and the upper floors for private apartments.

In France, architecture was influenced by the cultural cross-currents that spread through Europe at this time, characterized in Northern Europe by the use of the spiral staircase following German examples. The model for the French tower house was Vincennes, where the royal tower, begun in 1361, was a response to a clear programme: to provide a luxury dwelling protected by a military presence, with a clearly established hierarchy between the floors, progressing from spaces for utilitarian functions to spaces for living. Elsewhere, developments centred on the layout of a building and on the general conception of how a house functioned, and stairs would take a variety of forms in different dwellings, even those of princely or similar status. In aristocratic dwellings, the spiral staircase was accommodated within a distinctive stair turret, a prestigious feature that recalled the medieval keep. The new generation of grandees, now busily engaged in modernizing or rebuilding their châteaux, adopted the model of the rectangular tower house with turrets – one of them containing the staircase – and retained a military presence for protection in times of strife.

When he came into possession of the Hôtel d'Artois (later the Hôtel de Bourgogne) in Paris, Jean sans Peur (John the Fearless) carried out a programme of enlargement in 1409–11. In the north tower, a great spiral staircase in the tradition of the one built at the Louvre for Charles V by Raymond du Temple occupied nearly half the space. From the ground-floor entrance, the staircase climbed up to the second floor, serving both the tower and a building to the north. Access to the two chambers on the upper floors was from the top landing of the great spiral staircase via a second staircase housed within a raised turret. The Tour Jean sans Peur still stands today, a remarkable vestige of the aristocratic dwellings of the late Middle Ages.

LEFT
The two covered flights of the staircase to the Rathaus in Bern, Switzerland, built from 1406 by the German architect Heinrich von Gengenbach.

LEFT
The Tour Jean sans Peur, Hôtel de Bourgogne, Paris: a cross-section and perspective drawing of the staircase, plus floor plans for the various levels.

OPPOSITE
Vaulting in the staircase of the Tour Jean sans Peur, Paris. Boughs of oak and hawthorn intertwined with hop tendrils are emblems of the dukes of Burgundy.

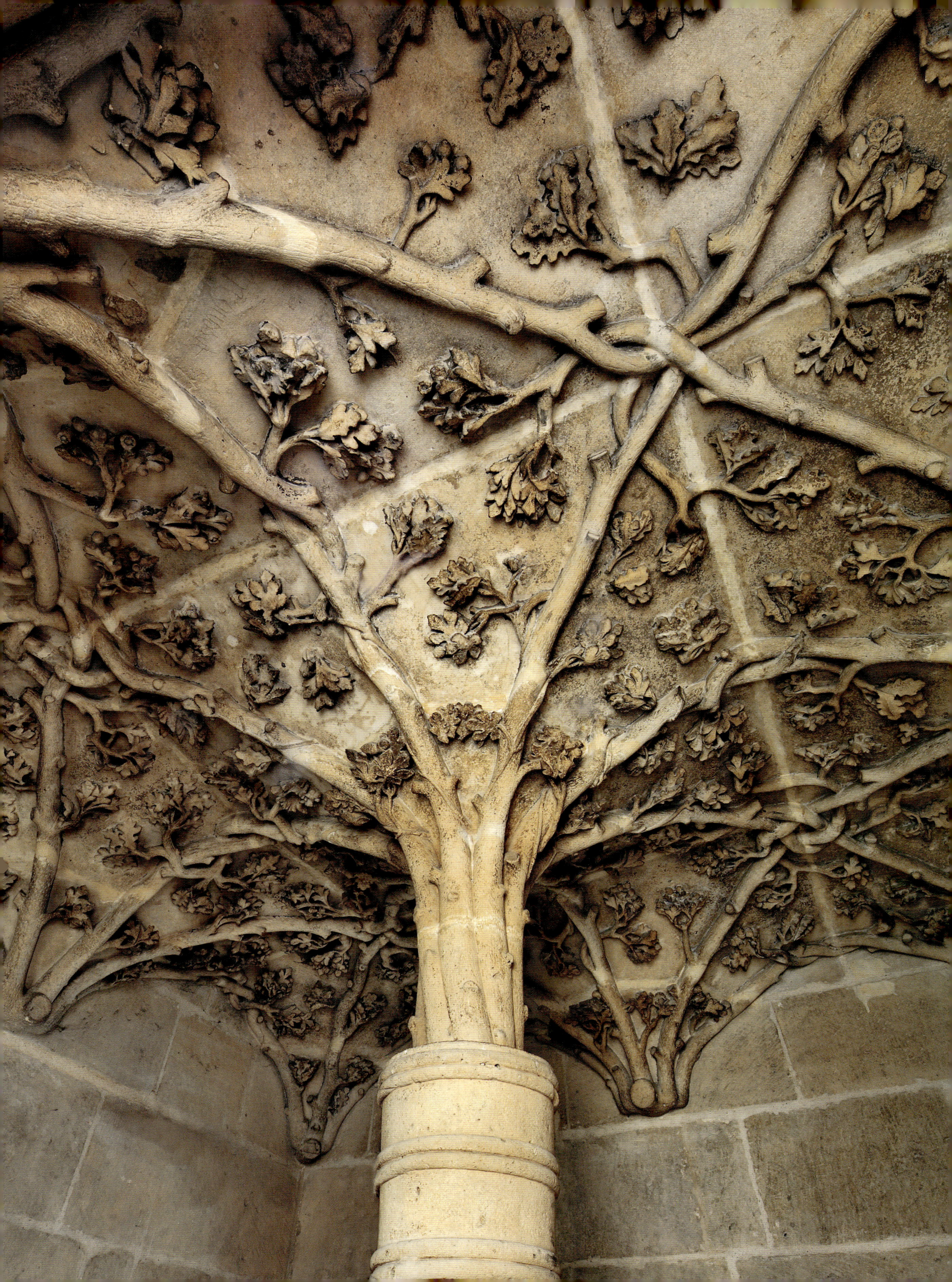

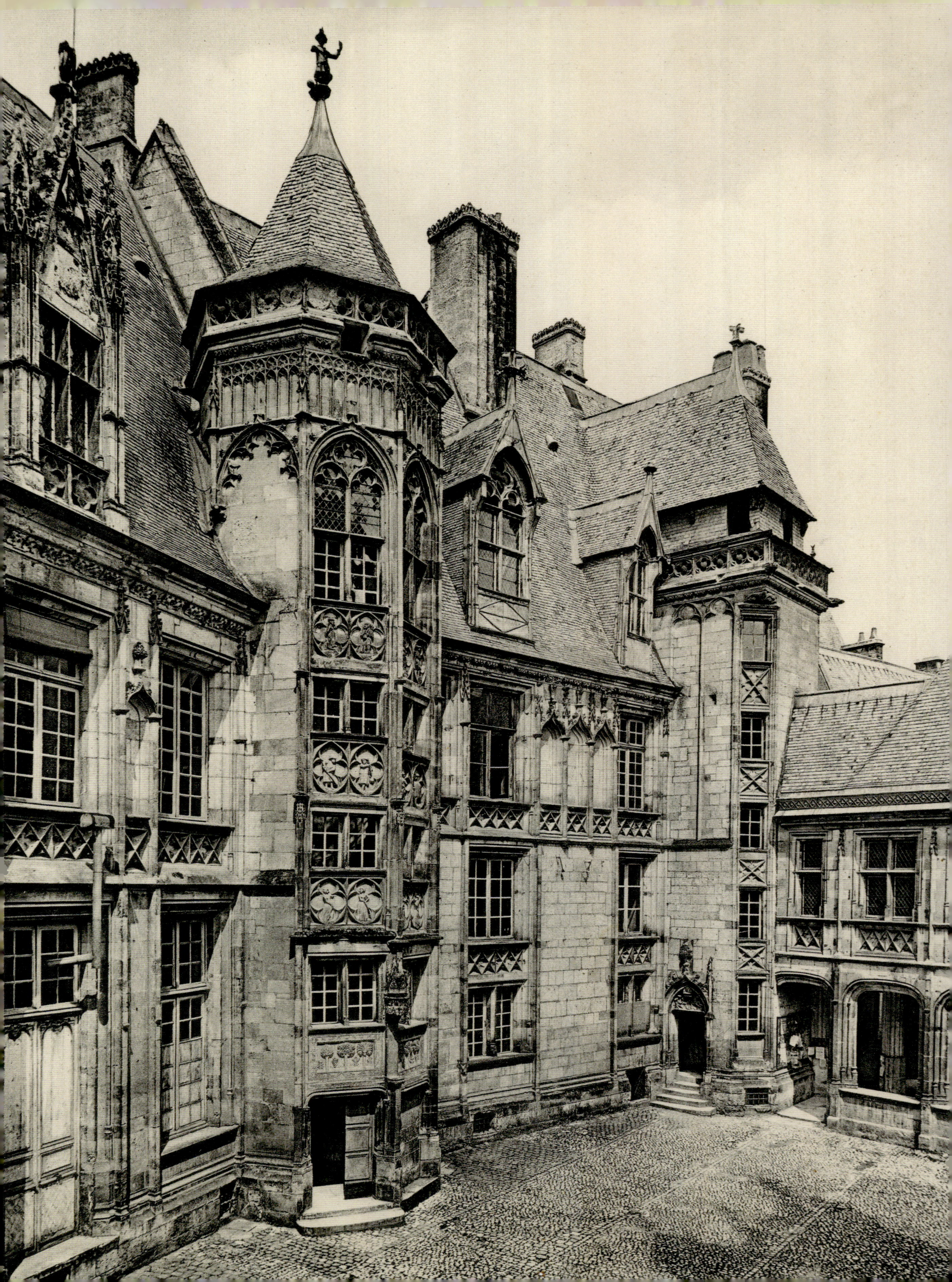

OPPOSITE
The turret housing the ceremonial staircase of the mansion built by Jacques Coeur in Bourges, one of the most sumptuous secular buildings of the Gothic period.

RIGHT
Staircase in the château of Châteaudun. This spiral stair, constructed as an integral part of the building in around 1510, marks a new departure. The broad diameter of the central newel favoured the use of Italianate decorative devices, including candelabra motifs.

OVERLEAF
Photograph of the courtyard of the Hôtel Binet, Tours, taken before 1932. This pair of timber staircases was added to the open gallery overlooking the courtyard in the late sixteenth or early seventeenth century, to serve the house built a century earlier.

THE HIERARCHY OF PUBLIC AND PRIVATE SPACES During this same period, dwellings became organized around two poles: the public and the private. The staircase ceased to be a purely functional structure and instead became an element in the carefully laid-out approach to ceremonial spaces. The doubling-up of communications systems between the ceremonial stair, reserved for noble visitors, and the secondary stair or stairs, destined for utilitarian purposes or for servants, prompted adaptation and reconstruction. In important buildings, the increasing numbers of spiral staircases conformed to a hierarchy within the plan, so as to establish more rapid communication between the various spaces. Rooms were now more numerous and formed a main dwelling area that reflected new developments in daily life. They were distinguished by their accessibility, which entailed making alterations to the main entrance and also, by extension, to the staircase.

The grand staircases of former years were replaced by the great spiral staircases of the late fourteenth and fifteenth centuries. These occupied pivotal positions in the dwelling, often situated in a projecting tower in order to leave the internal spaces unencumbered and to simplify the floor plan; they thus became a feature of the façade, and were positioned at the far end of a wing or in a corner formed by two wings. These spiral staircases influenced the arrangement of spaces throughout the building, making the approach to the first-floor public rooms more imposing, as in the mansion built by Jacques Coeur in Bourges.

The ceremonial staircase of the château of Saumur, incorporated into the main body of the building, is lit by daylight, which floods in through broad, open bays giving onto the courtyard, and has decorative parapets to the landings. The only surviving example of a fourteenth-century staircase of this type, it marks an important milestone in the development of domestic architecture, by virtue of the part it plays in the arrangement of the principal rooms. At Châteaudun, the great staircase of the Dunois Wing, begun around 1459, follows in the tradition of the Saumur staircase, consisting of a spiral built within a square well inside the building. The central newel is wider in diameter, which allows for a gentler and more spacious movement up and down, but also means that it can no longer be incorporated into the steps. The newel, constructed from courses of dressed stone, may be considered as a circular wall receiving the butts of the steps. This spiral staircase, positioned at the junction of two wings, provided convenient access – similar to that offered by a staircase with parallel flights – to the rooms that flank it by means of large rectangular landings. Its presence is signalled on the façade by broad, open bays, wider than the window bays, which open largely onto the courtyard and so allow daylight in. This combination of a main staircase constructed within a building with a portico was a new development.

From 1460, many buildings left ruined or abandoned during the Hundred Years' War were modernized or rebuilt. The internal staircase became an important feature of secular architecture. The spiral staircase rising from ground level in a separate circular or polygonal well, almost always occupying its own turret attached

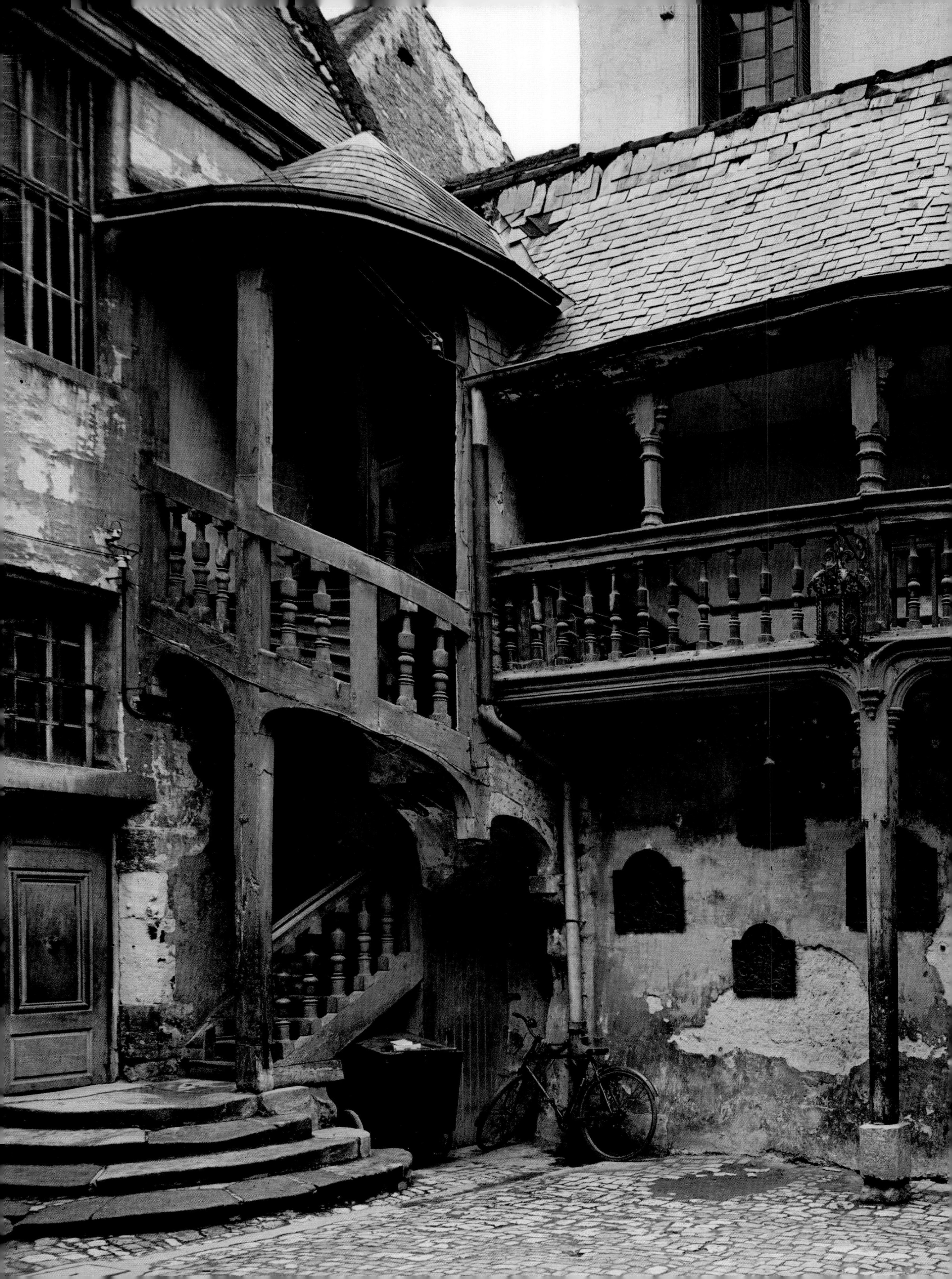

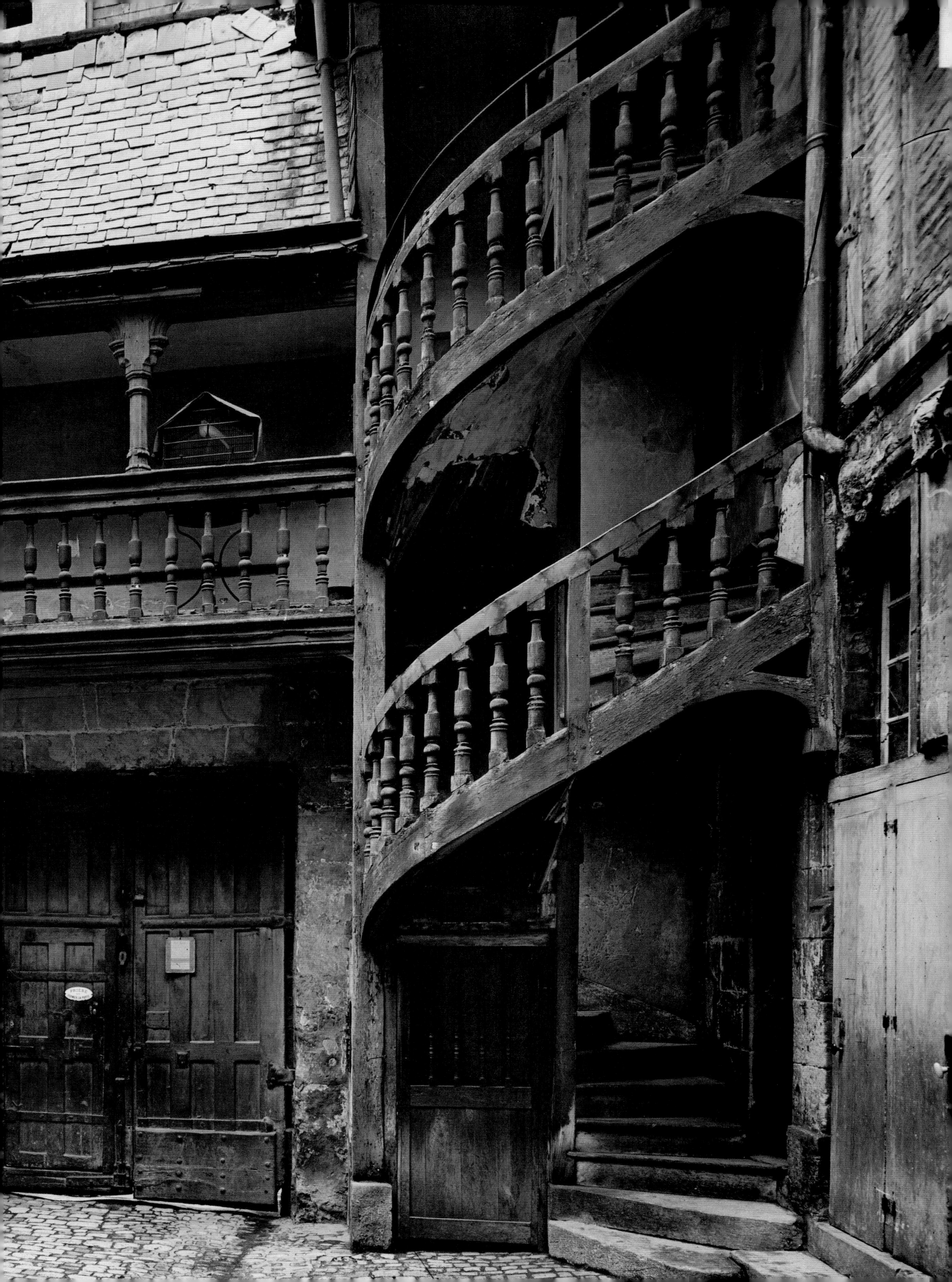

or half-set into the main building, remained dominant until the sixteenth century. With a few exceptions, it served a range of buildings from the grandest to the most modest. Its popularity may be explained by its simplicity of conception and its convenience. Like the straight staircase, it had the advantage of taking up little space. And even if its fan-shaped steps were slightly awkward to use, it was the only design that could be adapted to the constaints of old structures while also resolving the problem of the arrangement of rooms on different floors, since landings could be added at any point on its circumference.

The spiral staircase was built wherever it was needed, but in France it was usually positioned at the back of the entrance building, on axis with, and at the far end of a passage opening onto, the courtyard (rarely in a central position, as in northern Italy). Its tower, of wood or stone and distinguished by its tall silhouette, marked the juncture of two wings. It was lit by parallelogram-shaped bays that followed the pitch line. Its position enabled other wings to be added around the courtyard, which could be accessed either directly or via open half-timbered galleries.

The wooden staircase of the old Panier Fleury inn in Tours stands in the north-western corner of a small courtyard. It is attached to two façades, the older, northern one dating from the fifteenth century. This spiral staircase, with a landing on each floor, boasts balusters with moulded decorations. A narrow passage beneath the bottom bay links the courtyard with a corridor leading to the street. This staircase, which serves three floors, is typical of the evolution from the helical stair to the U-shaped stair. Pairs of straight steps are added for comfort at the top and bottom of each flight, which ends in a landing.

The houses known as *maisons à pondalez* (or *maisons à lanterne*) in Morlaix, Brittany, date from the first quarter of the sixteenth century and are a highly specific form of noble merchant urban dwelling, found nowhere else in Europe. Each dwelling consists of two buildings separated by a roofed courtyard. A spiral staircase of solid steps around a cylindrical newel, and a series of gangways or *ponts d'allée* attached to the staircase by means of a carved corner post rising the full height of the house, allowed movement between rooms that overlooked the street and those in the rear building.

LEFT
Staircase of the Maison de la Reine Berthe, Chartres. The spiral stair, probably built in the early sixteenth century, is contained within a semi-projecting half-timbered turret. Following Gothic tradition, its presence is signalled on the outside only by its sloping windows.

OPPOSITE
Staircase of the Panier Fleury inn, Tours: elevations; cross-section; plans of the ground and top floors; and a cutaway showing the staircase newel perpendicular to a landing.

FAR LEFT
Timber staircase in the Sinnwell tower, Nuremberg Castle, Germany. Housed in a thirteenth-century defensive tower, it led to a lookout post from which to guard against attacks from the east.

LEFT
Staircase of a typical house in Morlaix, of a type known as maison à pondalez *(Breton for* pont d'allée, *or 'gangway') or* maison à lanterne. *The spiral staircase, supported by the trunk of an oak tree some 10 metres (33 feet) tall, provided access to galleries linking the house buildings overlooking the street with those overlooking the garden.*

ÉLÉVATIONS

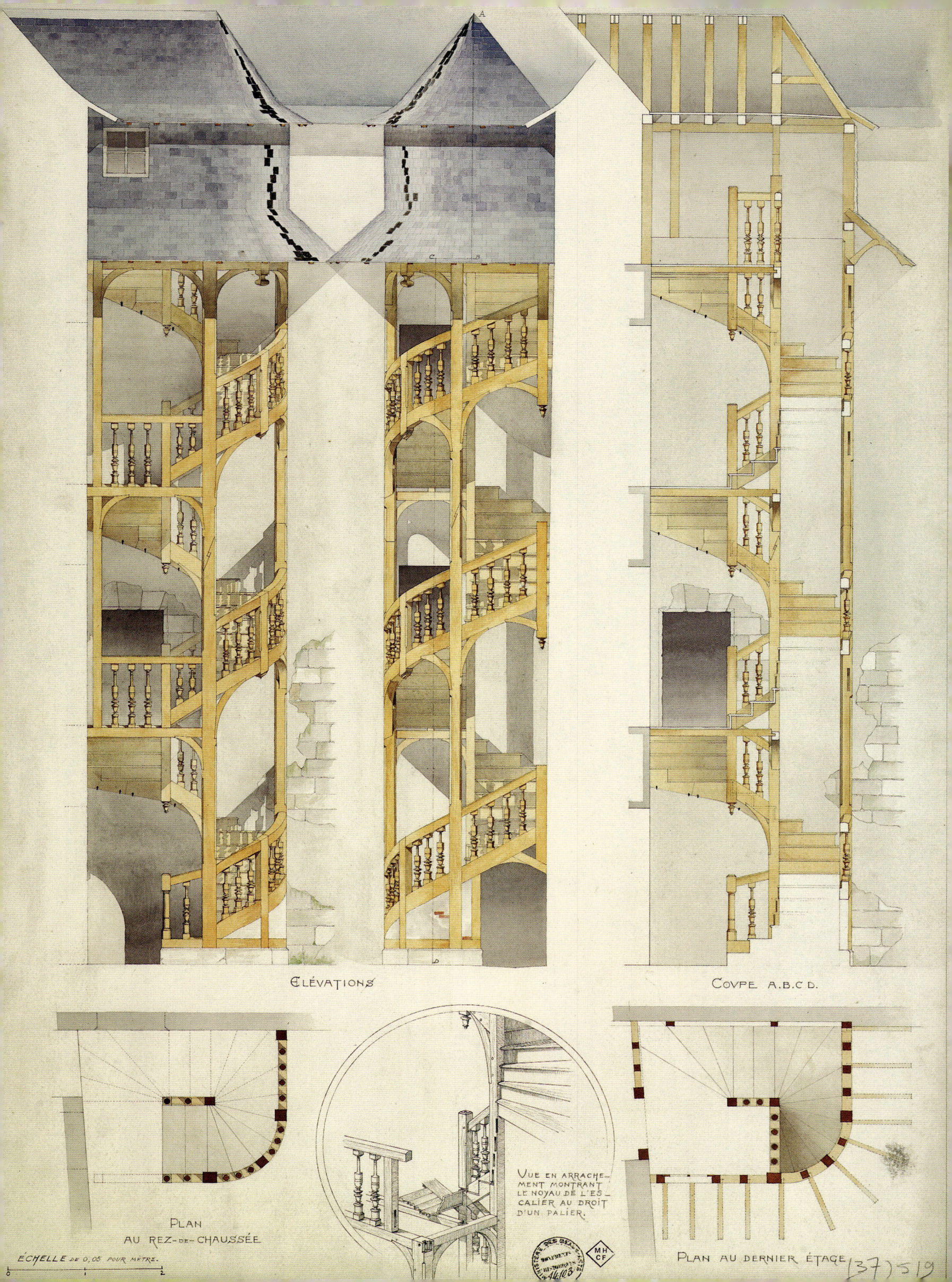

COUPE A.B.C.D.

PLAN AU REZ-DE-CHAUSSÉE

VUE EN ARRACHEMENT MONTRANT LE NOYAU DE L'ESCALIER AU DROIT D'UN PALIER.

PLAN AU DERNIER ÉTAGE

ÉCHELLE DE 0,05 POUR MÈTRE.

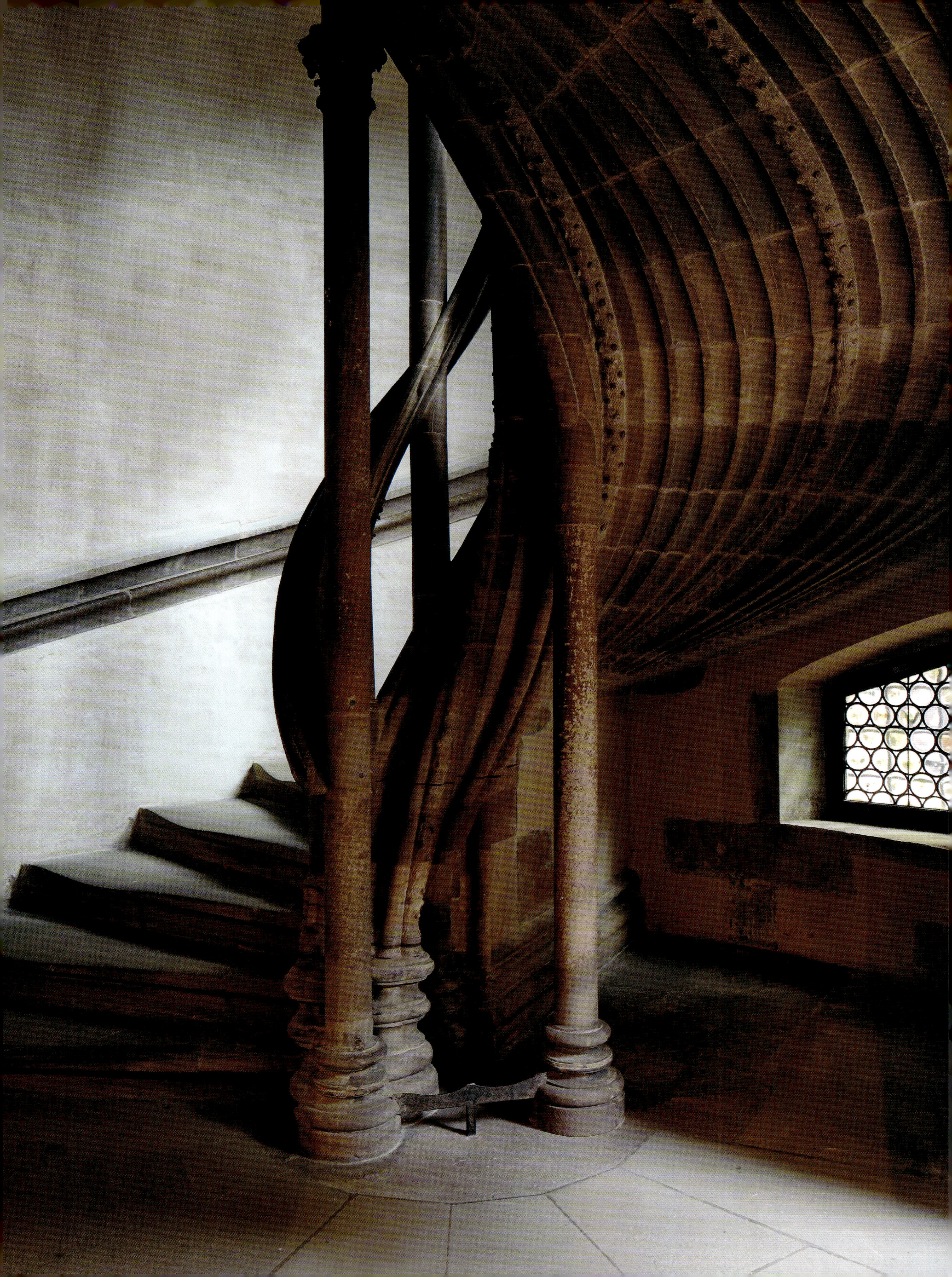

1100–1600 | 55

OPPOSITE
Staircase in the building that accommodates the Oeuvre Notre-Dame in Strasbourg. This stair, built by Hans Thomann Ulberger in 1578–85, consists of a newel in the form of a hollow spiral encircled by slender Corinthian columns. The underside of the steps is decorated with fluting and lopped branch motifs.

RIGHT
Perspective drawing of a helical staircase attributed to Philibert de l'Orme. With its hollow spiral newel encircled by slender columns, this stair displays a virtuoso command of both structure and decoration, combining a Renaissance vocabulary with echoes of the Gothic lexicon.

VARIATIONS ON THE SPIRAL STAIRCASE Germanic countries explored skilful structures with either open centres or hollow or solid newels. Some staircases had large-diameter or twin spirals, as at the castle of Graz (1499–1500), where the architect juxtaposed two helical stairs so that the flights crossed over in the middle, between the newels. The user passes from one flight to the other by climbing either clockwise or anticlockwise. In horizontal projection, these two staircases form the shape of an '8'.

Starting in the fourteenth century, the newel of a spiral staircase might be dispensed with in order to allow more space in very restricted sites. At the end of each step where it was closest to the centre of the staircase a tubular shape emerged from the handrail, leaving the newel space open.

The appearance of the hollow newel, in the form of a helix approximately 25–30 cm (10–12 inches) in diameter, revolutionized the structure of the staircase, since the newel was now replaced by open space. These open-spiral staircases were contained within circular, polygonal or square wells, and were composed of steps carved from a single block of stone, complete with stringers and stacked on top of each other as *tas-de-charge*: each fan-shaped step was self-supporting. Each riser overlapped the one below, on which it rested by its very edge, so forming a newel with offset sinusoidal sides. The other side was cut into the well facing, and the underside was left exposed. Mathurin Jousse describes an open stone spiral staircase in which 'the newel on which the small butt, or remainder, of the steps is hollow, so that an object dropped from the top may easily be seen falling to the bottom'.

From the end of the sixteenth century, this type of open spiral staircase with no newel post took over from the older spiral staircase as an alternative to straight flights of stairs, since in narrow and restricted spaces their steps were more open and convenient. It was an idea that became very widespread, notably in Alsace and Germany. In Strasbourg, the Musée de l'Oeuvre Notre-Dame, which has housed the cathedral works department since the thirteenth century, occupies two houses separated by a courtyard. A half-timbered hexagonal turret has been added to the eastern wing, in the corner of the courtyard. This Gothic turret encloses a helical stone staircase. Built under the direction of Hans Thomann Ulberger between 1578 and 1585, it is signalled from the outside by its stepped windows (p. 54). It serves two floors and is extended to join the southern buildings by a series of open, half-timbered galleries. The open spiral staircase is encircled by small Corinthian columns; on the underside of the steps, the ceiling is decorated with fluting and branches. The top landing has a balustrade and a vaulted roof in the Flamboyant style.

The Convent of Christ at Tomar, Portugal, contains eight cloisters built in the fifteenth and sixteenth centuries. The roof of the two-storey Cloister of John III forms a broad terrace connecting the monks' dormitory with the church. The first to work on the construction, from 1557, was the Spaniard Diogo de Torralva, but it was completed in 1591 by Philip II's Italian architect, Filippo Terzi. The first storey is reached by four helical staircases, one in each corner of the cloister.

THE EARLY ITALIAN RENAISSANCE In the early fifteenth century the northen regions of Italy were heavily influenced by the Gothic style, and by the

LEFT
Staircase in the Cloister of John III at Tomar, Portugal. Positioned in a corner of the cloister, this floating spiral stair with helical string gives access to the upper floor. On the roof terrace it is crowned with a sentry box in the form of a cupola.

OPPOSITE
In 1499–1500, an unknown master builder designed these two extremely unusual staircases for the castle of Graz in Austria. Two helical stairs rise side by side, to meet at a point that enables users to pass from one flight to another.

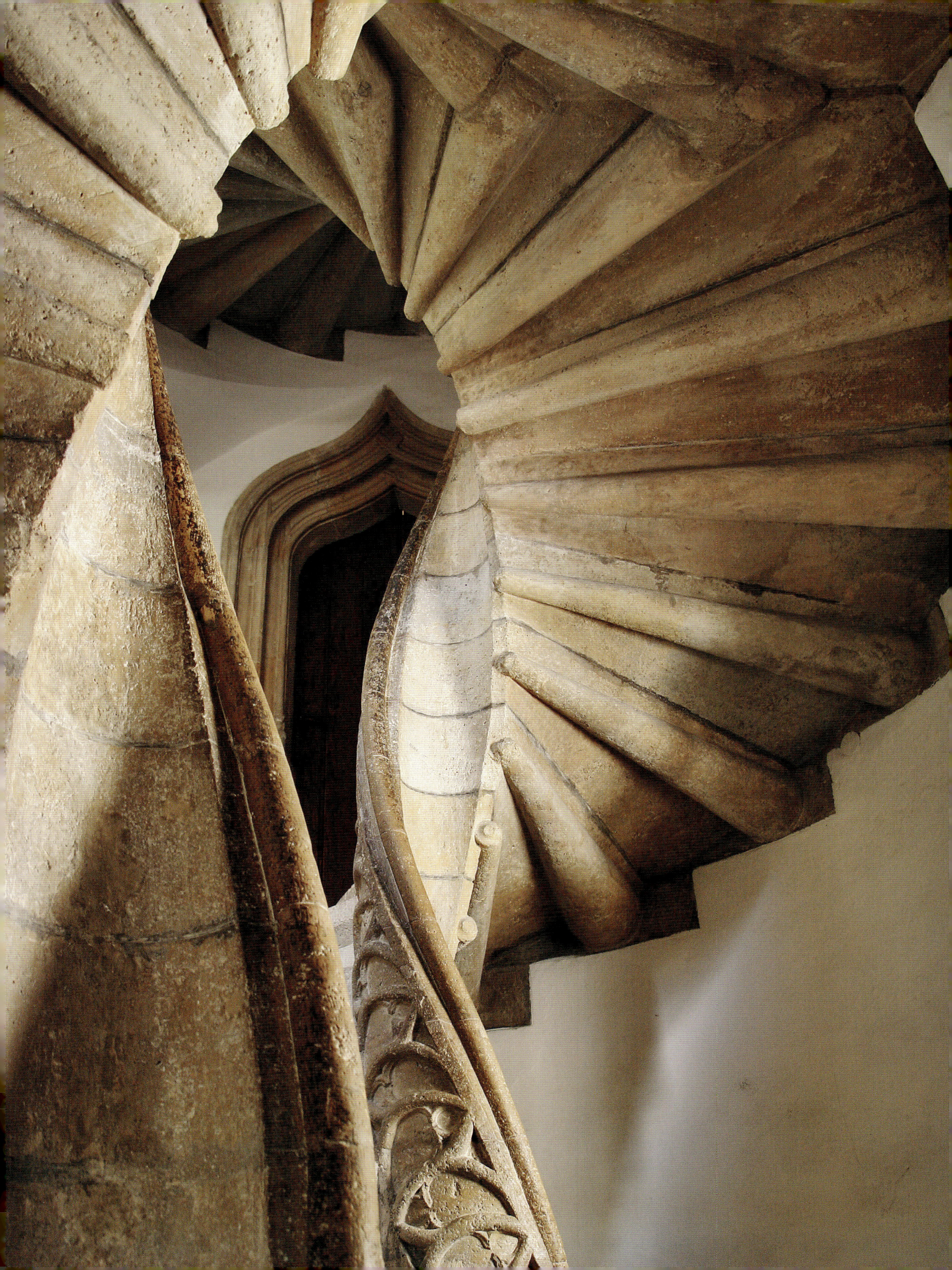

German artists established in Lombardy and the Veneto. Nobles and wealthy merchants lived in the cities, where the most characteristic form of secular architecture was the palazzo. This traditionally consisted of an inward-looking block arranged around an internal courtyard, square or rectangular in plan and massive in appearance, with broad loggias opening onto this central space. In buildings of some importance, staircases began to multiply and to change position and shape; transitional spaces were remodelled in order to improve the buildings' internal arrangements and to ensure easier communication, better adapted to the changing requirements of daily life.

The art of the Renaissance emerged and developed in Florence, where dwellings reflected the growing material comfort of secular life. Florentine architects strove to establish an organic link between the various elements making up the palazzo, among which the staircase enjoyed a place of special importance. The palazzo's internal plan followed straight lines and right angles; now a new type of staircase, with straight steps closed off by a dividing wall, replaced the spiral stair. Innovations included a larger stairwell, the search for the ideal relationship between the staircase and the arcades lining the courtyard, and a renewed vocabulary of the staircase. Elsewhere in Italy the spiral staircase clung on only in exceptional cases, such as the Palazzo Ducale in Urbino (1476) and the Vatican Belvedere (1516), where Bramante adopted it purely out of the need to design a ramp that could be negotiated on horseback, following the medieval custom.

In Venice, the staircase of the Palazzo Contarini del Bovolo (*bovolo* meaning 'snail' in the Venetian dialect) was commissioned from the architect Giovanni Candi by Pietro Contarini in 1499. The external helical staircase rises through four storeys, with galleries on each level. Its decoration – finely sculpted arcades of slender white columns that glow in the sun – is unique.

THE INFLUENCE OF ITALIAN TREATISES

The European 'discovery' of Italian models took place at a time when secular and civic architecture was undergoing a period of great experimentation, taking its inspiration from classical antiquity. The translation into Italian of Vitruvius' architectural treatise *De Architectura*, which appeared in 1521, formed a link between classical thought and the Renaissance. The earliest known survey of the subject, it has served as the theoretical basis for architects of all eras and had a considerable influence – notably on Leon Battista Alberti and Andrea Palladio. According to Vitruvius, architecture was a science based on mathematical thought, and was to be understood through both practice and theory. The manner in which a building was laid out established the proportions of its various constituent parts – the human figure being the principal source for the ideal proportions of classical architecture – and these different parts should be designed in a manner appropriate for their intended use.

The earliest Italian theoretical works became more widely read with the introduction of printing. In his treatise *De re aedificatoria* (*On the Art of Building*), which was first printed in 1485, Alberti argued that every building was a body in which all elements were connected; these elements were a response to the proportions upon which the beauty of the completed edifice depended. He recommended that staircases should be well lit, and that their dimensions should be appropriate to the

LEFT
*The spiral staircase of the Palazzo Contarini del Bovolo in Venice, built in 1499, gave its name to this branch of the family (*bovolo *means 'snail' in the Venetian dialect).*

OPPOSITE
The staircase of the former Palazzo Dandolo in Venice, now the Hotel Danieli. The building was constructed in the fourteenth century on the traditional palazzo plan. The staircase, which would originally have been open to the elements, occupied the corner formed by two wings and served the loggias.

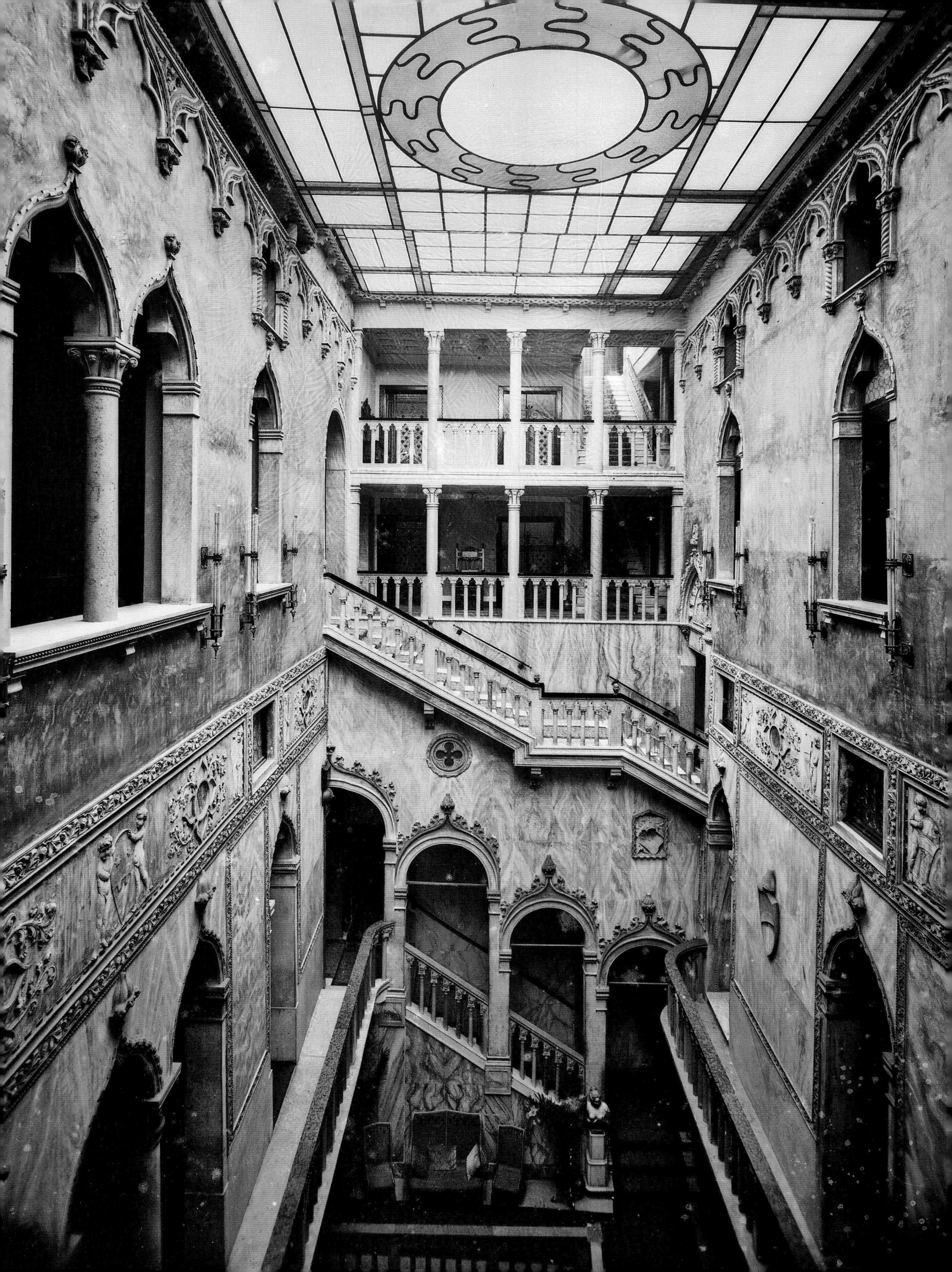

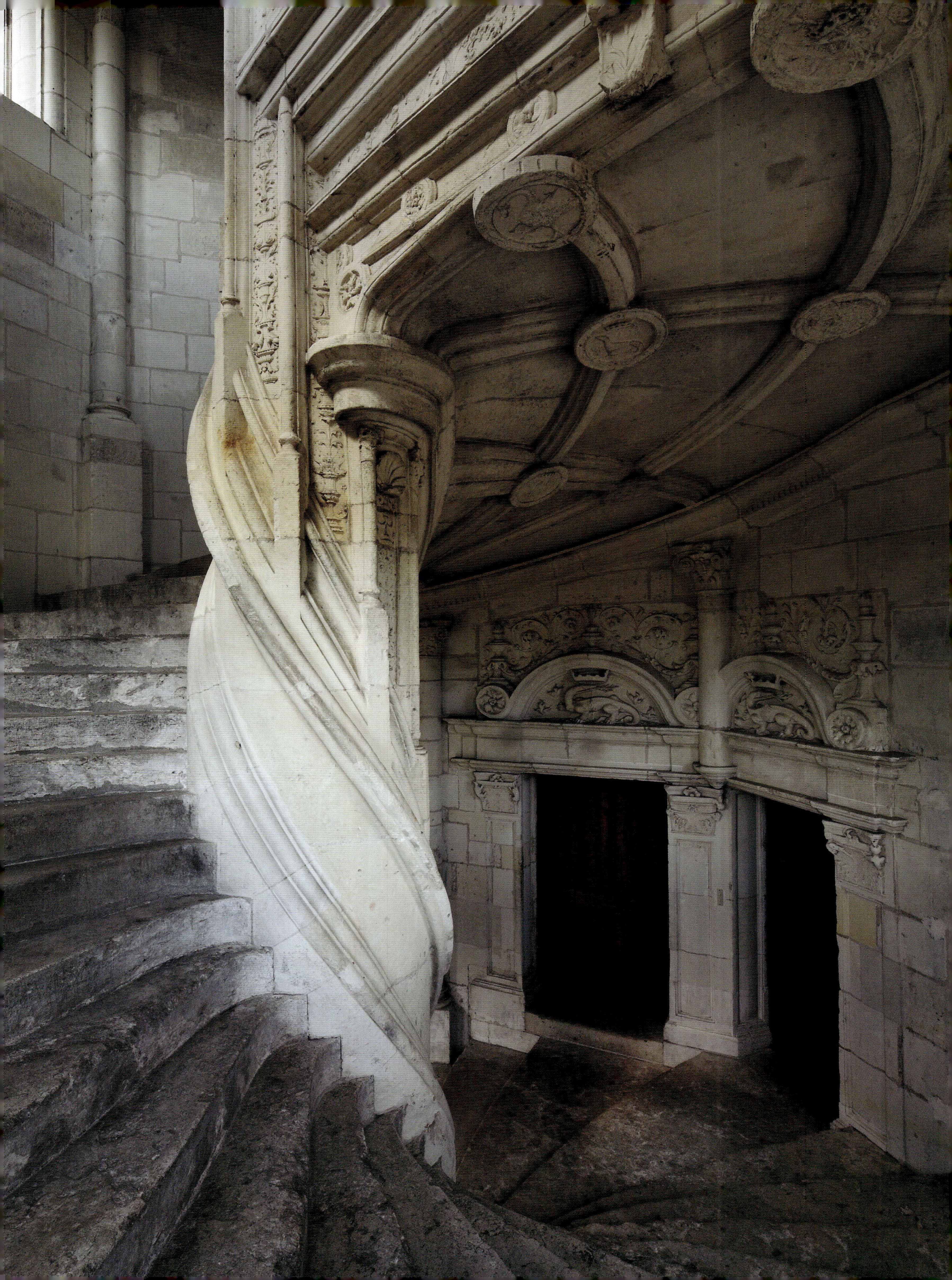

OPPOSITE
Though Gothic in essence, the staircase of the François I wing in the château of Blois is Italianate in decoration. The newel is embellished with narrow panels divided by slender columns, and the underside of the steps is pared back to form a smooth ceiling with a type of ribbed vaulting.

BELOW RIGHT
Built between 1515 and 1519, the staircase at the château of Blois is contained within an octagonal tower set into the façade – a structural arrangement that recalls the half-timbered turret. The walls of the stairwell are reduced, and the bays follow the pitch of the handrail.

OVERLEAF
The double staircase at the château of Chambord, which lies on axis with the keep, consists of two helical stairs rising around a broad newel with openings. Between the pillars, the bays are lit via the adjoining cruciform galleries.

PAGES 64–65
View into the lantern of the staircase at Chambord. The flat ceiling is embellished with coffering containing the monogram of François I and his emblem, the salamander. Flanking the generous windows are eight niches intended to hold statues.

importance of the site. The transition from the Middle Ages to the Renaissance was marked by a synthesis between two worlds and two ways of thinking about them, and between two styles that coexisted, separate but not exclusive. New and original investigations throughout Europe at the turn of the sixteenth century sought to establish the fundamental principles of regularity, symmetry and proportion, in marked contrast with the empirical practices of the previous era. The rediscovery of the merits of classical art focused attention on the perfection of the human body, at once natural and ideal. The influence of this new style and new conception of art was confirmed in Europe by the desire of princes to follow the Italian fashion. Artists established links with each other and travelled widely, thus encouraging the appearance of buildings imbued with a new spirit. With the reign of Charles VIII, who died in 1498, Italian forms began to appear in France.

TRADITION AND MODERNITY The introduction of Italian forms of decoration to France had no influence whatsoever on the architectural treatment of the staircase: in the early sixteenth century the large-scale spiral staircase housed in a separate tower was still in its heyday. The culmination of developments in architecture that took hold in the fourteenth century, it would remain the major feature of French architecture until 1520, when the first Italian-inspired staircases with straight flights appeared in the châteaux of the Loire Valley.

At Blois, the great spiral staircase of traditional Gothic construction was one of a group of structures adapted or built from scratch between 1515 and 1519 under François I. An addition to the original plan, and almost certainly an afterthought, it is ill-assorted with the rest of the façade. The spiral staircase, enclosed in an octagonal tower set into the building frontage, could be reached from the courtyard and declared its purpose through its unusual layout. The weight of the almost entirely open stairwell walls was transferred to the corner piers, with their rectangular flying buttresses, while the bays follow the pitch of the handrails. Within this structure, which recalls that of half-timbered turrets, the stairwell is roofed with a barrel vault that circles a broad newel constructed of courses of dressed stone. The independent winders were designed to be convex at the newel edge and slightly convex in the middle, so as to make them easier to use. They are cut back on the underside to create a smooth ceiling, whose carved decoration is the first example of its type on a French staircase. The stair culminates in a palm-tree vault with decorative ribs and pendant roof bosses. The sophistication of the decorative scheme echoed the increasing luxury of the French court and the growing splendour of royal ceremonial.

The development of the spiral staircase centred around an open space found its apogee at the château of Chambord, which marks the culmination of this tradition. It illustrates the fascination exercised over Renaissance architects by the staircase and confirms the international character of experiments on this theme. In 1518 François I planned to build a replacement for the stronghold of the Comtes de Blois at Chambord. It is thought that Leonardo da Vinci and Domenico da Cortona both worked on the plans for the new château, which was intended primarily as a hunting lodge. The original wooden model was laid

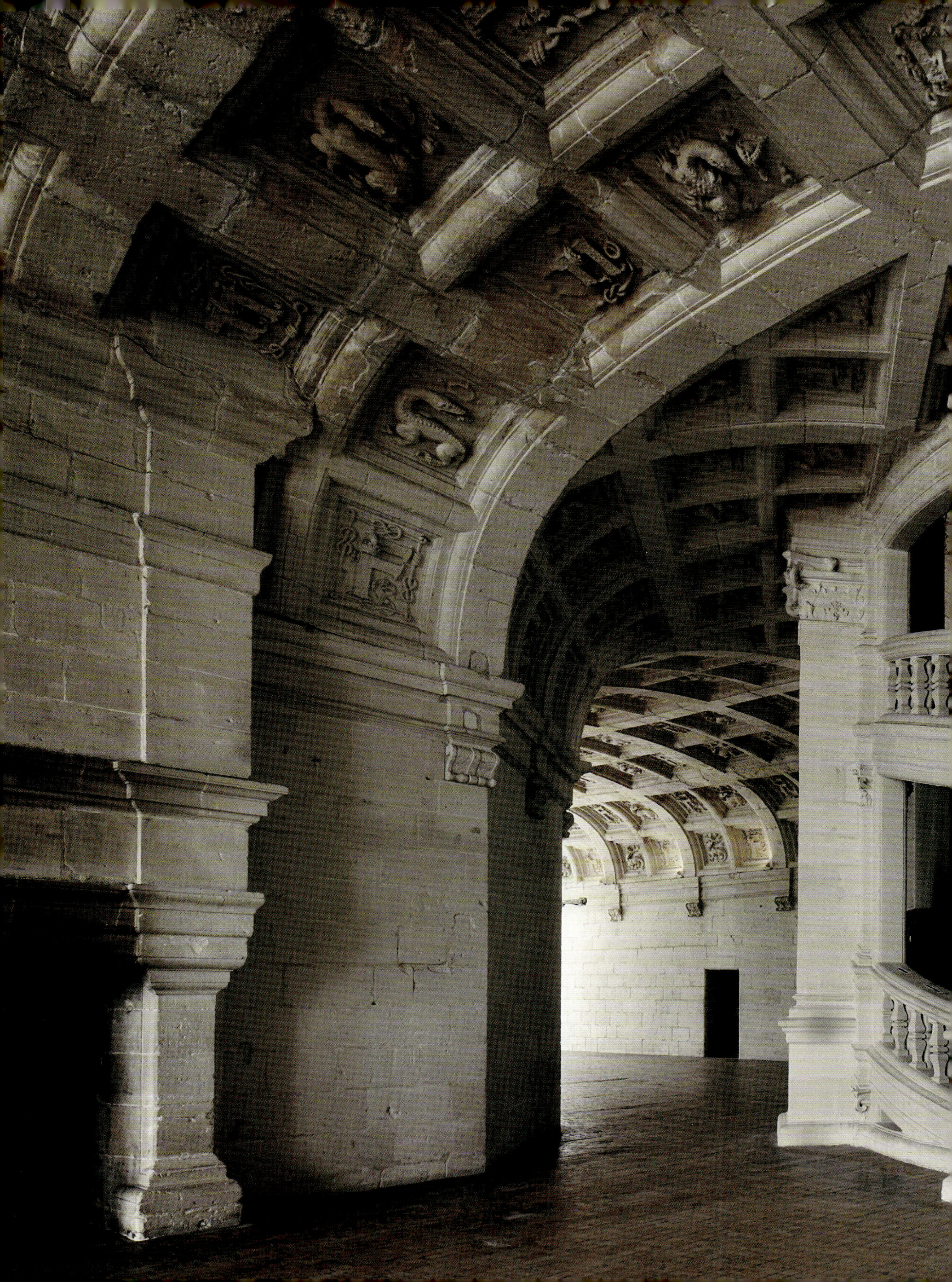

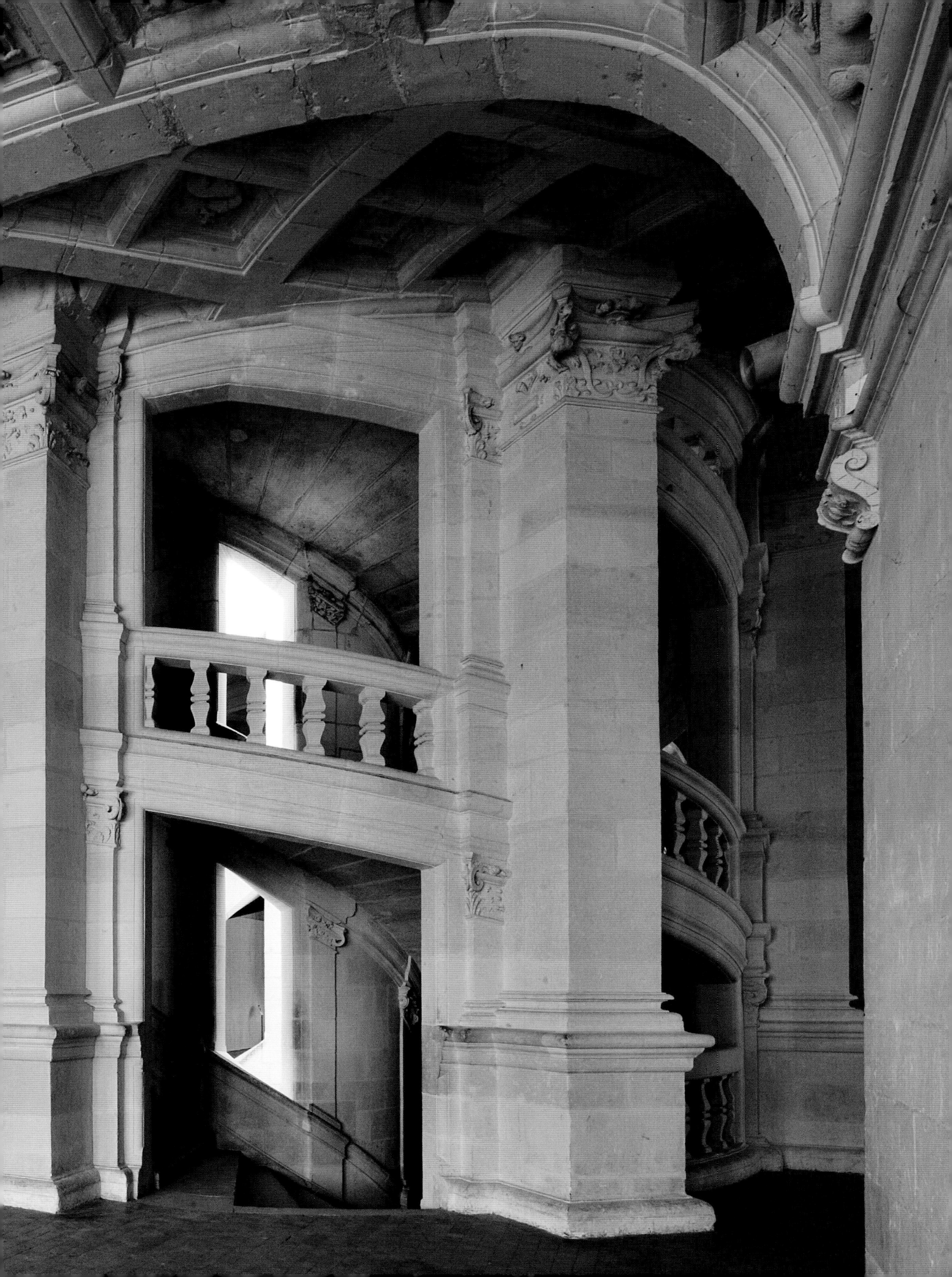

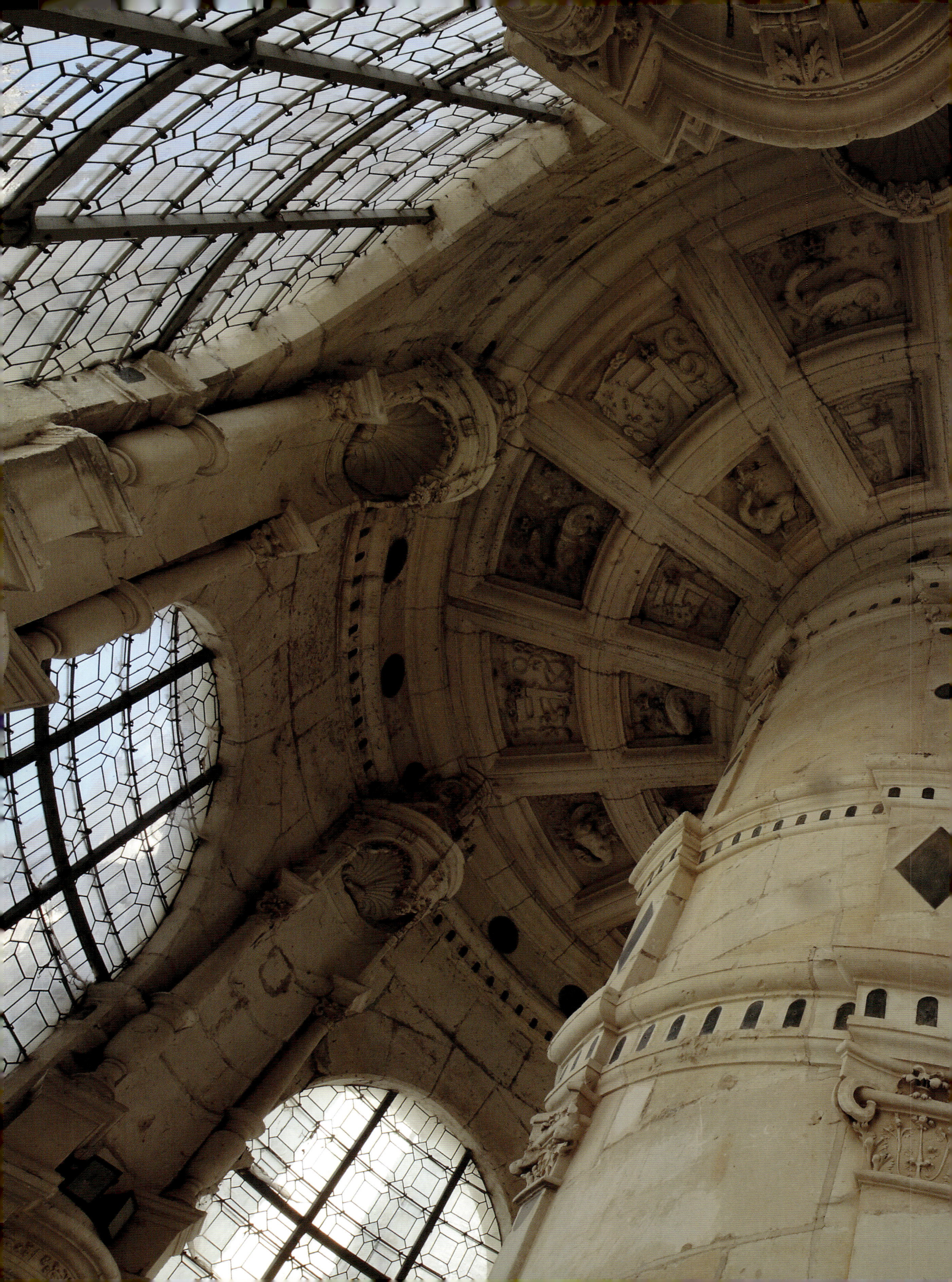

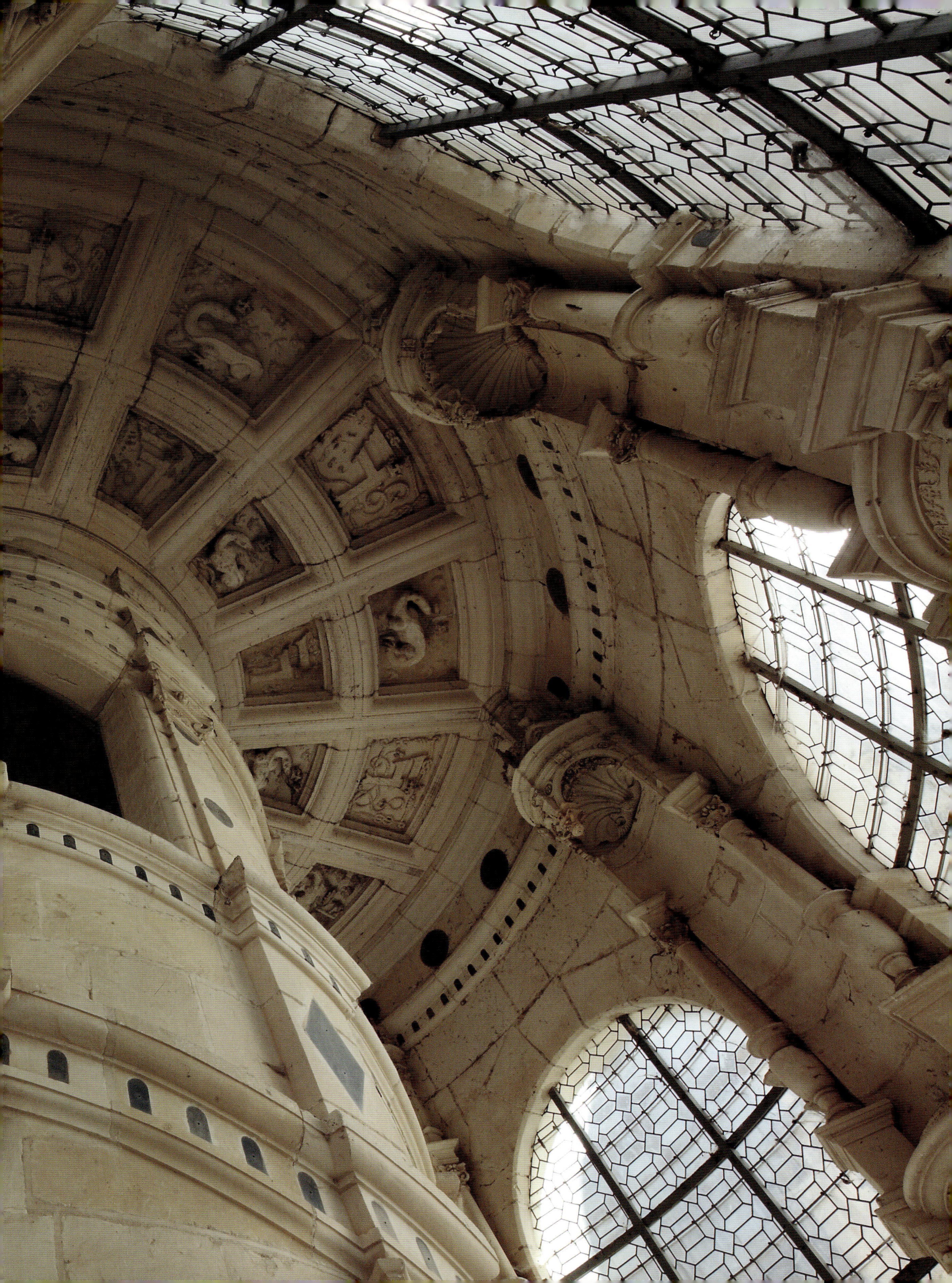

out on two main circulation axes that intersect to form a Latin cross, one of which housed a staircase with straight flights.

The overall conception of the plan, including the idea of a central staircase with four complete turns, developed between 1519 and 1521 and is attributed to Leonardo. In the eighteenth chapter of his *I Quattro libri dell'architectura* (1570), which is dedicated to 'staircases and their diverse varieties, [and] the number and dimensions of their steps', Palladio cites Chambord, though he had never seen it, and the image that supports the text confirms his interest. What attracted the architect was the ingenious nature of the design, which contrived to accommodate within a single stairwell four independent flights of stairs serving four separate apartments. In the final plan, the four flights were reduced to two, while still respecting and accentuating the centralized plan of the building and its internal symmetry.

This double staircase was built by French craftsmen. Composed of two helical flights, it rises around a broad open newel, positioned on axis with the keep and crowned by a lantern. In plan as in elevation, the pilasters placed inside and outside the stairwell are dictated by the complex structure that they embellish. Their diameter, which increases as they move out from the centre, is determined by the radius of the stairwell. In the apartments, the buttresses supporting the stairs are embellished on each floor, featuring broad pilasters that support the ceiling and are decorated with horizontal astragals and necking to the capitals. Those that follow the pitch of the flights, by contrast, have slanting bases and capitals. Within the stairwell the pilasters are grouped in threes, with the central pilaster projecting slightly. This design, logical in structure and dynamic in its aesthetic, may be compared with the flamboyant style championed by Philibert de l'Orme. The second floor in particular is remarkable for its coffered ceiling depicting François's royal symbols – a crowned 'F' and the salamander – accompanied by a knotted cord, emblem of his mother, Louise de Savoie.

The position of this staircase, invisible from the outside, is unique in sixteenth-century architecture. The stairs are lit from above by the lantern, and by borrowed light from the cruciform apartments. A small, second spiral staircase, attached to the flank of the larger one, gives access to the terrace at the foot of the lantern tower, where one of the capitals bears the date 1533. The lantern is topped with a fleur-de-lis, symbol of the French monarchy, instead of a cross.

The spiral staircase of the château of Les Granges-Cathus in the Vendée, built in 1525, is of interest for the novelty of its decorative vocabulary, which mingles the heraldic repertoire with allegorical subjects. This uninterrupted decorative scheme, on the underside of winders that have been pared right back, can only have been executed *in situ*. The project's two major innovations – continuous decoration and the coffered ceiling – were to pass into posterity as a standard feature of staircases with straight flights.

STAIRCASES WITH STRAIGHT FLIGHTS

Between the fifteenth and the mid-sixteenth centuries, as economic prosperity returned, the U-shaped staircase with straight flights became a widespread feature in châteaux. Supplanting the spiral as the principal staircase type and showing the influence of Italian models, it would develop in a remarkable fashion during the course of the sixteenth century.

The staircase with straight flights was enclosed in a special stairwell, whose structure was adapted to the framework of the partition and load-bearing walls between which it was inserted. Its position was an important factor

LEFT
Engraving of 1863 depicting the staircase at the château of Les Granges-Cathus at Talmont-Saint-Hilaire in the Vendée. Dating from 1525, this spiral stair is remarkable for the continuous sculpted decoration on the underside of its winders.

OPPOSITE
Double staircase by Leonardo da Vinci. The design of staircases of this type was linked with military architecture and the need to separate those going up from those going down for reasons of security. Leonardo was consulted on the planning of Chambord before 1519, and this idea may be seen in the wooden model produced by Domenico da Cortona.

escalera doble del castillo

schale docpie una per lo chastellano
laltra per i prouisionati

68 | A LESSON IN ARCHITECTURE

LEFT
Exterior of the staircase in the chapel wing at Chambord. Construction began under François I, continued under Henri II and was finally completed by Jules Hardouin-Mansart under Louis XIV between 1682 and 1686. The sculpted decoration at the staircase's uppermost level has been left unfinished.

OPPOSITE
The great lantern at the château of Chambord forms a vertical axis around which the staircase is arranged, in similar fashion to the central dome of a religious building. The polychrome effect of the inlaid slate motifs is of Italian inspiration.

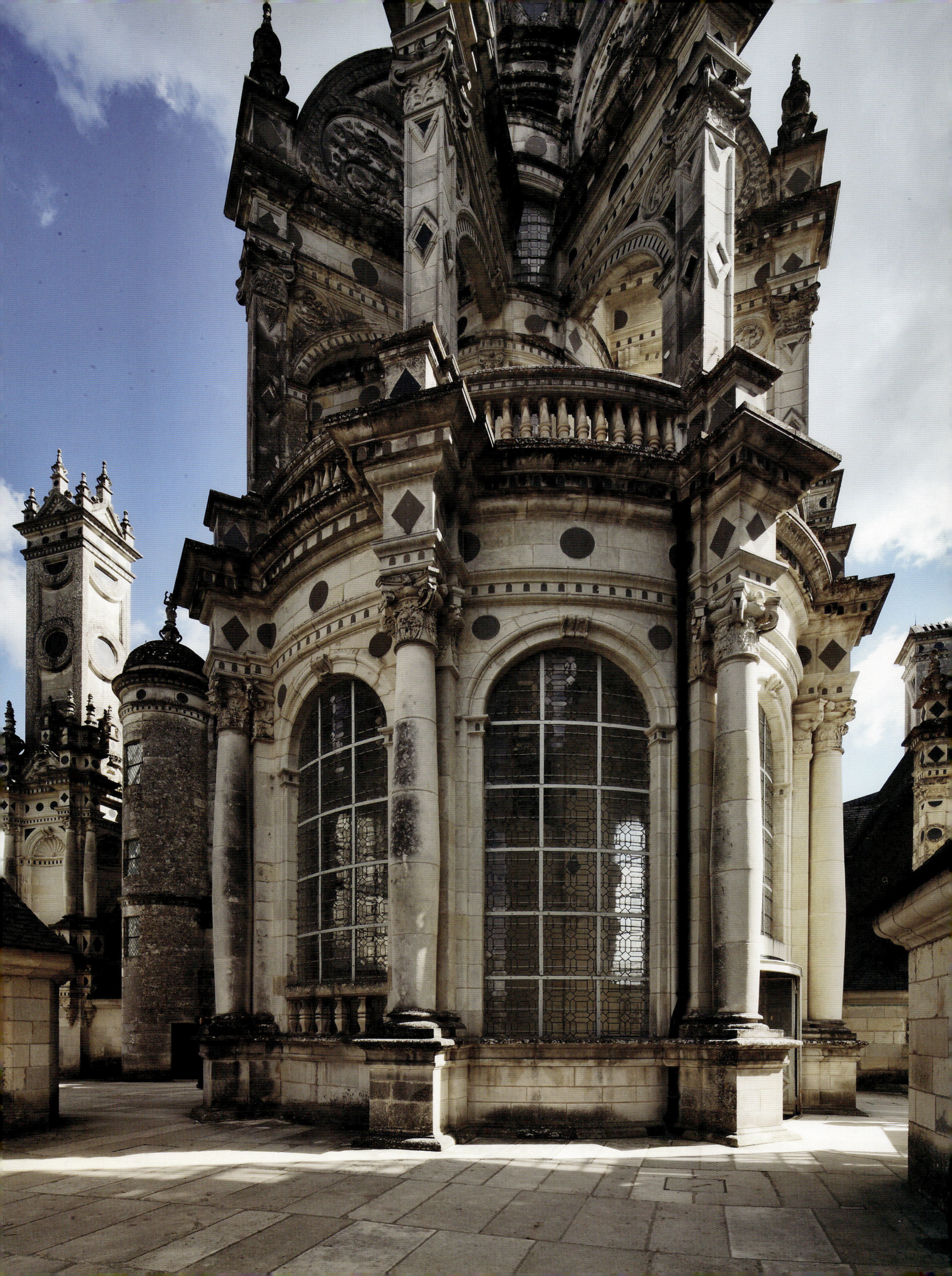

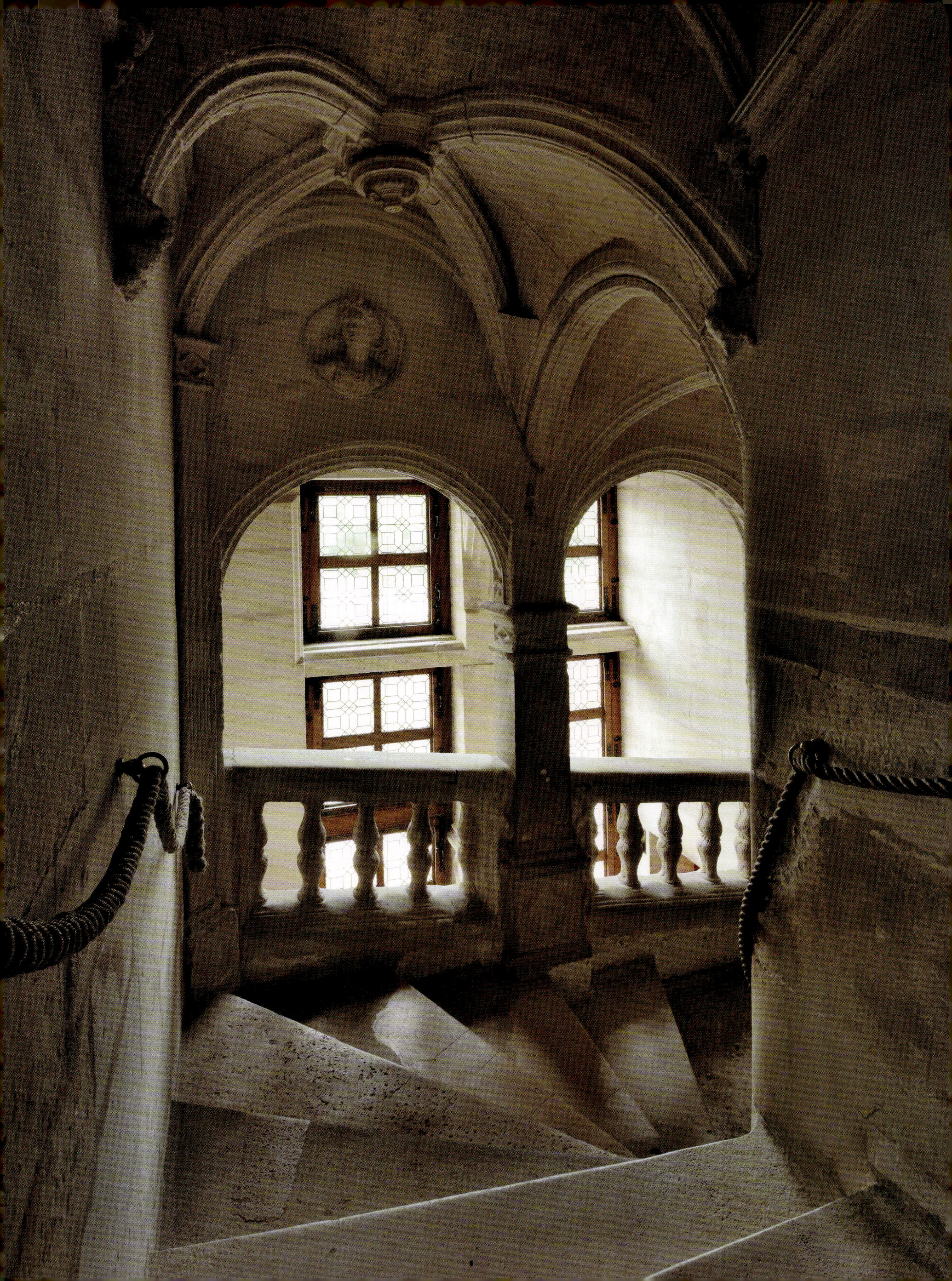

OPPOSITE
The staircase at the château of Chenonceau, consisting of straight flights positioned at the heart of the building (1521). As part of this new development, a new space designed to coincide with the façade was introduced at the turn on each half-landing.

RIGHT
Façade of the staircase at the château of Azay-le-Rideau. The presence of this integrated stair is signalled by a slight projection from the façade. The paired bays light the steps, and the landing forms a loggia, all in a pyramidal composition faithful to the decorative dormers of Northern European architecture.

in determining the division of the building's internal spaces. When arranged successfully, the landings that gave access to the different floors were contiguous with the façade, and their windows were on a level with rooms on the same storey. This type of staircase consisted of one or more straight flights, combined with a turning space at the top or bottom, and flared steps or winders. The return might be a quarter-turn or a half-turn, to the left or to the right. How best to integrate the stair into the building plan became a major pre-occupation of architects.

At Chenonceau, the château completed in 1521 replaced an older feudal dwelling and fortified mill. It was now a country retreat, designed for the purpose of leisure and recreation, and features that had formerly been defensive now became decorative. The staircase that leads up to the first floor was one of the first straight flights to be built. It rises through the centre of the building, perpendicular to the main corridor, the transparency of which it respects. This arrangement, which features a central gallery looking out over an expanse of water and opening up the staircase laterally, is to be found in Venetian palazzos. But what is unique here is the fact that, instead of being set behind the façade, the intermediate landing between floors is separated from it by a passageway communicating between the rooms onto which it opens by means of a clerestory. Had the intermediate landing been placed directly behind the façade, this would have created unevenly spaced bays. The bays on the axis are wider and topped with a split-level tall dormer window that lights the staircase. The spirit of innovation may be seen in the sloping barrel vaults that form the ceiling of each flight: they have coffers and roof bosses where the mouldings intersect, whereas the half-landings still have rib vaulting.

The U-shaped staircase is made up of parallel flights turning back on themselves without a central space, supported by the stairwell wall or two newels and giving access to more than one floor. The top and bottom landings are positioned one above the other. The height of the floors generally demands a half landing and a full landing above the point of departure. If the flights rise one above the other, a large longitudinal landing is required on each floor, positioned behind the façade and alongside the flight of stairs. The replacement of winder stairs with rectangular landings meant that winders could be dispensed with. Similarly, the lighting of landings made it easier to use the stairs; however, the openings on a level with the intermediate landings had to fit in with the bays of the façade in order not to disrupt the overall design. The simplest staircases consisted of two flights divided by a partition wall and a stairwell wall rising from the bottom level. The steps stretched between the walls like so many lintels and formed a sloping ceiling to the lower flight. This type of

LEFT
The vaulting on the landing of the staircase at Azay-le-Rideau retains a Gothic structure in its ribs and pendant bosses. Its innovation lies in the Italianate décor of salamanders, rosettes and antique-style figures.

staircase, which appeared at the château of Josselin in 1510 and at Bury in 1513, reached its finest expression at Azay-le-Rideau in 1518.

Built between two branches of the Indre between 1518 and 1527 but never completed, the château of Azay-le-Rideau is L-shaped in plan, consisting of a principal wing, which contains the staircase, and a shorter wing. The desire for symmetry is expressed on the façade of the main wing by an axial bay designed to light the landings without introducing any uneven levels. The staircase is an Italian U-shape in design, but the composition of the façade betrays a different influence: the staircases at Châteaudun, of which it is the ultimate development. Its bays, which are on four levels, do not align with the windows on each floor. This difference is explained by the position of the intermediate landings. The flights have flat caisson ceilings that are decorated with rosettes and classical-style medallions, intercut with diaphragm arches and pendant bosses that soften the grid pattern of the caissons.

Whether placed in a wing or signalled by its own dedicated façade, the staircase occupied a great variety of different positions during the first half of the sixteenth century. For many years, architects played on the contrast between concealed staircases and those that were put on show. By the end of the century façades were generally regular in design, and buildings were laid out around an axis of variable width and importance. While in more humble structures the lateral staircase remained the dominant form, the central staircase now reigned supreme in all great buildings.

The next development was the piercing of the newel wall. At the château of Montal in the Lot, wide openings in the stairwell wall let in light from large windows on the landings. Here, the desire to unify the stairwell led to a preference for empty space, and the importance of the supporting walls is minimized in some places. Elsewhere, their complete removal from the central space led to the realization of the floating staircase, the earliest known example of which is the staircase of four flights and a central space

OPPOSITE
Azay-le-Rideau's integrated staircase of parallel flights has a newel wall. The flat, sloping ceilings have coffered vaulting, formed by a straight central rib with transversal diaphragm arches ending in pendant bosses.

OVERLEAF
The staircase of the Biblioteca Laurenziana in Florence. The central section of this stair, designed by Michelangelo from 1524, has been likened to a solidified lava flow.

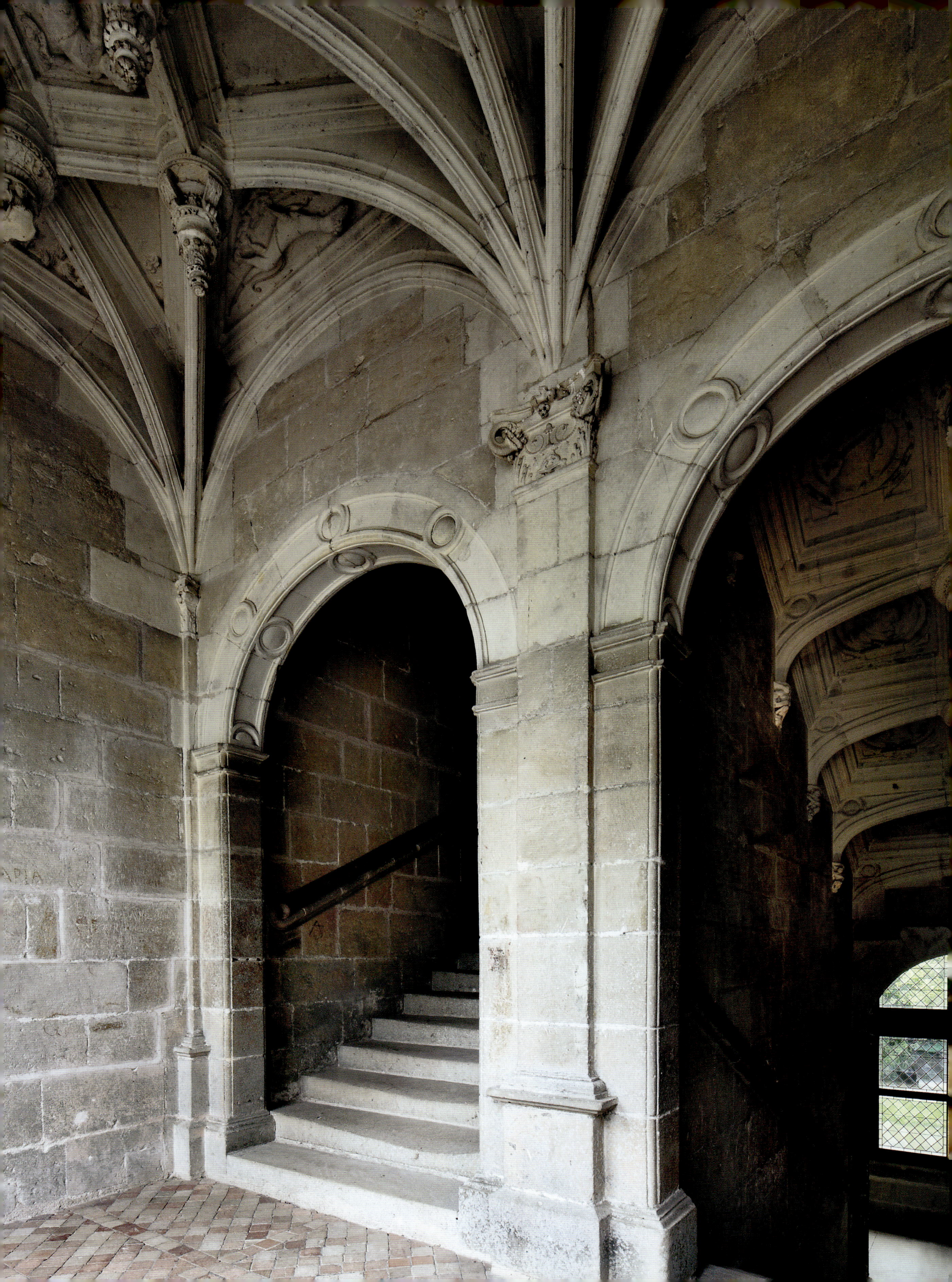

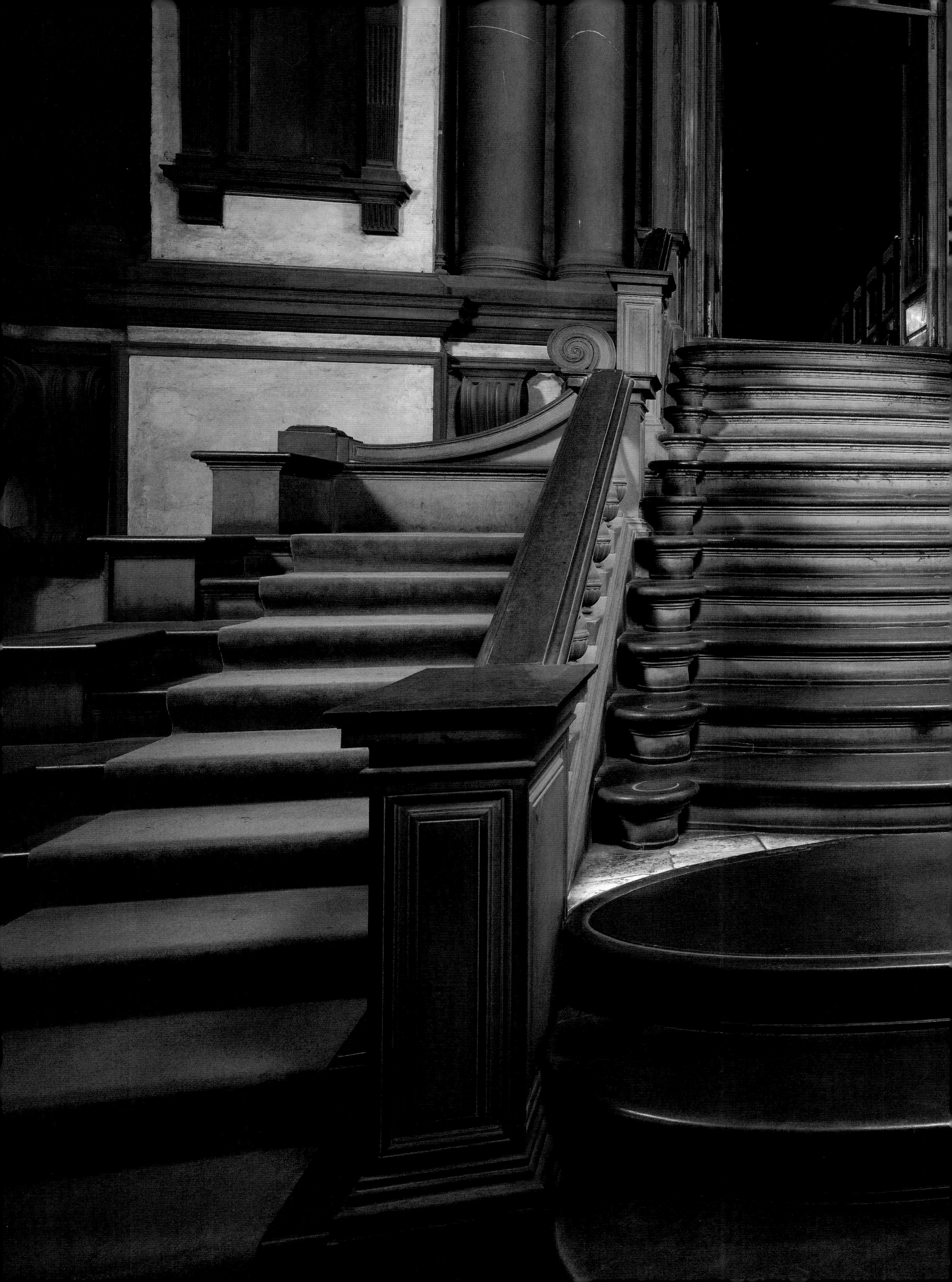

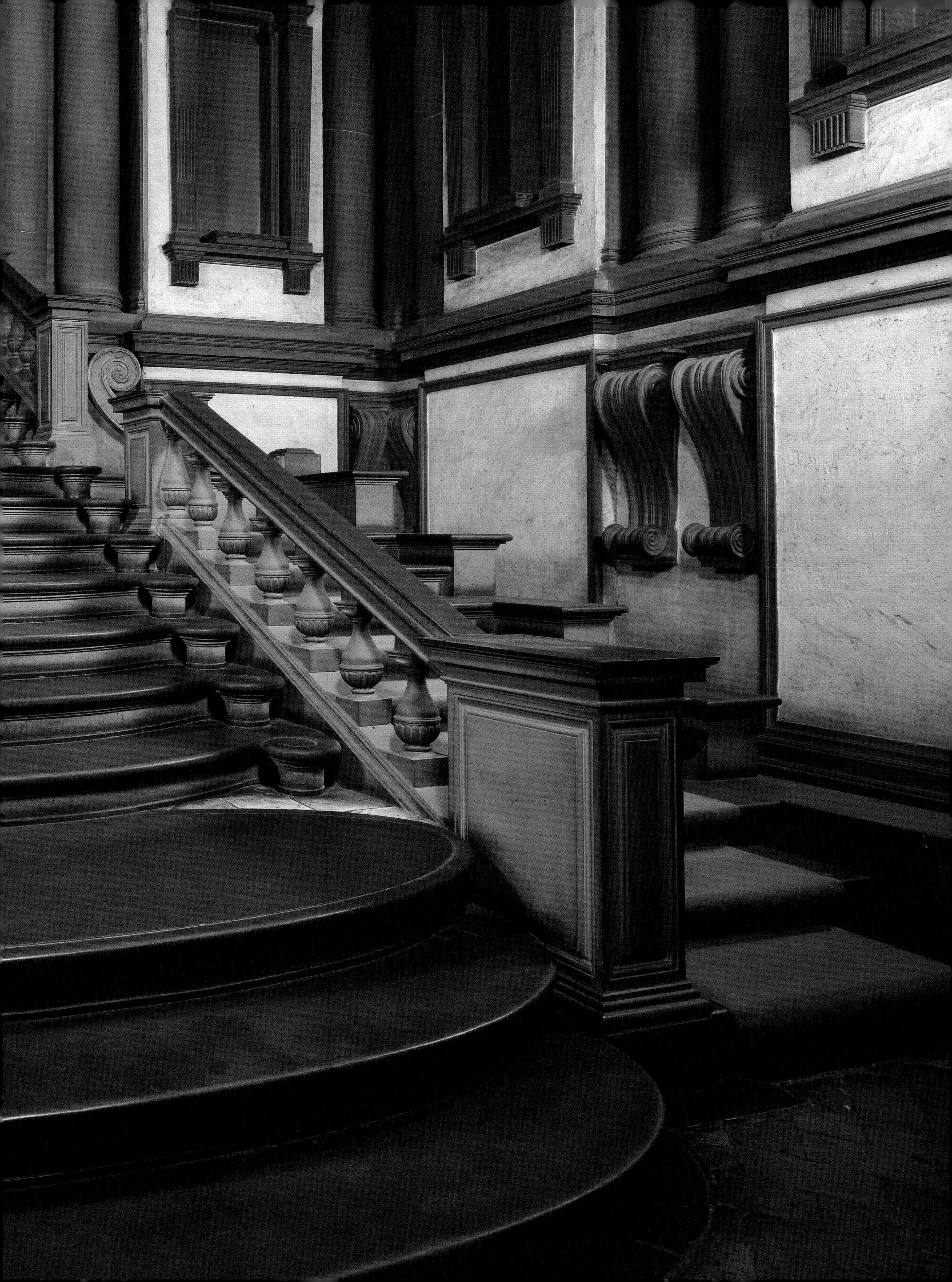

built in the clock tower of the Capitole in Toulouse. In Paris, Philibert de l'Orme designed the oval spiral stairs of the Tuileries, which would lead to the development of the classic French staircase.

MANNERIST ITALY The first signs of Mannerism in architecture appeared in Michelangelo's work for the Biblioteca Laurenziana, Florence, in 1524. But Michelangelo left the building unfinished when he departed for Rome in 1534, and the construction work – still to his designs – was entrusted to Giorgio Vasari and Bartolomeo Ammannati. The vestibule was completed in 1536, and the staircase not until 1557. Although it made use of classical features, the finished staircase was profoundly original. It highlighted the contrast between the low, deep space of the long library and the narrow, high space of the vestibule. Michelangelo wanted to create in users of the library a sense of strangeness and of isolation from the outside world. This feeling derives from the articulation of the walls, which are separated by twinned columns that support no weight but express power. It is as if they are imprisoned within their niches, and the bulging volutes below look as if they are being forced out of the stone under pressure. Between these niches blind windows reinforce a feeling of isolation. The forms are derived from classical antiquity, but the laws that normally govern their function are here deprived of meaning. A remarkable staircase, consisting of a central section that has been compared to a lava flow and secondary stairs on each side, leads gradually up to the reading room. To his contemporaries, Michelangelo's work signalled a break with the classicism of Vitruvius, elaborated a few years earlier by Bramante and the artists of Rome.

While civic architecture continued to produce palazzos, another programme developed in parallel: that of the country house or villa on a centralized plan, which was suited to a new lifestyle. This type of dwelling brought with it a different kind of relationship between the building and its site, and the development of the garden. At Caprarola, Cardinal Alessandro Farnese commissioned an imposing residence on the foundations of a pentagonal fortress designed by Antonio da Sangallo. There, Jacopo Vignola built an original work that took the form of an ambiguous compromise between an Italian palazzo, a villa and a French château. Started in 1559, the structure went up at such speed that it was virtually finished by the time of the architect's death in 1573. Preserving the pentagonal plan of the original fortress, its internal spaces were laid out according to a rational programme. At the centre of the dwelling is a circular courtyard on two levels, linked by a supported helical staircase in the spirit of Bramante's staircase at the Vatican Belvedere. This monumental stair rises to a third floor, supported by thirty pairs of Doric, Ionic and Corinthian columns, with a frieze of lilies – emblem of the Farnese family – decorating the spiral. The staircase was decorated between 1580 and 1583 by Antonio Tempesta, with landscapes provided by the brothers Bril.

As the Italian forms that characterized the Renaissance spread throughout Europe, so the spiral stair vanished from the repertoire of the monumental staircase. Yet, contrary to what might have been expected, it did not usher in the triumph of the U-shaped staircase. In Italy, France and Spain, new preoccupations led instead to the appearance of two previously unseen forms, more complex and rich in possibilities than the Italian model. The twofold desire for symmetry and for a greater sense of space within the stairwell would culminate, in Italy, in staircases with convergent or divergent flights, already seen in external stairs, and, in Spain, in the imperial staircase.

The upper part of the helical staircase of the Villa Farnese at Caprarola, Lazio, supported by paired columns designed by Giacomo Barozzi da Vignola in 1559. The motifs on the underside of the steps echo the overall decorative scheme devised by Antonio Tempesta and the figures on the ceiling.

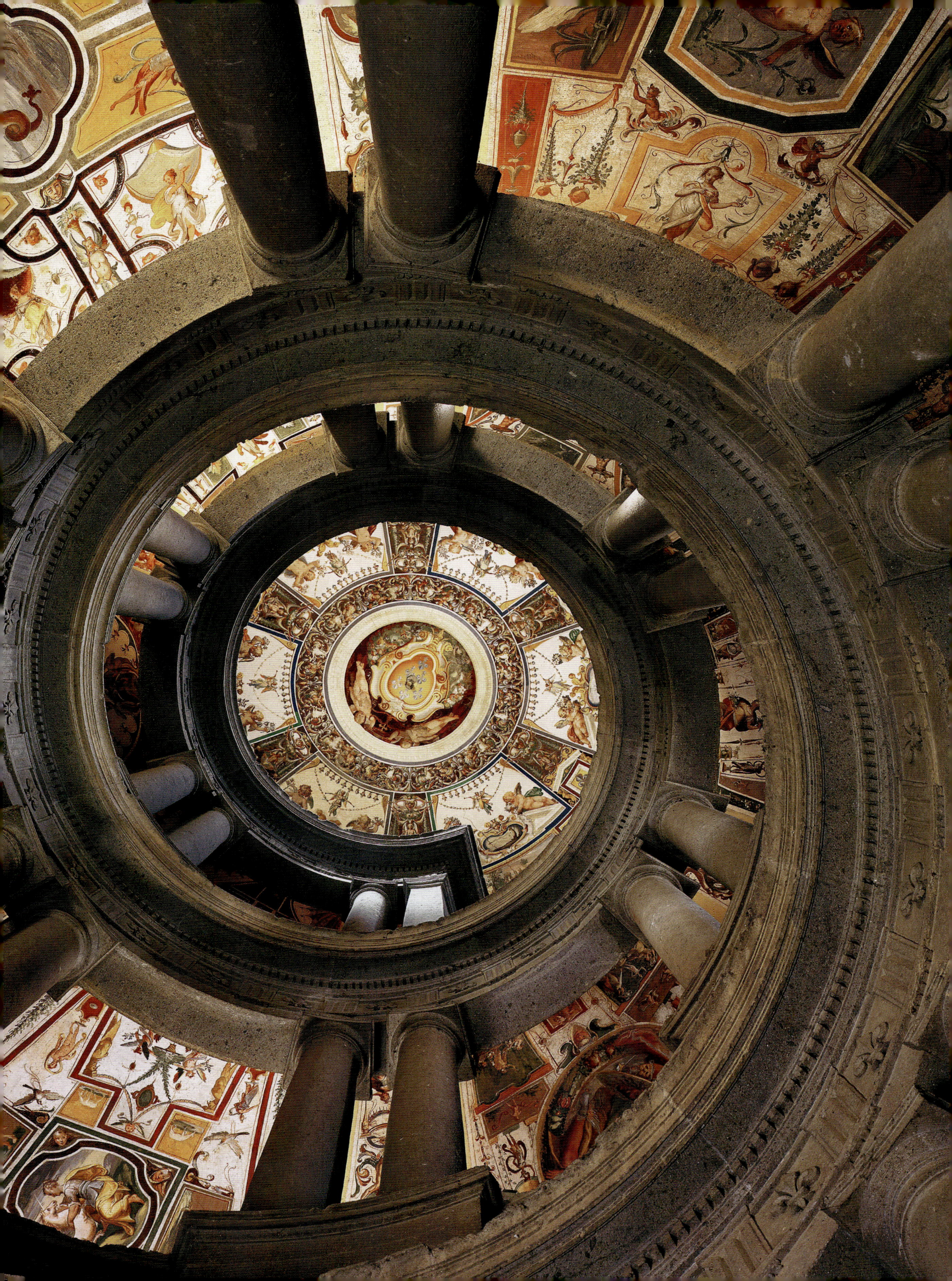

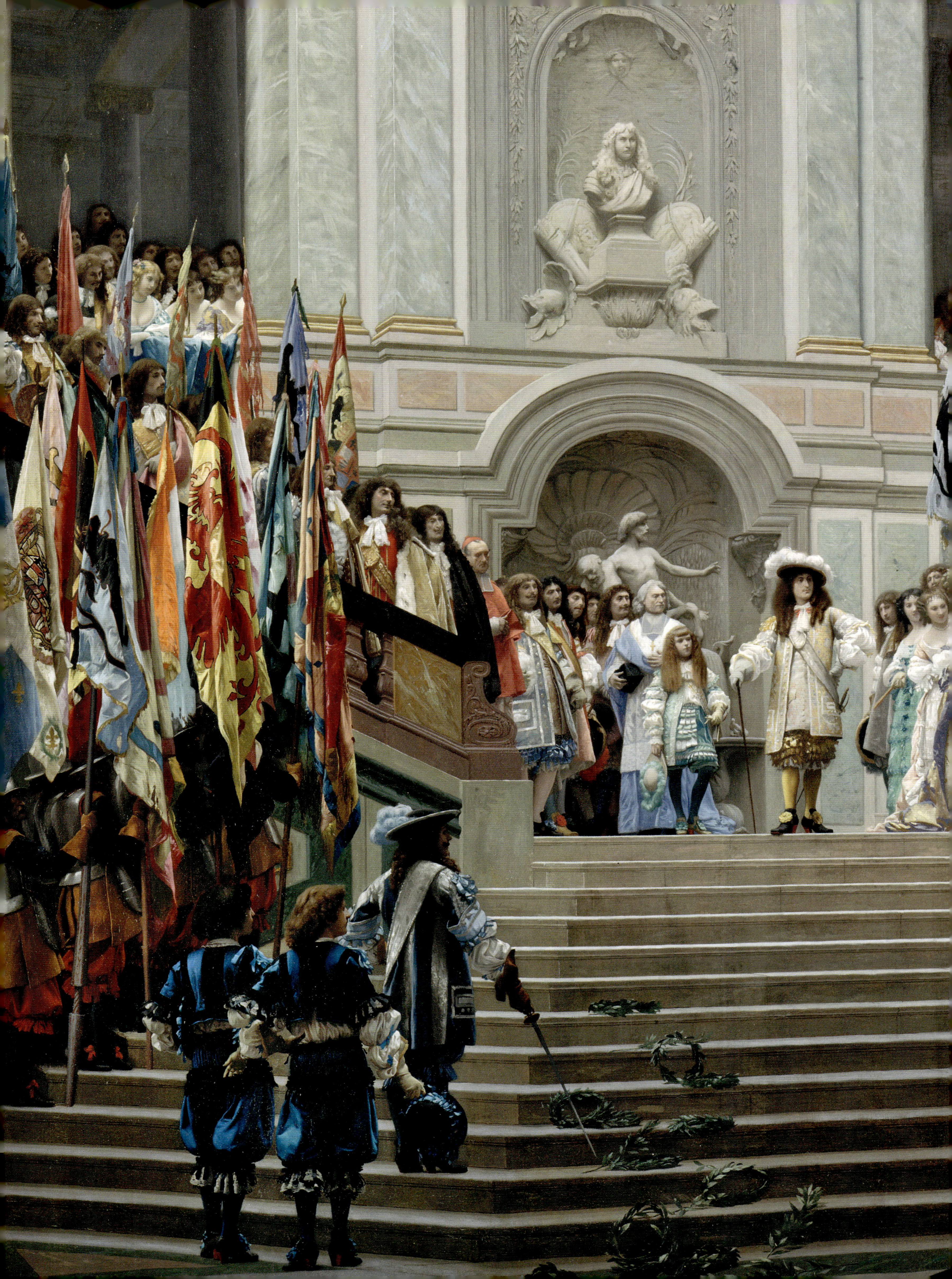

A Theatre of Power

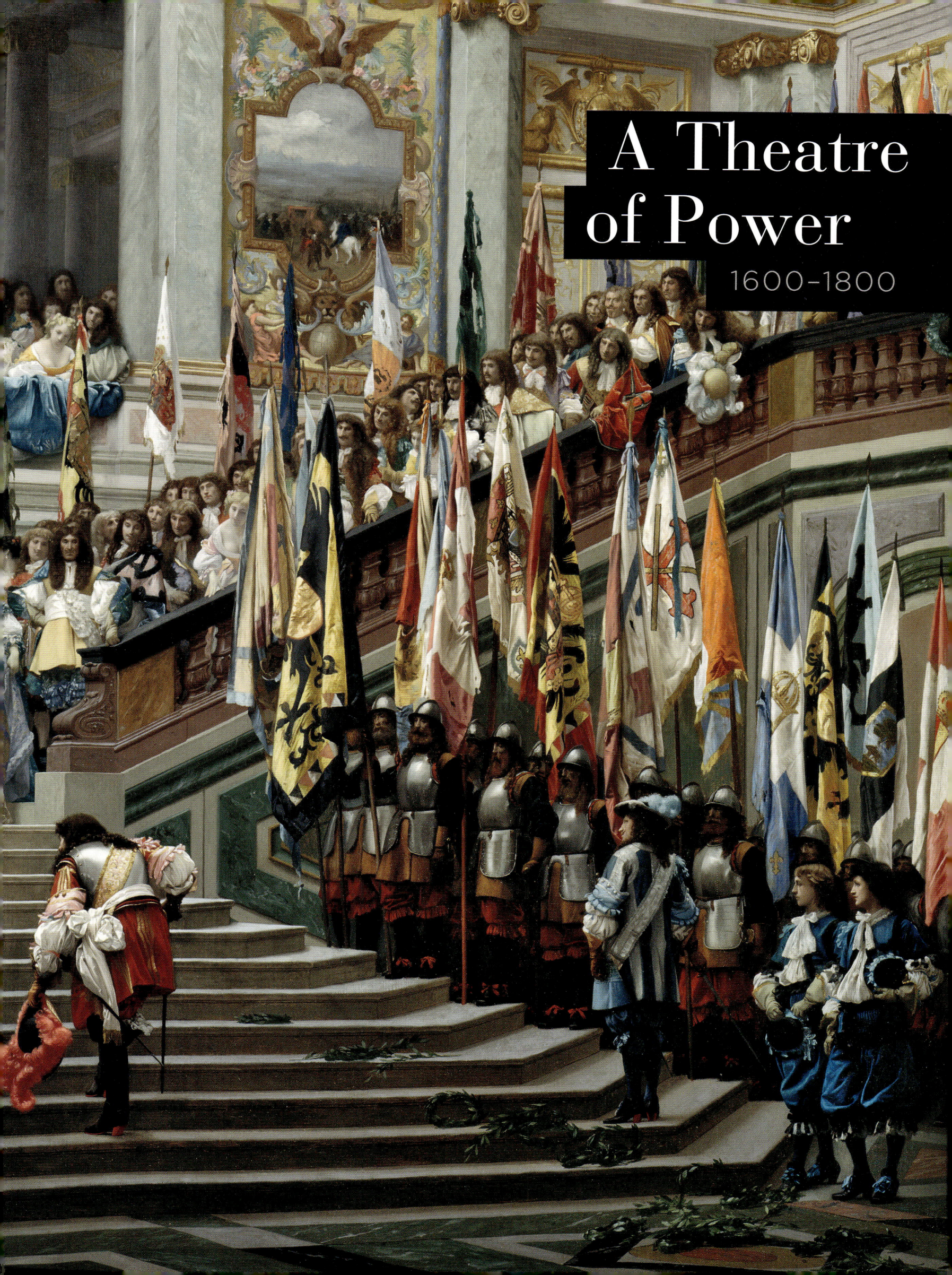

1600–1800

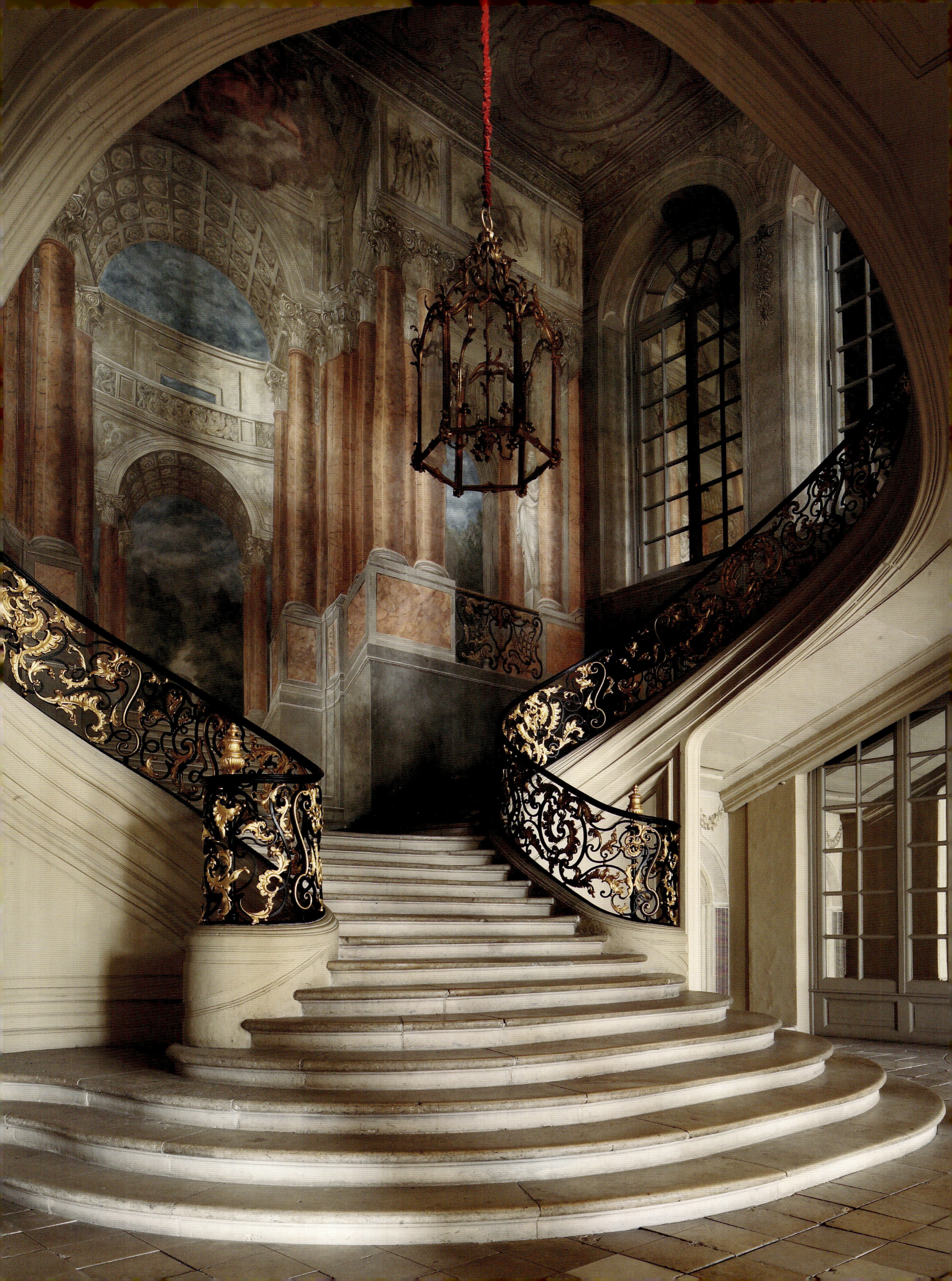

OPPOSITE
The staircase of the Hôtel de Ville in Nancy, built in 1755, has decorative wrought-iron balustrades by Jean Lamour. Above the landing rise trompe-l'oeil frescoes by Jean Girardet.

PREVIOUS PAGES
Jean-Léon Gérôme, Reception of the Grand Condé at Versailles, 1878; Musée d'Orsay, Paris. The scene takes place on the Ambassadors' Staircase, built by François d'Orbay and decorated by Charles Le Brun between 1672 and 1679. It was demolished in 1752.

The legend of St Alexis contains a very early example of the way in which the staircase could be transformed into a potent symbol of worldly power. Alexis was the son of a Roman senator who ran away from home on his wedding day, called by God to a life of pious asceticism. He travelled to Edessa in Syria, where he gave all his possessions away to the poor and spent the next seventeen years as a beggar, living off the alms he was given. Forced to flee once again after a miracle brought him unwanted fame, he returned to his father's house in Rome, where he went unrecognized. Offered shelter in the space under the stairs, he lived there like a dog in its kennel.

The story is a revealing one. St Alexis's strong faith gives him the strength to resist worldly concerns in order to devote his heart fully to God, a sacrifice beyond the capabilities of any ordinary soul. Treated as a slave in his own house, he retreats to a small, humble space. Yet, for St Alexis, the staircase is not just a place of refuge: most importantly, it is also an expression of power. Every day, St Alexis is literally trodden underfoot by those who used to love and respect him. Apart from reinforcing his lowly situation, this staircase is also a bridge that links his soul to God. It is impossible not to be reminded of such religious themes as Jacob's Ladder, used by angels to descend to earth and ascend to heaven, or the Presentation of Mary in the Temple, whose steps symbolize her heavenly destiny.

In the legend of St Alexis, the staircase functions as a potent sign of domination and of prestige, a twofold motif that would reach its culmination the European Golden Age. In England, the phrase 'below stairs' was used by Shakespeare and probably by others before him; and by the eighteenth and nineteenth centuries it had come to encapsulate the crushing social differences that separated the wealthy landed classes in their vast houses from the armies of toiling servants hidden away in their basements. This is the very essence of the seventeenth- and eighteenth-century staircase: an ostentatious and ever more ambitious indicator of the social status of its owner. An inheritance from classical antiquity raised to the peak of perfection by the architectural developments of the Renaissance, the ceremonial staircase as an expression of status would take on an even greater significance in the two centuries that followed. Once freed from technical constraints, the newly mastered floating staircase became a fundamental element in the decorative and building practices of the first half of the seventeenth century. From this point on it assumed a theatrical role of ever-increasing exuberance. The mastery of technique and sense of form that had been of such importance to Renaissance creations were now swamped and obscured by a Baroque profusion of decoration.

HARMONY IN THE SEVENTEENTH CENTURY In the early years of the Renaissance, with its concern for comfort and convenience, the monumental staircase reached no higher than the first floor, the *piano nobile*. In the seventeenth century, however, buildings became increasingly linked with their external environment, leading to the introduction of the vestibule, a space hitherto unknown in France, and the development of surprising contrasts between size and scale in various parts of the dwelling and its gardens.

Parisian architecture of the seventeenth century was permeated by a new spirit of grandeur, as expressed in numerous *hôtels particuliers*. An outstanding example was the Hôtel de Beauvais, built between 1655 and 1660 by Antoine Le Pautre. Although his staircase was not as light and sensual as those produced by François Mansart, here Le Pautre was nonetheless highly successful in adapting an irregularly shaped site. The arc-shaped courtyard was like a theatre auditorium, and the staircase was placed to one side, to the left of the entrance. Its elevation recalled the stairs at the châteaux of Maisons and Blois, whose balustrades were also of stone interlacing. The Hôtel de Beauvais was built for Catherine Bellier, lady-in-waiting to Anne of Austria, who had given her the land. It was here, from a balcony overlooking the street, that the queen mother and Cardinal Mazarin watched the entry into Paris of Louis XIV and the new queen, Maria Theresa of Austria. At the Hôtel Salé, built around 1660 for Pierre Aubert de Fontenay, who made his fortune from the salt tax, the spectacular effect of the interior is reinforced by the staircase's highly decorative wrought-iron balustrade. This novelty, which appeared around 1630, fundamentally changed the appearance of staircases, making them airier, while the balustrades themselves became a form of artistic expression in which France was to excel.

The staircase that was most emblematic of this period of lavish splendour was indisputably the Grand Degré, or Ambassadors' Staircase, at Versailles (p. 166). As part of the constant wave of alterations that took place at Versailles, Louis XIV laid out this staircase to provide access to the Grands Appartements. Built under the direction of François d'Orbay and Charles Le Brun between 1672 and 1679, it occupied the full height of the palace and was topped by a glass roof such as had never been seen before. The staircase consisted of an unbridled profusion of marbles and *trompe-l'oeil* paintings. On the wall above the two divergent flights was a pair of imitation tapestries painted by Adam Frans van der Meulen recalling French victories at Cambrai and Valenciennes. Figures leaned over a *trompe-l'oeil* balcony to welcome visitors as they climbed the steps. Personifications of a several different parts of the world were included. The symbolic and formal functions of the Grand Degré were a way of impressing both those who were well versed in complex iconography and visitors who were less familiar with the lexicon of royal power. Its message was not directed primarily at the French people, but rather at foreign delegations who might not have shared the same visual references as the French court. Luxury, on the other hand, was a language that was universally understood. Jean-Léon Gérôme's painting of the Prince de Condé's reception by Louis XIV at the foot of this staircase may be of doubtful historical veracity, but it certainly conveys the architecture's dramatic power.

The Queen's Staircase, pendant of the Grand Degré, has survived virtually intact and gives us an idea of the appearance of the Ambassadors' Staircase. Although it is comparable in neither scale nor function, its decorative programme is the same, featuring coloured marbles and *trompe-l'oeil* paintings, and a frescoed figure dressed in oriental costume welcomes visitors from within a grand faux-architectural setting echoed by painted landscapes (these were destroyed in the nineteenth century when the arches were knocked through).

These two staircases are masterly expressions of the splendour of Versailles – the ideal palace that inspired imitations throughout Europe. Here, as elsewhere, the staircase played a central role in reinforcing notions of power at its very heart.

OPPOSITE
The staircase of the Hôtel de Beauvais, built in the 1650s by Antoine Le Pautre for Catherine Bellier, principal lady-in-waiting to Anne of Austria. The carved stone balustrade is decorated with interlaced motifs recalling those at the châteaux of Maisons and Blois.

LEFT
The staircase of the eighteenth-century Hôtel du Maréchal de Tallard, on Rue des Archives in Paris; photograph by Eugène Atget, 1901.

OVERLEAF
The Queen's Staircase at Versailles, built to plans by Louis Le Vau and completed in 1680. Its coloured marbles and trompe-l'oeil *architecture were originally complemented by painted landscapes, destroyed in the nineteenth century to create an arcade.*

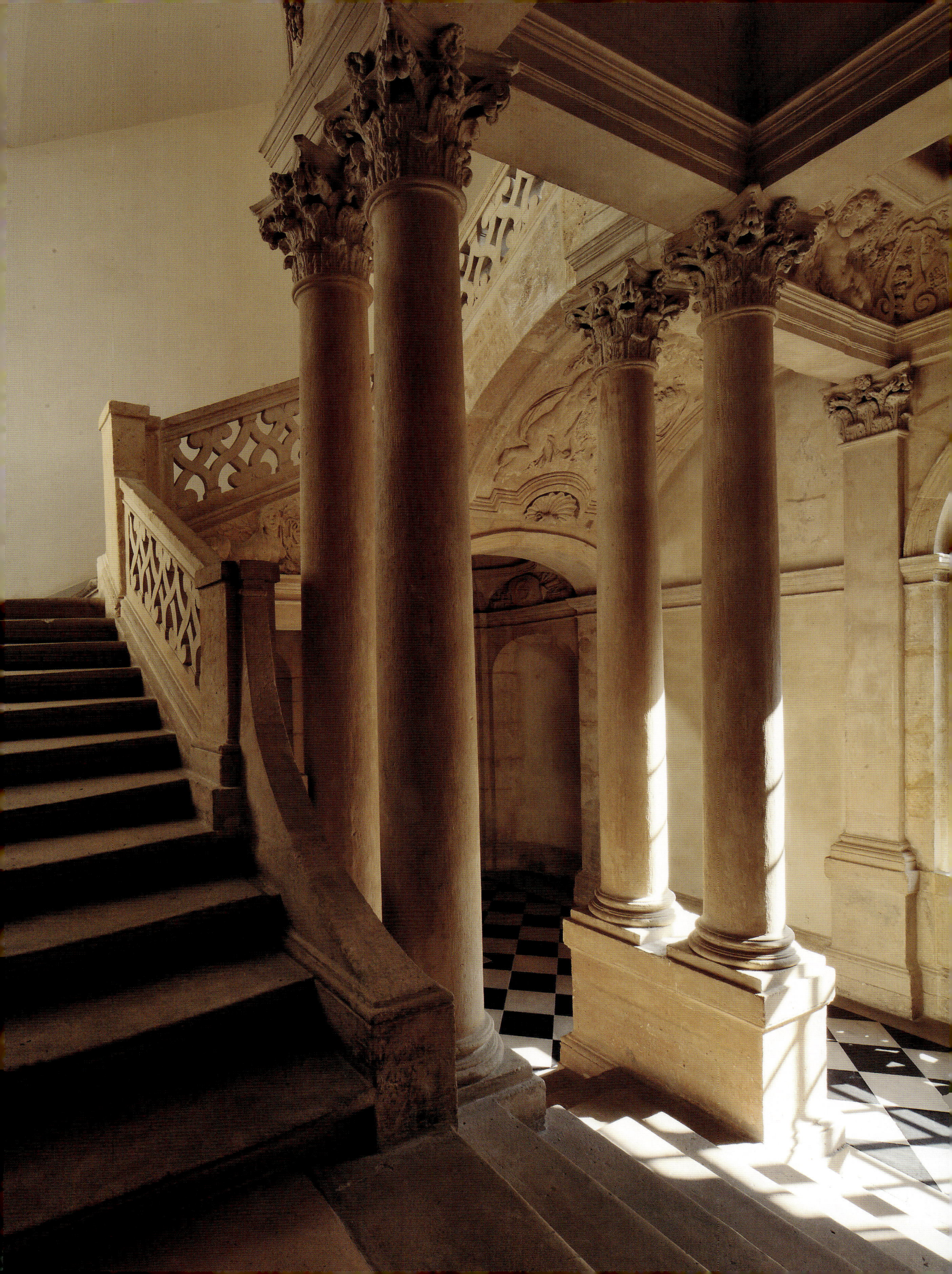

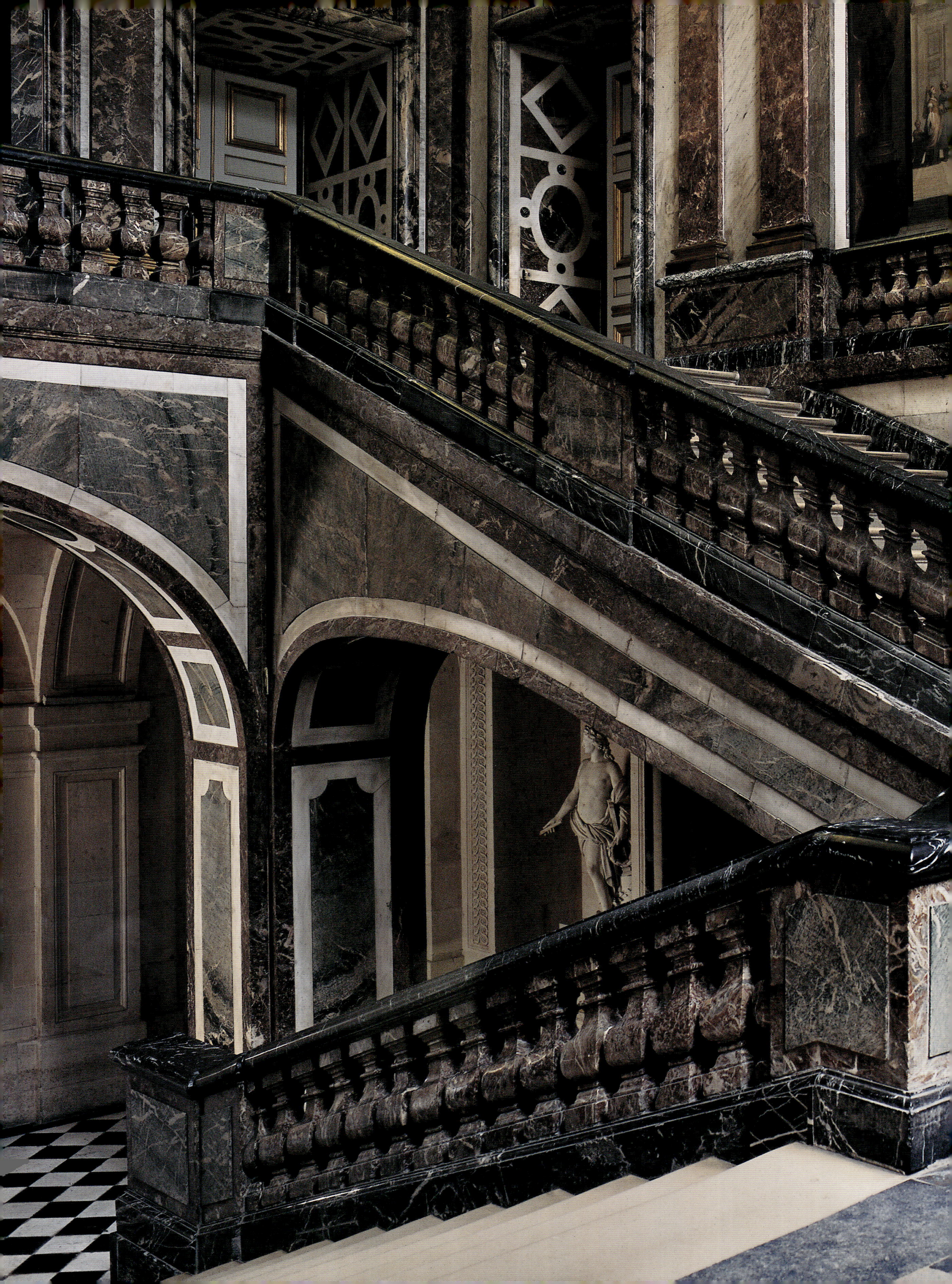

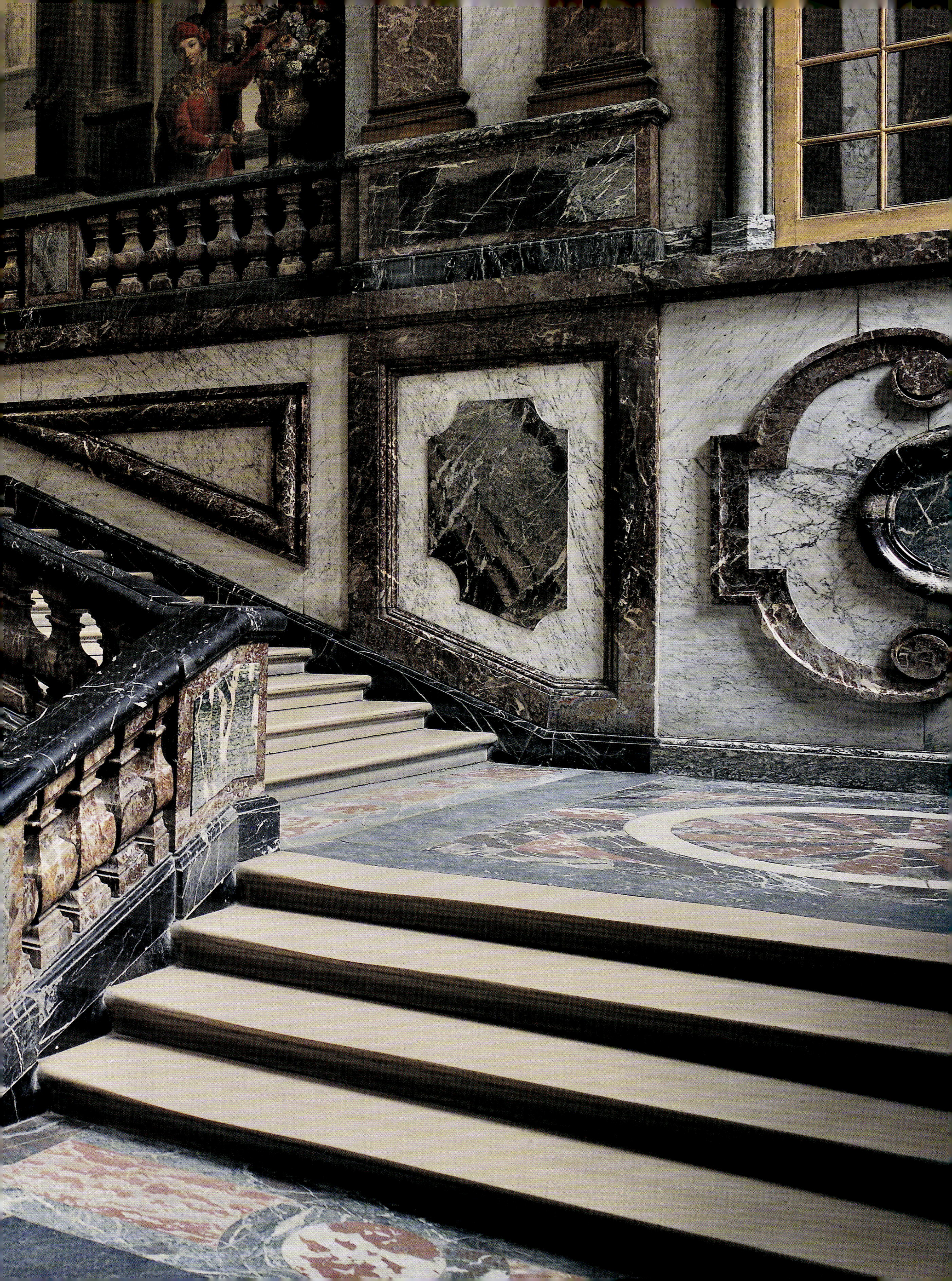

LEFT
At Powis Castle in Wales, the staircase forms part of a sequence of Baroque ceremonial rooms decorated by Antonio Verrio in the 1670s.

BRITAIN: COATS OF ARMS AND *TROMPE-L'OEIL*

English staircases, which were distinguished by their almost universal use of wood, flourished in the early seventeenth century following the arrival of Renaissance influences from the Continent. As the historian Henri Sauval has noted, 'The early seventeenth century saw the full development of the Elizabethan grand staircase, one of the typical features of which was its tall newel posts topped with heraldic beasts.' At Knole in Kent, the main staircase, built between 1603 and 1608, combined two styles. The balustrade was Renaissance in style, while the carved interlacings and heraldic beasts on the newel posts could already be described as Jacobean. These wooden leopards hold between their paws a shield bearing the arms of the Sackvilles, cousins of Elizabeth I, who had come into possession of the house in 1566. In addition to the staircase's grisaille decoration are heraldic motifs that borrow colours from the family's coat of arms. The finest example of this genre is to be found at Hatfield House in Hertfordshire, the Jacobean mansion built in 1611 for Robert Cecil, the first Earl of Salisbury, where the balustrade is richly carved with a profusion of heraldic sculpture. In that same year, Robert Peake commissioned the first English translation of Sebastiano Serlio's *First Book of Architecture* – a work that could not fail to influence English builders and open their eyes to the Italian model being promoted by Inigo Jones. One of the great English architects, Jones encouraged fresh ideas by importing Renaissance principles. After several journeys to France and Italy, he drew inspiration from designs he bought from a pupil of Palladio for the Queen's House at Greenwich, which was built around 1615. The house contains a superb cantilevered staircase known as the 'Tulip Staircase', now as famous for a ghostly apparition caught on camera by a Canadian couple in 1966 as for its virtuoso architectural flair and role within the earliest Neoclassical building in England.

As the English staircase evolved and the carved decorations on its balustrades were abandoned, the focus shifted to the walls, which were now covered in *trompe-l'oeil* paintings. It was at this point that, in order to allow these decorative schemes more room, the staircase became broader. As the architectural historian Nathaniel Lloyd pointed out, 'The stairs (which were once squeezed into a small space even in the most important of houses), now designed in the full Italian manner, assume such prominence that the largest room in the house, with a height of two storeys, is devoted to them.'

At Powis Castle in Wales, the first Marquess of Powis remodelled the interior to create a sequence of Baroque state rooms with a grand staircase as one of their highlights. The discreet balustrade yielded pride of place to paintings by Antonio Verrio depicting, among other scenes, Venus descending from heaven in a chariot. Born in southern Italy, Verrio had worked with Le Brun at Versailles and was the first to introduce this type of Italianate decorative painting to England.

Other notable houses subsequently adopted the same style of décor, making the late seventeenth century a golden age of decorative painting. Hanbury Hall in Worcestershire was built in the early eighteenth century by the Chancery lawyer Thomas Vernon. He commissioned the wall and ceiling paintings for the hallway and staircase (overleaf) from Sir James Thornhill, who later worked on the grisaille scheme in the cupola of St Paul's Cathedral in London. His works for the staircase at Hanbury depict scenes from the life of Achilles, while the ceiling features classical deities. Mercury points

OPPOSITE
The staircase at Knole, at Sevenoaks in Kent, built in the early years of the seventeenth century. The singular animals bearing heraldic devices on the balustrade are characteristic of the Jacobean style.

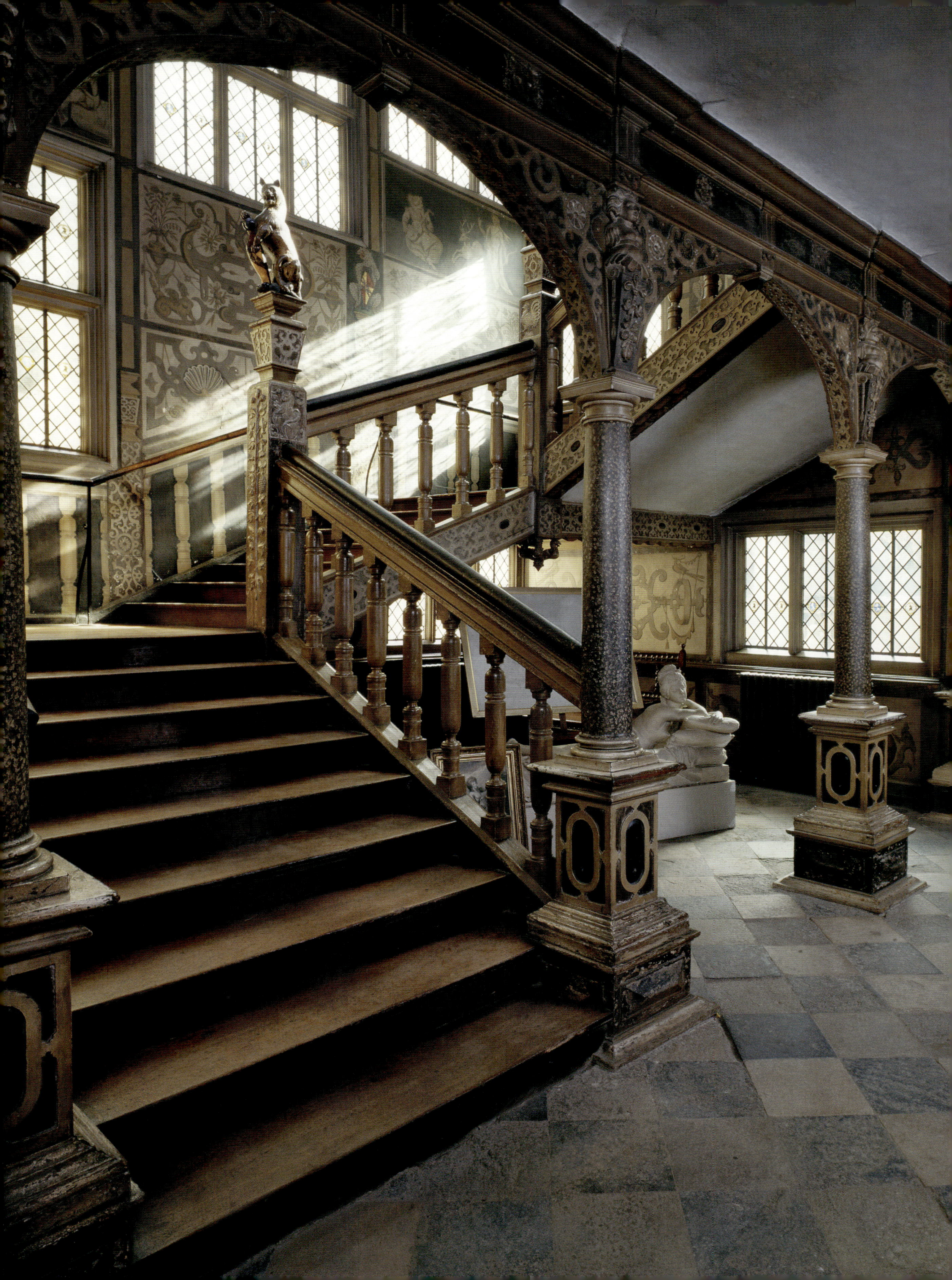

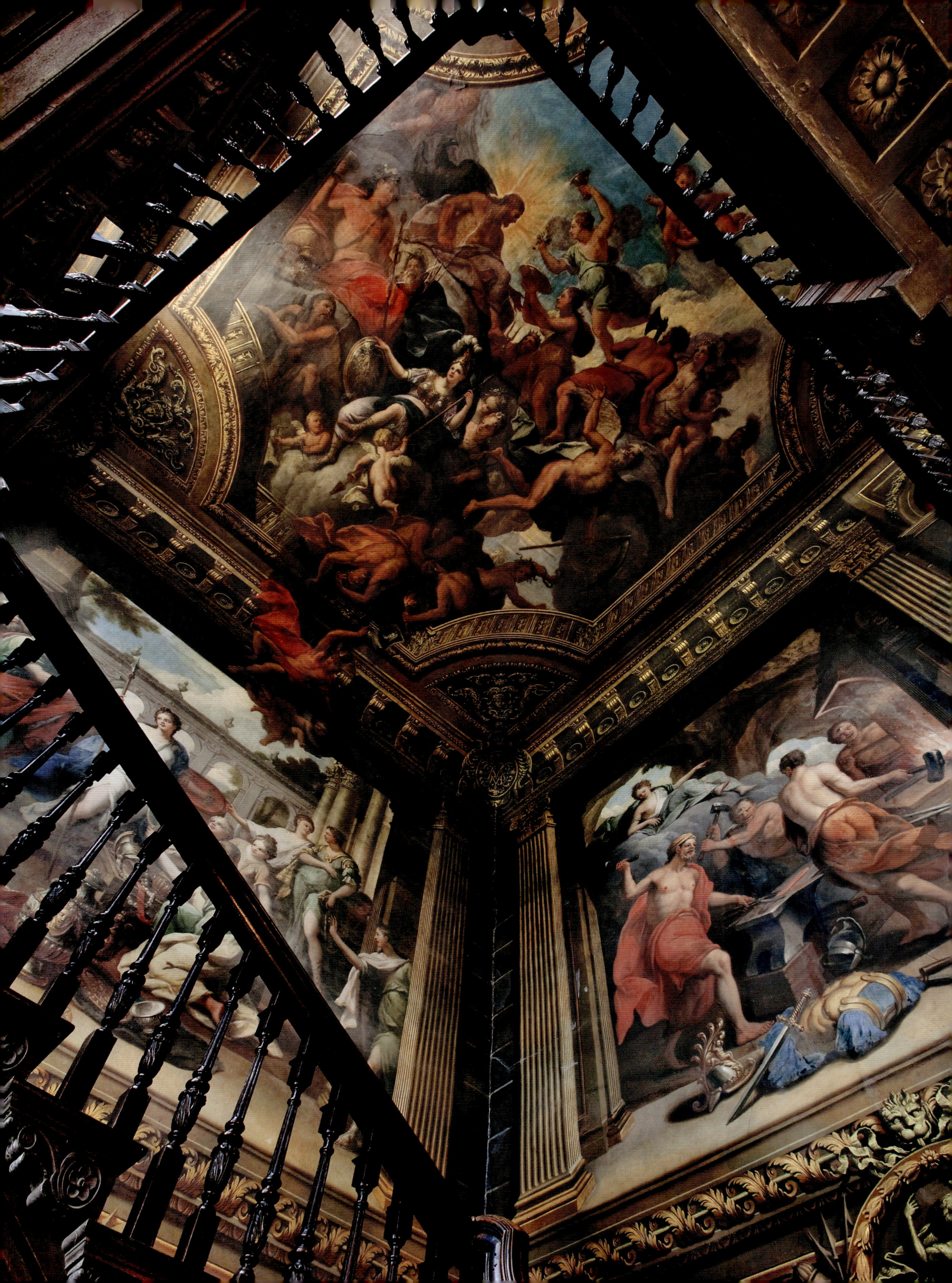

OPPOSITE AND RIGHT
The staircase at Hanbury Hall in Worcestershire. It was decorated c. 1710 for the lawyer Thomas Vernon by Sir James Thornhill, who produced a series of paintings relating to the life of Achilles.

OVERLEAF
The monumental staircase of the Palazzo Canossa in Mantua, built in the seventeenth century and refurbished in 1779 by Paolo Pozzo. The spirit of the Baroque emerges here in the figures that greet the visitor on the landing.

towards a painting of the Reverend Henry Sacheverell being cast to the Furies, who prepare to burn him. This dates the work to 1710, when Sacheverell, a Tory, was being tried for sedition, having published two sermons accusing the Whigs of neglecting the interests of the Church and of putting it in danger (the sermons were publicly burned at the Royal Exchange in London). Far from being of purely anecdotal significance, this detail demonstrates the importance of the decorative scheme beyond its purely ornamental and aesthetic qualities. While some messages might be conveyed through complex mythological symbolism, others were clearly displayed for all to see, taking on a political dimension that is lost today.

ITALY AND SPAIN: THE BAROQUE STAIRCASE In Italy, cradle of the Baroque, the staircase was less a place of exuberant artistic expression than a grandiose expression of power. Surprisingly, unadorned stone and sculpture were preferred, as at the Palazzo Canossa in Mantua, Lombardy, which was ruled by the powerful Gonzaga family. The *piano nobile* is reached by a grand staircase featuring two large hounds (dogs being the family emblem) on the landing that watch over a pair of return flights. The balustrades are topped by a series of statues, including Jupiter casting a thunderbolt, that enliven an otherwise rather stiff ensemble. This arrangement can be found also at the Palazzo Reggia in Caserta, built some fifty years later, although the treatment is more monumental. A pair of lions stands guard

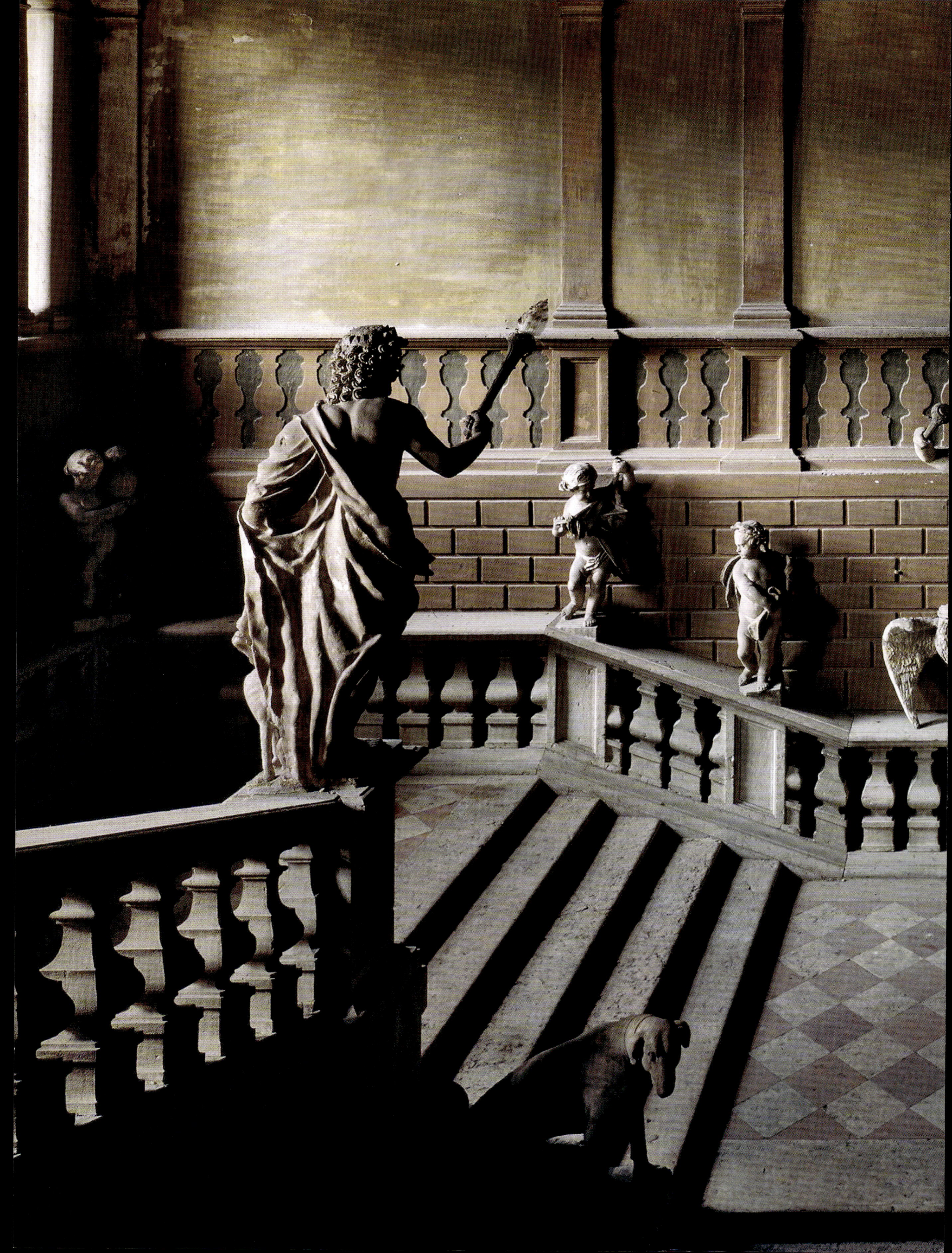

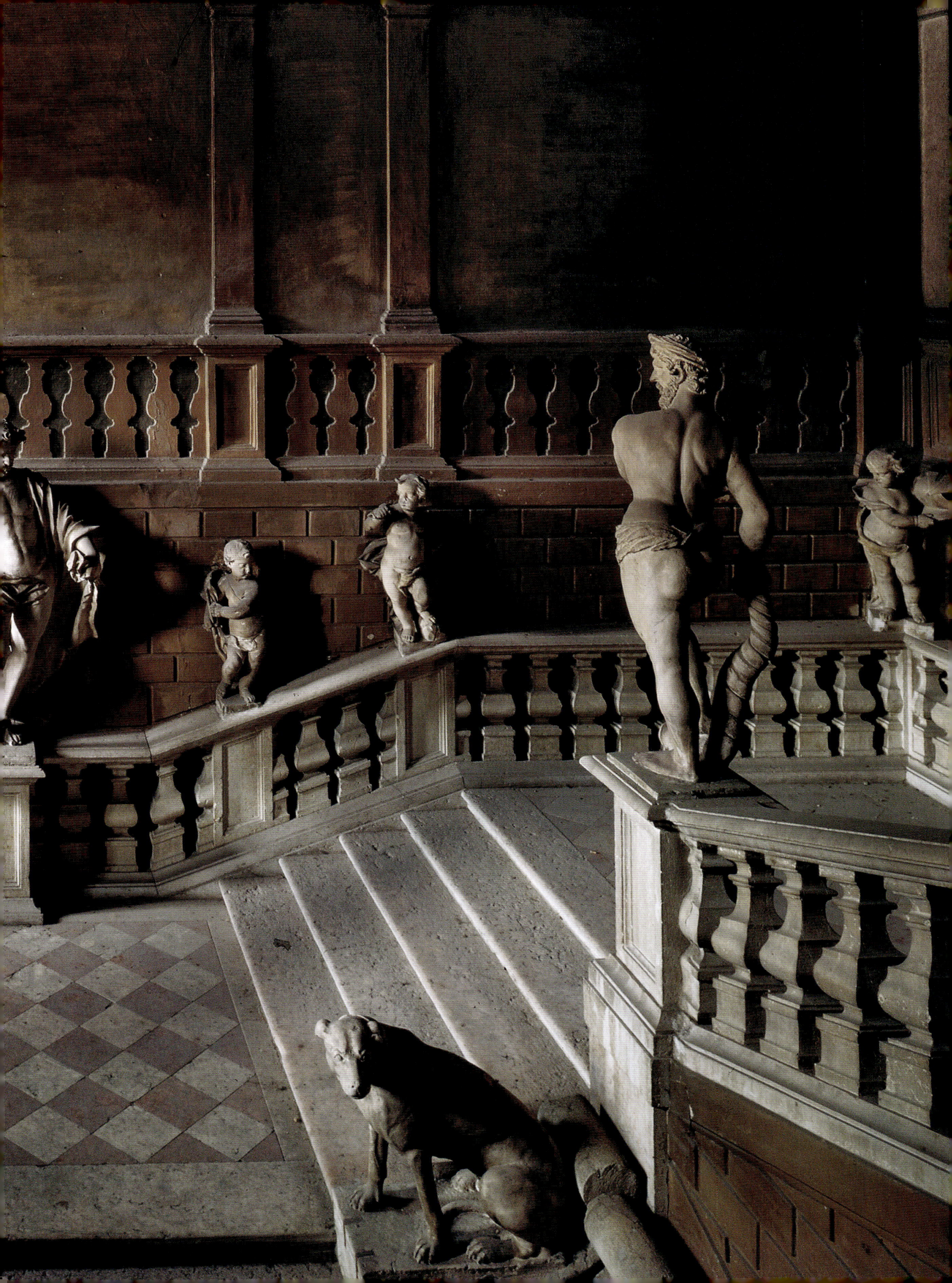

LEFT
The grand staircase of the Palazzo Reale in Naples, begun c. 1650 to a design recalling the great ceremonial staircases of Renaissance Spain.

over an imposing staircase, its scale befitting the status of the ruler for whom it was built: Charles de Bourbon, Prince of the Two Sicilies.

In Naples, the Palazzo Reale was one of the principal residences used by the Bourbon kings before and during the Kingdom of the Two Sicilies – a state that united Sicily and Naples under the Spanish crown. The grand staircase was begun in 1651 by Francesco Antonio Picchiatti, on a model recalling the great ceremonial staircases of the Spanish Renaissance. Its outstanding feature is undoubtedly its magnificent white marble balustrade, carved with a profusion of plant motifs contained within geometric forms. It is impossible not to be reminded of the Ambassadors' Staircase at Versailles, which followed a similar plan except for the final returns. Although there is no documented link between the two examples, Philip IV of Spain, who was also king of Naples, was none other than the father of the Infanta Maria Theresa, whom Louis XIV was to marry in 1659, thus sealing the Treaty of the Pyrenees and ending twenty-five years of war with France.

In Rome, Bernini, genius of the Baroque, created one of the virtuoso staircases of the age. A protégé of the highest patrons in the land, he succeeded Carlo Maderno as chief architect to St Peter's after his death in 1629. In 1657 Bernini suggested the idea of a colonnade to the office of the Fabric of St Peter, which oversaw the basilica's administration and building works, and was then under the management of Cardinal Barberini. The success of this enterprise, and the confidence with which Bernini's work had long been viewed, may explain why, at the start of work on the Scala Regia in the Vatican in 1663, he submitted no plans to the Fabric – or at least as far as we are aware, since there are no records of any discussions having taken place. The original staircase, designed by Maderno, Bramante and Antonio da

Sangallo, was dark and impractical. According to T. A. Marder, 'The report by Carlo Fontana on the new Scala Regia, written a generation after its construction, described the earlier, poorly lit "Scala Maestra" as an uninterrupted descent that tested the courage of the pope and the endurance of his porters. In short, this staircase did little to enhance the dignity of the papal palace.' Bernini considered this staircase his greatest challenge. Working within an inconvenient and unpropitious space, he perfected the Baroque art of illusion. The staircase was irregular, squeezed between the palace and the basilica, and starved of external light. Bernini designed a colonnade, recalling the one in St Peter's Square, which supports a barrel vault that narrows as it rises, creating an illusion of considerably greater depth than is actually the case. Bernini's great technical achievement lay in his ability to adapt the vaulting to the constraints of the space without causing any distortion, notably by playing on the proportions of the columns that climb the staircase. It evokes the majesty of the papacy – a point further underlined by the

RIGHT
The Scala Regia in the Vatican, begun in 1663, is one of Bernini's greatest masterpieces. It narrows as it rises, so creating a false perspective and a powerful illusion of height.

statue of Constantine placed at its foot. Visitors are reminded of the power and presence of the faith, which are given sublime material form by an artist of matchless skills.

In Spain, the triple helical staircase in the former monastery of Santo Domingo de Bonaval, Santiago de Compostela, was an expression of the Baroque at its most profound and intellectual. Here, it is not the profusion of decoration that is dizzying, but rather, when one views the stair from below, a vertiginous sensation of being drawn upwards. Its lines swirl and interlace to form a powerful, complex image of pure and sincerely held faith, which may follow different routes and yet still arrive at its celestial destination. Doubtless inspired by Chambord, these three staircases at the heart of a religious foundation, linking different aspects of the monks' lives, might also be viewed as symbols of the Holy Trinity – a single essence divided into three distinct and yet inseparable states.

THE MASTERY OF EXTERNAL SPACES The mastery of space and symbolism displayed by seventeenth- and eighteenth-century architects was employed also in external staircases. We are familiar with the Italian taste for terraced gardens, which boasted rippling water and playing fountains in harmony with the landscape; according to the historian John Templer, 'many of the spatial theories that exploit stairs in the interiors of Renaissance and baroque palaces first appeared in garden design, and clearly some of these great interior designs were intended to represent the spatial effects of the garden stairs'. While it is true that some internal staircases may look like an extension of external stairs, the outside staircase has its own specific characteristics, which include monumentality. Liberated from the visual barrier of walls, it could develop almost unhindered, and architects very quickly grasped that its essential asset was its potential height. Outside, the staircase could rise as high as it wanted, and take as many detours and diversions as it liked. In Portugal, the restoration of the monarchy in 1640 prompted the nobility to display their renewed power in such graceful constructions as the magnificent pool in the grounds of the Palace of the Marquesses of Fronteira, near Lisbon. It is flanked by steps and lined with superb *azulejos*, which not only enliven the gardens, but also embellish the palace's internal staircase. In this garden, designed around 1670 by João Mascarenhas, the first Marquess of Fronteira, the enamelled tiles surrounding the pool depict mythological scenes as well as portraits of the marquess's forebears, bringing his illustrious pedigree to the attention of the enlightened visitor in a way that is both subtle and attractive.

OPPOSITE
The steps at the sanctuary of Bom Jesus do Monte, in Braga, Portugal. Built between 1722 and 1760, they lead up to the church at the top of the hill, guiding pilgrims along a highly dramatic ascent.

LEFT
The steps in the gardens of the Palace of the Marquesses of Fronteira near Lisbon, built c. 1670. They flank a pool and a series of mythological scenes composed of glazed tiles.

OVERLEAF
The external staircase of Troja Palace in Prague, built in the 1680s by the architect Jean-Baptiste Mathey, who introduced Roman Baroque to Bohemia. The statues depict the battle between the gods and the Titans.

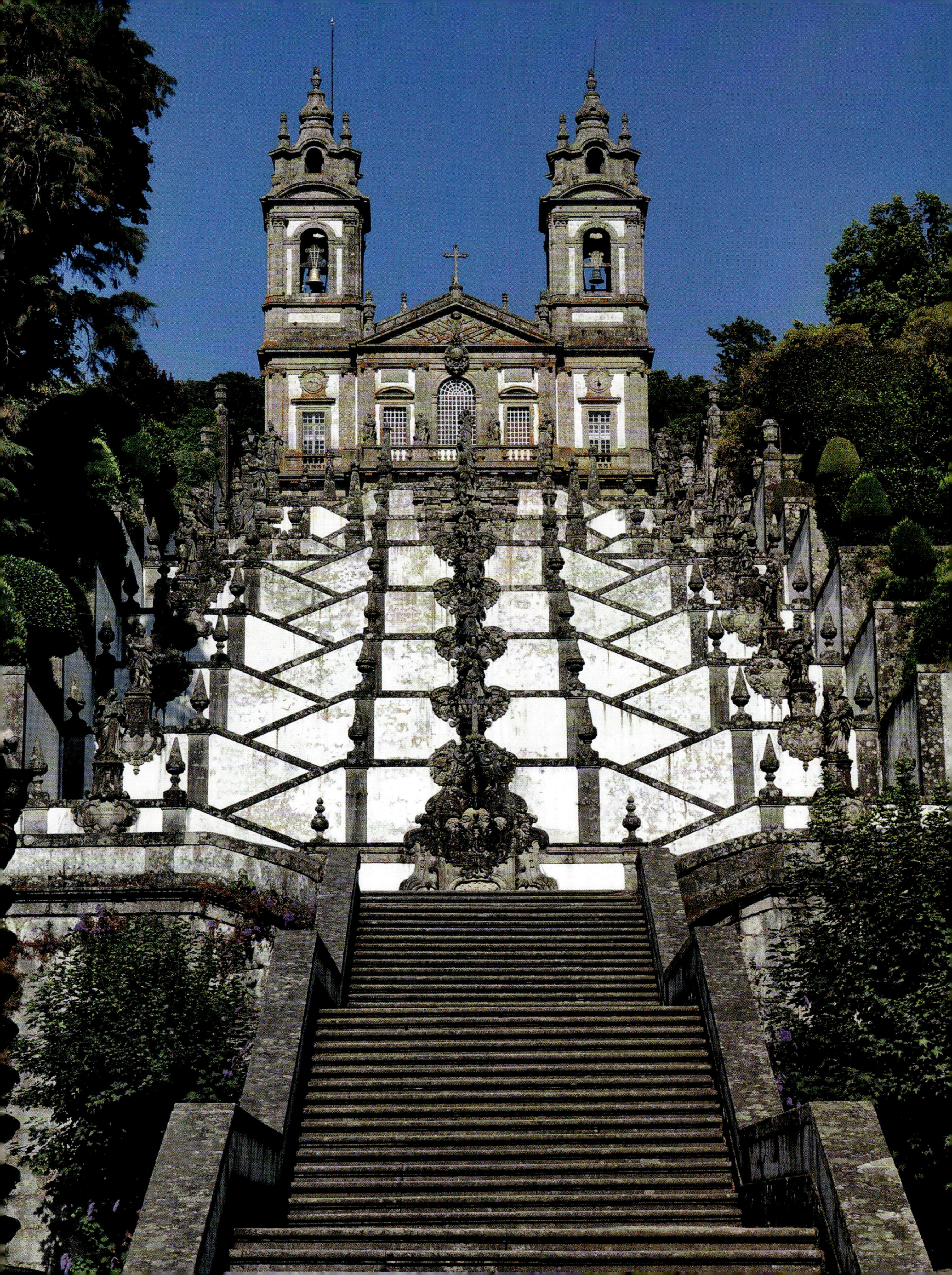

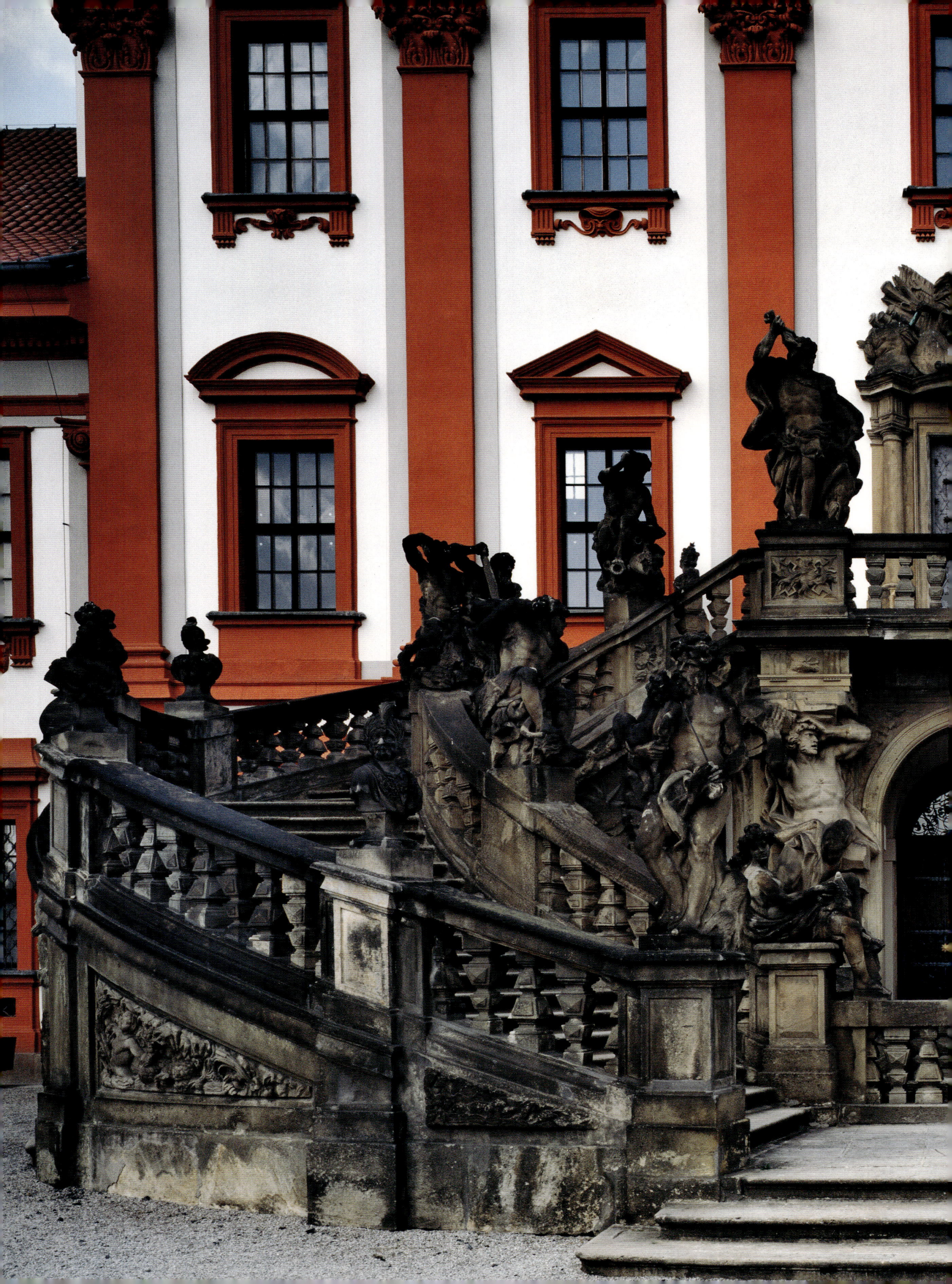

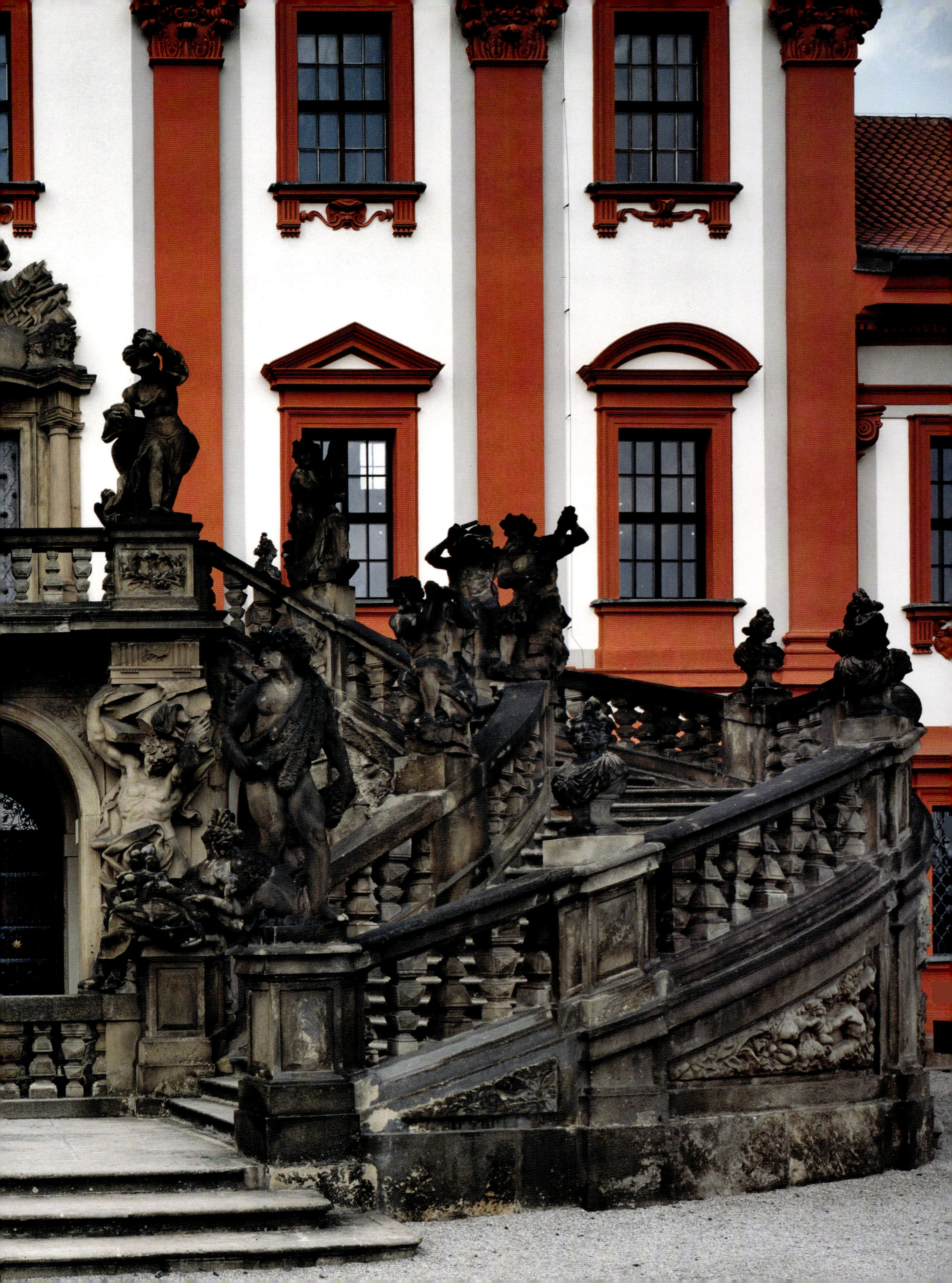

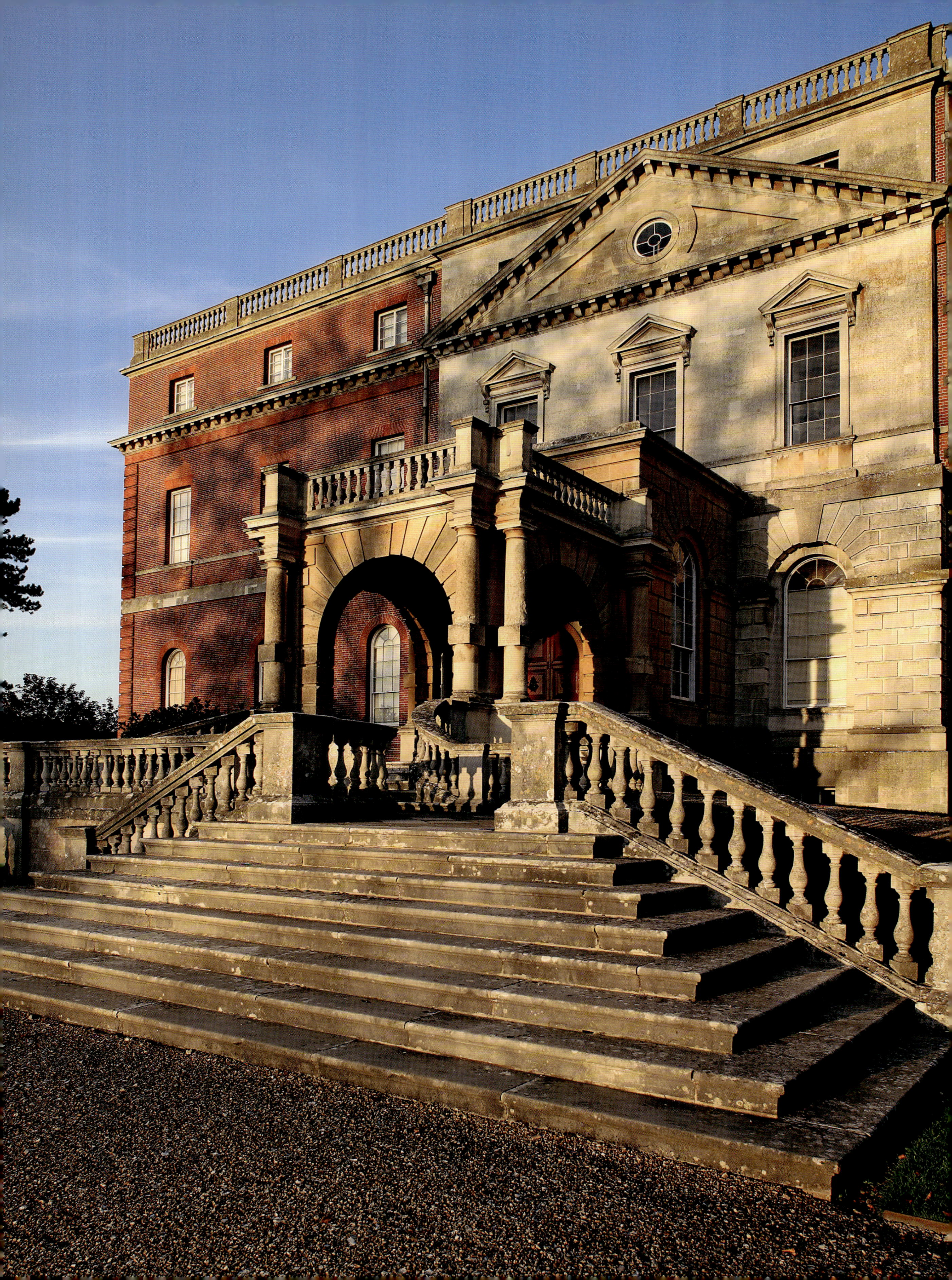

OPPOSITE
The entrance steps at Clandon Park in Surrey, built in the 1720s by Giacomo Leoni.

RIGHT
The horseshoe-shaped staircase in the Cour du Cheval Blanc at the palace of Fontainebleau, completed by Androuet du Cerceau in 1634 in a Mannerist style.

OVERLEAF
The staircase at the abbey of Prémontré in the Aisne, built in the first half of the seventeenth century, is an exceptional elliptical spiral, testifying to the accomplished elegance of French architecture in the Age of Enlightenment.

At Braga, in the north of the country, is the shrine of Bom Jesus do Monte (p. 95), one of the most unusual Catholic sanctuaries in Europe, where an exterior staircase assumes spectacular dimensions. As pilgrims climbed the more than 600 steps, they were encouraged to contemplate the contrast between the material and spiritual worlds, and would stop before small chapels on the landings illustrating scenes from the Passion of Christ. The complex theatricality of this vertical *Via Crucis*, in which each step was a striving towards God, was designed to instil an atmosphere of meditation and devotion. The scheme recalls the *Scala Sancta* in Rome, twenty-eight marble steps traditionally thought to have come from the praetorium in Jerusalem. Believed to be the steps that Jesus climbed in order to meet Pontius Pilate, they are scaled by the faithful on their knees. First commissioned around 1720 by the archbishop of Braga, the shrine of Bom Jesus do Monte originally had a single staircase, at the top of which stood a Baroque church (later demolished and replaced with the Neoclassical structure we see today). Two more staircases were added during the century, winding up almost to the summt and embellished with statues and fountains illustrating the five senses and the three theological virtues: faith, hope and charity. The programme therefore represented a journey of the senses and of the heart, whereby the faithful distanced themselves from the material world with the aid of a staircase leading to the spiritual realm. The theatrical element is here a concrete expression of faith – a book of images that are as luminous and eloquent as the teeming frescoes of the Roman Baroque. The remarkable drama of this Portuguese site finds an echo in an identical arrangement at Lamego, east of Porto, where the same interlocking, labyrinthine lines reach up to the church, creating a sensation of unattainability that dissipates as the pilgrim climbs upwards.

But an external staircase may also be one of the first architectural features a visitor encounters on approaching a grand house. Having taken their lead from Renaissance models, architects in the seventeenth and eighteenth centuries presented the exterior stair as a prelude to the splendours to come, using it to attract attention to the centre of the façade. One famous example is the horseshoe-shaped staircase at the palace of Fontainebleau. Built to replace a similar structure by Philibert de l'Orme, it has presided over the Cour du Cheval Blanc since 1634, when Jean Androuet du Cerceau completed its reconstruction. The distinctive shape enables carriages to turn round with ease between its two flights. The site is known to history as the 'Cour des Adieux', recalling Napoleon Bonaparte's appearance at the steps in 1814, shortly after his abdication, in order to bid farewell to his guard as he left for exile on Elba. If staircases are synonymous with power, they may also illustrate dramatically a fall from power.

In the same the spirit as the arrangement at Fontainebleau, the façade of the Troja palace in Prague is largely occupied by a pair of monumental curved stairs in dark stone that contrast strikingly with the red and white of the façade, lending the building a subtle verticality. The palace was built between 1679 and 1691 by Jean-Baptiste Mathey, a Dijon-born architect summoned to Prague by Count Václav Vojtěch Šternberk. He drew his inspiration from Italy and France and thus introduced the Roman Baroque to Bohemia. In the style of the Baroque stairs of Italy, the external staircase is embellished with statues depicting the battle between the gods and the Titans (pp. 96–97).

In England, the external staircase at Clandon Park, Surrey, built in the 1720s by the Italian architect Giacomo Leoni, is probably no more than an architectural whim, comparable to one of the follies to be found in the gardens. A curious pair of twinned stairs meet beneath a portico sheltering the house's main door. Leoni was an admirer of Alberti and Palladio, and this may have been a stylistic exercise aimed at magnifying the entrance: visitors need not even take the stairs, since just behind the steps the driveway leads directly up to the portico.

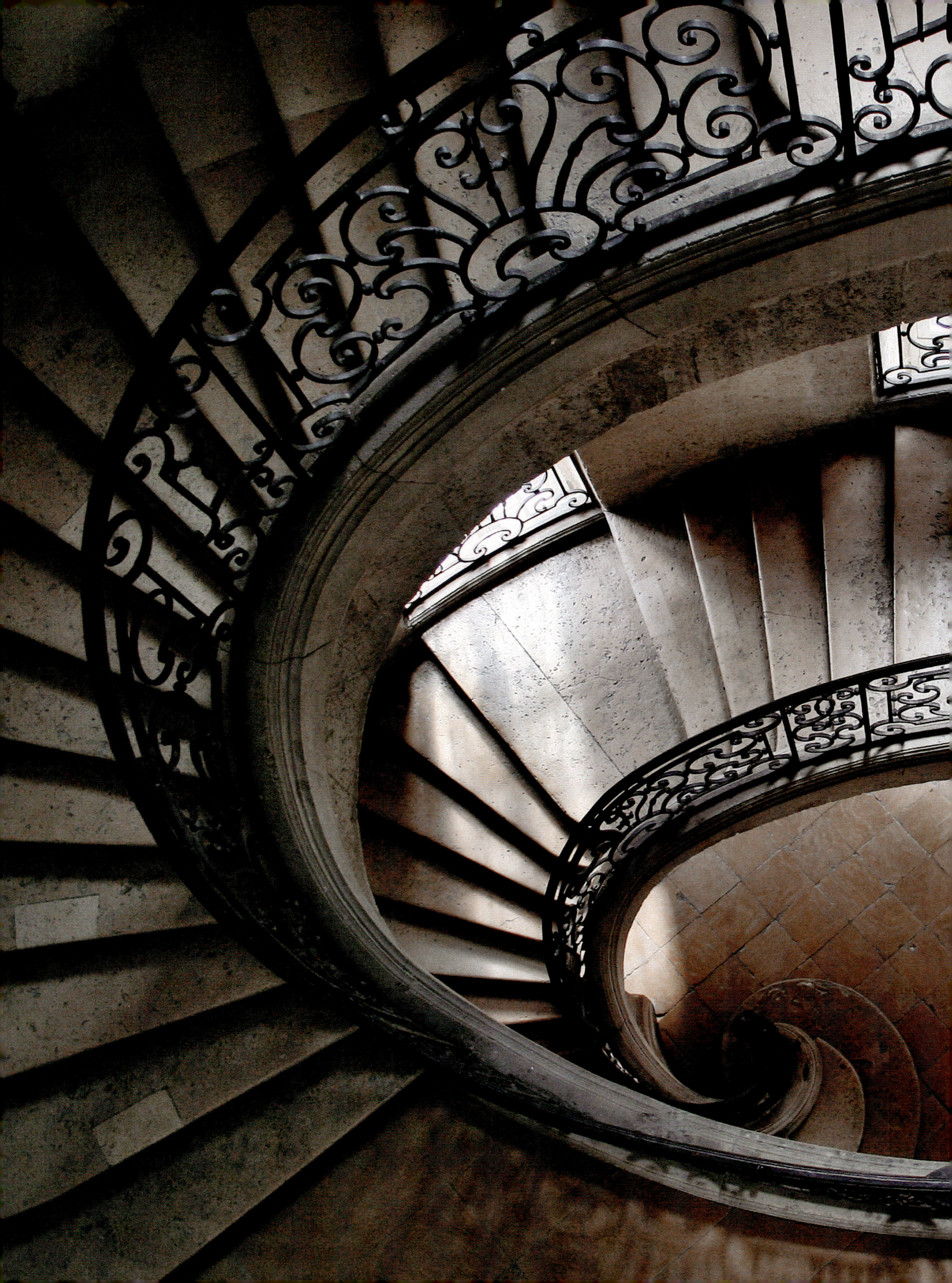

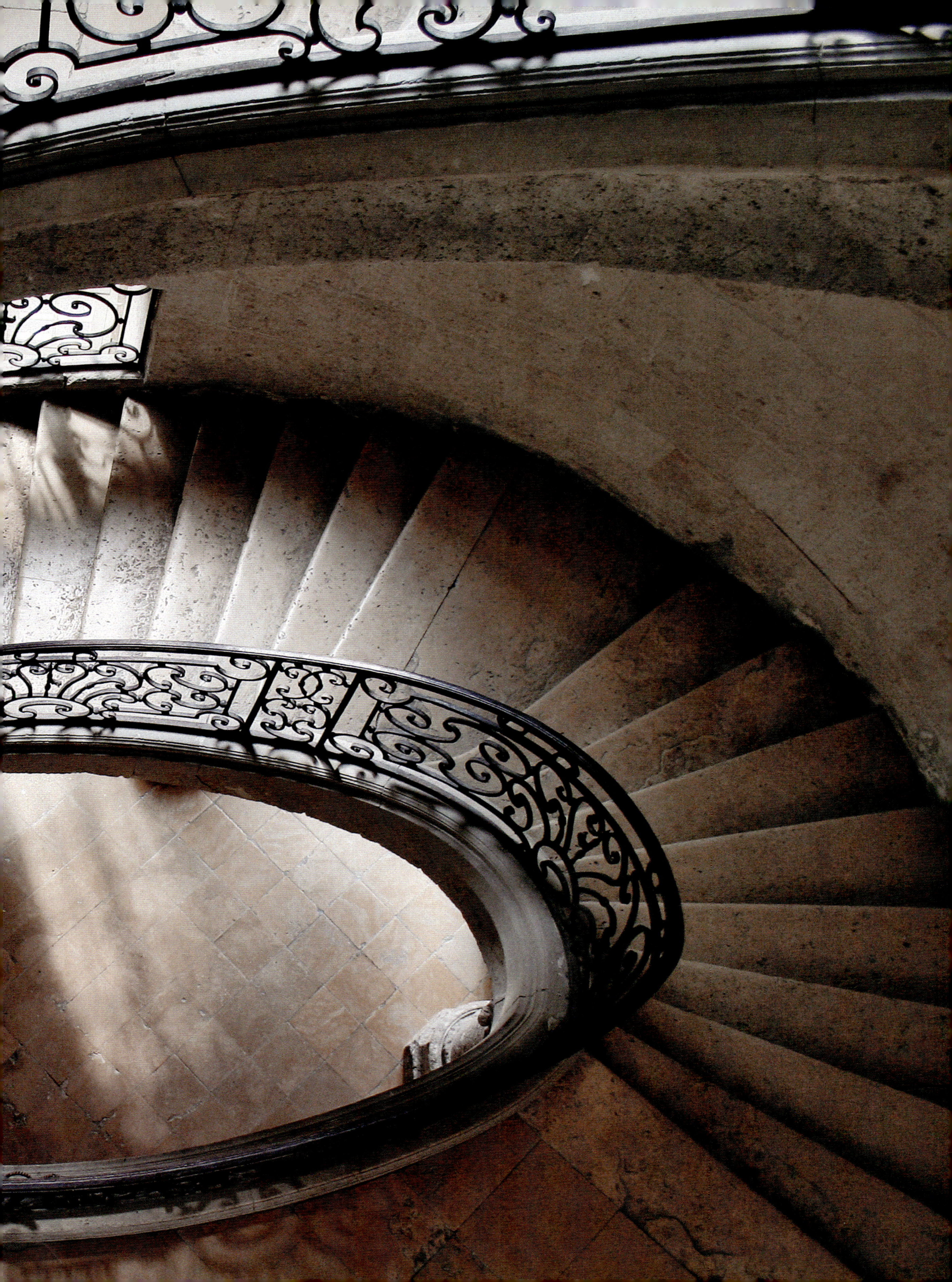

NEOCLASSICAL HARMONY IN FRANCE The French staircase of the eighteenth century was measured and restrained in style. Following a few attempts to introduce Rococo elements in the 1710 and 1720s, visible essentially in the balustrades, there was a rapid move towards the elegant simplicity of Neoclassicism. The seventeenth-century staircase, with its pure lines and refined theatricality, reached its pinnacle with the designs of Louis Le Vau and François Mansart, and was so successful that its basic form survived virtually unchanged throughout the following century. The essential characteristic of these staircases was their remarkably harmonious combination of stone and wrought iron. Skilled craftsmen produced ironwork of astounding quality, creating scrolls and arabesques of the utmost sensuality that were imitated – though not necessarily understood – throughout Europe.

French abbeys made particularly sublime use of this combination. Here, architects understood, as had the medieval stained-glass makers before them, the mystical power of light on stone and of tapering shadows on steps. Staircases in the residential wings always extended to the top floor rather than stopping at the *piano nobile*, as was the custom in private dwellings. Not only did they serve state rooms, but these staircases were also and above all a means of circulation for the religious community. They provided a symbolic passage in which an ascent towards God might be discerned in an architecture of such purity it seemed to verge on the divine.

In the twelfth century, Norbert of Xanten founded an abbey in the forest of Saint-Gobain, now in the department of the Aisne, at a place called Prémontré. The monks belonged to the Augustinian order, which centred on communal life, an experience that was essential for a true understanding of the meaning of charity. The monastery was rebuilt in the eighteenth century, and the living quarters were endowed with a remarkable elliptical staircase of unusual elegance (pp. 100–1).

The Abbaye aux Hommes, founded in Caen by William the Conqueror, was also refurbished in the second half of the eighteenth century. The staircase seems to float above its supporting arches, soaring upwards in a luminous space, the scrolls of its balustrade silhouetted gracefully against the bare stone.

LEFT
Built in the 1760s, the grand staircase of the Abbaye aux Hommes at Caen gave the monks access to the library and their cells. The immaculate purity of the design is characteristic of French abbeys of the eighteenth century.

RIGHT
The staircase of the Petit Trianon at Versailles, built in the 1760s by Ange-Jacques Gabriel for Madame de Pompadour. The gilt wrought-iron balustrade, of outstanding craftsmanship, is decorated with Neoclassical motifs.

The composition as a whole is one of astonishing purity, representing both the abbey's power and the vow of silence imposed within its walls.

At Versailles, Ange-Jacques Gabriel's less restrained Petit Trianon, built for Madame de Pompadour, boasts a staircase of 1769 with a gilded wrought-iron balustrade displaying early Neoclassical motifs; the monogram of Marie Antoinette was added in 1787. This example, built for a mistress and inherited by a queen, expresses the discreet, almost intimate quality of the refuge used by Marie Antoinette to escape the court's stifling etiquette.

At the château of Bénouville, built in a triumphant Neoclassical style around 1775 by Claude-Nicolas Ledoux, one of the most talented architects of his age, a monumental staircase is set in a square space that rises through the building's full height. The space is treated as though it were an external one, featuring bare stone, columns, pilasters and small windows to the attic storey, as on a château façade. This impression is reinforced by the powerful flights of stairs, with their stone balustrading. Even the ceiling suggests the illusion that the staircase is open to the sky: the cupola has *trompe-l'oeil* coffering pierced by an oculus, as at the Pantheon in Rome, which opens onto a magnificent painted sky. This serene architecture typifies a century in which enlightened gentlemen viewed architecture as the accomplishment of perfect good taste. Through their ability to appreciate it, they were raised to the ranks of the elect.

RIGHT
The staircase of the château of Bénouville, completed c. 1775, is Claude-Nicolas Ledoux's masterpiece and an exemplar of the Neoclassical style.

ROCOCO EXCESS The Rococo was a style of richness and exuberance that, mingled with the Baroque, spread through a large part of Europe. While some countries, such as France, refused to yield with good grace and quickly denounced its ornamental excesses (even though French examples were relatively modest compared to those of neighbouring countries), others opted to express their prestige through a delirious riot of form and colour. In 1754 Charles-Nicolas Cochin, an engraver and member of the French academy of painting and sculpture, noted scathingly in *Le Mercure de France* that 'we call these things "forms", but we forget to add the epithet "bad", which is inseparable from them. Yet we allow [artists] to peddle these deformed goods to any provincial or foreigner who is sufficiently poor in connoisseurship to prefer our modern taste to that of the last century.' A softer-toned, less tormented and more anodyne version of the Baroque, the Rococo found fertile ground in Germany, Austria and Russia, where a different sensibility accorded the staircase a spectacular place amid decorative schemes of unbridled splendour.

In Germany, the staircase at Schloss Bruchsal in Baden-Württemberg, built in the 1720s, displays a Baroque style on the threshold of the Rococo. Completed by Johann Balthasar Neumann for the Prince-Bishop of Schönborn-Buchheim, the staircase is a superb composition that plays on gradations between light and shadow. Highly unusual in plan, it consists of two symmetrically arranged flights set within an oval, a motif common in Neumann's work and ultimately inspired by Borromini. The ellipses overlap to meet above a grotto, an original feature that was decorated with frescoes by Giovanni Francesco Marchini between 1731 and 1736.

In Austria during the same period, the Prince-Archbishop of Salzburg entrusted the rebuilding of the Mirabell Palace to the celebrated architect Johann Lukas von Hildebrandt. Construction took place between 1721 and 1727. In the remodelled staircase, the most surprising and remarkable feature was without doubt the balustrade, which had 'cherubs astride a froth of volutes, capering and gambolling on foaming marble waves that tumble down the stairs, lending the existing structure exuberance and movement' (Charles-Nicolas Cochin). This balustrade is one of the most original ever conceived. Architects in general concentrated more on the wall and ceiling decoration, assigning balusters or wrought-iron arabesques to the balustrade and declining to explore the form any further. Practical considerations probably prevented this curious experiment from being repeated on other staircases, and the antics of Baroque cherubs were reserved for equally decorative but less entertaining schemes.

One of the most remarkable staircases of the German Rococo was created by Neumann at Schloss Augustusburg in Brühl, near Cologne, for Clemens August of Bavaria, Archbishop-Elector of Cologne and a distinguished patron of the arts. Augustusburg and its grand hunting lodge are without doubt among Neumann's most ambitious creations. Although the Belgian architect François de Cuvilliés – one of the masters of the Bavarian Rococo, whose masterpiece was the Amalienburg hunting lodge near Munich – was in charge of the building work, it was Neumann who was responsible for the staircase (p. 113). Clemens August would certainly have been aware of his outstanding reputation, and perhaps of his exceptional work at Bruchsal; like many prominent figures before him, the Archbishop-Elector was anxious to demonstrate his own influence and personality through the construction of a grand staircase

LEFT
Johann Balthasar Neumann's staircase for Schloss Bruchsal in Baden-Württemberg (c. 1728) is subtly Baroque in style, verging on the Rococo.

OPPOSITE
In Salzburg, Austria, Johann Lukas von Hildebrandt remodelled the grand staircase of the Mirabell Palace in the 1720s to create one of the most original stairs in the Rococo style. Its balustrade is full of cascading movement and is topped with capering cherubs.

OVERLEAF AND PAGES 108–9
Composed of two symmetrical flights contained in an elliptical plan, the staircase at Bruchsal plays skilfully on the transition from darkness to light: the steps flank a vestibule painted to suggest a grotto (pp. 108–9), while the pink-and-white flights are flooded with light.

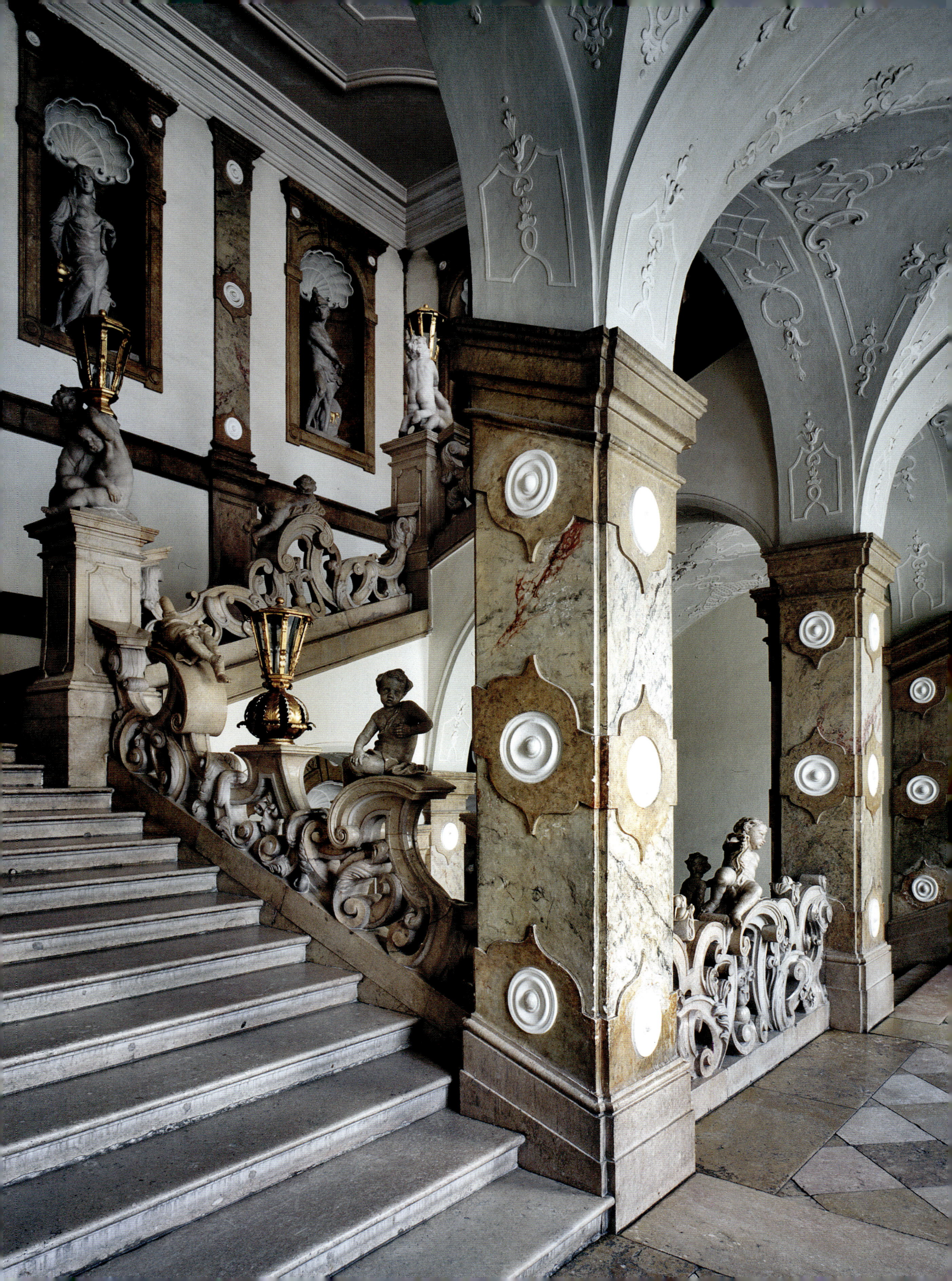

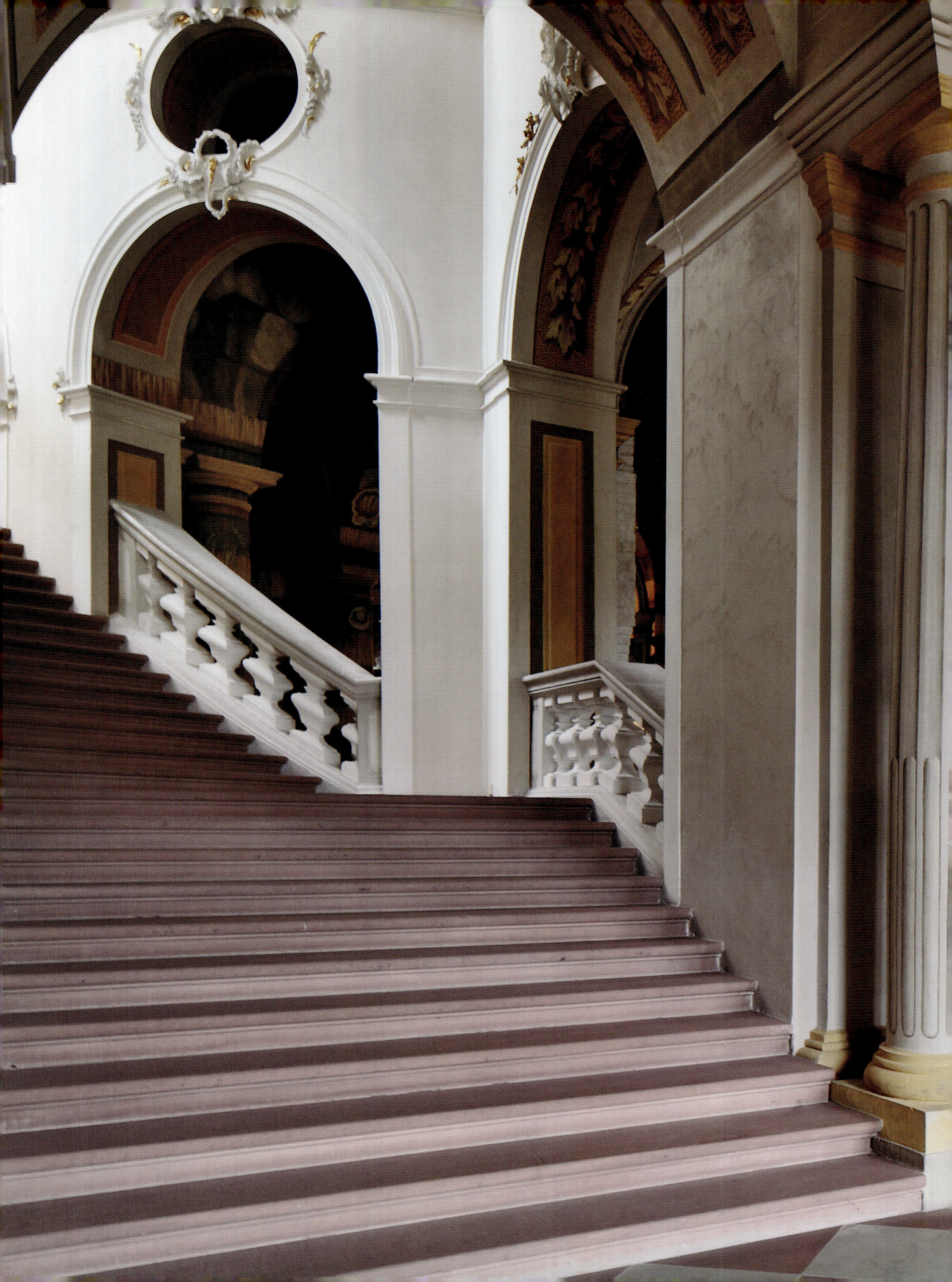

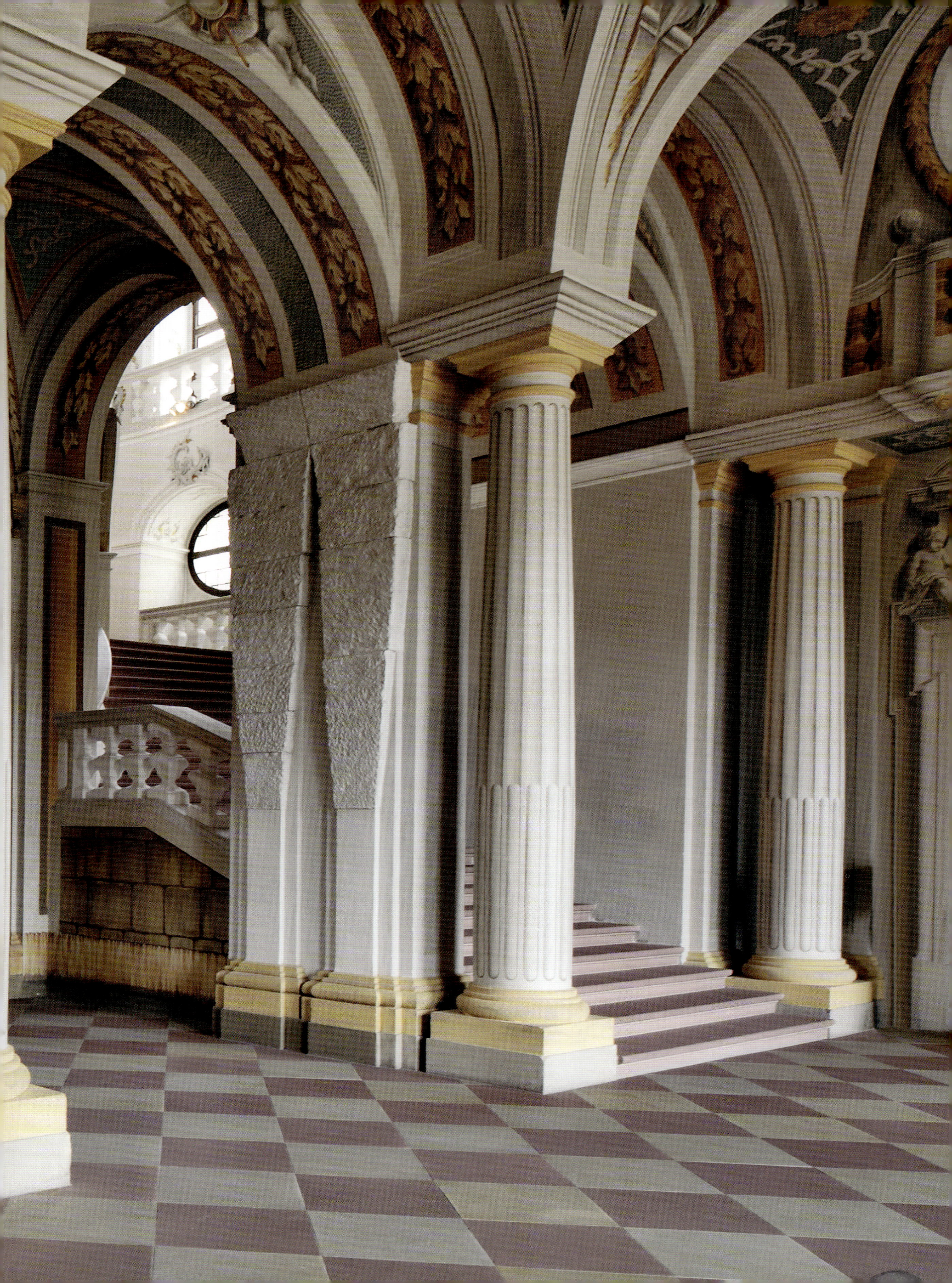

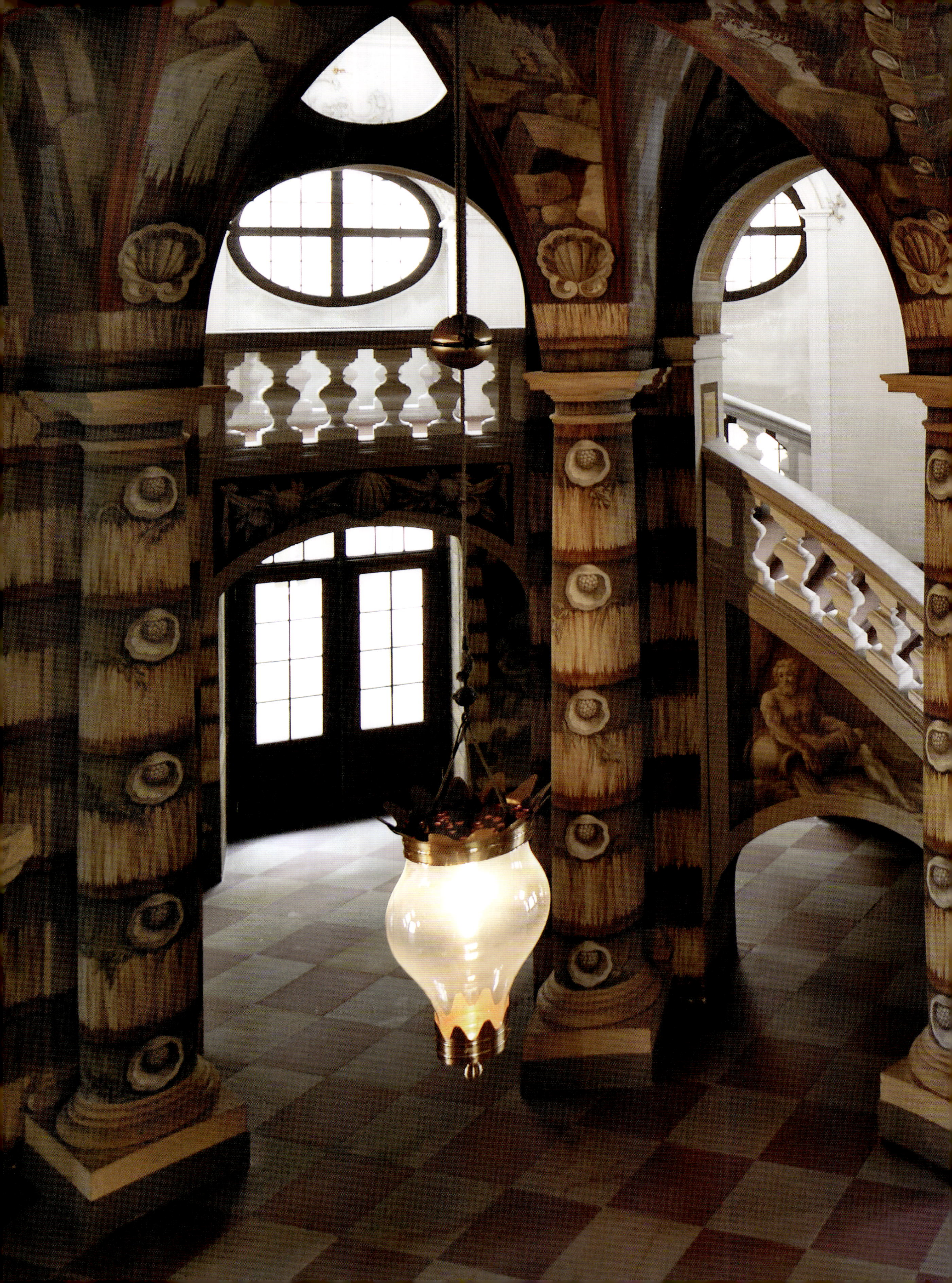

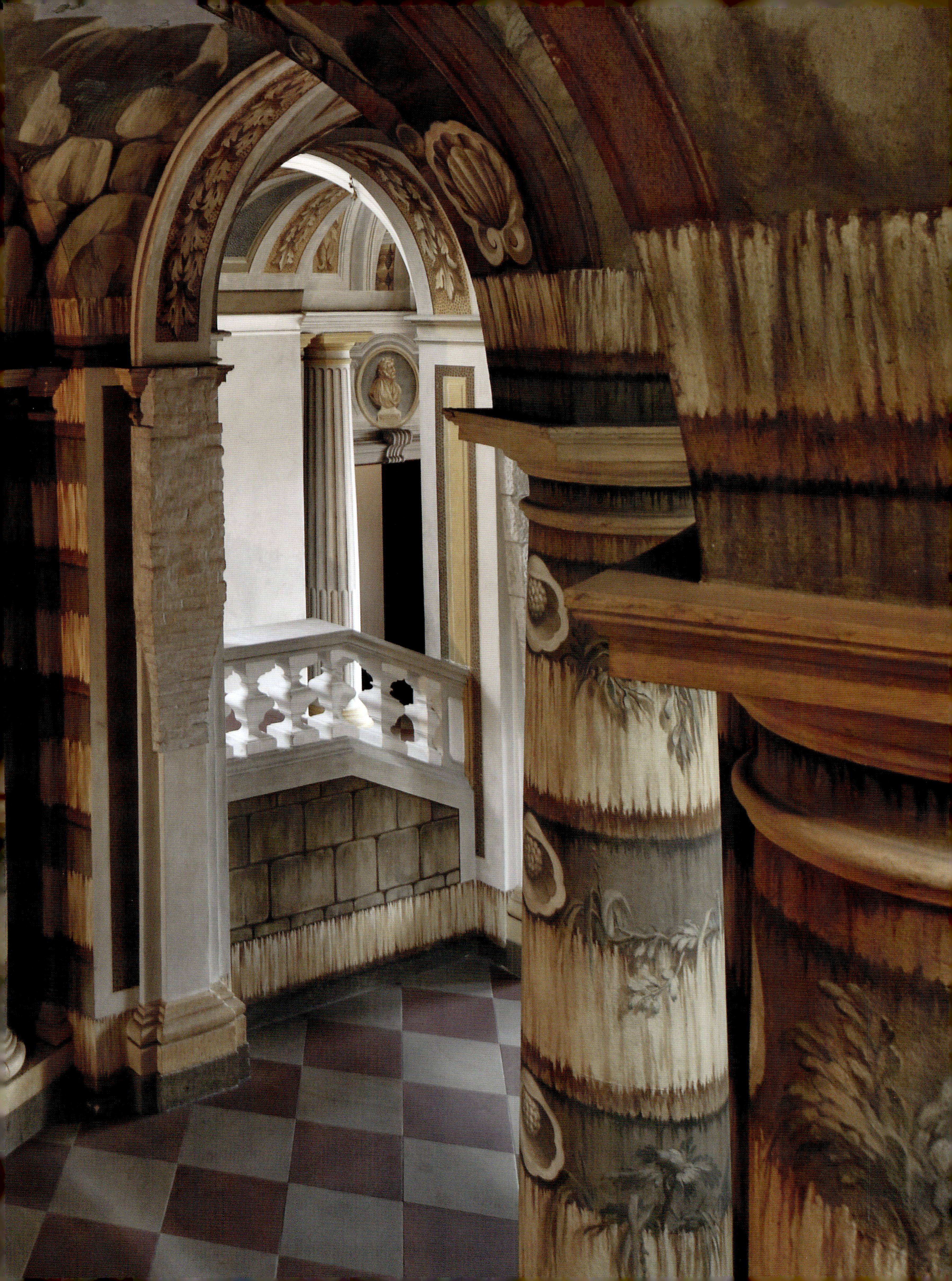

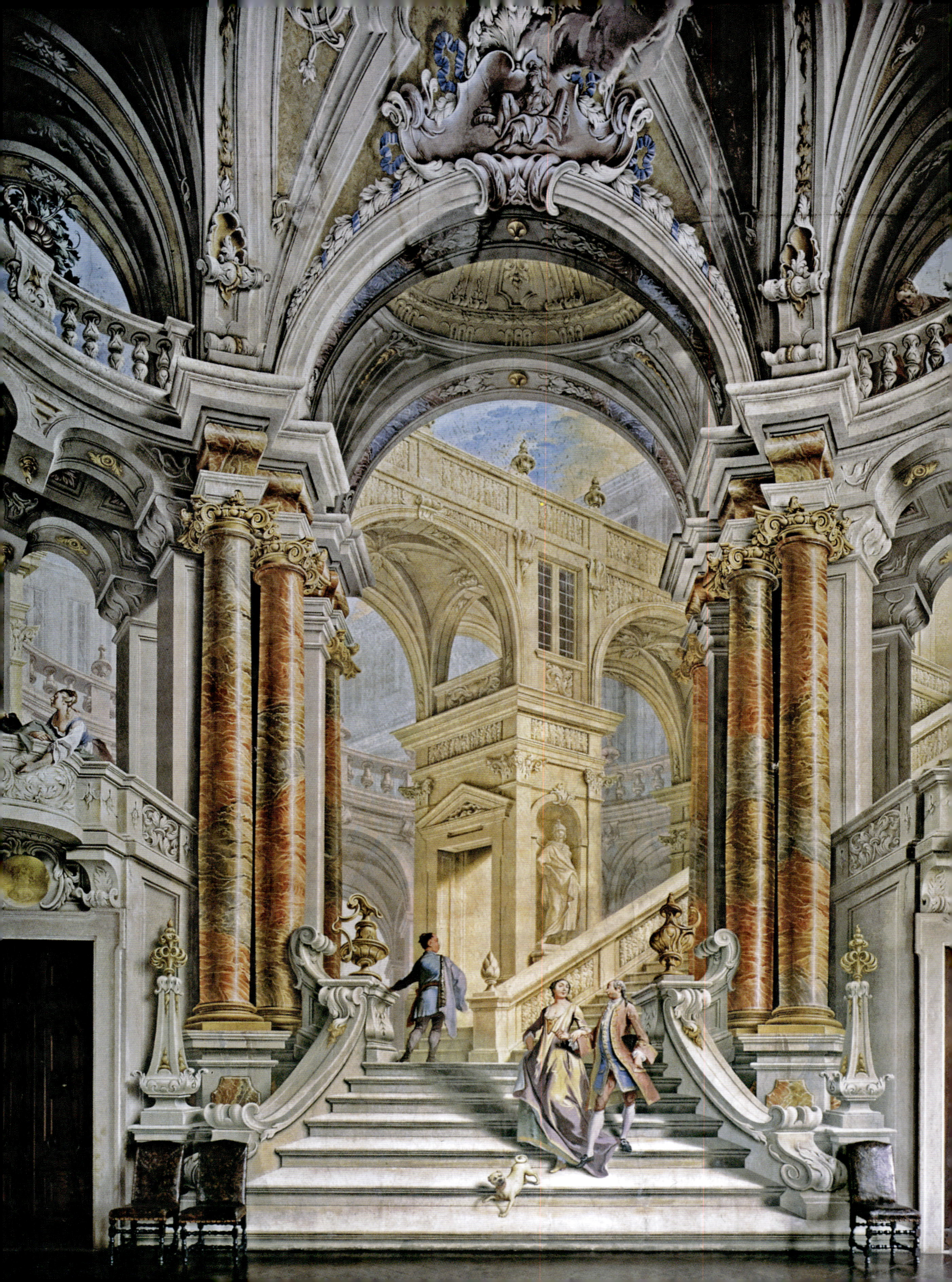

OPPOSITE
Trompe-l'oeil fresco painted in 1745 by Carlo Carlone for the Villa Lecchi in Montirone, Lombardy, depicting a court scene in an imaginary architectural setting. Great skill was needed to create the illusion of perspective for the staircase.

RIGHT
Plate from Andrea Pozzo's work on the art of trompe-l'oeil *(1693), in which he included several depictions of staircases in imagined architectural settings.*

that would lead up to the palace's ceremonial rooms. The result – harmonious, inventive and yet in impeccably good taste – marks a milestone in the history of art. Like all flamboyant, extravagant creations it has had its critics, but its breathtaking decorative profusion, its warm and lively palette of colours and its rich repertoire of Rococo ornamentation all add to the surprise effect intended by Neumann. The visitor is received in the same spirit that reigned at the Ambassadors' Staircase in Versailles, via an entrance hall with a relatively low ceiling, from which only the first flight of steps and part of the decoration above are visible. Gradually the space shifts as the visitor climbs upwards, to reveal, all of a sudden, a cascade of stucco trophies and other decorative details. The whole ensemble is crowned with an immense cupola surrounded by a wrought-iron balustrade and painted in *trompe-l'oeil*, suggesting that the ceiling opens up onto a terrace giving views of an idealized firmament peopled with gods and allegorical figures. The paintings and ceiling are by the Italian-born artist Carlo Carlone, who worked for a period in Germany, attracted by the many building projects for princes who wanted to express their power in a new style. Carlone had trained in Venice in the illusionistic tradition established by Andrea Pozzo, the brilliant artist responsible for the breathtaking *trompe-l'oeil* paintings on the ceiling of Sant'Ignazio in Rome, painted in 1685. In the 1690s Pozzo had published his *Perspectiva pictorum et architectorum*, a handbook of *trompe-l'oeil* art in which several plates show staircases and their architectural settings. Carlone drew inspiration from this treatise in 1745, when he painted one of the frescoes at the Villa Lecchi at Montirone in Lombardy, depicting a court scene unfolding at the foot of a staircase in a fabulous architectural setting. The correct perspective and movement of stairs are among the most difficult features to capture and convey using *trompe-l'oeil*, but Carlone here demonstrates a considerable mastery of the imaginary space he has created.

The palaces of Austria and Germany offer a rich, fascinating and comprehensive range of examples of the German Baroque, which was concerned less with the beauty of materials than with the visual effects that could be created when they were brought together. At Brühl, most of the marble is in fact imitation and made of scagliola, an Italian technique combining powdered gypsum, glue and pigments. No expense was spared, by contrast, on the *trompe-l'oeil* paintings, for which the most outstanding artists were commissioned. Thus the powerful dynasty of the Prince-Bishops of Würzburg, who had already built Schloss Bruchsal, commissioned the Venetian Giambattista Tiepolo to provide the frescoes for Neumann's grand staircase in their palace at Würzburg (p. 112). Between 1751 and 1753 Tiepolo painted an immense fresco, measuring 30 by 18 metres (98 by 59 feet), depicting the four corners of the earth on the staircase ceiling.

THE STAIRCASE IN RUSSIA: A EUROPEAN AMBITION In Russia, the reign of Peter the Great was characterized by his determination to open his empire up to Europe, so transforming it into a brilliant Western power. This enlightened ruler, who understood that the arts were an excellent tool for conveying political importance, travelled through Europe on a historic diplomatic mission. This 'grand

112 | A THEATRE OF POWER

ABOVE
The great staircase of the Würzburg Residenz, by Balthasar Neumann. In the 1750s Giambattista Tiepolo covered the ceiling with a fresco depicting the four corners of the earth.

RIGHT
At Schloss Augustusburg in Brühl, near Cologne, Neumann built one of the most extraordinary of all German Rococo staircases. The delirious profusion of decoration is complemented by the disorientating drama of the design, with its mastery of interlocking spaces inherited from the Baroque.

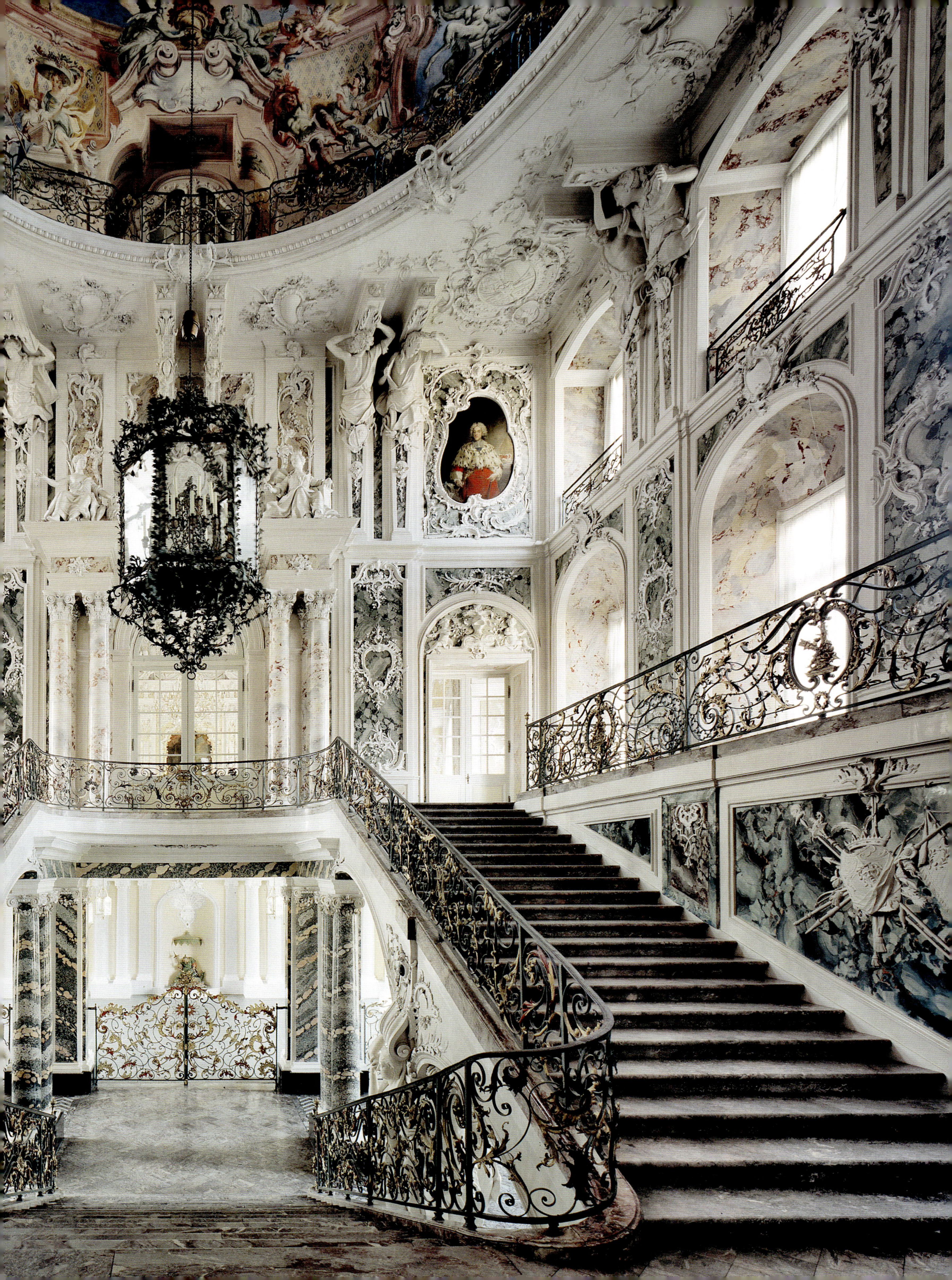

embassy', undertaken in 1697–98, had the twofold purpose of seeking European alliances against the Ottoman Empire and gleaning information about European models. Having resolved to create a window onto the West within Russia, he founded the city of St Petersburg, to which he attracted engineers and artists from throughout Europe. Peter wanted to modernize Russia by modelling it on a European ideal of culture and refinement, pursuing this aim through numerous projects he conceived for the new city. He did not return to France, a country that fascinated him, until 1717, when he visited in Paris (which he found a disappointment) and Versailles, where he noted down everything he saw, later taking its arrangement of six broad, radiating avenues as his plan for St Petersburg. He travelled under the aegis of the Duc d'Antin, director of the Bâtiments du Roi, and on his return to Russia took with him the talented sculptor Nicolas Pineau, who introduced rocaille work and the French style to Russia. The Peterhof Palace near St Petersburg, overlooking the Gulf of Finland, would be powerful ammunition for the ruler of a country that hitherto had been regarded by certain European powers – notably France – as archaic.

The grand staircase at Peterhof was completed in 1752 by Bartolomeo Rastrelli during the reign of Elizabeth I. Rastrelli had arrived in Italy around 1715 with his father, an artist of lesser renown who had joined the court of Peter the Great at a time when the city offered many opportunities for building work and was a less competitive environment than Italy. Rastrelli's name is indelibly linked with a graceful Baroque style of Italian inspiration, which also incorporated a Russian element that he understood and expressed with consummate skill. He was commissioned by the Empress to build a staircase at the Winter Palace, which he completed in 1762 (overleaf). Known as the Jordan Staircase (on the Feast of the Epiphany, the Tsar would process down it to bless the waters of the Neva, in remembrance of Christ's baptism), this jewel of the Russian Baroque rises through the full height of the palace. It is watched over from above by the gods of Olympus, in a ceiling painting by Diziano Gasparo, while statues of gods and other allegorical figures enliven the spaces beneath the mirrors and the gilded embellishments.

After the Winter Palace was destroyed by a terrible fire in 1837, the Tsar asked Vassili Stasov to restore the staircase, following Rastrelli's plans in every detail. Only two features are not faithful to the original: the white marble balustrade was replaced by one in gilt bronze, and grey granite columns replaced the pink stone of the originals. (Pink was certainly more in keeping with the earlier style, which banished sombe colours from its light-filled spaces.) In her memoirs, Catherine the Great recalled being struck less by the beauty of Rastrelli's staircase than by its sheer size and the inconveniences it presented in the cold of the Russian winter: 'At the Winter Palace, the Grand Duke and I were accommodated in the apartments that we had already occupied. The Grand Duke's rooms were separated from my own by an immense staircase that also served the Empress's apartments. In order to reach his rooms, or for him to reach mine, we had to cross the staircase hall, which was not, especially in winter, the most convenient of arrangements.' It was perhaps those glacial memories that prompted Catherine to commission Charles Cameron to design a staircase in mahogany, warmer than marble, for the palace of Tsarskoye Selo, built in the 1750s. This structure, which replaced another Rastrelli creation, was replaced in its turn in 1860. In his book on the palaces of Tsarskoye Selo, Emmanuel Ducamp records how Catherine, having decided 'to annex the southern part of the palace for her personal use and to refurbish it to suit her own tastes . . . demolished the state staircase that occupied the far end of the building and led to the five antechambers of the Golden Enfilade, and replaced it with another at the very centre of the palace, on the site of Elizabeth I's former Chinese Room.' Brought to power by a coup d'état that overthrew her husband in 1762, Catherine was a woman of cultivated taste and prodigious energy. 'The new empress was endowed not only with unerringly good taste in matters of art,' notes Ducamp, 'but also with an understanding of how the creation of a sophisticated world around her could serve her image and reputation.'

The palace of Tsarskoye Selo, near St Petersburg, is indelibly linked with the history of Russia through its sumptuous splendour. It is one of the most accomplished expressions of the quest for insurmountable glory that obsessed eighteenth-century rulers. 'In modifying a small existing palace and transforming it into a new palace of vast proportions for Empress Elizaveta Petrovna, daughter of Peter the Great, Rastrelli took into account both the status of the building, destined to become the Empress's official residence, and the character of the woman who commissioned it,' writes Ducamp. While the Baroque

OPPOSITE
The grand staircase of the Peterhof Palace near St Petersburg, completed by Bartolomeo Rastrelli in 1752 during the reign of Empress Elizabeth I. It demonstrates the Italian inspiration that underpinned the Russian Baroque.

OVERLEAF
One of the finest examples of Russian Baroque interiors: the ceremonial staircase, or Jordan Staircase, in the Winter Palace, St Petersburg, built by Rastrelli in the eighteenth century and re-created after the 1837 fire.

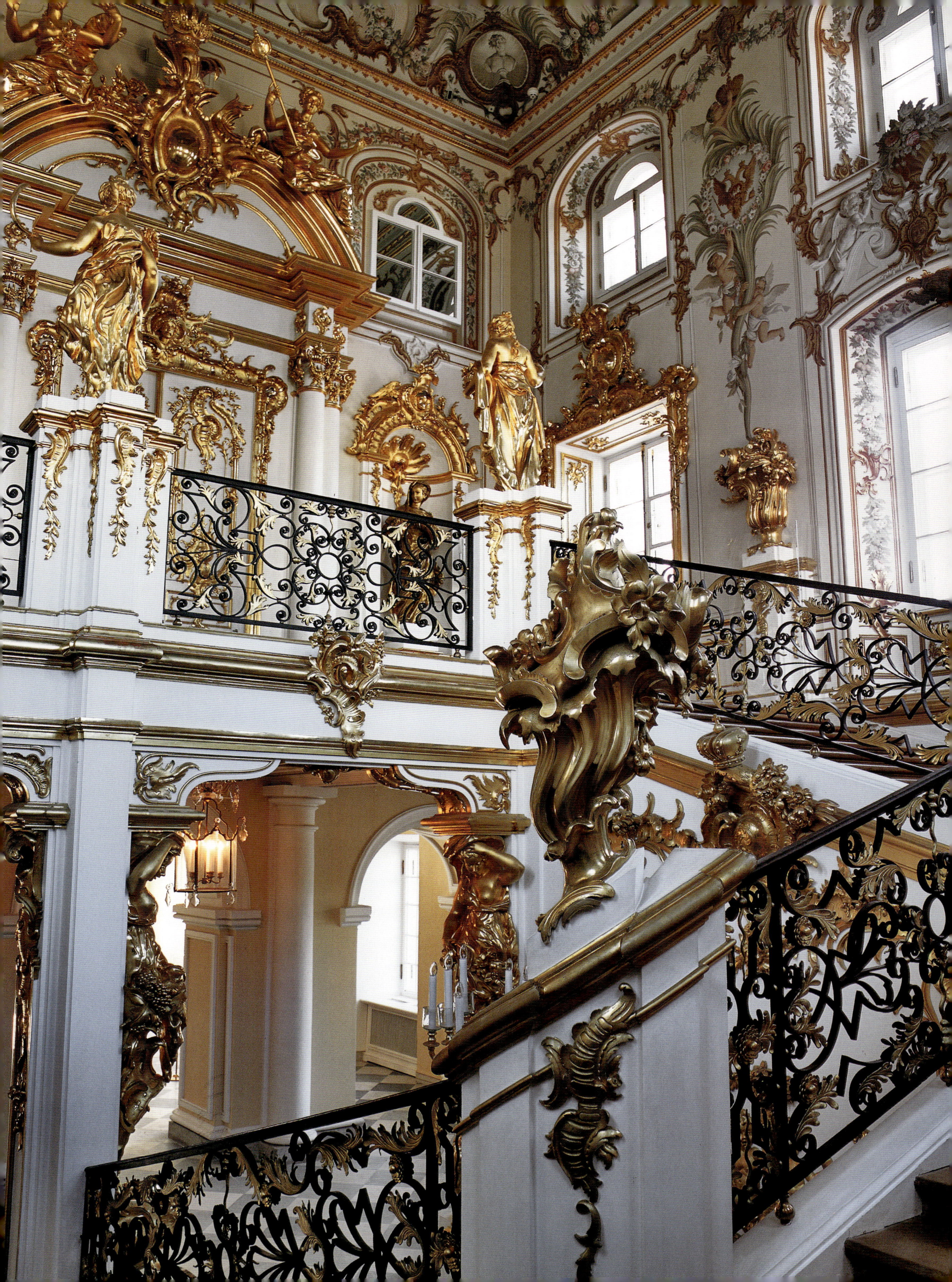

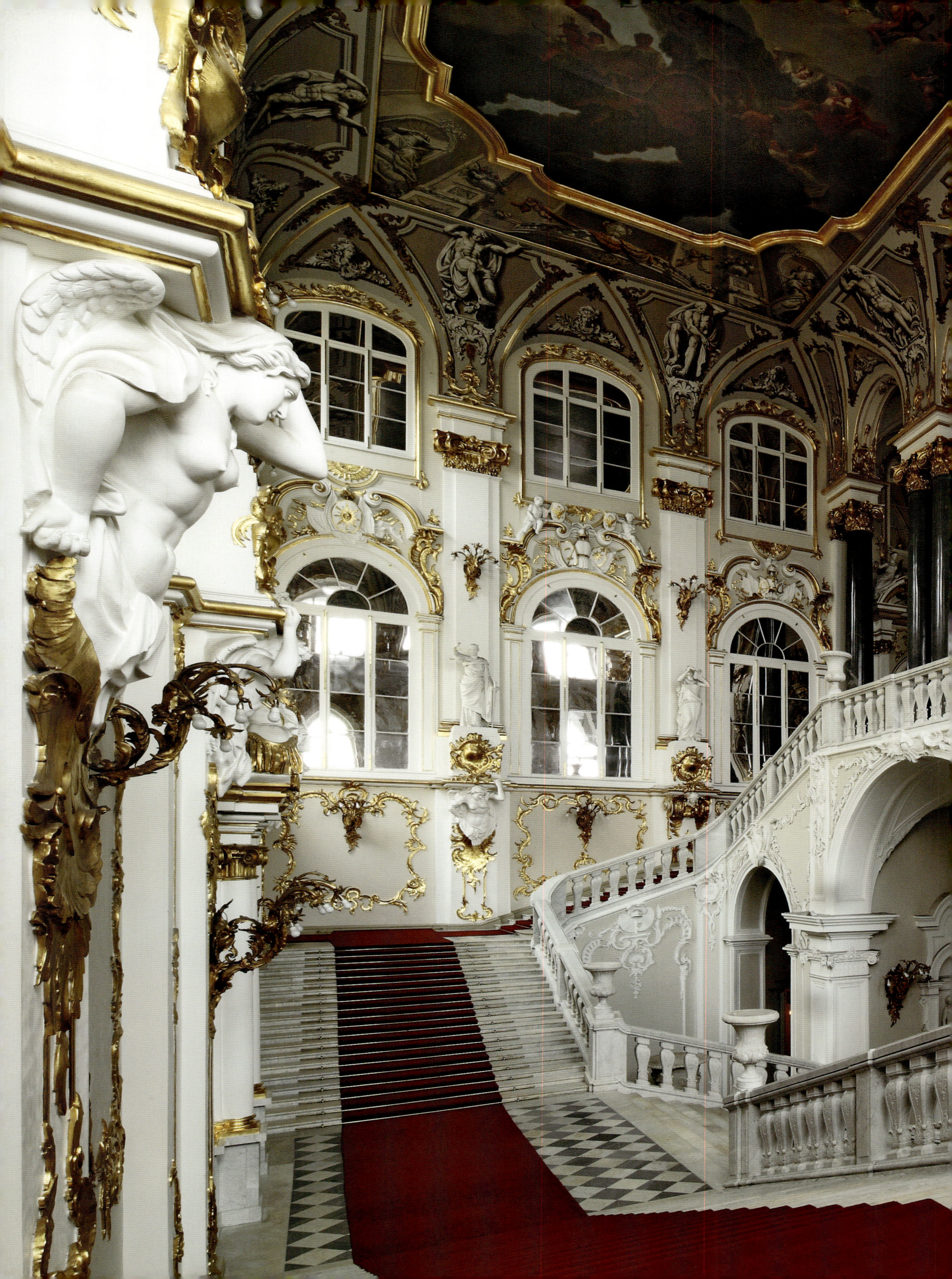

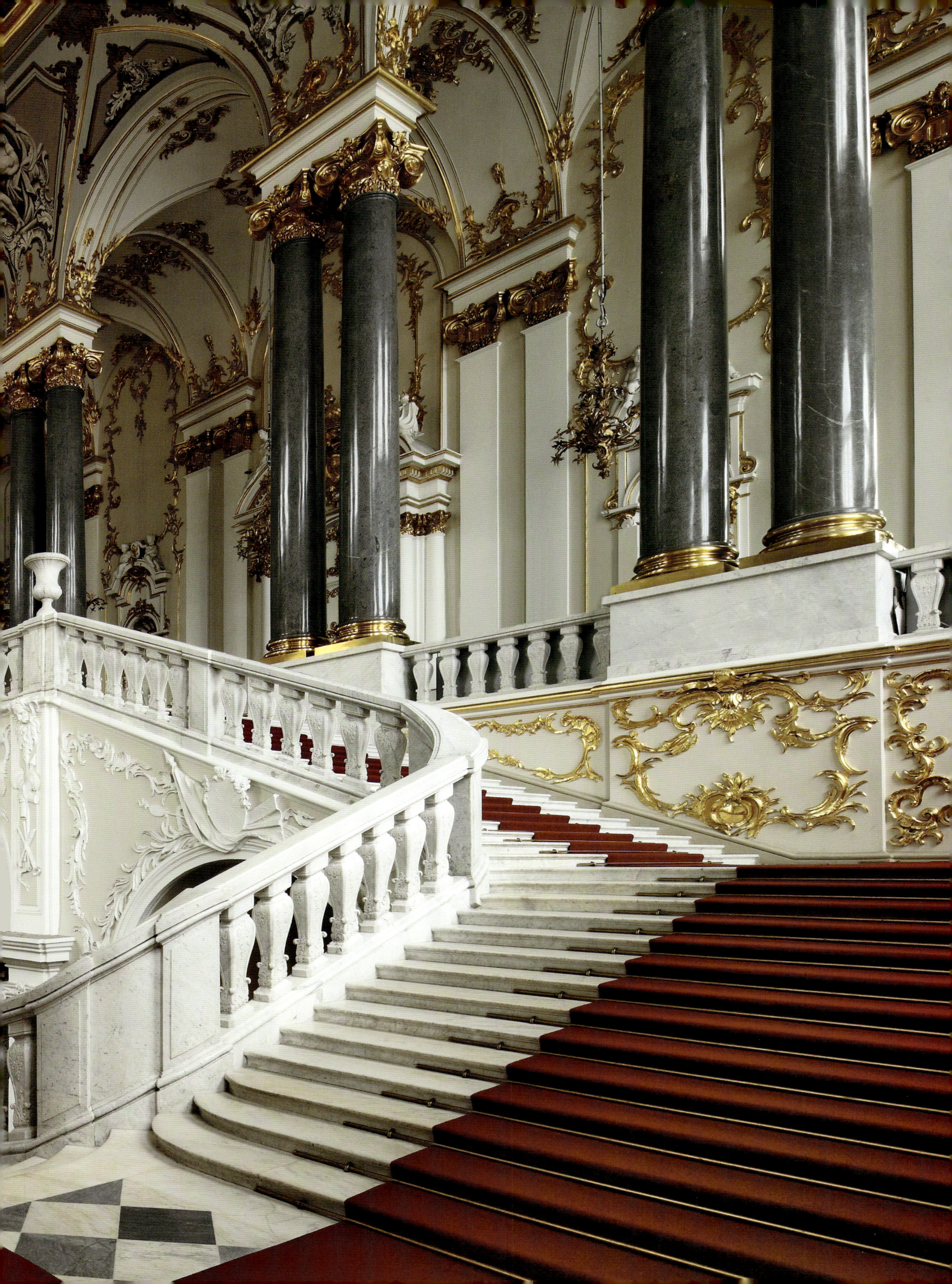

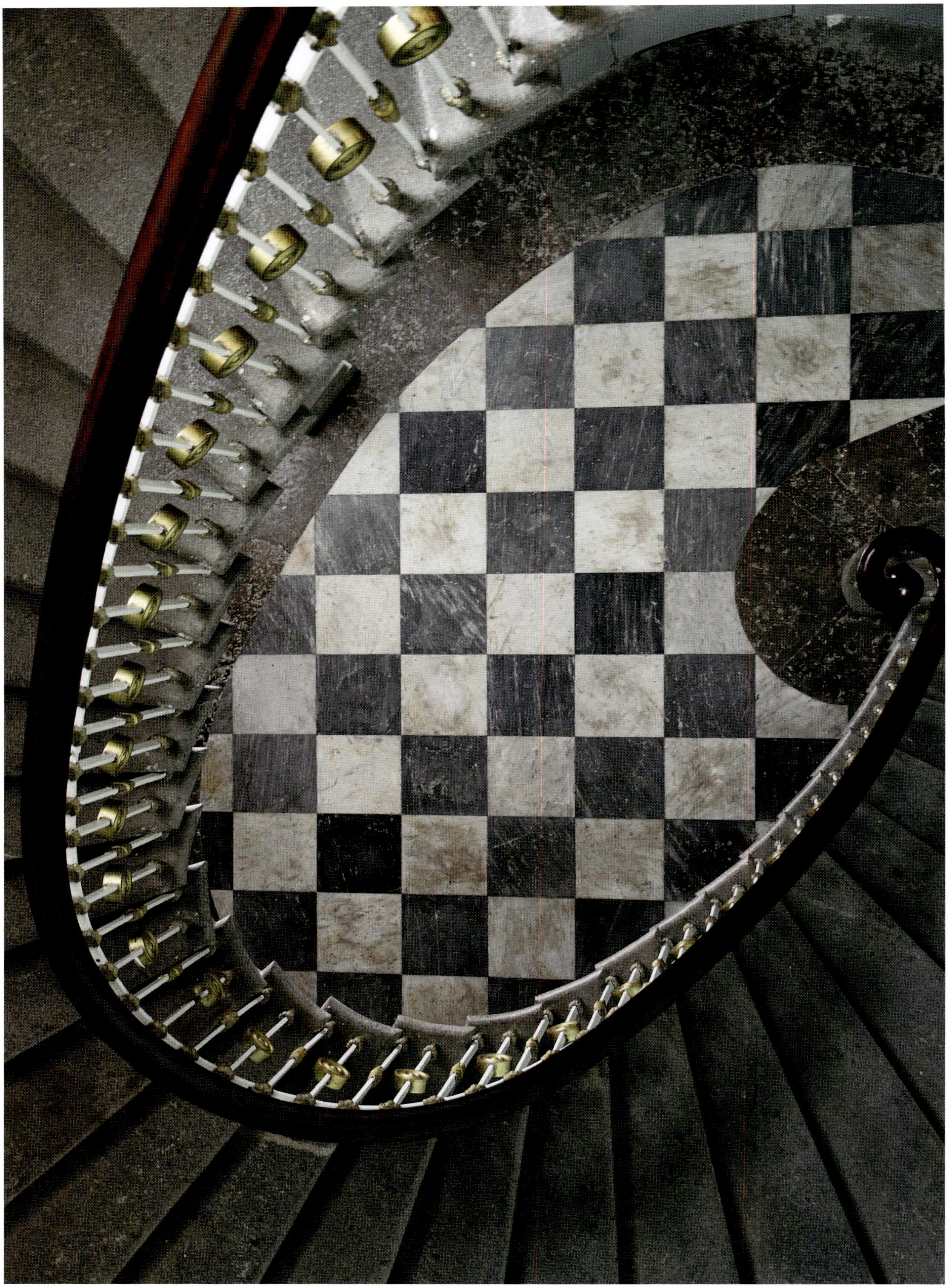

OPPOSITE
The staircase in the Cold Baths Pavilion at Tsarskoye Selo, designed by the architect Charles Cameron in a classical style at the command of Catherine the Great (1782). The stairs are in granite, while the handrail is in mahogany, then very much in vogue in Europe.

creations of Rastrelli are linked with the reign of Elizabeth I, who turned Tsarskoye Selo into a unique site, the reign of Catherine the Great was marked by her passion for antiquity and for the Neoclassical spirit that had swept Europe since the excavations at Herculaneum and Pompeii. She commissioned Charles Cameron, the Scottish-born architect recruited by one of her agents charged with finding European architects to work on the palace, to alter some of Rastrelli's interiors in the 1750s. But his most important commission was for a Neoclassical building close to the palace. The construction of his Cold Baths, which include the luxurious Agate Rooms, from 1782 formed part of the decorative programme for the private apartments.

These suites were unique in their originality and recalled Roman imperial palaces through their use of rich and unusual materials. The ground floor houses the baths, while the first floor is devoted to a number of rooms for leisure and relaxation, including a room lined in red jasper, a library and a hall opening onto a hanging garden. A staircase curves gracefully up to the first floor. From 1784 Cameron added an external open gallery sheltering Greek and Roman busts, which became one of Catherine's favourite walks. A straight flight of steps, flanked by statues of Hercules and Flora, initially led to the bathing pavilion, but there was no direct access from the gallery to the garden. Cameron therefore added a staircase of two curved flights, to spectacular effect. The gallery thus appeared to rest on the plinth of an austere classical temple, which some brilliant modern hand had softened with sensual curves that drew the eye upwards. Even in the private realm of her bathing pavilion, Catherine remained conscious of her status as Empress of all the Russias and intended to show it. Peter the Great's new empire, envisaged less than a century earlier, had perhaps failed to make the social progress he had wished for, but henceforth its art could vie with the greatest creations of the West. It was a crucial advantage, of whose importance the tsars were fully aware. On a political stage ruled by court etiquette, investing colossal sums in the arts was the first step to diplomatic success.

BRITISH GRANDEUR AND SIMPLICITY In Britain, the first half of the eighteenth century was characterized by an architectural movement known as the English Baroque. It was a distinctive style, based on the Palladian vocabulary introduced by Inigo Jones in the seventeenth century. Far removed from its continental cousin, which played on sensuality and curves, the English Baroque 'was not invariably angular, far from it, but its majestic power was imbued with a seriousness and gravitas that are sometimes ponderous and always severe, giving palaces the appearance of mausoleums or cenotaphs: this is

RIGHT
The steps and curved staircase leading up to the gallery of the Cold Baths Pavilion at Tsarskoye Selo, by Charles Cameron, 1784–87.

the Baroque of Protestantism. The *joie de vivre* is missing, but not the grandeur,' writes André Parreaux. At Seaton Delaval Hall in Northumberland, Sir John Vanbrugh – one of the style's most distinguished practitioners – built for Admiral George Delaval (who did not live to see the house finished) a staircase of extraordinary lightness and austerity. Dating from the 1720s, it declares Vanbrugh's desire for an architecture that was grandiose but glacial, in which movement was somehow crystallized within the building's monumental power. It should be remembered that Vanbrugh was also a playwright; and even if his writings have little in common with his buildings, he had a highly individual sense of the theatrical. This can be seen in his built work, particularly at Blenheim Palace in Oxfordshire, where the magnificence of the façade is at once both austere and dramatic.

This imperious architecture was followed by the arrival of pure Palladianism. It was the age of the country house, which represented an outward expression of a family's influence and served as the administrative centre of their (often vast) estates. The architect William Chambers became the chief practitioner of a style of architecture imbued with classical restraint and dignity. Having studied under Jacques-François Blondel in Paris, he travelled to Italy. He was initially disappointed when, in 1775, the commission to design Somerset House, London, was awarded to William Robinson, but following the latter's death he began work on the building that was to house the Royal Academy, the Royal Society and the Navy Board, among other august institutions. The most complex part of the building was the south wing, which housed the Navy Board and overlooked the Thames. It contained a dramatic stair known as the Navy Staircase (p. 122), where curved, cantilevered flights split apart and rejoined to soar upwards, bridging the void of the stairwell. This dizzying and extremely daring structure highlighted the glory of the British Navy, reminding users that Britain controlled an immense empire thanks to its domination of the seas.

A similarly masterly handling of space from the same period can be found at Home House, Portman Square, London. Elizabeth Gibbons, born in the West Indies to a plantation-owner father and married to the eldest son of the Governor of Jamaica, entrusted work on this townhouse to James Wyatt in 1776. The following year his place was taken by Robert Adam, the most famous of the brothers who lent their name to the classicizing style they founded. The principles of the Adam style, whose decorative vocabulary included sphinxes, griffons, medallions and grotesques, were published in volumes that other artists and architects looking for inspiration could consult. At Home House, the staircase rises through the building's full height and is roofed by a glass dome, which replaces the false painted skies crowded with gods of earlier styles. Here, the staircase again soars into the void in a bravura exercise, surrounded by architecture of an airy lightness, embellished with imitation marbles and classical-style grisailles.

One of the most eccentric English staircases is to be found at Claydon House in Buckinghamshire, built for Sir Ralph

LEFT
The audacious staircase at Home House, in Portman Square, London, decorated with imitation marble and grisaille panels, was designed by Robert Adam in 1777.

OPPOSITE
For his austerely elegant staircase at Seaton Delaval Hall in Northumberland, Sir John Vanbrugh took his inspiration from the Palladian style introduced by Inigo Jones a century earlier.

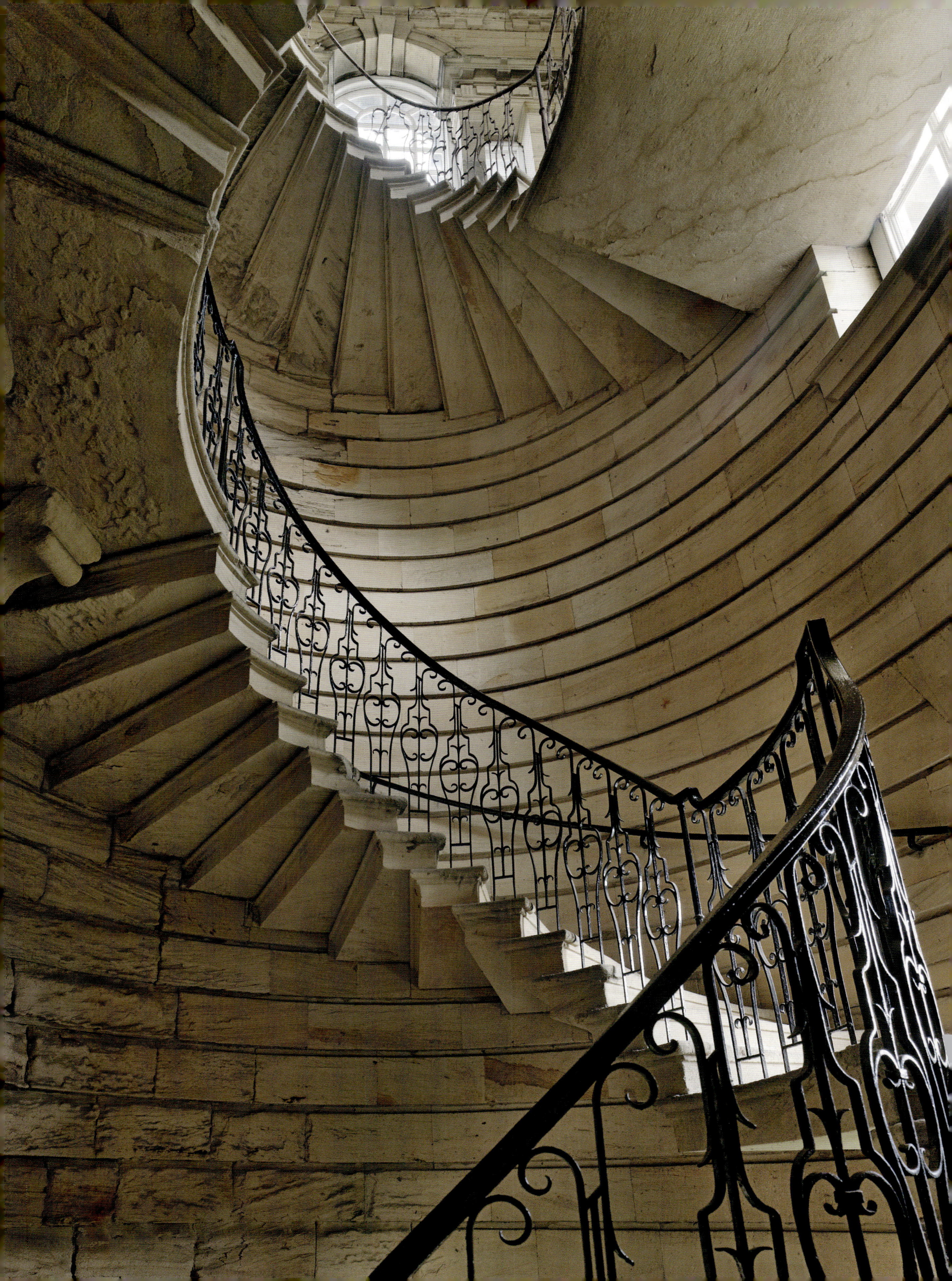

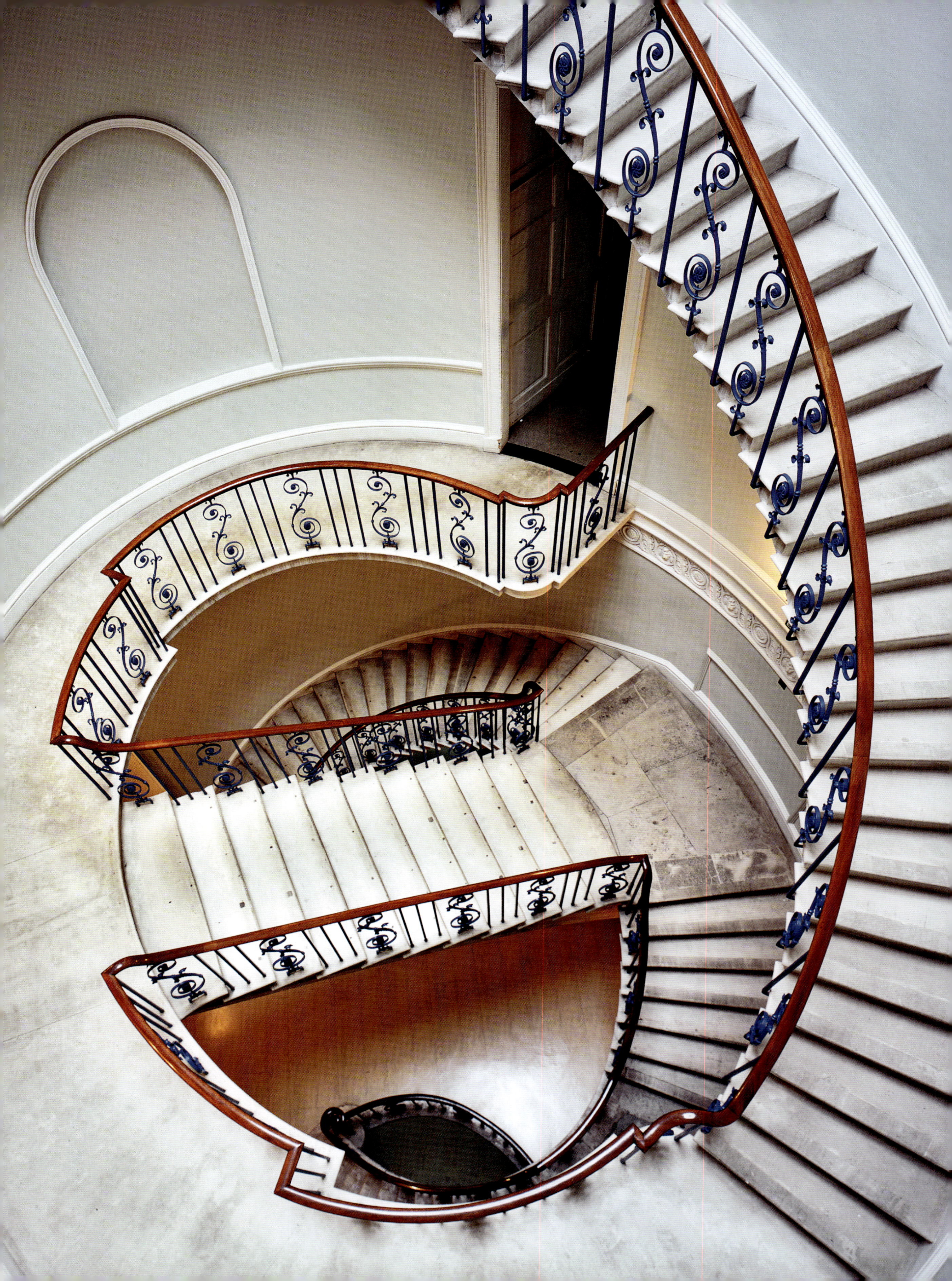

OPPOSITE
The Navy Staircase (later renamed the Nelson Stair) of the Navy Board at Somerset House, by William Chambers, c. 1775.

Verney between 1757 and 1771. In a major departure from anything that had been seen before, the staircase was completely inlaid, both above and below, with an intricate marquetry design of boxwood, ivory and ebony, while the balustrade was a decorative confection of wrought-iron flower garlands and ears of corn that rustled like a field of wheat in a breeze as the household went up and down. The staircase here is no longer just an imposing architectural feature, but enjoys the status of a rare piece of furniture, a curiosity – like a collection of precious objects – to be displayed to visitors. As in the rest of Europe, the staircase in Britain became an object of prestige and ritual; and in the context of the British country house it further reinforced the owner's success or ambitions to power.

CASCADES AND FOUNTAINS: WATER AND STONE Among the frequently extravagant staircases of the seventeenth and eighteenth centuries, some examples were taken to extreme lengths in an unabashed quest for monumentality. The gardens of Versailles and of Sanssouci in Potsdam, for instance, are unambiguous and conspicuous displays of power. At Versailles, the two majestic flights known as the 'Cent Marches' (Hundred Steps), which flank the Orangerie, built in the 1680s by Jules Hardouin-Mansart to shelter Louis XIV's precious trees, form an imposing cascade of stone – an apparently impregnable wall guarding the palace terraces (pp. 126–27). At the palace of Sanssouci, the effect may not be quite as powerful, but the intention is the same. Built for Frederick the Great of Prussia, the

RIGHT
Inlaid throughout in a marquetry design of boxwood, ivory and ebony, the staircase created by Ralph Verney for Claydon House in Buckinghamshire was completed in 1771. The exquisite wrought-iron balustrade is a virtuoso creation featuring flower garlands and ears of corn.

palace was more for pleasure than for ceremony. Even so, 120 steps link its terraces in a symmetrical arrangement, creating a vista that invites comparisons with that of Versailles. The same idea inspired the monumental steps leading up to the church of Trinità dei Monti in Rome. Now known as the Spanish Steps, this design, by an otherwise little-known architect called Francesco de' Sanctis, was completed in 1726 after long delays caused by diplomatic difficulties. It forms a magnificent prelude to the church that crowns the hilltop.

External staircases were not only an important feature of urban planning, but could also play more unusual roles. The designers of Renaissance gardens had already made a connection between steps and flowing water. 'Water steps', which combined both elements, graced many gardens, reaching their apogee in the monumental cascades found in a number of grand European gardens. In France, although the celebrated examples at Rueil and Pomponne have now vanished, the one at the Parc de Saint-Cloud near Paris still survives. The upper cascade at Saint-Cloud was constructed to a design by Antoine Le Pautre between 1660 and 1665, while the lower cascade was laid out to plans by Mansart in 1698. This remarkable hydraulic project was not merely an outstanding adornment to a magical garden; it was also, just like numerous internal staircases, an expression of its owner's social status. The water gushing down its steps served to remind guests of the huge expense involved in bringing such a project to completion and keeping it running.

As in the previous century, when the language of architecture was used convey power and wealth, so European grandees of the eighteenth century strove to assert their learning, culture and influence by commissioning architectural schemes on a scale that matched their own ambitions. Seeking to affirm their own identity and to declare their political triumphs through buildings and decorative schemes – as Louis XIV had done at Versailles – the European nobility became aware of the importance of pomp and display, both public and private, in society. In this unceasing quest for grandeur, the staircase was a highly effective, trusted tool. As John Templer wrote: 'These stairs cannot be considered simply as sumptuous means to pass from the ground to the reception rooms. They became an end in themselves – resplendent art objects, the jewel in the crown.'

OPPOSITE
The steps leading up to the palace of Sanssouci, built in Potsdam for Frederick the Great of Prussia from 1745.

LEFT
The water staircase, a feature inherited from the Renaissance, assumed a new dimension in France in the second half of the seventeenth century. This example – the upper cascade at Saint-Cloud – was completed by Antoine Le Pautre in 1665.

OVERLEAF
Flanking the Orangerie at Versailles, the Cent Marches (Hundred Steps) form an impressive stone cascade guarding the palace terraces: a masterful expression of the absolute power of the monarchy.

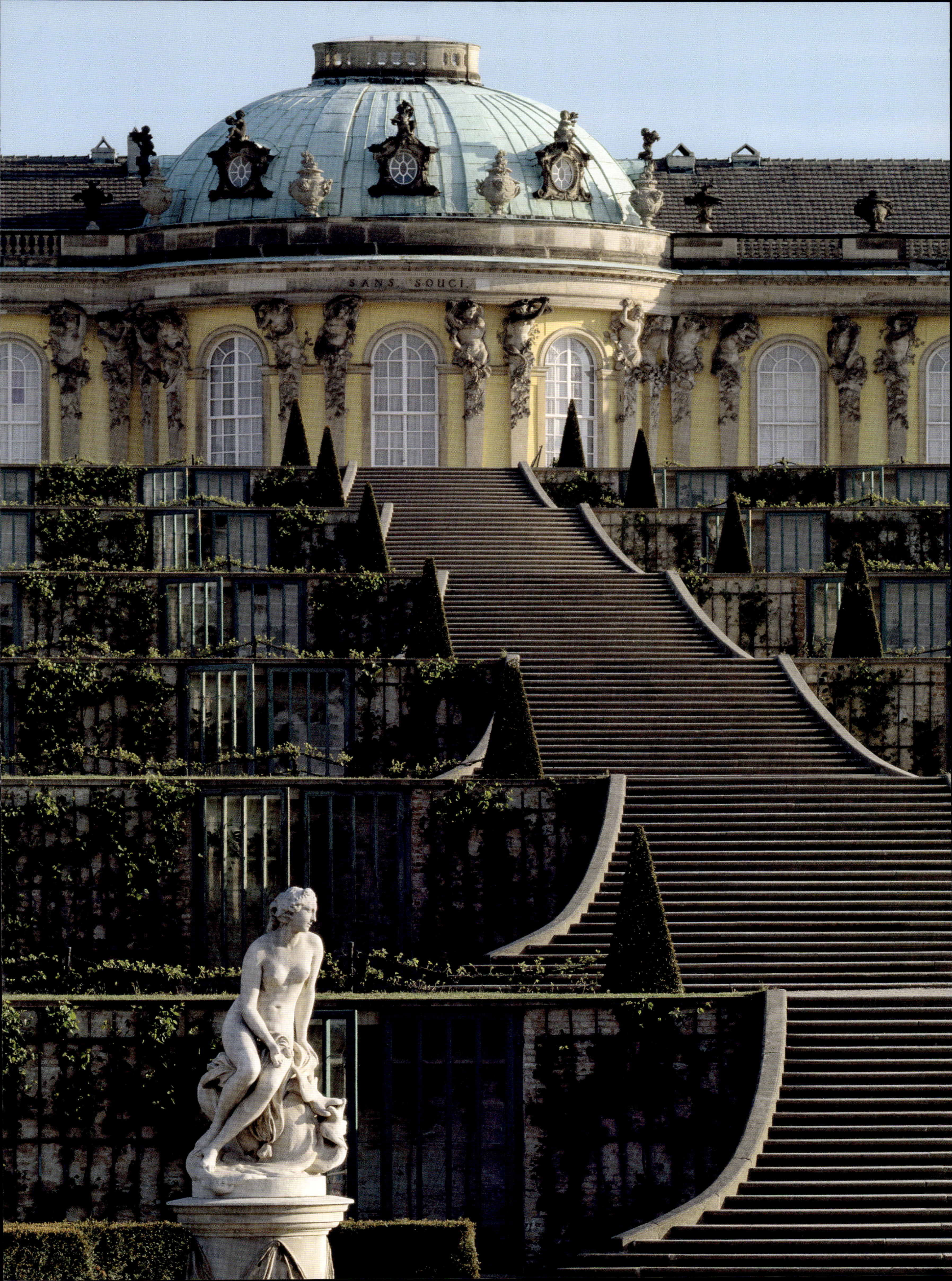
SANS SOUCI

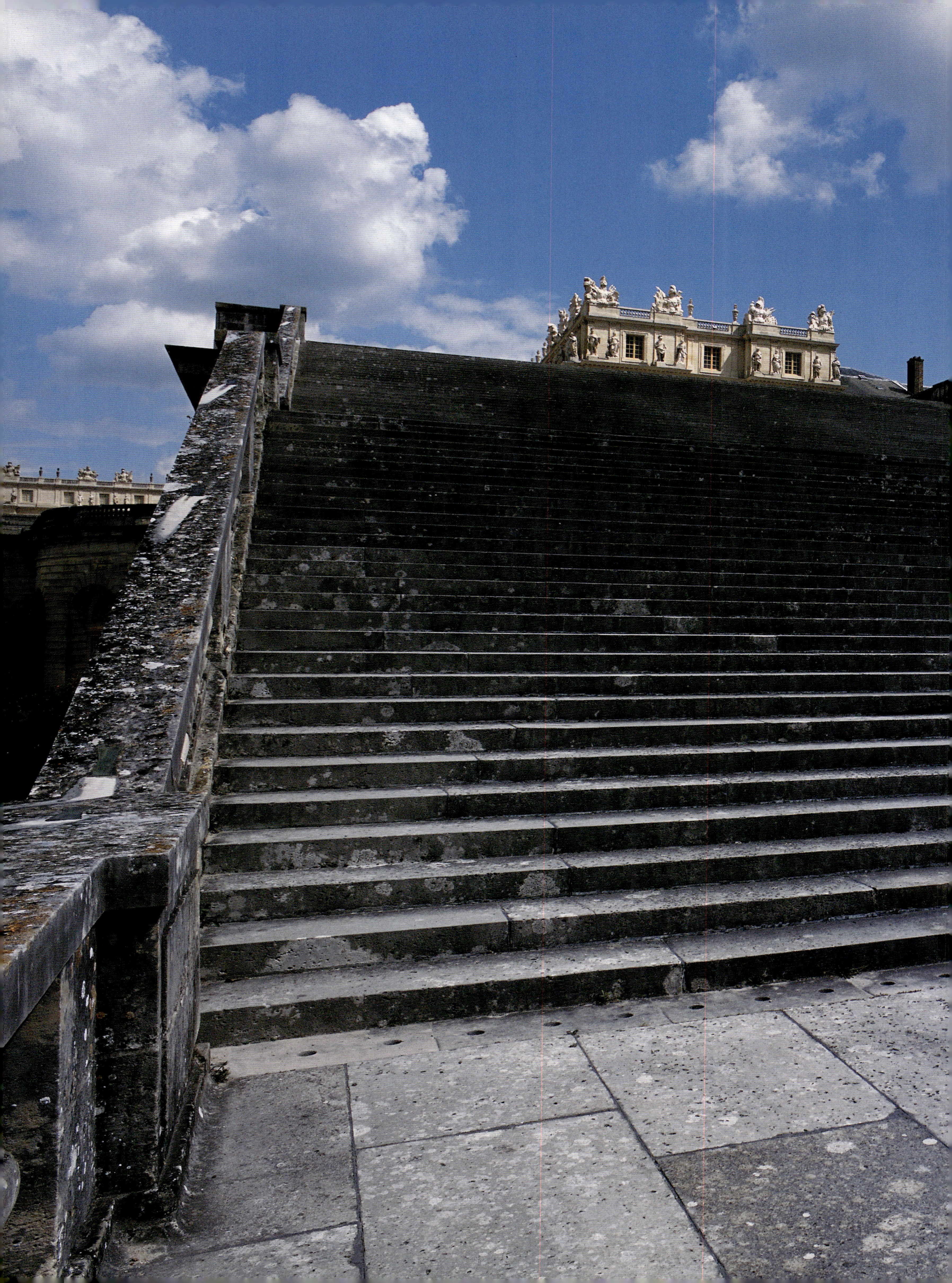

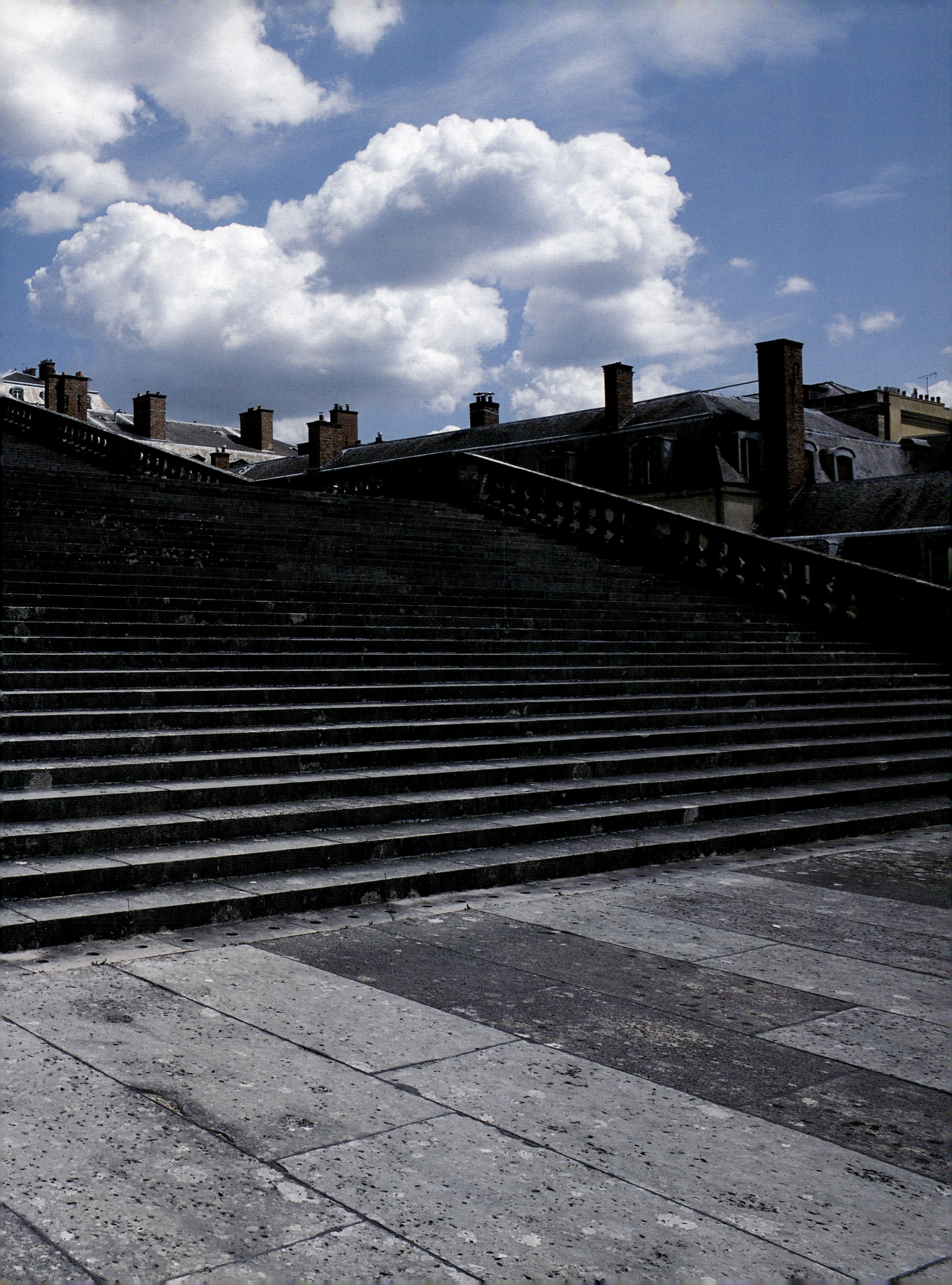

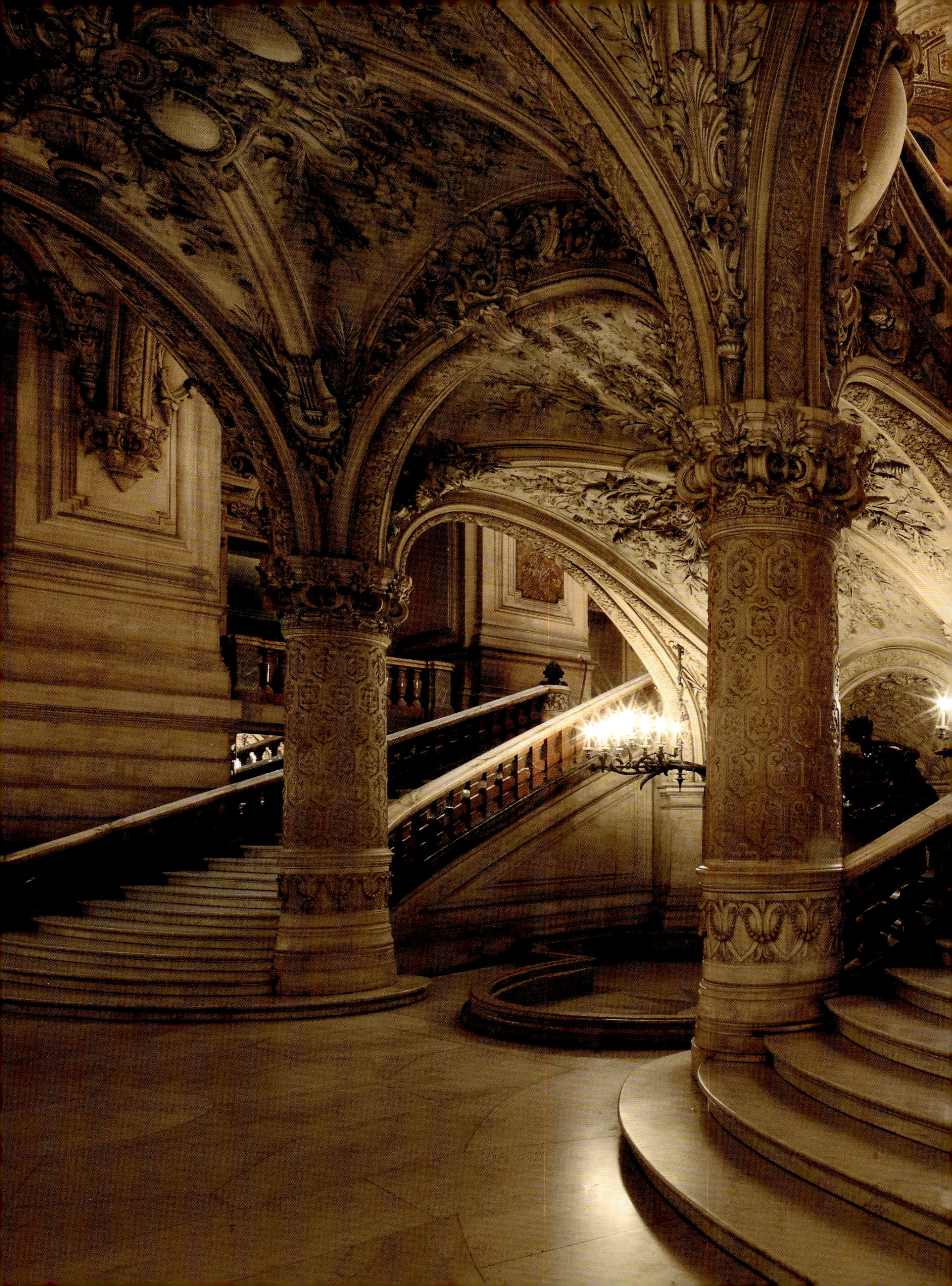

The Apotheosis of Ornament

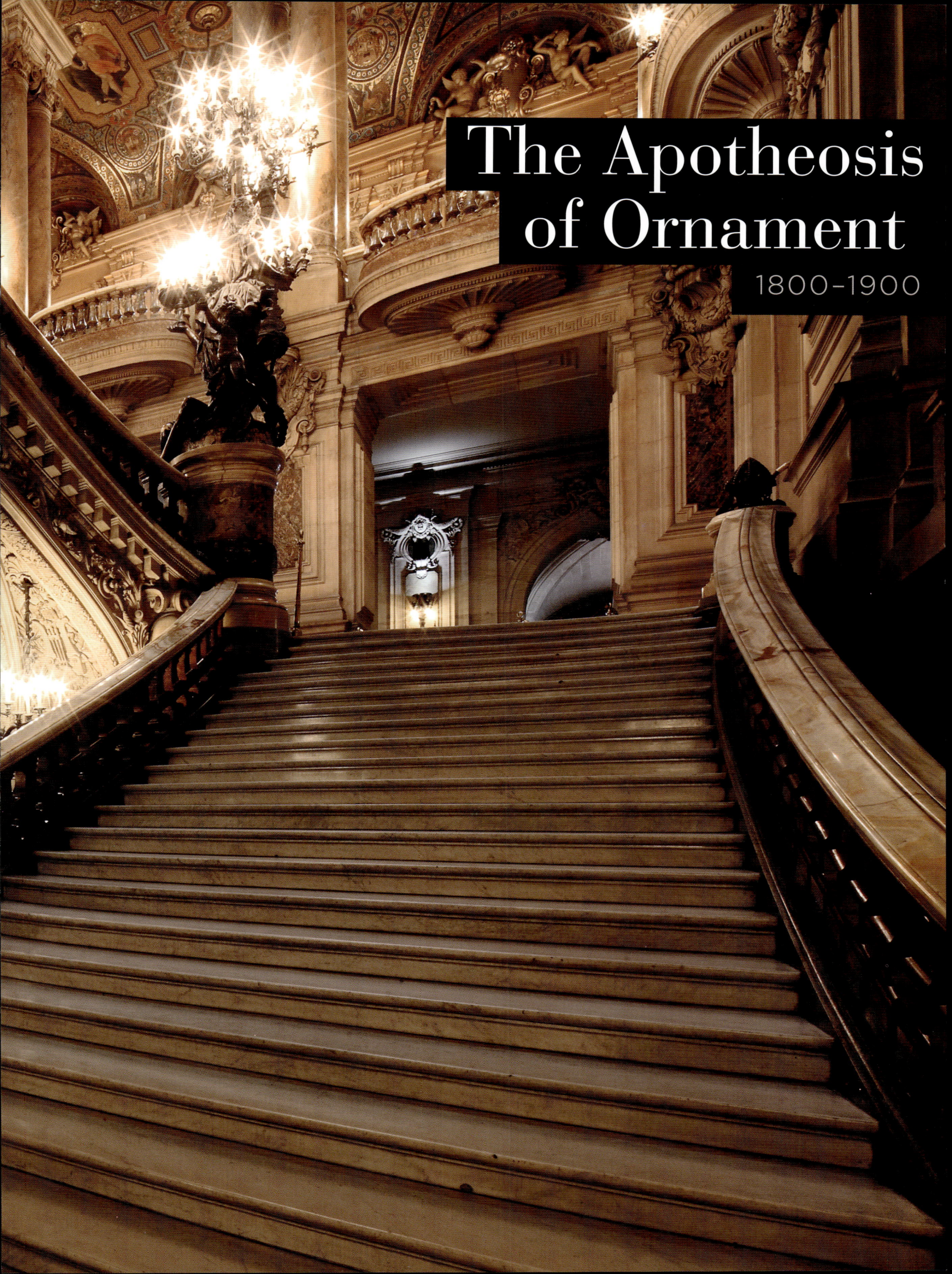

1800–1900

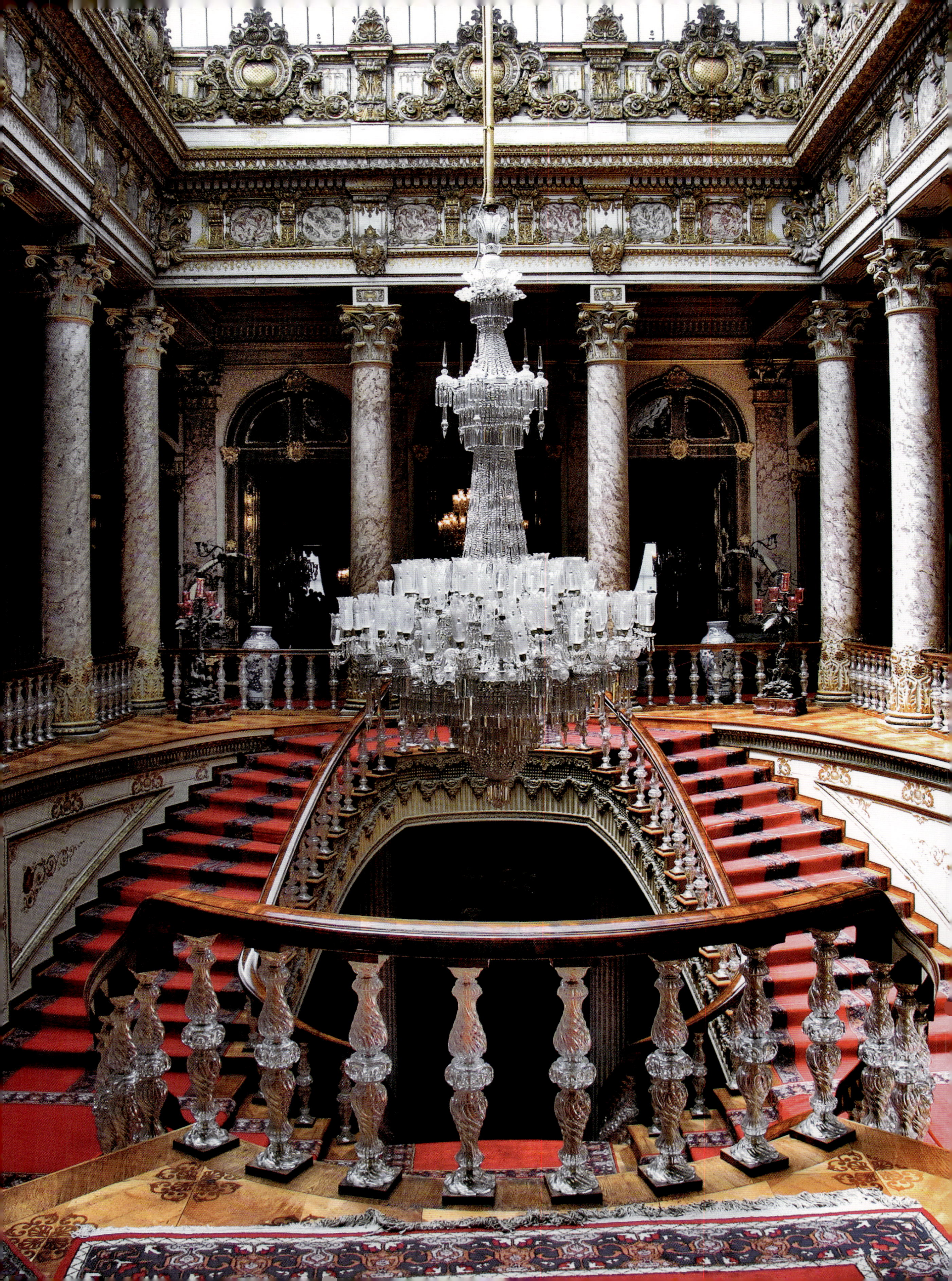

PREVIOUS PAGES
The staircase of the Paris Opéra, by Charles Garnier, completed in 1875. On the underside of the stairs Garnier camouflaged the metal structure with decorative stucco imitating stone carvings. Luxuriant vegetation enhances the grotto-like appearance of this space, which houses a bronze stature of the Pythia *by Marcello.*

OVERLEAF
The herculean proportions of the Opéra staircase moderate the extravagance of its decorative scheme. After innumerable obstacles, including the necessity of reopening disused quarries, Garnier gave pride of place to French marbles.

On 6 April 1904, the newspaper *Le Journal* carried an astounding news story: the grand staircase of the Paris Opéra had vanished. 'There had been a performance of *Die Walküre* the night before. After the performance the audience, exquisitely moved, had descended Charles Garnier's famous staircase. Indeed, had the Grand Staircase been absent at this hour this could hardly have failed to prompt innumerable comments, many of which would certainly not have passed unnoticed, but would on the contrary have resulted in the immediate appointment of a commission of enquiry.' The theft could only have taken place during the night. The missing item was rapidly tracked down, to 'an opulent and historic residence in the district of Saint-James'.

The affair of the 'stolen' staircase, as reported by the humorist Alphonse Allais, lampooned the extraordinary degree of importance that the staircase had assumed during the course of the nineteenth century, of which Charles Garnier's masterpiece remains the most dazzling example. Furthermore, the fact that the missing monument had been tracked down to a private mansion highlighted a trend that had spread throughout Europe and America as the century progressed. Encouraged by an unprecedented degree of prosperity, the nouveau-riche middle classes were now rushing to claim for themselves the trappings that had formerly been the preserve of the aristocracy – and foremost among these was the grand staircase. Grandees and wealthy aristocrats, rich bankers and industrialists now aspired to nothing less than the splendours of royalty. In London or Vienna, Madrid or Paris, Milan or New York, the finest modern mansions all possessed staircases fit for a king. The Count Boni de Castellane had availed himself of his wife's fortune (she was from the Singer family) to re-create the magnificence of Louis XIV's court at Versailles in one of the most sumptuous residences of Belle Époque Paris. He described with waspish glee the anachronistic ceremonial that he imposed at the height of the Third Republic, positioning himself at the top of his marble staircase as though he were the Sun King receiving the Siamese ambassadors: 'On party nights I would stand at the top of the stairs so as to enjoy the best view of people's expressions as they climbed up. The red marble steps were slippery. On one occasion, the Princesse d'Yssembourg fell, and I can still hear her cry of pain. So concentrated were they on not falling over, that our guests were unable to indulge in the scathing criticism that they were otherwise disposed to direct at our house.'

At the Paris Opéra – one of the temples of Parisian high society – the architect, Charles Garnier, had been kinder to the ladies, providing them with large mirrors before their crucial ascent of the steps: 'Yes, *mesdames*, yes, I have thought of you in installing to right and left these large unframed mirrors, filling the whole of the faux bays. It is only right that, before climbing these stairs, in full view of all your admirers, you should have a moment to put the final touches to your elegant costumes, to lower your

OPPOSITE
The crystal staircase at Dolmabahçe Palace in Istanbul, completed in 1856.

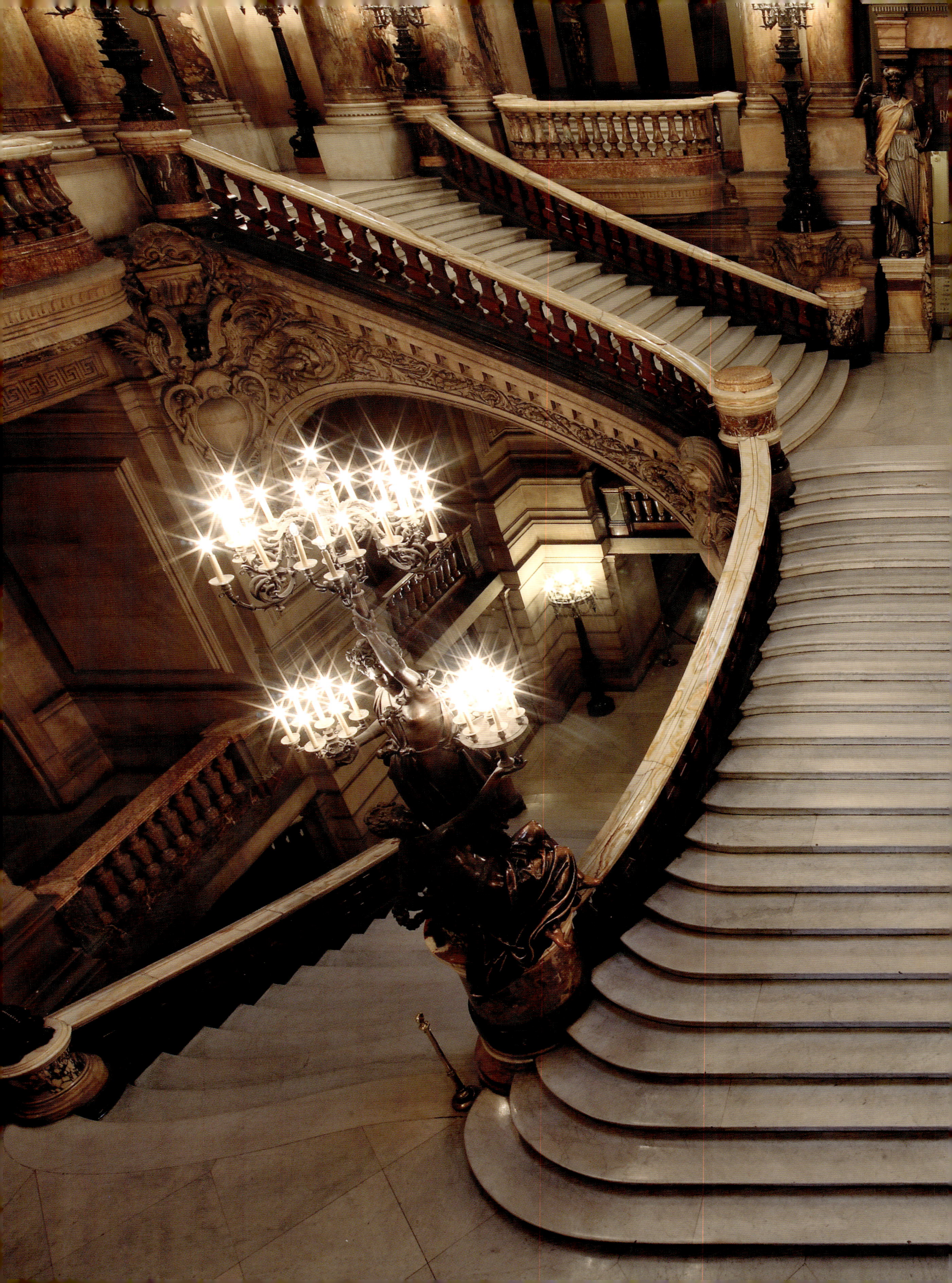

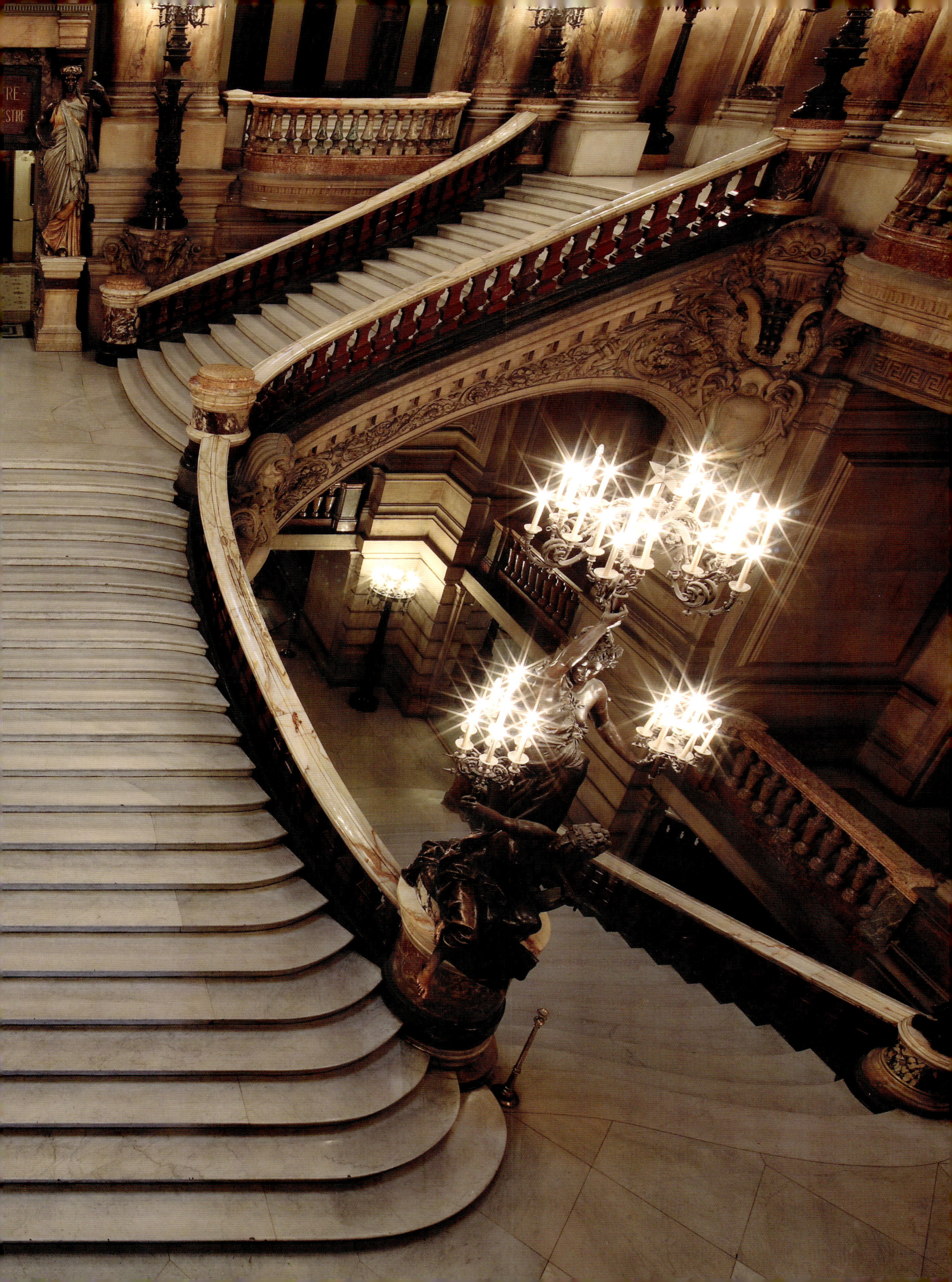

hoods and to plump up the pleats in your skirts.' To see and be seen: this was what the grand staircase was all about. This was theatre within the theatre, an interior complete with balconies arranged like boxes to offer the best vantage point over a glittering, constantly moving tableau. As the actress Cécile Sorel famously asked at the foot of the stairs in the Casino de Paris, 'Did I come down well?' But in good society the descent was of less consequence than the all-important ascent. The staircase had assumed such a major role in the rituals of high society that the rules governing its use applied even on the high seas: the first-class accommodation on every ocean liner built after the 1890s boasted a grand staircase in its proper place. A third handrail positioned in the centre of the first and broadest flight offered elegant lady passengers strategic extra support in case of choppy weather. Within the confines of a sea-going vessel, the staircase's large central void gave the illusion of a vast open space.

LEFT
The staircase on the ocean liner Olympic, *sister ship to the* Titanic *and the* Britannic, *built in the naval shipyards of Harland and Wolff in Belfast between 1908 and 1911.*

THE STAIRCASE AS SOCIAL STAGE The growing importance of the staircase went hand in hand with increasingly subtle divisions in a house's domestic arrangements, which in the nineteenth century attained an unprecedented level of complexity. Service stairs became a commonplace feature of middle-class homes and rented residential properties. The corollary of this adoption by the middle class of arrangements formerly reserved for the aristocracy was the perfection of the country house, which reached its apogee in Britain in the early decades of the century. Robert Kerr, a Victorian architect and theorist of the English country house, spelled out the rules governing vertical circulation in great detail: 'The principal staircase, as a rule in any good house, is understood to be closed against the passage up and down of the servants. A second staircase accordingly is provided, called commonly the back stairs. It runs generally from bottom to top of the house – from the basement to the uppermost storey.' This

LEFT
Eugène Lami, The Hall of the Château of Ferrières, *1860. The château was rebuilt in 1853 by Sir Joseph Paxton, with decorations and interior design by Lami.*

would concentrate 'first, all the traffic of the servants to the bedrooms; secondly, all the nursery traffic; thirdly, a great deal of the family traffic, which avoids the principal staircase for the sake of privacy, especially that of the young men; and fourthly, the traffic of the servants, in part at least, to their own bedrooms.' In the most substantial residences, the sheer number of functions allotted to the back stairs led to the creation of further staircases. There could therefore be a dedicated servants' stair (or even, if the staff were numerous, one for male servants and another for female servants), and another for the family. These refined degrees of segregation between masters and servants, and between men and women, were occasionally pushed to even daintier distinctions, such as the 'young ladies' stair' (which connected the rooms belonging to the mistress of the house to the young ladies' bedrooms) and the 'bachelors' stair' (by which 'single men can reach their own rooms, from perhaps dirty weather outside, without using the chief thoroughfares'). Behind the pretexts of convention and hygiene (young men having a tendency to return from the hunt and other sports caked in mud), there lurked the ever-present Victorian obsession with the niceties of morality. Lily Bart, heroine of Edith Wharton's *The House of Mirth* (1905), learns to her cost that she has been spotted leaving a bachelor's rooms: being seen on the wrong staircase could jeopardize a girl's chances in the marriage stakes.

RIGHT
The staircase on the public concourse of the Palais de Justice, Paris, by Joseph-Louis Duc with Théodore Dommey, begun in 1854 and rebuilt after 1871.

OVERLEAF
Léon Biet, a pupil of Charles Percier, designed the staircase giving access to the Bibliothèque Mazarine in 1823. It is a masterpiece of Parisian Neoclassicism.

THE CULT OF ANTIQUITY As a favoured backdrop for society and its rituals, the staircase naturally remained an architectural feature of particular importance. 'Everyone is familiar with the ugly and inconvenient chicken-coop ladders that serve as the staircase in most of the modern houses in London,' said Edward Middleton Barry, architect of the Theatre Royal in Covent Garden; 'and nothing marks more clearly than the design of the staircase the difference between an architectural composition and a builder's box.' The bugbear of the century was the 'winder' staircase, which saved space but was both unaesthetic and – since its steps narrowed towards the newel – hazardous. Sir George Gilbert Scott compared the stone staircase found in most modern British houses, with its polished mahogany handrail

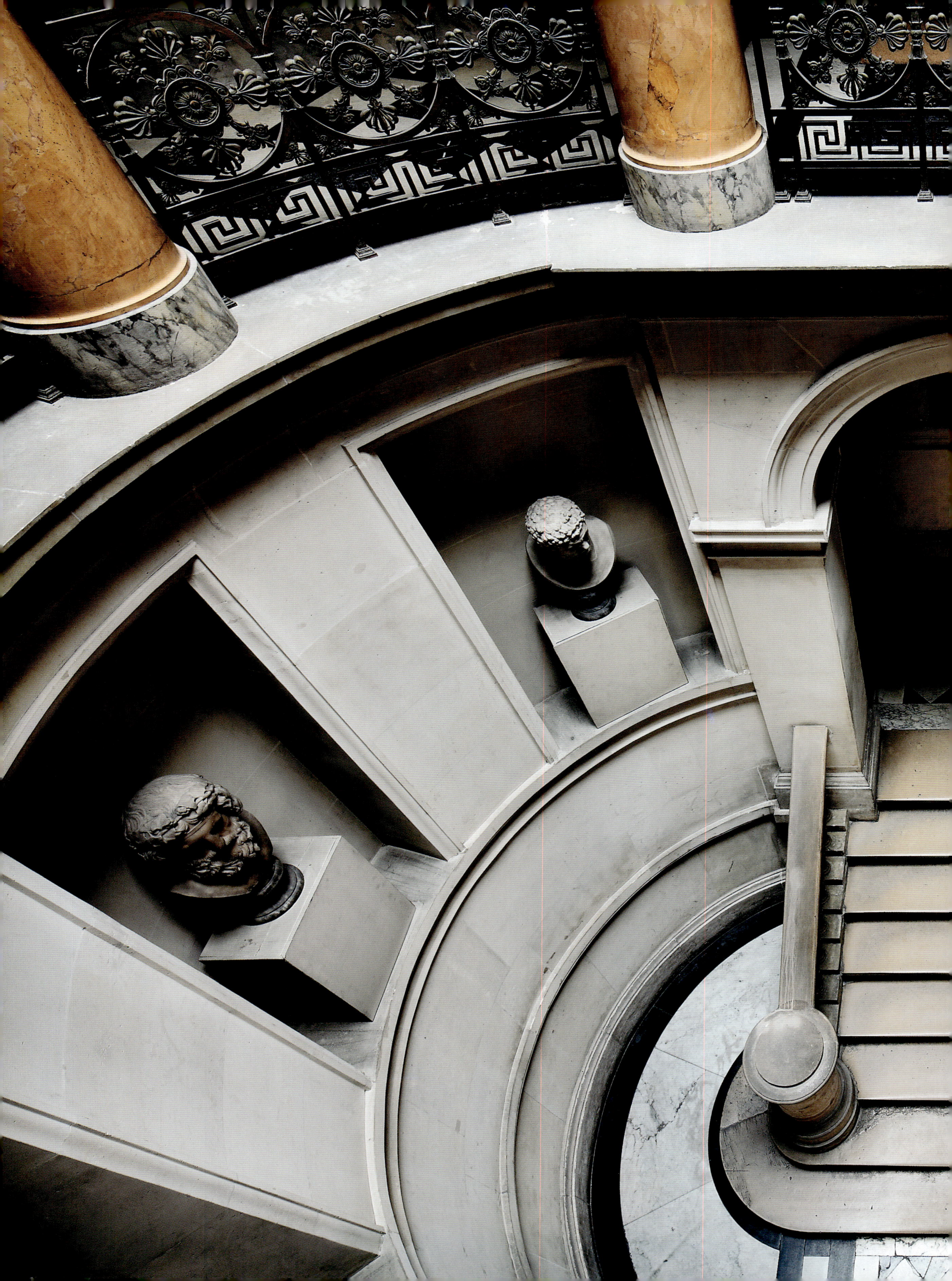

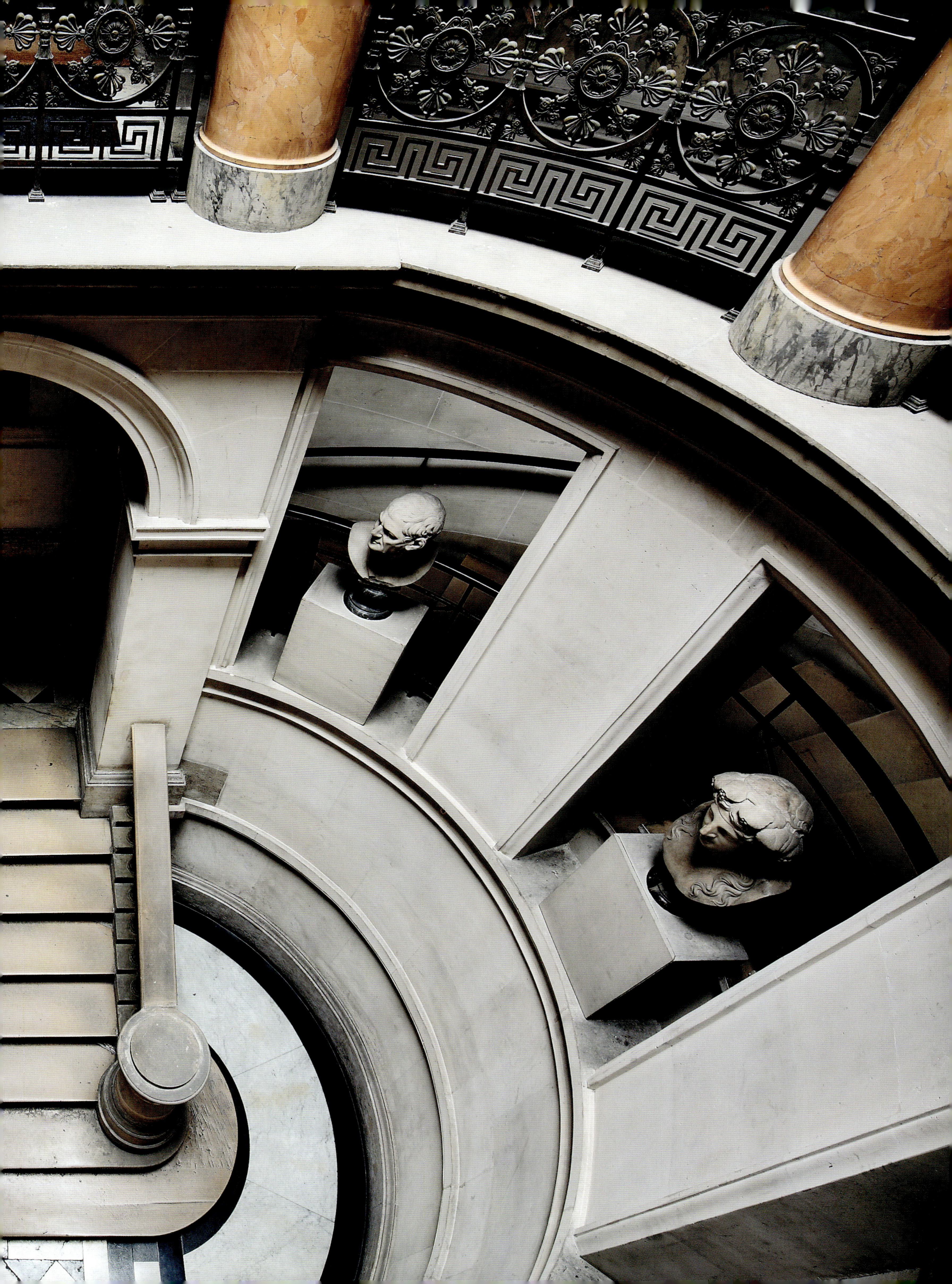

neatly coiled around a central void, to a 'cornu ammonis' – an ammonite fossil – and lamented that his attempts to give it some style had been in vain: alas, it 'still looks sleepy, as if its only duty were to show you the way to bed'.

For the first two decades of the nineteenth century, the great models inherited from European Neoclassicism in the 1770s remained largely unchallenged. It followed, therefore, that this was the style staircases adopted. Over the years, some of their lines became harder and finer, and some of their forms simpler; a cooler approach emerged, influenced by a more scholarly awareness of archaeological discoveries. For Joseph-Louis Duc, the architect of the Palais de Justice in Paris from 1840, architecture was above all the 'religion of form', and therefore should remain 'faithful to the tradition from which no type of architecture is exempt: Antiquity'. The example of classical architecture – with its smooth walls setting off the beauty of dressed stone or marble veneer, its geometric shapes, its cupolas and its coffered ceilings – was ubiquitous, found everywhere from Paris to St Petersburg and from London to Washington.

The difficulty encountered by the acolytes of classicism was that the Ancients had omitted to treat the staircase with the generosity of scale required by modern societies: 'In Roman buildings,' noted Viollet-le-Duc, 'with the exception of theatres and amphitheatres, staircases were relatively narrow and few in number. Moreover, the Romans used straight flights and spiral stairs; but they do not appear (in interiors at least) ever to have considered the staircase as a monumental decorative motif, as has been the case in modern times.' The requisite grandeur therefore had to be sought elsewhere. Antiquity was duly revisited, but through the prism of Italian architects from the fifteenth and sixteenth centuries, notably Bramante and Palladio, British Palladian examples, and the grand style of the ceremonial staircases at Versailles and Caserta. Architects accepted these compromises while still aiming for a style of 'classical purity' – the first step on the way to the eclecticism of the second half of the century. Among the most imposing models of nineteenth-century classicism are the straight barrel-vaulted staircase, rising between two walls as in Italian Renaissance palazzos, and a variation on the theme with three handrails. This was the design adopted by Charles Percier and Pierre Fontaine for the staircase of the Musée Napoléon (the Louvre), judged 'one of the finest of its type'. Approached through a pillared hall, the staircase's massive scale impresses the visitor, representing the power of the man who had commissioned it. The 'imperial' staircase, inspired by that at El Escorial, near Madrid, and equipped with a central open space from which to take in the whole ensemble, remained the preserve of palaces and a handful of grand public buildings.

Yet the straitjacket of imposed forms and references by no means excluded original creations. In 1823, in the Bibliothèque Mazarine at the Institut de France, Léon Biet built a remarkable staircase set in an elliptical space (pp. 136–37). This majestic construction, which serves one floor only, is embellished with a weighty procession of Tuscan columns, wrought-iron panels, niches and statues in the classical style, all lit from above by a glass lantern. The formal simplicity and elegance of the great eighteenth-century models, such as the floating staircase *à la française*, undeniably remained in favour throughout the nineteenth century. Viewed from above, the staircase in the north wing of the château of Versailles – built by Charles Questel in 1851 (pp. 140–41) – is virtually indistinguishable from its *ancien régime* forbears, with a spaciously designed string, restrained moulding and a handrail supported by wrought-iron balusters. Viewed from below, however, it reveals a structure first used in the seventeenth century: 'The flights and landings', explains Paul Planat, 'are supported by arches that intersect to form the string, and the pressure these superimposed arches exert on each other is carried out to the external walls of the stairwell thanks to a highly ingenious design and skilful bonding.' The architect highlighted this structural aspect of the design by placing pendant

OPPOSITE
A watercolour by Eugène Viollet-le-Duc of the new staircase at the Palais des Tuileries, c. 1830–35. A variation on the grand staircase of the Musée Napoléon (1807–12) and built by the same architects, this stair was designed by Percier and Fontaine for Louis-Philippe.

LEFT
A second view of the Tuileries staircase painted by Viollet-le-Duc. The iron structure of the ceiling allowed light to flood in through enormous skylights. Percier and Fontaine's staircase and first-floor gallery were destroyed when the palace was burned down in 1871.

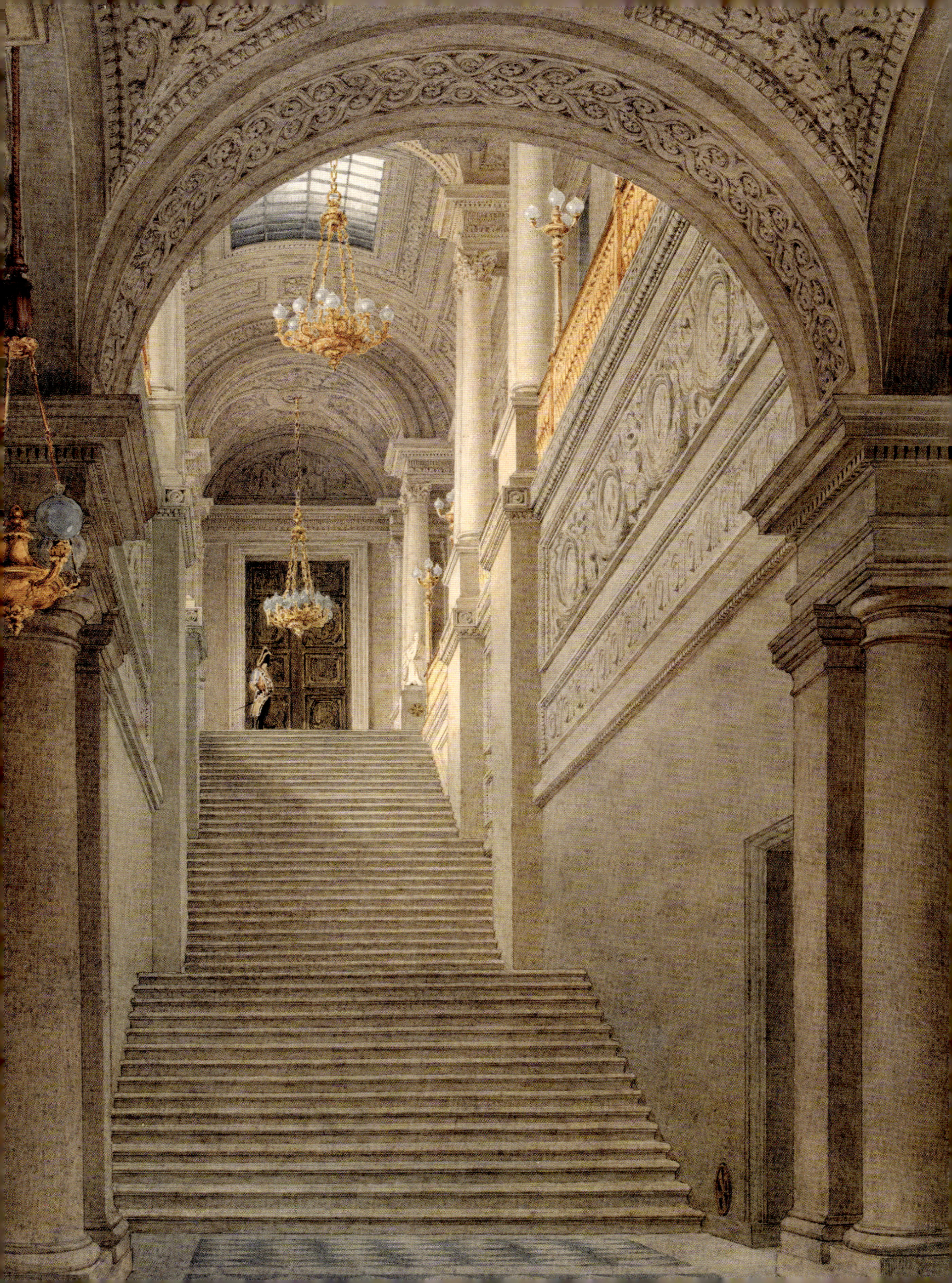

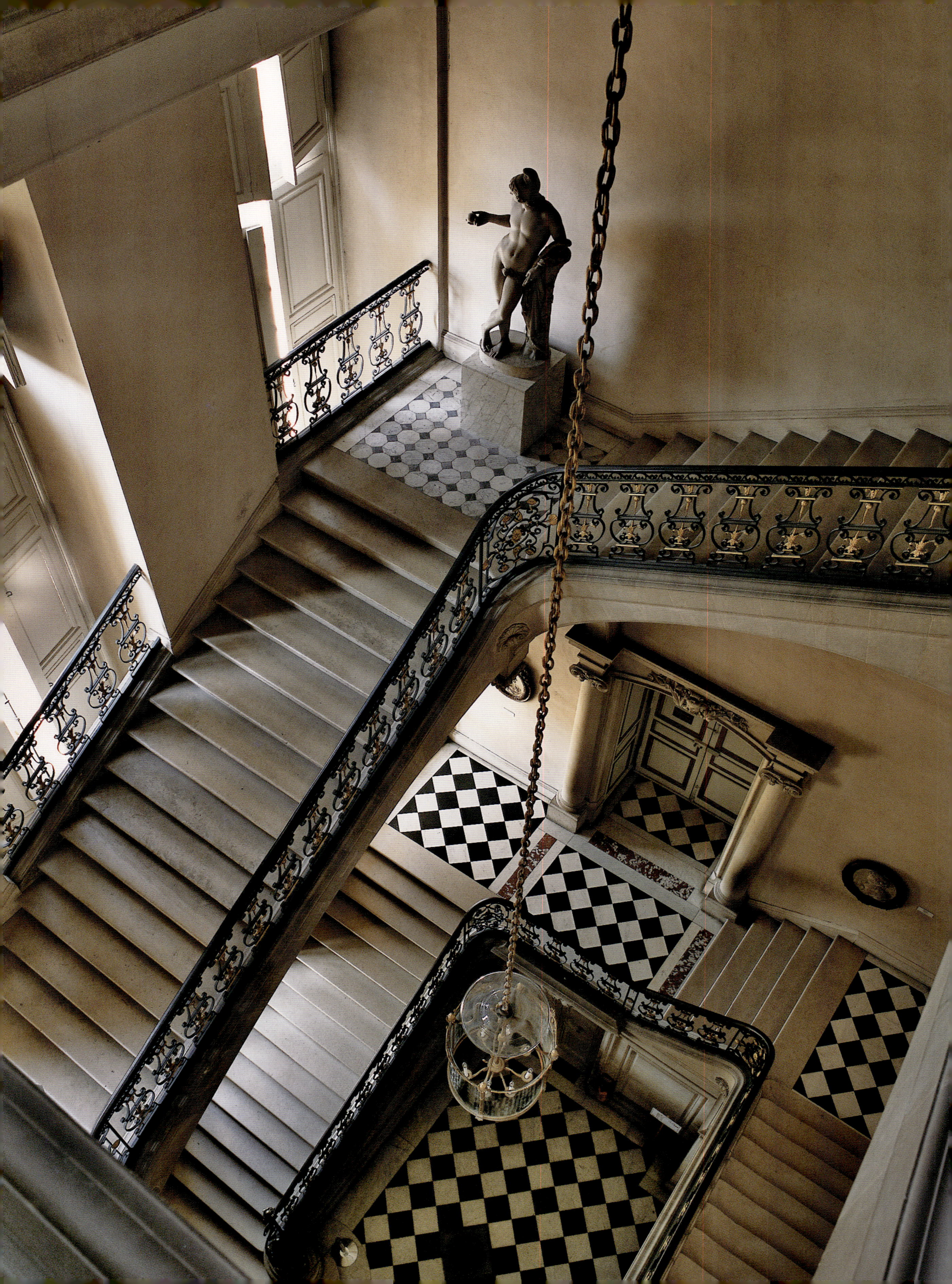

OPPOSITE AND RIGHT
In his staircase in the north wing of the château of Versailles, built in 1851, Charles Questel freely mixed seventeenth- and eighteenth-century models. On the right is a detail of the arches that form the string.

TOP
Built in University City, Missouri, in 1903–4 by Herbert C. Chivers, the Woman's Magazine Building and its virtuoso staircase showcased the wealth of the Lewis Publishing Company. When its founder, Edward G. Lewis, became the city's mayor, the building was used as the town hall.

ABOVE
Designed by the engineer Francisco Xavier Esteves and opened in 1906, the Lello & Irmão bookshop in Oporto, Portugal, retains its original neo-Gothic décor. The spectacular swooping curves of the cast-iron staircase recall the Paris department stores of the Second Empire.

RIGHT
Henri Parent, architect to Paris high society, designed the grand staircase for the Hôtel André (1868–76; now the Musée Jacquemart-André) with panache, creating a dazzling extrapolation of eighteenth-century models.

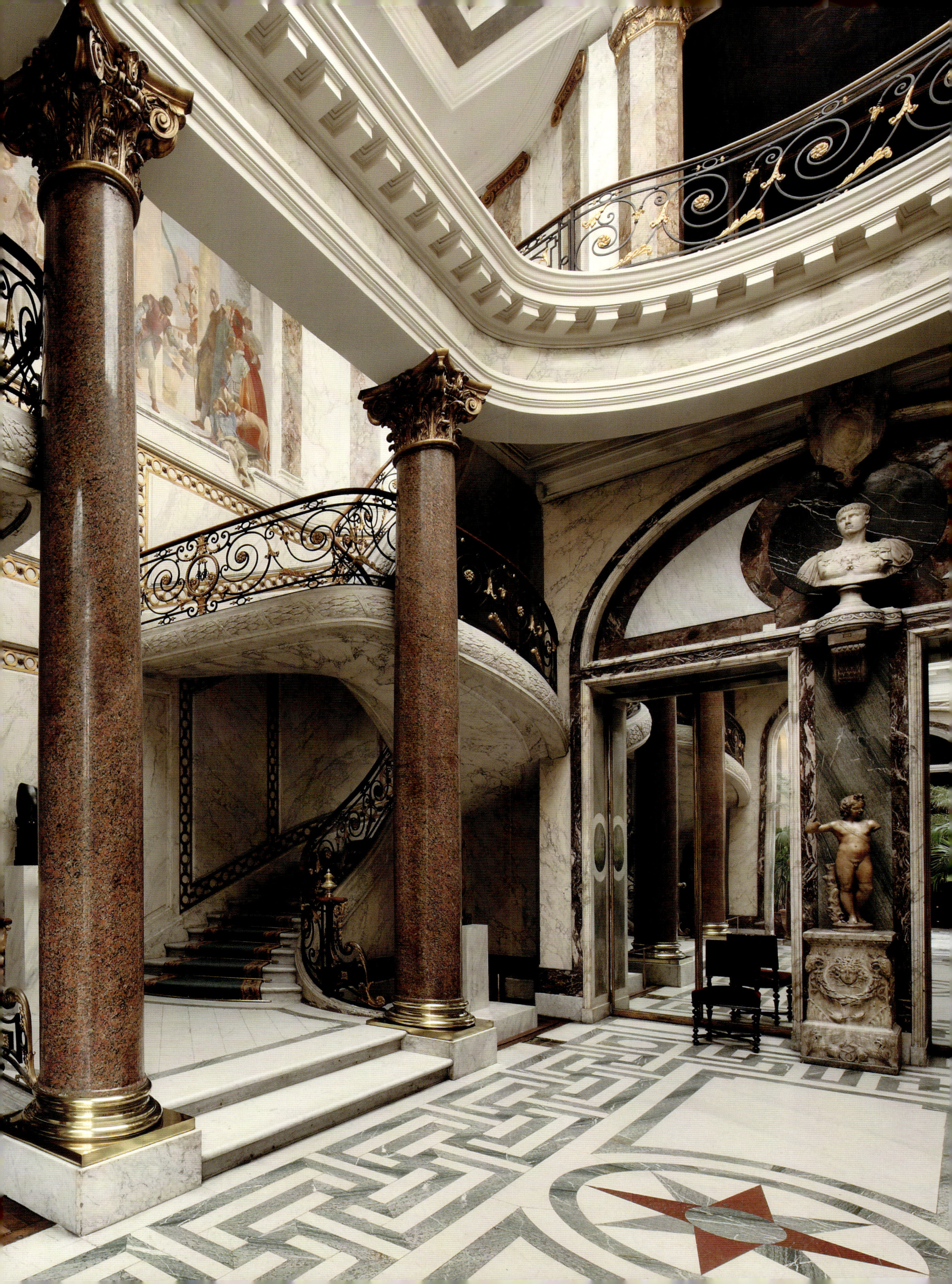

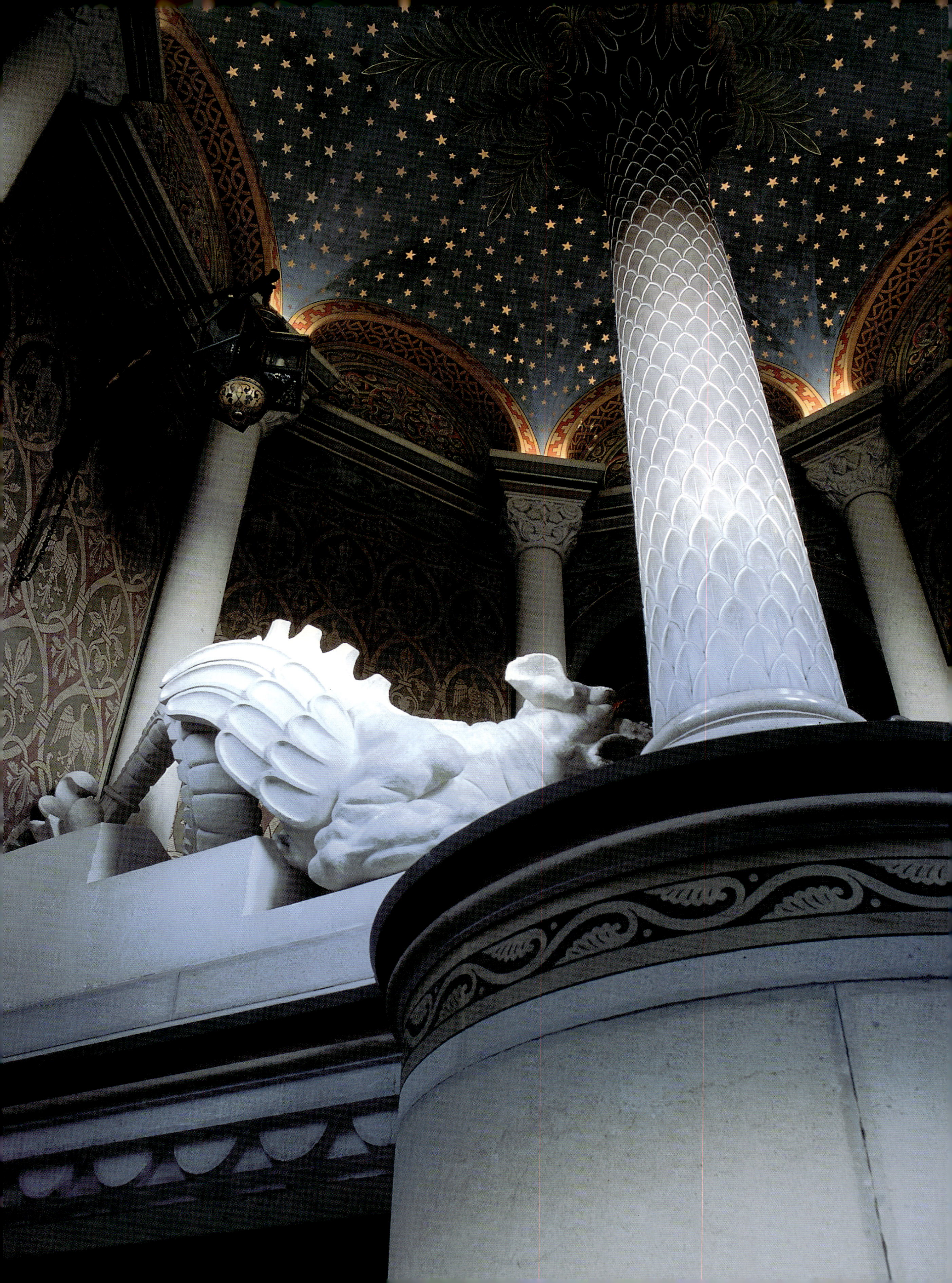

1800–1900 | 145

OPPOSITE
The staircase leading to the apartments of Ludwig II of Bavaria in his castle at Neuschwanstein, built by Edward Riedel, Christian Jank and Georg Dollmann. The decorations, a hybrid of the Gothic and the exotic, were designed by Julius Hofmann in 1881.

RIGHT
The nineteenth century produced an avalanche of publications to feed a growing interest in architecture. This illustration of the Elizabethan grand staircase at Aldermaston Manor, in Berkshire, is from Joseph Nash's Architecture of the Middle Ages (1838).

RIGHT
The Grand Staircase in Penrhyn Castle with Two Hunting Dogs, lithograph by G. Hawkins, 1846.

bosses in carved stone at the intersection of the arches. He also displayed a spirit of inventiveness in devising new combinations of traditional elements, an approach typical of artists who worked in the eclectic style.

Classicism – sometimes nobly austere, sometimes politely 'Pompeian', sometimes combined with elements from the Renaissance or other eras – remained popular throughout the century. This 'international style', loosely associated with civic virtue, was as appropriate for the senate building in Helsinki (1822) as it was for the town hall in Winterthur (1863–69), where Gottfried Semper endowed the grand staircase with a broad balustrade of stone latticework.

FROM GOTHIC REVERIES TO THE TRIUMPH OF ECLECTICISM In parallel with the comparatively linear evolution of Neoclassicism, the development of the Gothic Revival in architecture, followed by a vogue for other styles – from Roman Revival to Byzantine Revival, via every national variation on the Renaissance from Flemish Mannerism to Spanish Plateresque – transformed the 1840s and 1850s into a veritable showcase of different styles. The German architect Heinrich Hübsch, who in 1828 published a book entitled *What Style Should We Build In?*, was not alone in his perplexity. This tremendous diversity was reflected in staircase designs. Penrhyn Castle in Wales, rebuilt by Thomas Hopper in two campaigns, first in 1820–37 and then again in 1840–50, is not only one of the largest castles in Britain, but also – through its early adoption of the Norman Revival style – one of the most remarkable of the nineteenth century. In the great ceremonial staircase (pp. 146–47), Renaissance in structure, Hopper mingled European and Middle Eastern influences freely. In this he was following the wishes of its owner, George Hay Dawkins-Pennant, who had inherited a fortune from sugar plantations in Jamaica, and whose uncle had rediscovered the ruins at Palmyra and Baalbek. Even Indian influences have been detected. As it rises, the magnificent grey stone gives way to paler decorative stucco, including a number of grotesques. This heroic and 'barbarous' fantasy was designed to thrill and awe visitors who delighted in the brooding Gothic novels of Horace Walpole and his followers.

Revived in the late eighteenth century and initially interpreted in the picturesque manner, the Gothic style was to prove an enduring rival to Neoclassicism. Early incarnations were literary and romantic, and their decorative details were loosely inspired by medieval forms. In the second half of the nineteenth century, Ludwig II of Bavaria's whimsical Gothic castle at Neuschwanstein (1868–84) was the archetypal example of this fantasy medieval architecture, conceived like a stage set. Described as a 'miniature Neuschwanstein',

LEFT AND OPPOSITE
Worthy of the Gothic novels of Horace Walpole or Matthew G. Lewis, the grand staircase of Penrhyn Castle in Caernarvonshire, Wales, takes its inspiration from the Middle Ages of myth and legend. Designed by Thomas Hopper in 1820–37, it was completed in 1850.

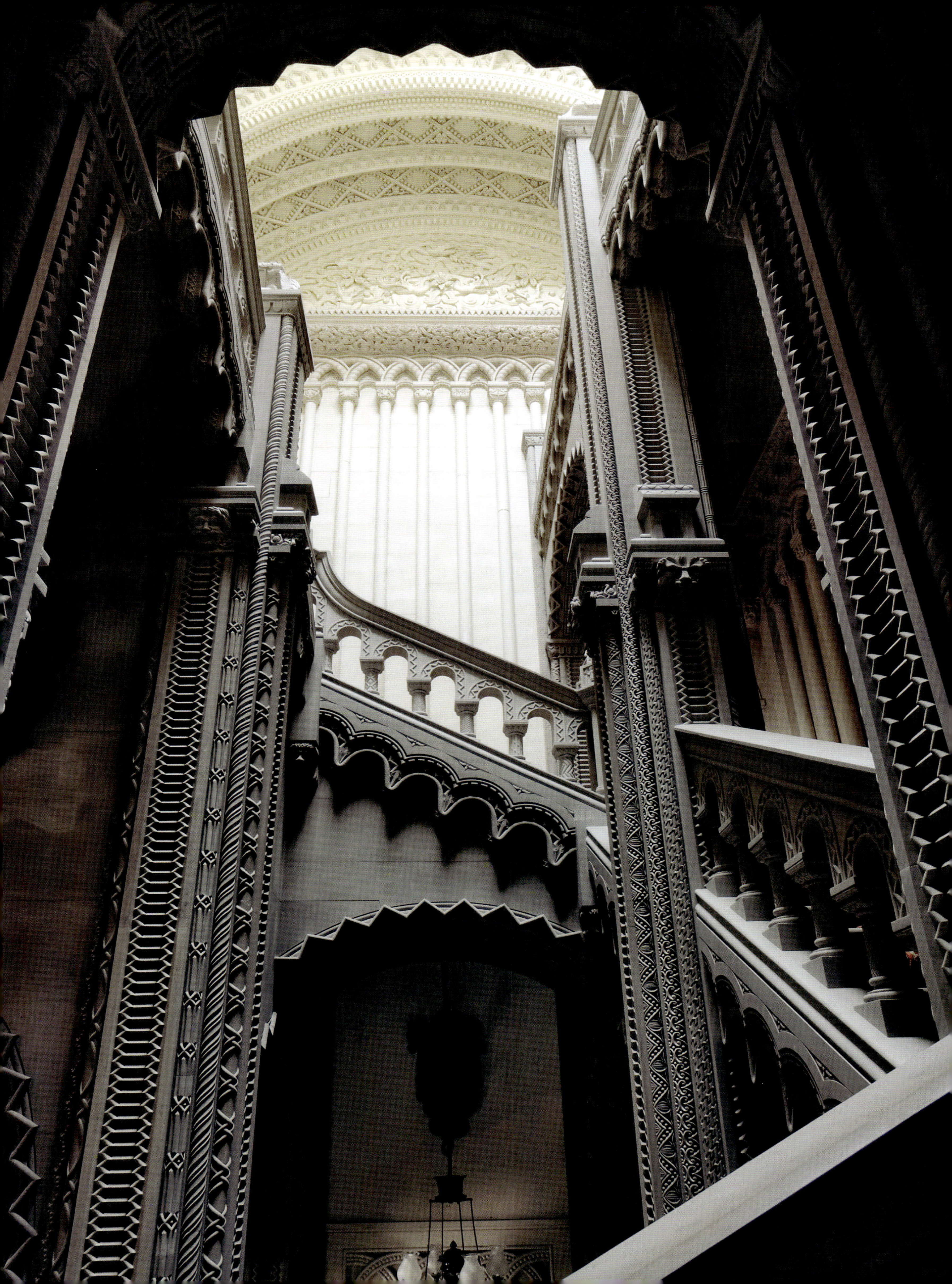

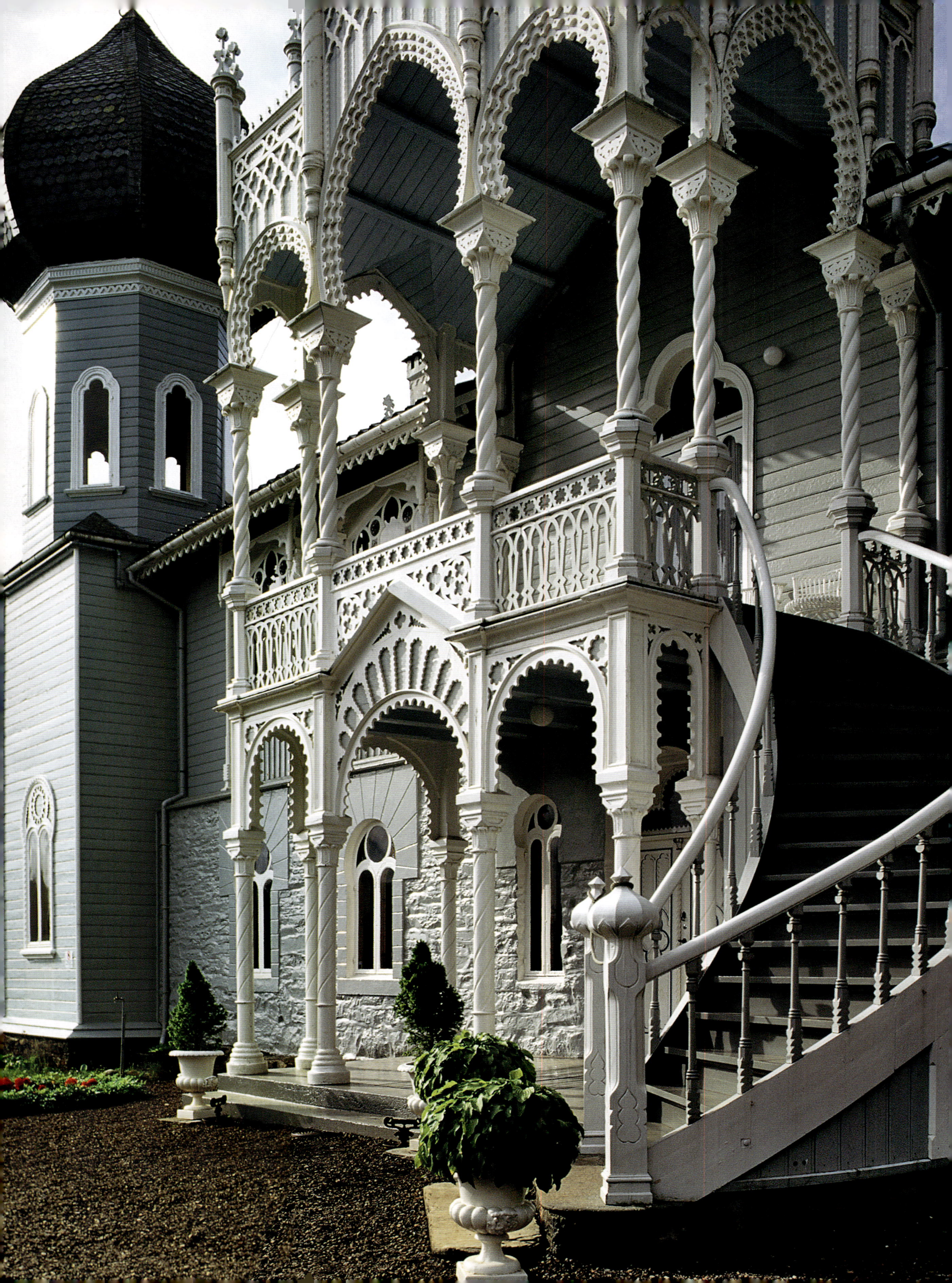

1800–1900 | 149

OPPOSITE
External staircase of the house of the violinist Ole Bull, at Lysøen, Norway, 1840s.

RIGHT
Like Karl Friedrich Schinkel in Germany, Vassili P. Stasov did not hesitate to make use of use cast iron. This staircase is in the chapel wing of the Catherine Palace at Tsarskoye Selo (c. 1820).

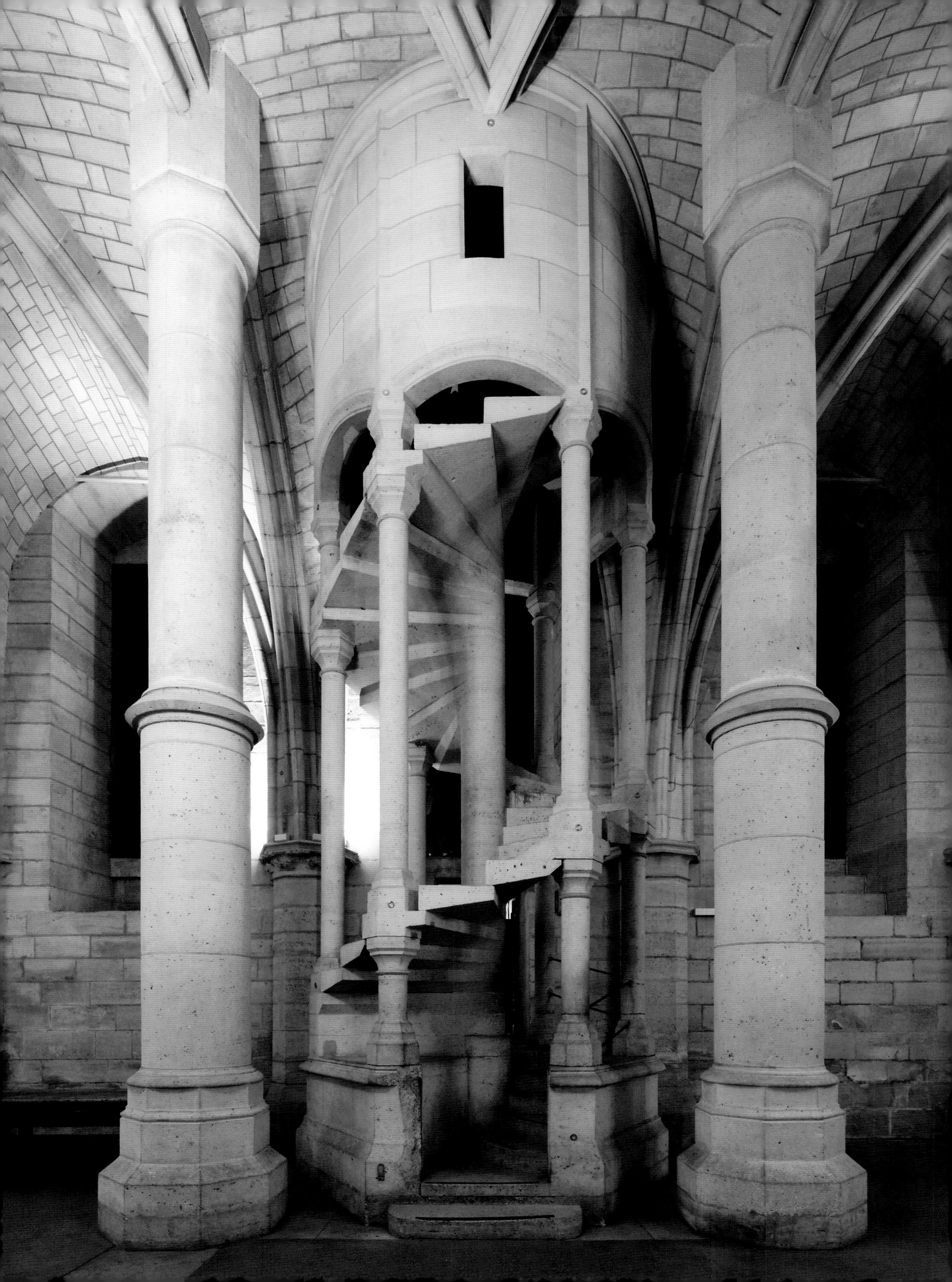

OPPOSITE

A bravura stylistic exercise, the spiral staircase of the Salle des Gens d'Armes in the Conciergerie, Paris, also served to support the roof vaults (c. 1852–54).

Castello Mackenzie, built by Gino Coppedè in the hills above Genoa between 1893 and 1905, offers a later example of this world of chivalric make-believe. It boasts one of the most magnificent Gothic Revival staircases in Europe, a bravura confection of solid marble, frescoes and superlative decorative sculpture. For the architectural historian Carroll Meeks, it was 'an example of the almost total lack of restraint or originality which led into the *Stile Floreale* and Futurism'.

At the other end of the scale from these works of medieval fantasy, the spiral staircase in the Salle des Gens d'Armes in the Conciergerie, Paris, designed in 1852 to support the ceiling, betrays a serious archaeological approach worthy of the engravings in Viollet-le-Duc's *Dictionary of Architecture*. Gothic architecture, with its clearly expressed structure, appeared to be an art of truth and to support rationalist ideas. Identifiable from outside, staircases were housed in turrets or projecting avant-corps topped with separate roofs. The line of the windows that lit them followed the diagonal pitch of the steps. The chief 'crime' of classical architecture, as denounced by numerous architects, was to have the string of the staircase deliberately cutting across the windows. A small castle of medieval inspiration near Helsingborg in Sweden, where the principal staircase was housed in a square tower, received Viollet-le-Duc's wholehearted approval. On the façade, four narrow windows set on the diagonal followed the pitch of the handrail, clearly signalling its presence: 'Simple façades, severe as the harsh Swedish climate, are open indications of the internal arrangements, which is a quality to which we should give our particular attention.'

In practice, medieval models were imitated more faithfully in service stairs, where the spiral continued to do its job perfectly well, than n ceremonial staircases. In practice, proponents of both the Gothic Revival and Neoclassicism came up against the same stumbling block: the lack of ancient models that could be adapted to modern needs. 'Here,' wrote Gilbert Scott, 'we are left almost wholly to follow our own developments, as the staircase was a part somewhat neglected in medieval buildings, especially in England. Abroad, we find it treated more boldly; but, generally, it may be said that the staircase did not become developed as a feature of first-rate importance till the sixteenth century.' The same view led Henry Havard to conclude: 'We may proclaim it with justifiable pride: the staircase is an invention of modern art.'

RIGHT

The great architectural theorist Eugène Viollet-le-Duc designed the external staircase at the château of Pierrefonds (1858–69) on a scale befitting an imperial residence of the Second Empire; photograph c. 1870.

FROM RENAISSANCE TO BAROQUE: THE SUBLIME DEATH THROES OF CLASSICISM

As great historic examples, the staircases at Blois and Chambord were to enjoy an astonishing degree of popularity in the second half of the nineteenth century. To reach the upper floors of Waddesdon Manor in Buckinghamshire, built in 1876–83 for Baron Ferdinand de Rothschild, Hippolyte Destailleur designed two Chambord-style spiral staircases around elaborately moulded central newels. Housed in a pair of symmetrically arranged turrets lit by stone lanterns, they form a picturesque feature on the building's north façade. The architect Julien Guadet reminds us, however, that in the Middle Ages turret staircases were not closed to the elements: 'The bays that lit them were open, and when later they were closed, this could not be done without distorting the nature of these semi-external features.' He concluded: 'Study these staircases, therefore, but remember that you must not reproduce them.' Happily, his advice was widely ignored. Far from encumbering himself with such scruples, Destailleur pierced the stair turrets at Waddesdon with large modern bays that opened in the French manner.

For the Paris head offices of Crédit Lyonnais (1876–83), William Bouwens van der Boijen created an extraordinary staircase, circular in plan and loosely inspired by Chambord (pp. 62–63). Situated some way behind the entrance pavilion on the Boulevard des Italiens, this is a double staircase, as at Chambord, but here the second flight is suspended above the first and is of metal. As at Chambord, those going up and those going down arrive at the same floor without encountering each other. The stone staircase was reserved for management and prestigious clients, while the workforce – it need hardly be said – was relegated to the iron one. Henri Germain, president of this august banking institution, had moreover decreed that walls between offices should be abolished, as they 'served merely to allow employees to read their newspapers'. Appalled by the distance from the entrance lobby on the boulevard to the staircase, the management submitted Bouwens's proposal to a number of architects in 1881. An approving Charles Garnier declared that the staircase could be situated 'neither on the boulevard, where space is too valuable, nor in the public concourses, which must retain their function and their grandeur; the staircase must be sited where it has been positioned, in the centre of the building, halfway between its two extremities. If the public is obliged to walk a certain distance to reach it, this is no cause for regret; it will ensure that Crédit Lyonnais is seen and known.' The delayed appearance of a staircase after an approach through vast glazed halls thus became a key feature of ostentatious displays.

The equally dramatic grand staircase of the Tribunal de Commerce in Paris (1858–64; p. 156) has a curious history. To please Emperor Napoleon III, the architect Auguste Bailly had been told that it was essential to imitate the Renaissance style of the town hall at Brescia. But to satisfy Baron Haussmann,

LEFT AND OPPOSITE
It behoves a bank to impress its shareholders and customers. For the Paris headquarters of Crédit Lyonnais, William Bouwens van der Boijen designed a grandiose variation on the double staircase at Chambord, which opened in 1883. The principal staircase is echoed above by a second staircase in iron, reserved for the bank's employees.

OVERLEAF
Built between 1853 and 1861 by Andrei Stackenschneider for the son of Nicholas I, the colossal marble pile of the grand staircase in the Nikolaievsky Palace, St Petersburg, is a weighty statement of imperial power.

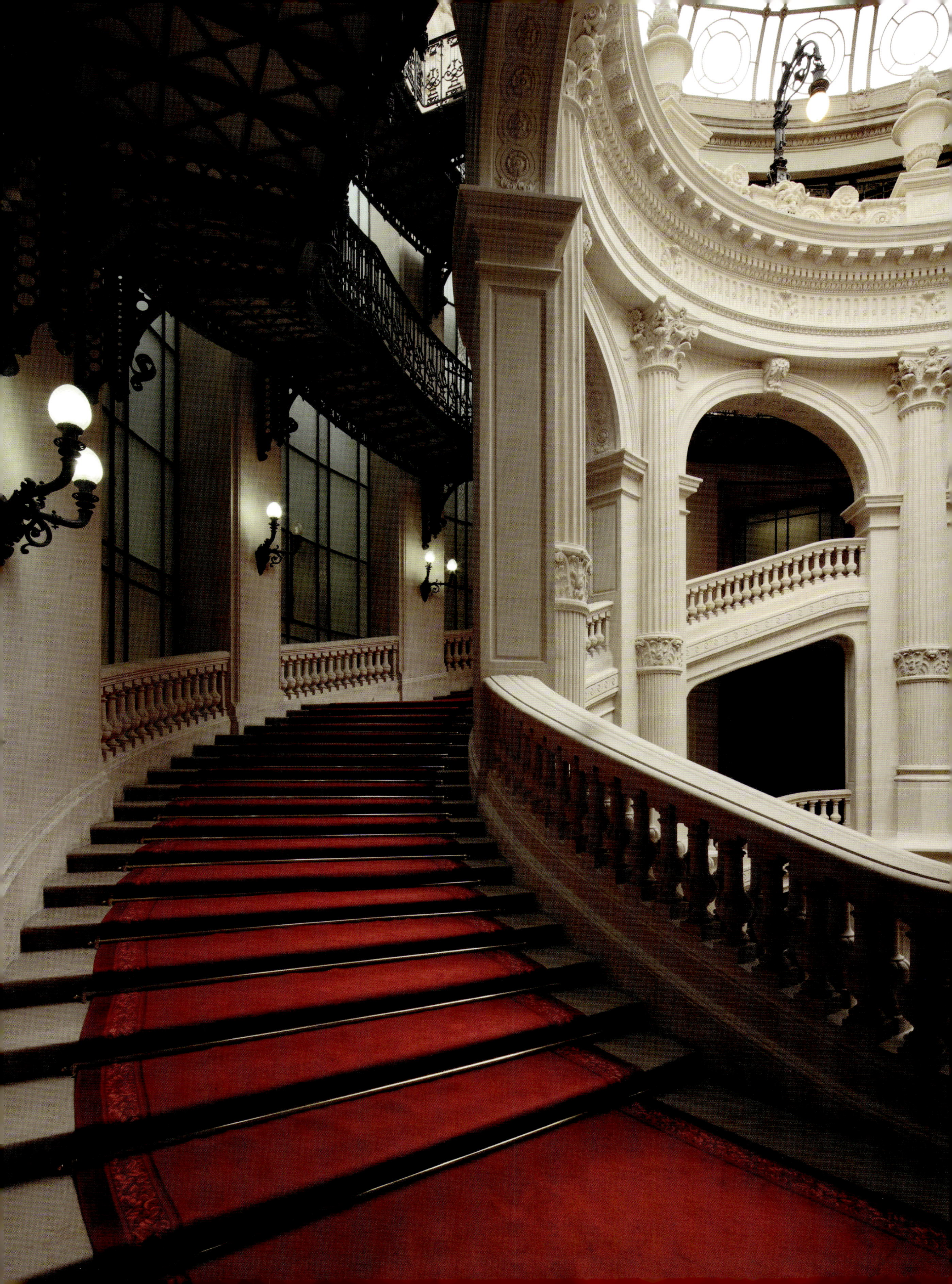

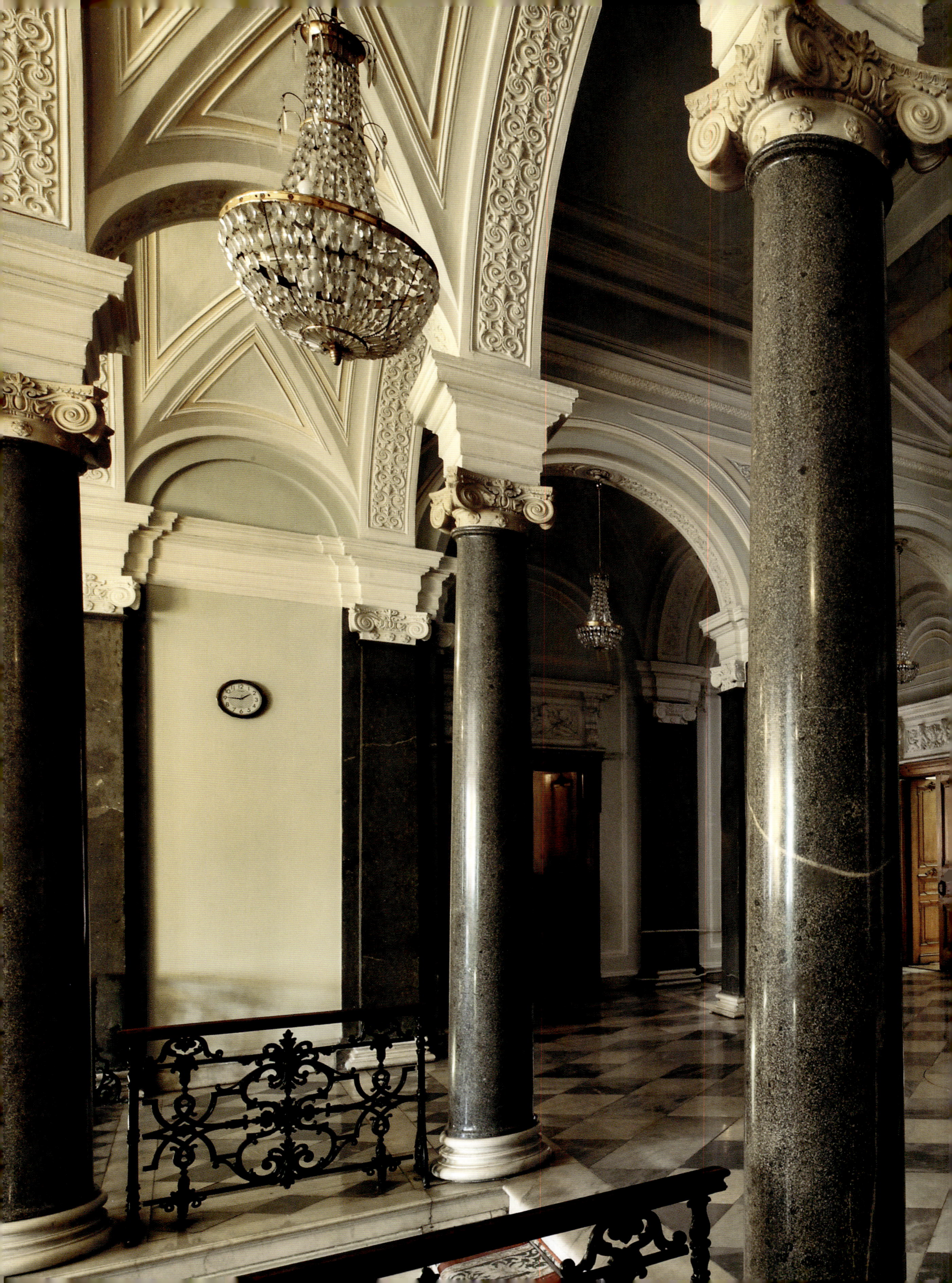

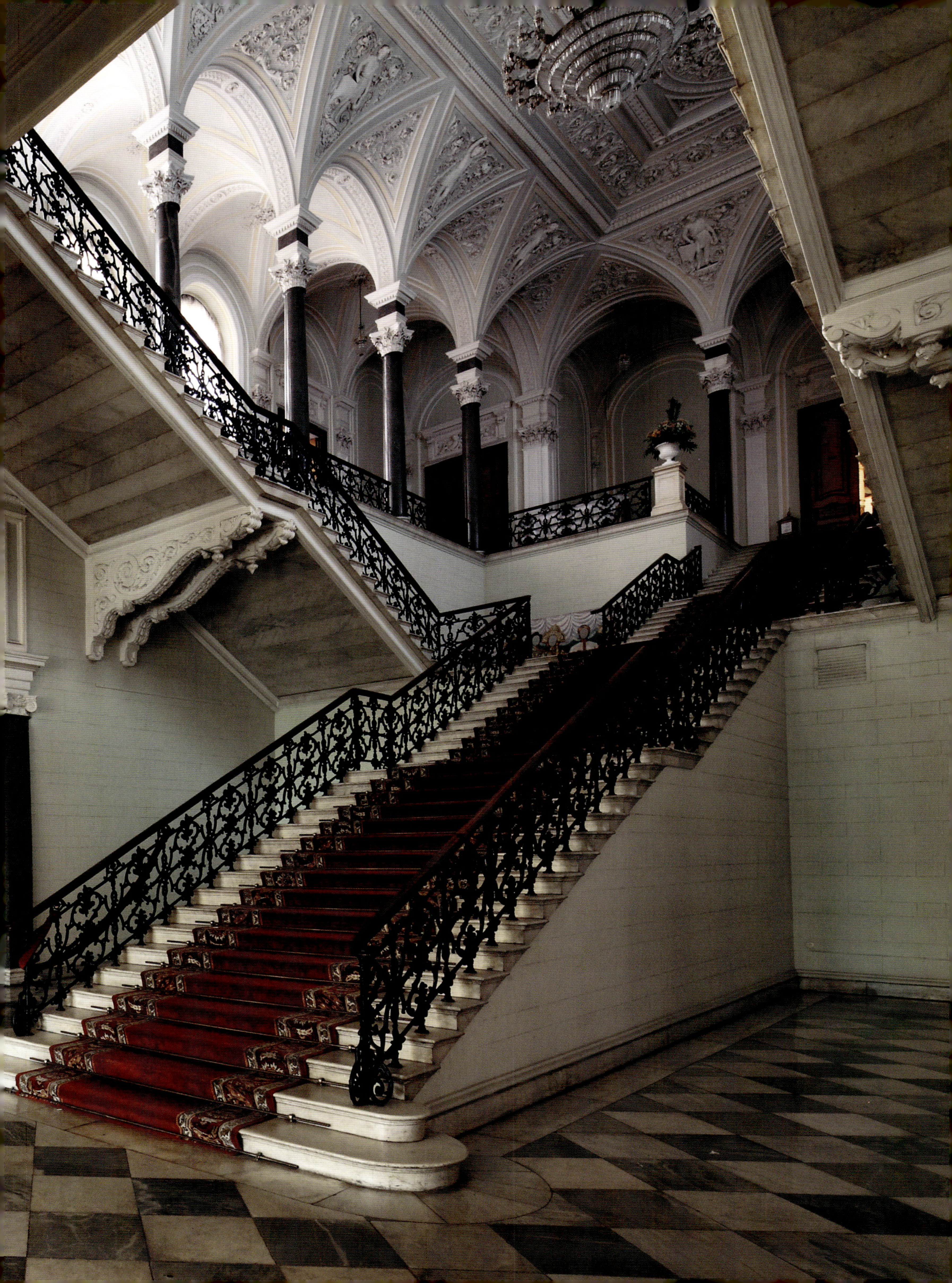

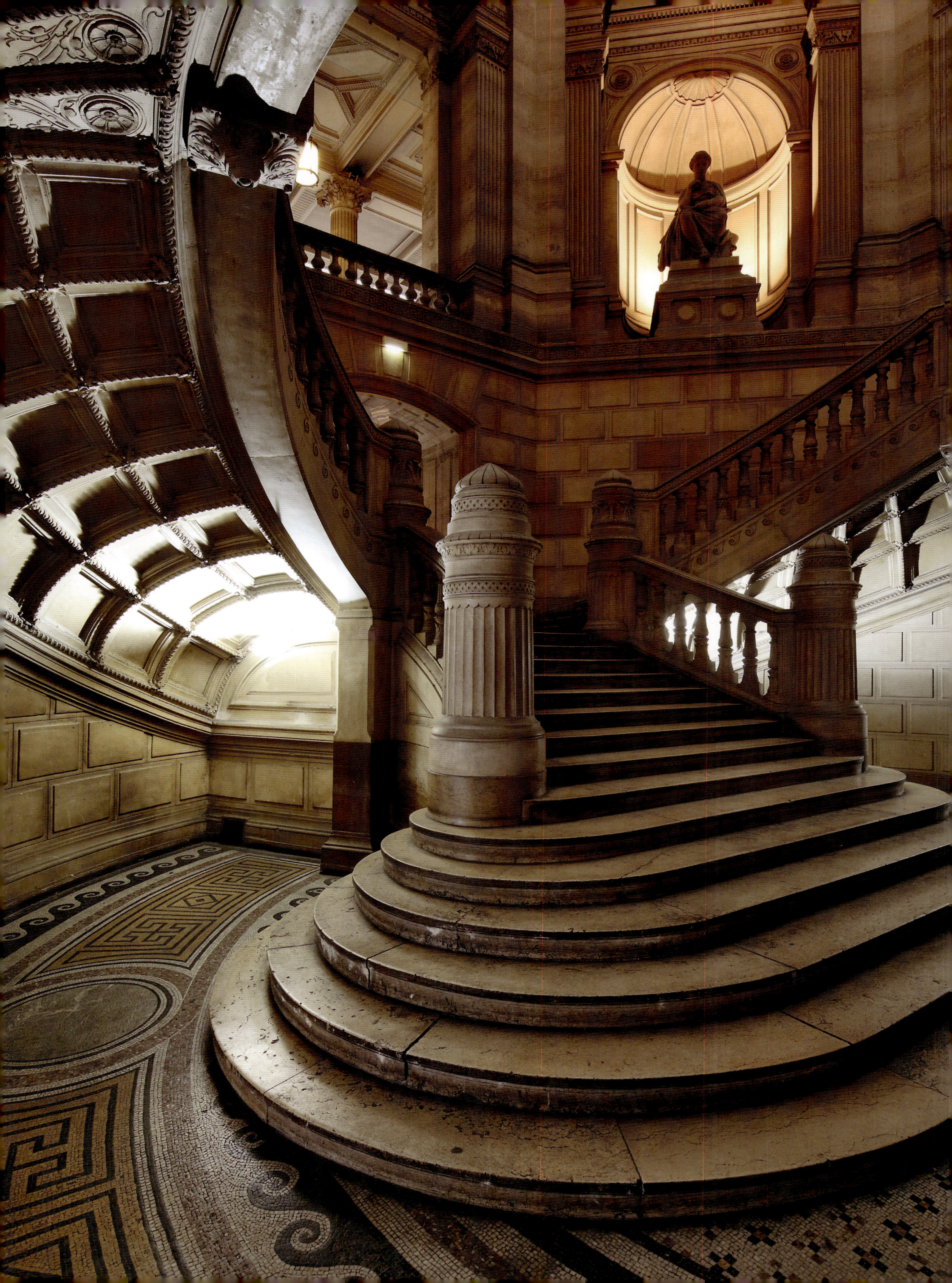

OPPOSITE
Ordered by Baron Haussmann to top the Paris Tribunal de Commerce with a large dome, Auguste Bailly filled the superfluous space beneath it with this remarkable staircase (1858–64), supported by a spiral vault.

RIGHT
The staircase at Centraal Station, Antwerp (photomontage). Each country had its own interpretation of the Renaissance style. For this monumental staircase, built between 1895 and 1905, Louis de la Censerie drew his inspiration from Flemish models, such as the Rubenshuis in Antwerp.

Prefect of the Seine, he also had to design a monumental dome (absent from the initial design) to create a picturesque prospect from the Boulevard de Sébastopol. To fill the huge space lit by this architecturally redundant feature, and to give access to the first floor only, Bailly created a magnificent staircase of two curved flights, with a diameter of 12 metres (40 feet). The surrounding decoration is a lavish affair of stone balustrades, pilasters, niches filled with statuary, and caryatids. Underlining the opulence is a remarkable detail: the steps are cantilevered. Above, the skilfully carved coffering follows the staircase's curves.

Every country developed its own version of the Renaissance style. At Peles Castle near Sinaia in Romania, built for Prince Karl of Hohenzollern-Sigmaringen (later King Carol I), it took on a Germanic flavour. The ceremonial hall and grand staircase (pp. 158–59), designed by Karel Liman in 1911, took their inspiration from two famous historic monuments in Lübeck: the church of St Jacob and the town hall. To the principal staircase, made of wood, Liman added a sumptuously carved spiral stair between the first- and second-floor galleries. Trained in Prague and Munich, Liman was a peerless architect and decorative artist, who had also worked on the Palais Albert Rothschild in Vienna, one of the most opulent palaces in Europe (now demolished). The choice of wood rather than stone for the staircase of a large-scale royal palace may seem a surprising one, but this was, after all, a summer residence in a picturesque 'chalet' style; and wood also evoked a traditional German ambience better than stone. The extraordinary wooden staircase leading to the private apartments of the Comtesse de Béhague, in her Paris residence rebuilt by William Destailleur from 1893 (now the Romanian Embassy), displays the same desire to create spectacular effects by adapting historic models: it has a balustrade composed

158 | THE APOTHEOSIS OF ORNAMENT

LEFT AND OPPOSITE
Designed by the architect and interior designer Karel Liman, the spiral staircase in the great hall of Peleș Castle in Sinaia, Romania (1911–14), was inspired by the Germanic models favoured by the first king of Romania, Carol I, who belonged to the Hohenzollern dynasty. The castle was built in a picturesque 'chalet' style as the summer residence of the Romanian sovereigns.

OVERLEAF
The grand staircase of the Vladimir Palace in St Petersburg, built by Aleksandr Rezanov for Grand Duke Vladimir, third son of Tsar Alexander II, from 1867. This dramatic staircase branches off to give access to the mezzanine theatre and the reception rooms.

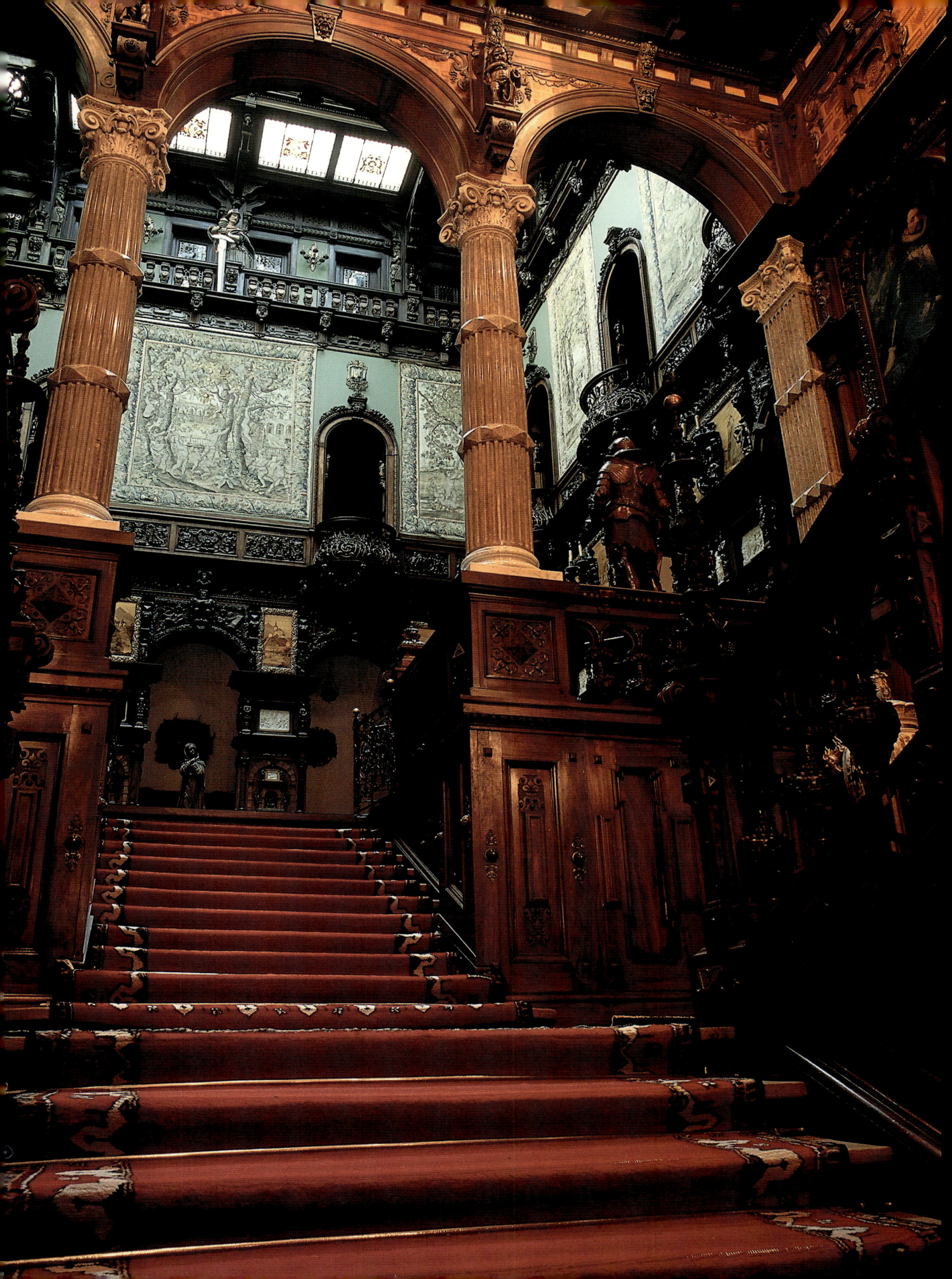

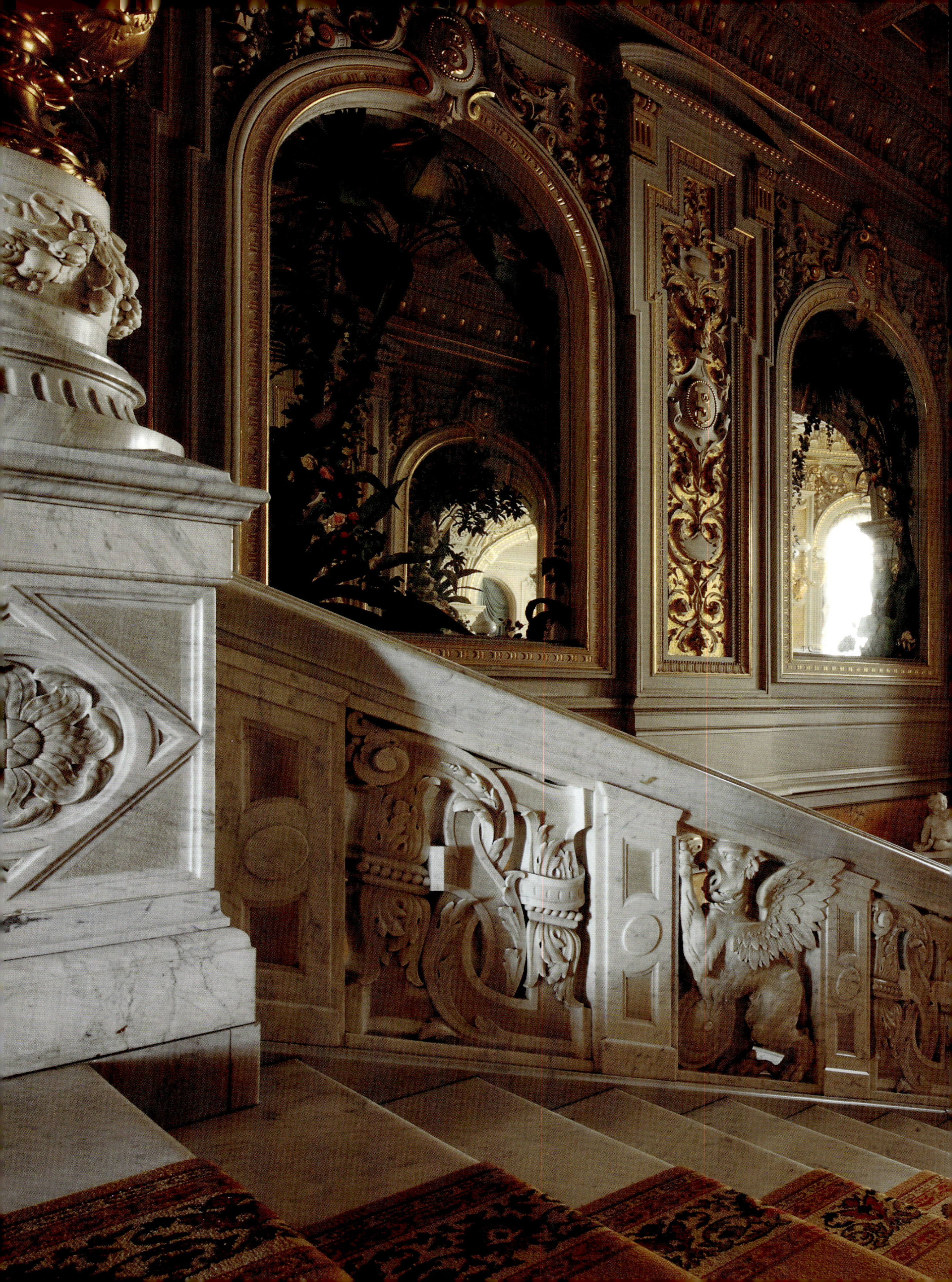

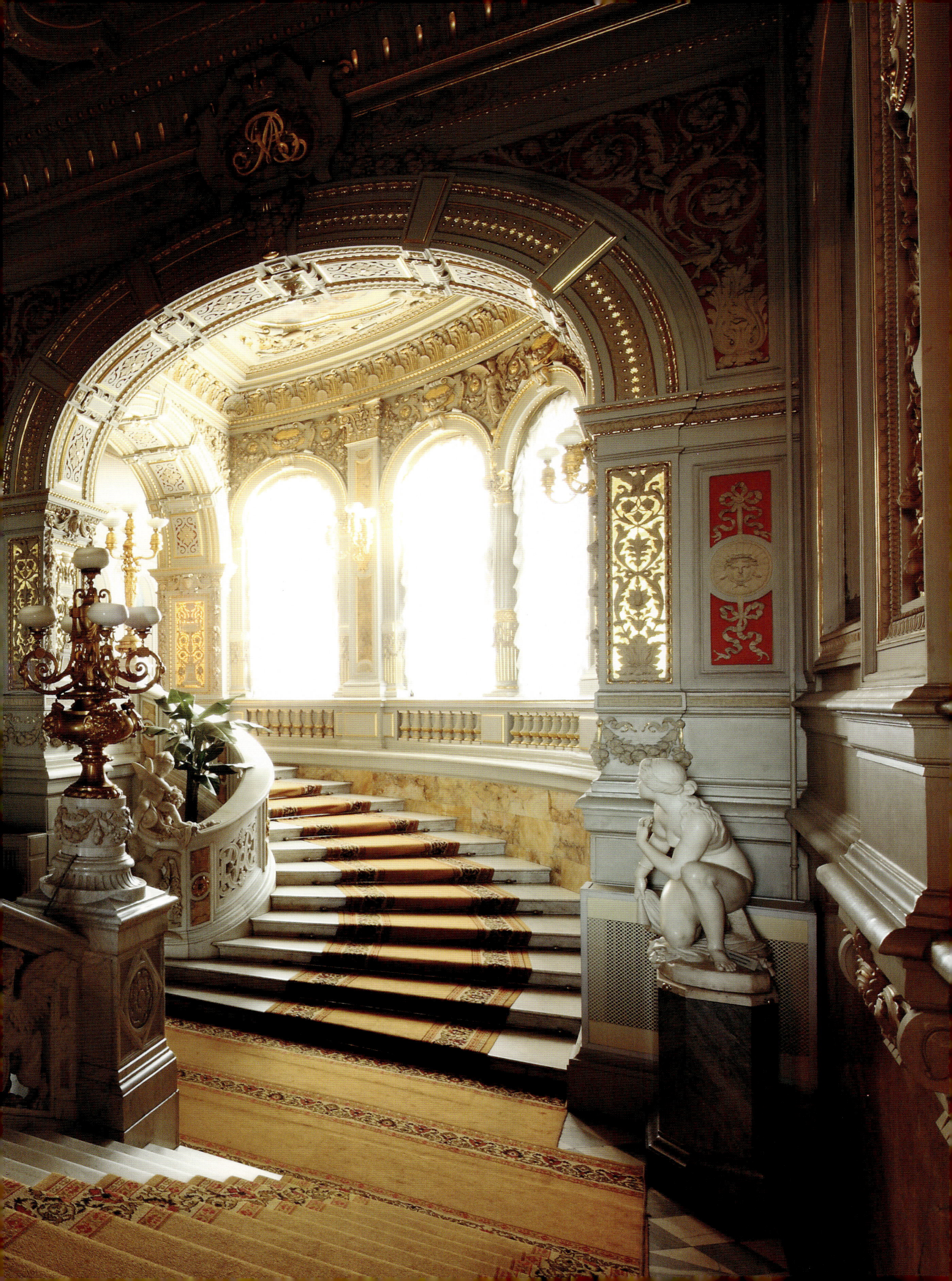

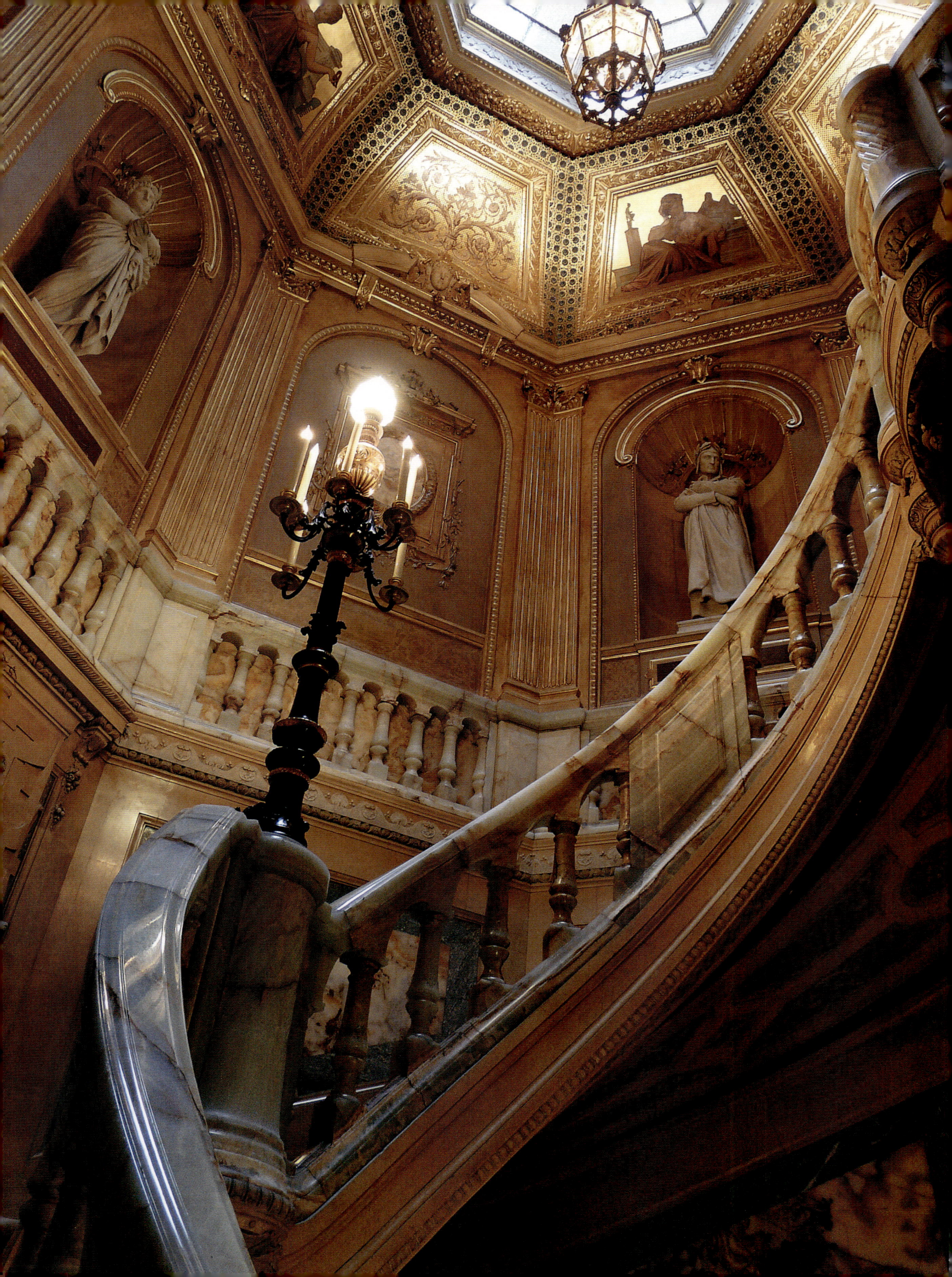

OPPOSITE
In accordance with the wishes of his client, one of the most celebrated courtesans of her time, Pierre Manguin spared no expense in the lavish decoration of the grand staircase – known as the Onyx Staircase – of the Hôtel de Païva (1856–68) on the Champs-Elysées. This sumptuous building is now home to the Travellers' Club.

RIGHT AND FAR RIGHT
A staircase in wood leading to the private apartments of the Comtesse de Béhague, and the marble grand staircase in the entrance hall. The Hôtel de Béhague (1893–1904) – today the Romanian Embassy in Paris – was designed by William Destailleur.

OVERLEAF
The grand staircase, also called the Cedar Staircase, at Harlaxton Manor in Lincolnshire, built in the 1830s and 1840s. The paternity of this precocious masterpiece of the Baroque Revival remains a mystery: it is attributed variously to Anthony Salvin, William Burn and David Bryce.

of original eighteenth-century French and Flemish elements. In Belgium, the Flemish Renaissance style was used with equal success in Centraal Station in Antwerp, with its monumental internal staircase (p. 157) – a spectacular composition of polychrome marble and stone by Louis de la Censerie – and for Pieter Dens's staircase at the Hôtel de Ville, built in the courtyard of the sixteenth-century building to which a glass roof had been added. Another Renaissance-inspired building, the Hôtel de Païva in Paris (1856–68), displays an eclectic range of influences, and was fondly described by the Goncourt brothers in 1866 as resembling a 'hideous knick-knack in Turkish-Renaissance style'. The colossal sums this building swallowed up – 6 million gold francs – was the same amount as was spent on Viollet-le-Duc's rebuilding of the château of Pierrefonds. The architect, Pierre Manguin, spared no expense in the decoration, hiring the painter Paul Baudry, the sculptor Albert-Ernest Carrier-Belleuse and some of the finest Parisian artists of the age. Setting the staircase within an octagonal space, Manguin added a cupola to illuminate this confection of marble and onyx, which by night glittered in the light of bronze candelabra. On the first floor, the apartments of the Marquise de Païva – a famous courtesan and a multimillionairess thanks to her lover, Count Henckel von Donnersmarck – were arranged around the staircase, which formed a hub at the centre of the house. Théophile Gautier is sometimes credited with one of the bons mots inspired by the scandalous marquise and her famous stairs: 'Like virtue, vice has its degrees.'

BAROQUE EUPHORIA If the Renaissance inspired many staircases in Europe and America, borrowings from the Baroque, which first appeared in the 1830s, were rarer. The most astonishing example is without doubt Harlaxton Manor in Lincolnshire, an enormous castle built from 1832 by Anthony Salvin in Elizabethan style and completed by William Burn. For the grand Cedar Staircase (pp. 164–65), the owner, Gregory Gregory, abandoned the building's original style. In a tribute to the German and

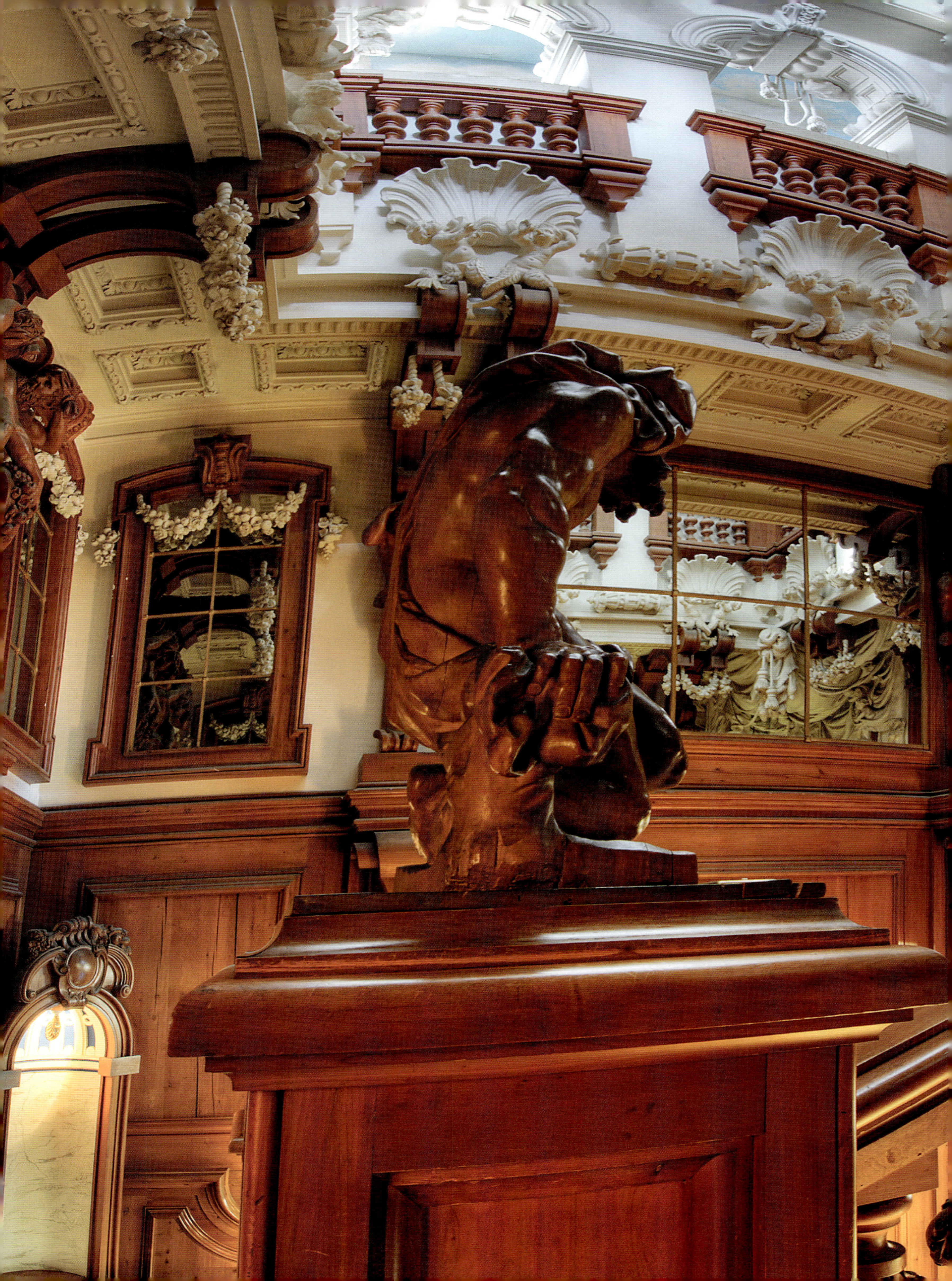

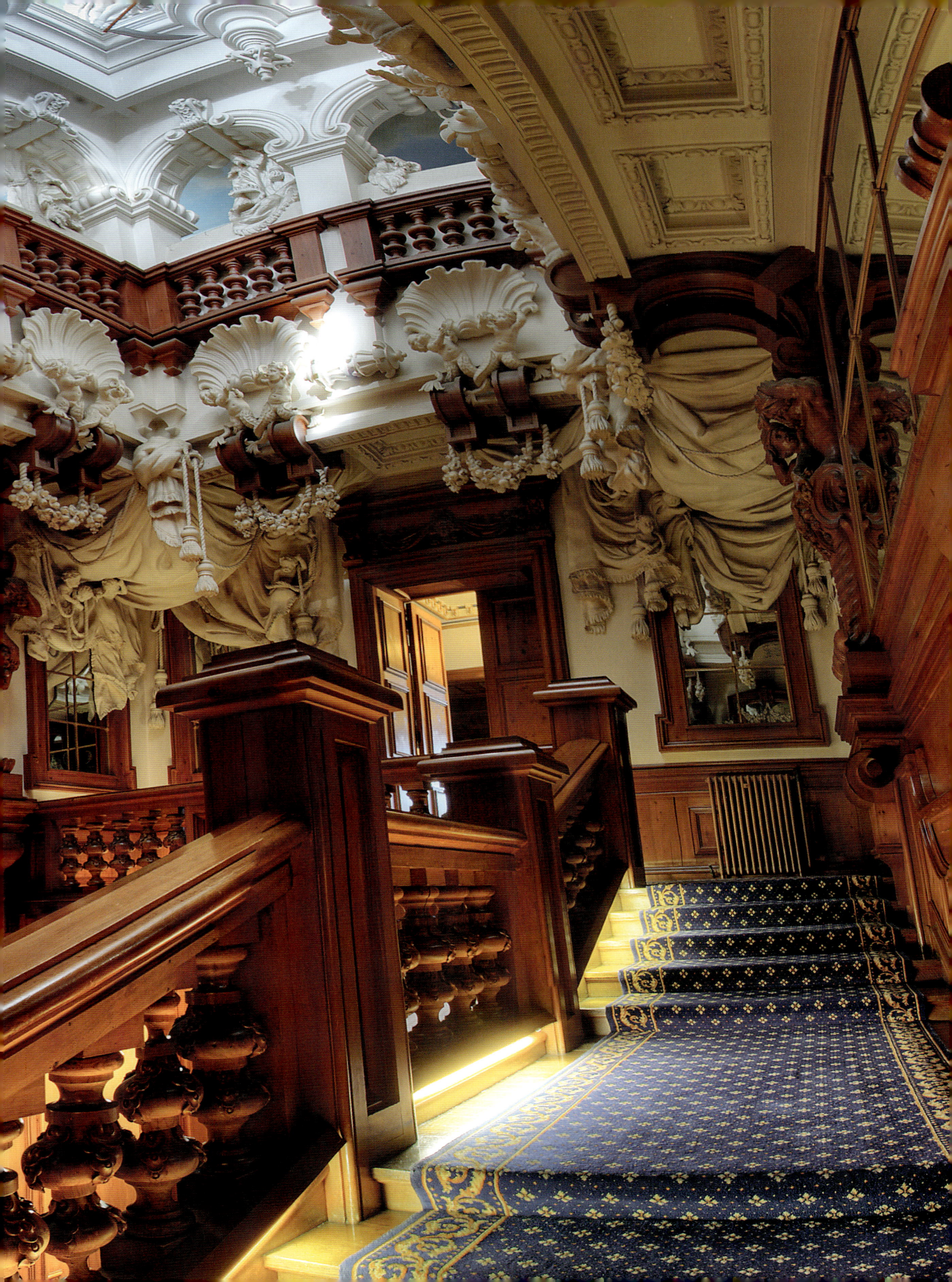

Austrian Baroque, the staircase ceiling is swathed in heavy stucco draperies, thronged with muscular atlantes and besieged by chubby-cheeked cherubs. Close inspection of the details reveals the influence of the famous Asamkirche in Munich, a tour de force by the Asam brothers and one of the undoubted masterpieces of the Baroque. Who was responsible for this idiosyncratic creation? We know that Salvin travelled to Munich and Nuremberg, probably at Gregory's behest. The less colourful Burn, meanwhile, had as his right-hand man the talented David Bryce, who designed several buildings in the Baroque style. What is certain is that Gregory, a great landowner, squandered his entire fortune on building Harlaxton. He died unmarried, and this was his sole extravagance.

The legendary Ambassadors' Staircase at Versailles, composed in a less delirious Baroque style, had been demolished in 1752 on the orders of Louis XV, but nonetheless enjoyed a remarkable revival in the late nineteenth and early twentieth centuries. More or less precise copies were to be found at Schloss Herrenchiemsee, built by Ludwig II of Bavaria (from 1876); the Palais Albert Rothschild in Vienna, designed by Hippolyte Destailleur (also 1876); the Hôtel de Castellane in Paris, also known as the 'Palais Rose', designed by René Sergent (1896–1902); and the Palais d'Egmont in Brussels, by Octave Flanneau (1906–10). It also inspired Sir George Gilbert Scott's Ambassadors' or Grand Staircase at the Foreign Office in London – which he boldly roofed with cupolas lined with Byzantine mosaics – and the marble staircase of the Hôtel Potocki in Paris (now the Chambre de Commerce et d'Industrie), by Jules Reboul (1878–84). Equally rich in its decoration of marble veneer, the Queen's Staircase at Versailles (pp. 84–85) also inspired later versions, notably at the Hôtel de Béhague, described above (p. 163), and at the Hôtel de La Rochefoucauld-Doudeauville, altered by Henri Parent in 1875 (both in Paris).

These splendid marble halls and staircases, imbued with nostalgia for the royal courts of vanished eras, lingered on in the architecture of the great cinemas until the late 1920s, chiefly in the United States. Of the Paramount Theater on Times Square, New York (1926), the luxurious masterpiece of the Rapp brothers, the designer Harold W. Rambusch observed: 'The great majority of those who frequent our cinemas have very limited means. Their interiors are modest, and the cinema gives them the possibility of believing that they are the wealthy classes in luxurious surroundings . . . No king or emperor has ever wandered through more sumptuous places than this.' It was a dream of luxury and grandeur made accessible to the working classes.

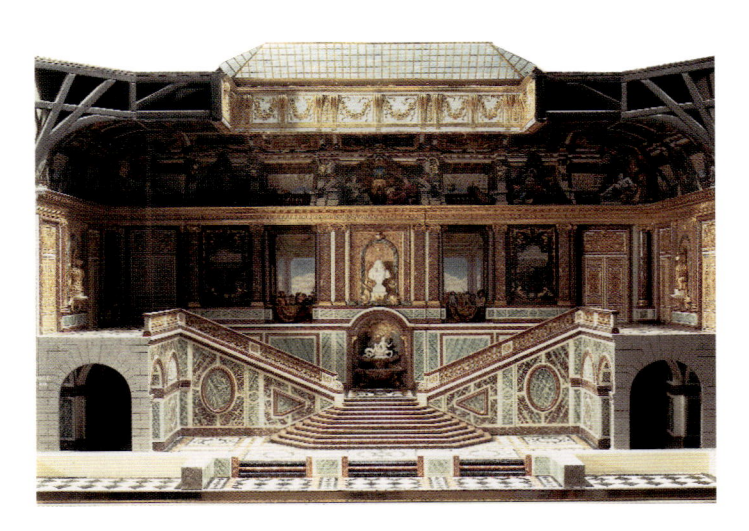

STAIRCASES OF THE CENTURY

Can the staircase designed by Charles Garnier for the Paris Opéra, inaugurated in 1875, be described as Baroque? The architectural historian Ian Sutton described it wittily as 'a child of the Beaux-Arts, though a distinctly disobedient one', since it mingles borrowings from classical architecture, the Renaissance and Baroque art 'like ingredients stirred into a soup' in order to make an unusually dynamic composition. As for Garnier, who had to face a tidal wave of criticism, he described it mischievously as 'un robuste gars' ('a solidly built fellow').

LEFT
Maquette of the Ambassadors' Staircase, Versailles, designed by François d'Orbay and Charles Le Brun in 1672–79.

BELOW LEFT
The grand staircase at Schloss Herrenchiemsee in Germany, inspired by the Ambassadors' Staircase. It was designed by Georg Dollmann in 1876; photochrome 1901.

RIGHT
The 'Million Dollar Staircase' in the Capitol Building, Albany, New York (1876–99), is supported by a sequence of round arches – a remarkable tour de force by one of the greatest of American architects, Henry Hobson Richardson; photochrome 1902.

He drew his inspiration for the stair's design chiefly from Victor Louis's Neoclassical staircase at the Grand Théâtre in Bordeaux, but also from staircases in the wealthy palazzos of Genoa. Garnier's powerful structure, punctuated by the monolithic marble columns of the first floor, valiantly holds its own against a profusion of decorative detail, raised to glowing heights by the use of countless different types of marble and multicoloured onyx. But the most remarkable quality of this world-renowned staircase lies in the unprecedented generosity of its proportions. The foyer and staircase together occupy a space as large as the auditorium itself.

The great western staircase of the Capitol Building in Albany, New York, famous throughout America as the 'Million Dollar Staircase', is not only one of Henry Hobson Richardson's masterpieces, but also one of the most accomplished works of the entire century. This is another 'solidly built fellow'. Construction of the Capitol Building had been started by Thomas Fuller, and when Richardson took over he was obliged to respect the Renaissance style adopted by his predecessor. The building's external outlines display some features reminiscent of sixteenth-century French châteaux, but for the external staircase and the western staircase Richardson had no hesitation in adopting the late Romanesque Revival style that had made his reputation. The western staircase is supported by a bold sequence of round arches that offer visitors an ever-changing spectacle as they go up and down the steps. This structural tour de force is complemented by a profusion of carved decoration; as the project developed, a lavish gallery of portraits was carved out of the stone walls (hence the staircase's popular name). When he was commissioned to rebuild the Allegheny County Courthouse, Pittsburgh, in 1883, Richardson used the same system of round arches to support the courthouse steps. Simpler in its decoration, this staircase emerges as all the more masterful in its design.

STEPS TO GLORY In the second half of the nineteenth century, a vogue for building on a colossal scale swept through architecture in the public domain, and sometimes in the private realm, too. External staircases were not immune. Along with its great central dome, the double flight of steps leading up to the United States Capitol in Washington, DC, enlarged by Thomas U. Walter in 1850–65 (p. 168), are an expression of national power. Others were to adopt similar dimensions, such as the great ramps and steps sweeping up to the parliament building in Vienna. In Germany, Leo von Klenze placed his Walhalla, constructed near Regensburg in 1830–42 during the reign of Ludwig II, on a grandiose stepped plinth. The latter is arguably the true monument, rather than the well-mannered – and comparatively diminutive – Greek temple that it supports.

In Rome, the design of the monument to Vittorio Emanuele II avoided this pitfall by ensuring that the building was no less colossal than the steps leading up to it. The competition for this monument to one of heroes of Italian unification had been won in 1885 by the French architect Henri-Paul Nénot, who built the new Sorbonne. Though well suited to this type of grandiose project by virtue of his training at the École des Beaux-Arts, Nénot was dismissed from the project in favour of an Italian, Count Giuseppe Sacconi. The site chosen, on the northern slope of the Capitoline Hill, had the merit of linking ancient and Renaissance Rome with the modern city. But the rock on which this colossus was to sit

LEFT
Loretta Young and Joseph Cotten on the steps of the Capitol in Washington, DC, from the film The Farmer's Daughter *by H. C. Potter (1947).*

proved to be riddled with ancient quarry workings, necessitating ruinously expensive consolidation works. Among the era's other spectacular staircases for urban spaces, the most celebrated is without doubt the Odessa Steps (also known as the Potemkin Stairs), which link the Ukrainian city of Odessa to its harbour. Designed in 1825 by two Neoclassical architects, Francesco Boffo and Avraam Melnikov, they were built in green sandstone from Trieste in 1837–41. In his film *Battleship Potemkin*, Sergei Eisenstein made masterly use of this dramatic setting (p. 18).

Among civic buildings, the central law courts of the great capitals were also expected to function as manifestations of national pride. Larger than St Peter's Basilica in Rome, the Palais de Justice in Brussels is an especially formidable pile. 'Outside it's a colossus, inside it's a monster,' was the verdict of Verlaine, who coined the terms 'babélique' and 'michelangesque' to describe it. One could be forgiven for mistaking this extraordinary building, erected between 1868 and 1883, for the funerary monument of a megalomaniac. But it was the pride of a young nation, as the Belgian minister for justice declared in 1873: 'It will be the finest, if not to say the only, monument of the nineteenth century.' From a square named after the building's architect, Joseph Poelaert, visitors climb steps 80 metres (262 feet) wide and cross two colonnades to reach the Piranesian public concourse. But the most spectacular steps lead from the entrance on Rue des Minimes, where Poelaert exploited the steeply sloping terrain to create the Babylonian Escalier des Minimes (p. 170).

IRON: A HIDDEN BEAUTY From the seventeenth century on, metal was used frequently in the construction of staircases, most usually for the wrought-iron handrails that often made stairs so decorative. Honed to perfection in France in the second half of the eighteenth century, this locksmiths' art returned to prominence in the second half of the nineteenth. When cast iron made its appearance in British buildings of the eighteenth century, it was initially used as a cheap substitute for decorative details that would previously have been in wrought iron or stone, such as balusters, balconies and gates, as well as handrails. But from the early nineteenth century, cast iron made it possible to introduce grand flights

OPPOSITE
The steps of the monument to Vittorio Emanuele II in Rome, photographed by the writer Leonid Andreiev. It was erected from 1885 by Giuseppe Sacconi; autochrome from 1914.

1800–1900 | 169

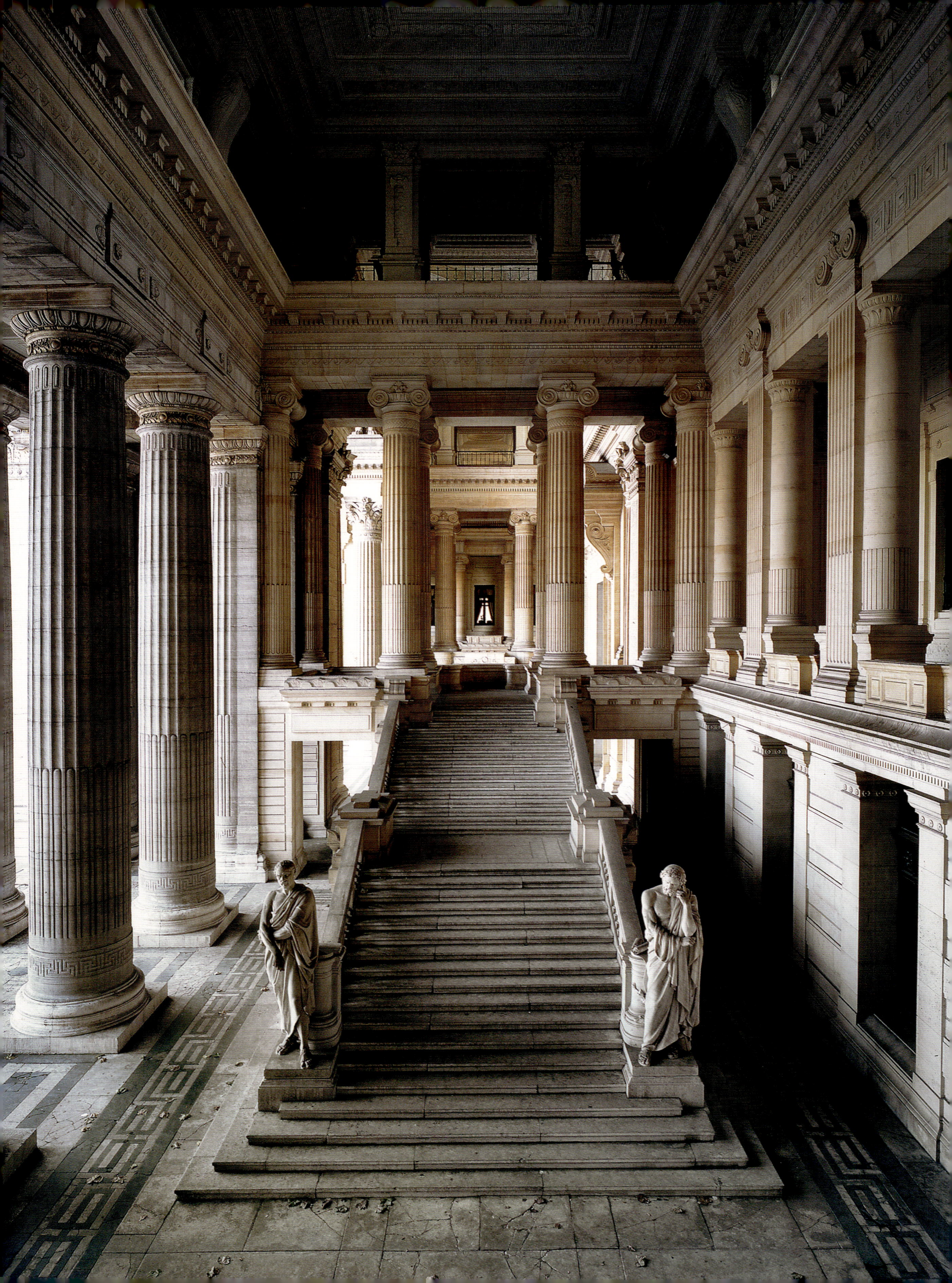

1800-1900 | 171

OPPOSITE
'Outside, it's a colossus; inside, it's a monster,' was Verlaine's verdict on the Palais de Justice in Brussels, built by Joseph Poelaert (1868–83). Pictured here is the central staircase.

RIGHT, ABOVE AND BELOW
Of the three architects involved in the building of the Library of Congress in Washington, DC, Edward Pearce Casey, who worked there from 1892, was responsible for the design of the grand staircase, which featured painted decorations by Elmer Ellsworth Garnsey and stucco work by Albert Weinert. The balustrade is carved with putti bearing attributes of learning among the garlands of fruit.

OVERLEAF
The stairs in the central hall of the Natural History Museum, London, by Alfred Waterhouse (1871–81). Here and throughout the museum, the bold use of a cast-iron structural framework is disguised with terracotta facings in a Romanesque style.

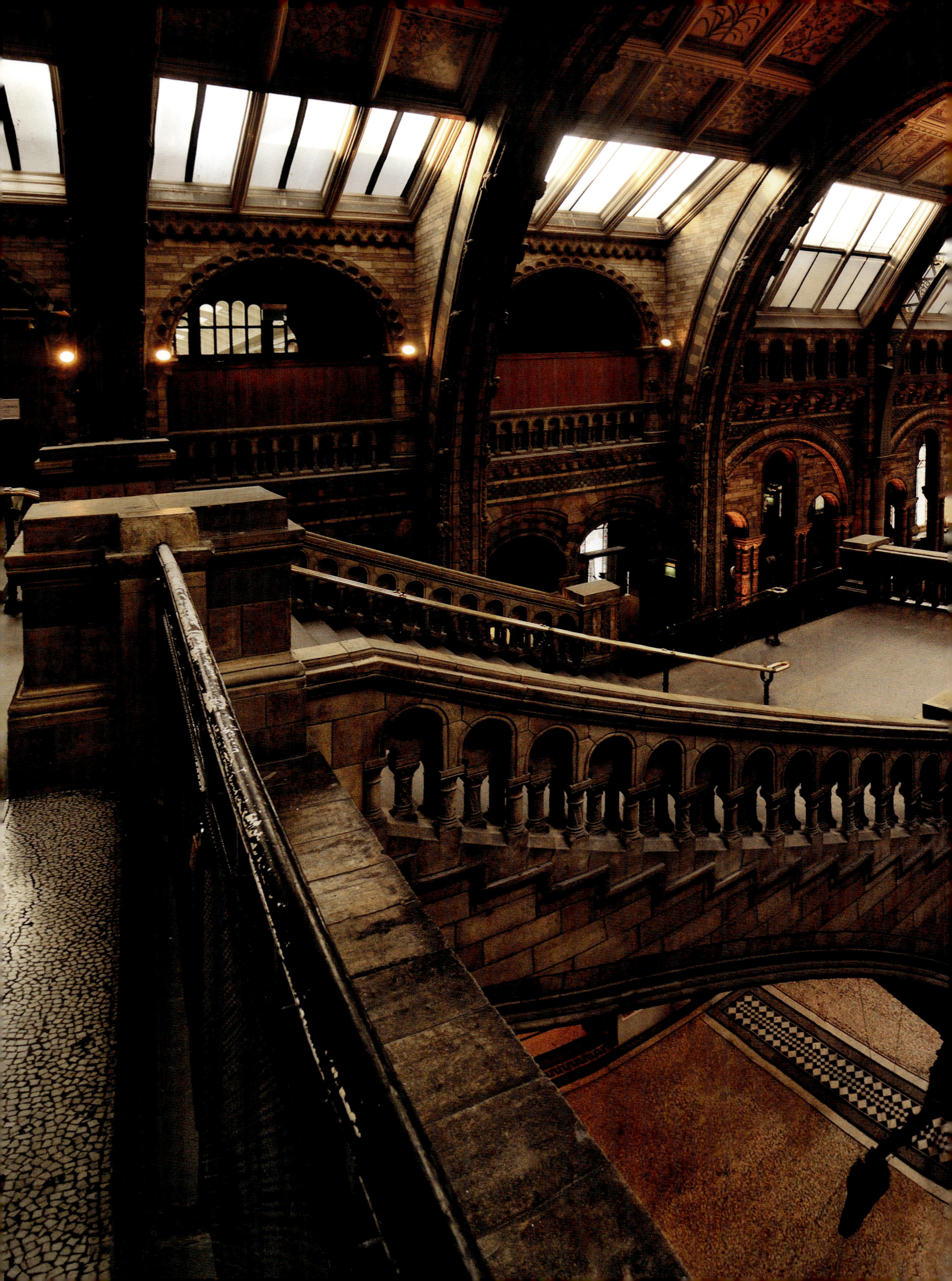

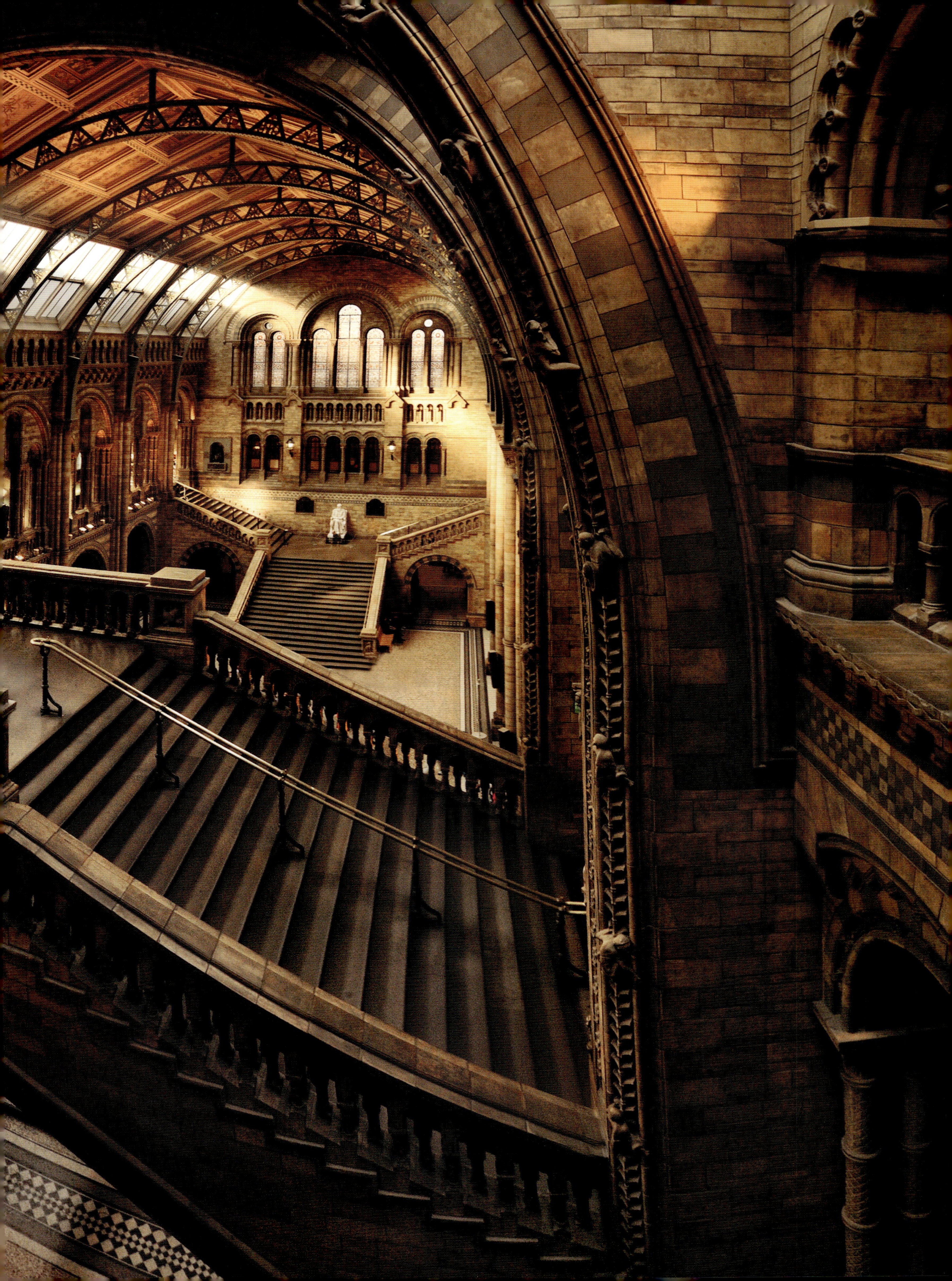

of the imagination into decorative schemes. At the Royal Pavilion in Brighton, the oriental folly built for the Prince Regent in 1815–22, John Nash designed the grand staircase in cast iron to imitate bamboo. Writing in 1864, the architect Léonce Raynaud observed: 'Cast iron is perfectly suited to the construction of staircases, and is quite frequently used for this purpose.' On the subject of floating staircases in this material, he noted that they were 'capable of great solidity and were more durable than stone staircases'. Moreover, he explained that the open steps, with their grooved treads, helped prevent slipping, citing as an example the grand staircase of the Théâtre Montansier in Paris. The main foundries in Europe (such as Walter Macfarlane & Co. in Glasgow) and in North America exported staircases in kit form throughout the world, in an extraordinary variety of shapes and decorative detail. In spiral staircases each step was cast as a single piece, with the central newel and riser attached; the parts simply slotted into each other. Particularly elegant staircases of this type may be seen in the Palm House at Kew Gardens, and in the greenhouse of the palace of Schönbrunn in Vienna, their delicate forms rising

FAR LEFT
Photograph showing the metal staircases leading down to the platforms at Pennsylvania (Penn) Station, New York (1905–10). The magnificent cast-iron train shed, concealed behind an opulent façade by McKim, Mead & White, was demolished in 1963.

LEFT
Engraved cross-section showing the central staircase of the Bon Marché department store in Paris, enlarged in the 1870s by Louis-Charles Boileau.

gracefully among the fronds of the tropical plants. Others are more discreet, hidden inside lighthouses and such tall monuments as the statue of Notre Dame de France in Puy-en-Velay, the Statue of Liberty and the Campanile in Venice. In great railway stations, including the Gare d'Orsay in Paris or its New York cousin, Pennsylvania (Penn) Station, the design of the main façade – the former by Victor Laloux, the latter by McKim, Mead & White – deployed the full grandiloquence of the classical repertoire as taught at the École des Beaux-Arts. But in the vast, glazed engine sheds, built by engineers, the iron staircases that led down to the level of the tracks were exposed, unadorned, reduced to their simplest possible function.

New York fire regulations required the construction of metal fire escapes from 1860, and by the 1920s painters and photographers had transformed this everyday feature of the American urban landscape into a veritable aesthetic object (p. 175). Until the construction of the Empire State Building in New York, Paris boasted the tallest staircase in the world: the 'Tour de 300 mètres', as the Eiffel Tower was initially known. We tend to forget that it was supposed to be a temporary structure, designed to be demolished after the Exposition Universelle of 1899 had ended. For monumental iron staircases of palatial proportions we must turn to the great department stores. The standard was set by Le Bon Marché, which was enlarged by Louis-Charles Boileau in 1873 and 1876, and endowed with a majestic double staircase

OPPOSITE
Apartment buildings on Greene Street, New York. Metal fire escapes – a legal obligation introduced in 1860, following disastrous fires in two tenement buildings, with great loss of life – became an iconic feature of the city's streetscape.

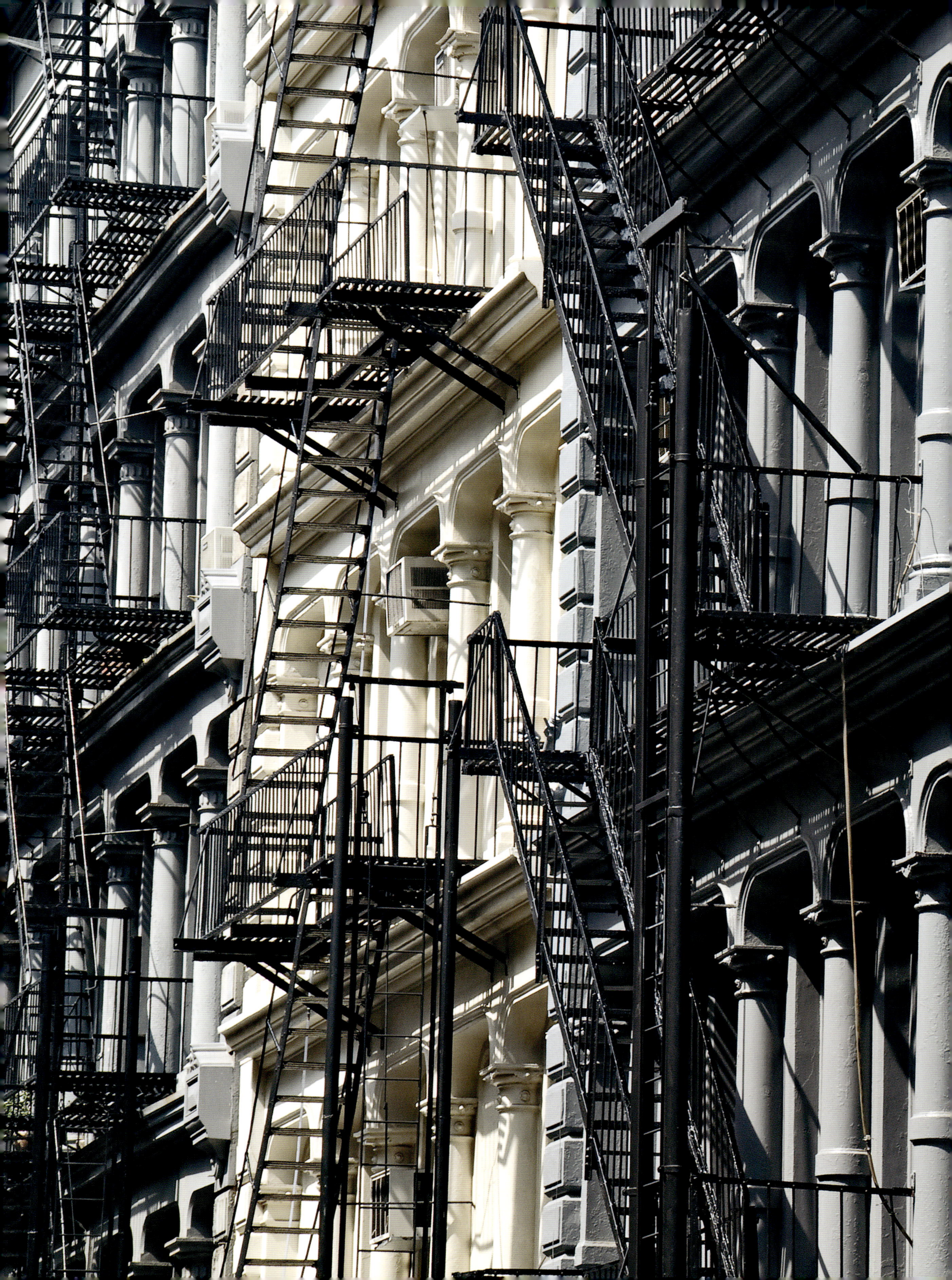

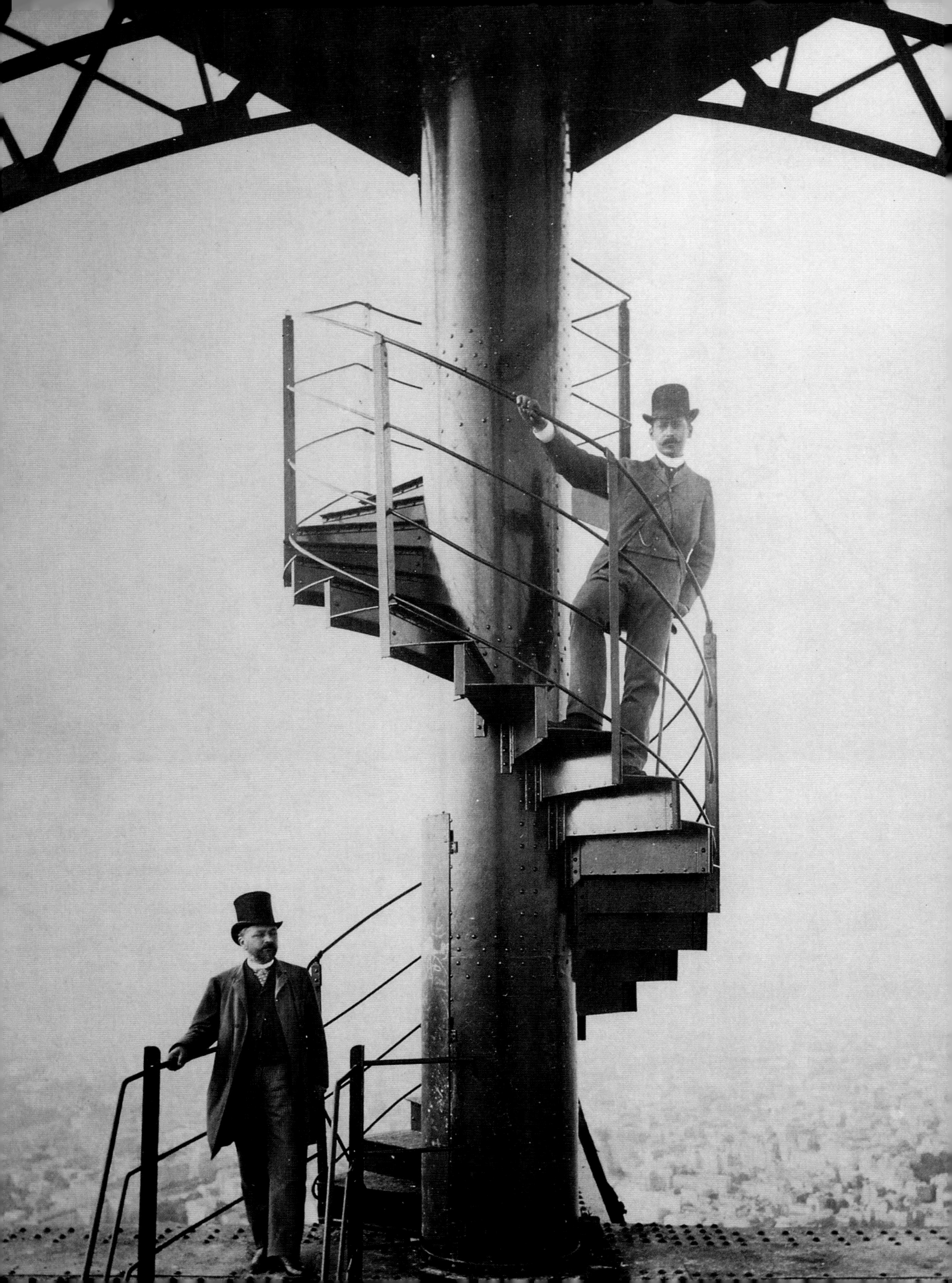

OPPOSITE
Gustave Eiffel with his son-in-law and collaborator Adolphe Salles on the spiral staircase between the upper platform and the summit of the Eiffel Tower, photographed in 1889, the year of its inauguration.

ABOVE RIGHT
One of the cast-iron spiral staircases in the State Law Library of Iowa in Des Moines (1884).

BELOW RIGHT
The stairs linking the first- and second-floor studios in the Musée Gustave Moreau in Paris, designed by Albert Lafon (1895).

occupying the centre of the building, described by the architect as 'an immense iron stairwell' (p. 174). The tall, airy trading space of Le Printemps, rebuilt by Paul Sédille in 1881–82, housed a gigantic central staircase that was among the most spectacular of the century. The decoration of the store's staircases and bridges was sumptuous in the extreme, combining carved wood, pink-veined stone, white marble and red Languedoc marble with wrought and laminated iron. The finishing touch to this dizzying ensemble, which was crisscrossed by a network of iron bridges, was a magical lighting system composed of dozens of electric globes. The new Printemps was hugely influential both in France and abroad, and may have inspired the Cleveland Arcade, a vast shopping gallery with two internal staircases.

With a few outstanding exceptions, in general the nineteenth century made little use of cast iron and metal in 'noble' architecture. However, given the considerable technical difficulties involved in building large stone staircases, one could be forgiven for wondering why this was not the first area to benefit from advances in manufacturing.

In the first half of the century, the great Karl Friedrich Schinkel was one of the few architects to give iron a prominent role in a domestic context, using it in the principal staircases of some of his dwellings. His staircase for the Prinz-Albert-Palais in Berlin (1830–33, demolished) was an unabashed display, featuring handrail, treads and risers in decorative, pierced cast iron, embellished with an elegant repertoire of palmettes and foliage designs. In around 1820, for the chapel wing of the Catherine Palace at Tsarskoye Selo, the architect Vassili P. Stasov adopted a very similar Neoclassical style for a remarkable cast-iron staircase alternating single and double flights over three storeys (p. 149). This creation is contemporary with the slender cast-iron balustrades that embellish the canal bridges of St Petersburg. (The imperial capital had been one of the first cities in the world to employ cast-iron balustrades, first installing them in the eighteenth century.) Later, taking advantage of advances in laminated iron, Sir George Gilbert Scott eagerly combined this material with the stone vocabulary of the purest thirteenth-century Gothic. His Midland Grand Hotel (1868–76), which graces the iron train sheds of St Pancras Station in London with its fairytale turrets and pinnacles, boasts one of the most stunning Gothic-style stairs in Europe (pp. 180–81). The slender, sinuous structure winds boldly upwards in a virtuoso composition that make a virtue of exposed metal girders, their industrial lines embellished with Gothic-inspired foliage and ribbons. Scott was disappointed that it did not inspire more imitations: 'Metallic construction is the great development of our age, and it speaks ill for the taste of our architects that they have done so little to render it beautiful.' Lifts, or 'ascending rooms' – still a novelty in London – complemented the stair. The great windows and ribbed vaulting are treated with all the sumptuousness of a cathedral, despite the limited budget imposed by the Midland Railway company.

Always abreast of the latest technological innovations, the great Viollet-le-Duc published a number of projects in which he combined medieval architectural forms with exposed metal components. But they remained on paper. At the Château d'Eu in Normandy, he did succeed in creating an iron staircase of great elegance, but it was reserved for the servants only. Very often, metal was restricted to a secondary role. And when it was used as a supporting element in prestigious projects, it had to be disguised. An age that had retreated into a scholarly historicism preferred not to see it. Yet it was thanks to the iron structure of their vault, pierced by large glazed areas, that Percier and Fontaine – having overcome their long-held aversion to the use of metal – were able to light the staircase at the Tuileries so generously at the beginning of the century. It was thanks to a framework made entirely of iron that, in his Natural History Museum in London (1871–81), Alfred Waterhouse was able to introduce a vertiginous staircase into the space of the central hall, forming a bridge between the first- and second-floor galleries (pp. 172–73). While the great hall's iron structure is left partially exposed, that of the staircase is camouflaged, like the entire building, with terracotta tiles decorated with Romanesque motifs. The balustrades are especially remarkable, consisting of a triple row of small columns and arcatures. Such a bold approach would have been well-nigh impossible in stone, especially since the budget was constantly being cut back. At the Paris Opéra, Garnier had used an iron structure to reinforce his grand staircase, though it of course remained invisible. You have to climb the seven flights of stairs in the administration building to see bare metal used as part of the mixed construction. The stairs are iron, but the steps are veneered in wood: as Garnier wrote, 'It is important that these steps should not be different in nature from the floors, boxes, corridors or stage, especially for the dancers, who could slip if there were alterations to the floor covering. If this were to be in stone, it would moreover give their feet, so lightly shod, an unpleasantly and perhaps harmfully cold sensation.' Thus the architect who was capable of creating the most grandiose of great staircases was also attentive to the smallest practical details, such as the effect of his stairs on the dancers' feet.

LEFT
The decorative scheme of the grand staircase of the Villa Achilleion in Corfu, designed by Alexander von Warsberg and built by Raffaele Carito and August von Bukovich (1891), is Pompeian in inspiration, down to the finest details.

OPPOSITE
The steps in the Passage Pommeray in Nantes, designed by Jean-Baptiste Buron and Hippolyte Durand-Gosselin (1841–43). Lit by vast glazed panels, the shopping arcade is here endowed with a monumental decorative scheme worthy of a palace.

SALSA
LSA NOVA
GALERIE REGNIER
BILLET
GRAND T
BONNES AFFAIRES

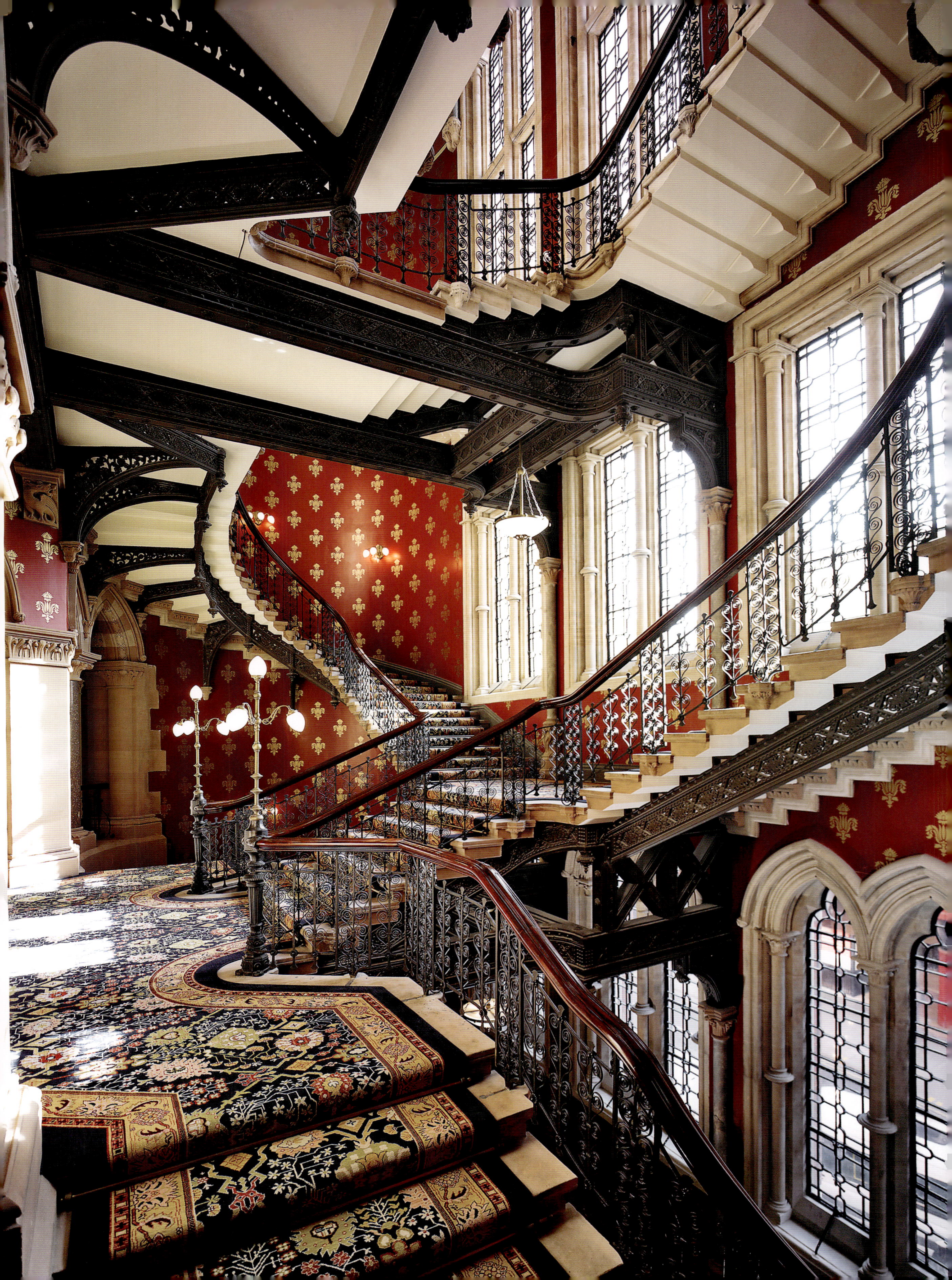

OPPOSITE AND ABOVE
The staircase of the Midland Grand Hotel – now the St Pancras Renaissance Hotel – in London (1868–76). Sir George Gilbert Scott, restorer of Britain's great Gothic cathedrals, was keen to showcase the beauties of cast iron in this dazzling essay in historicism.

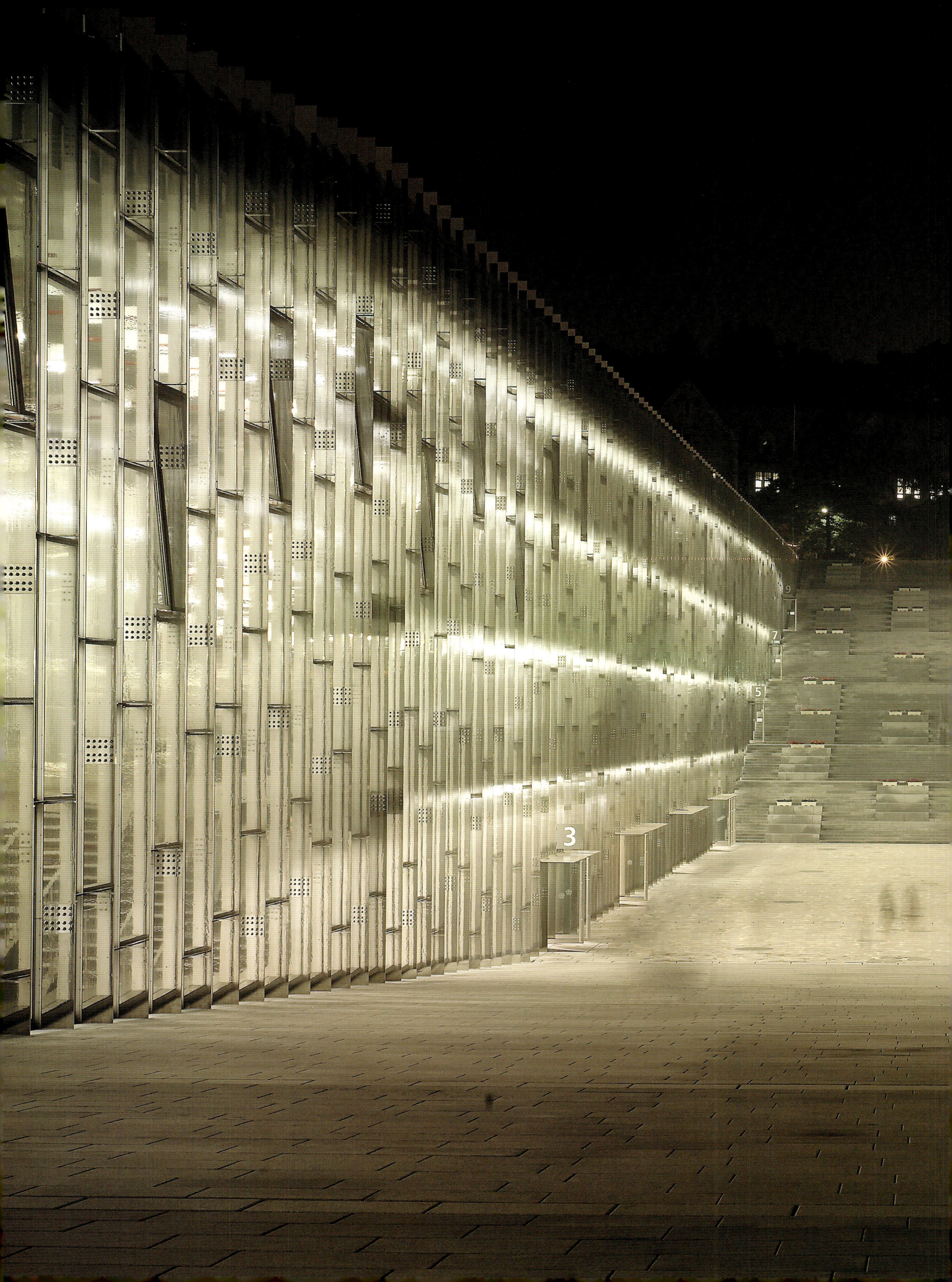
3

From Art Nouveau to the Present Day

1900–NOW

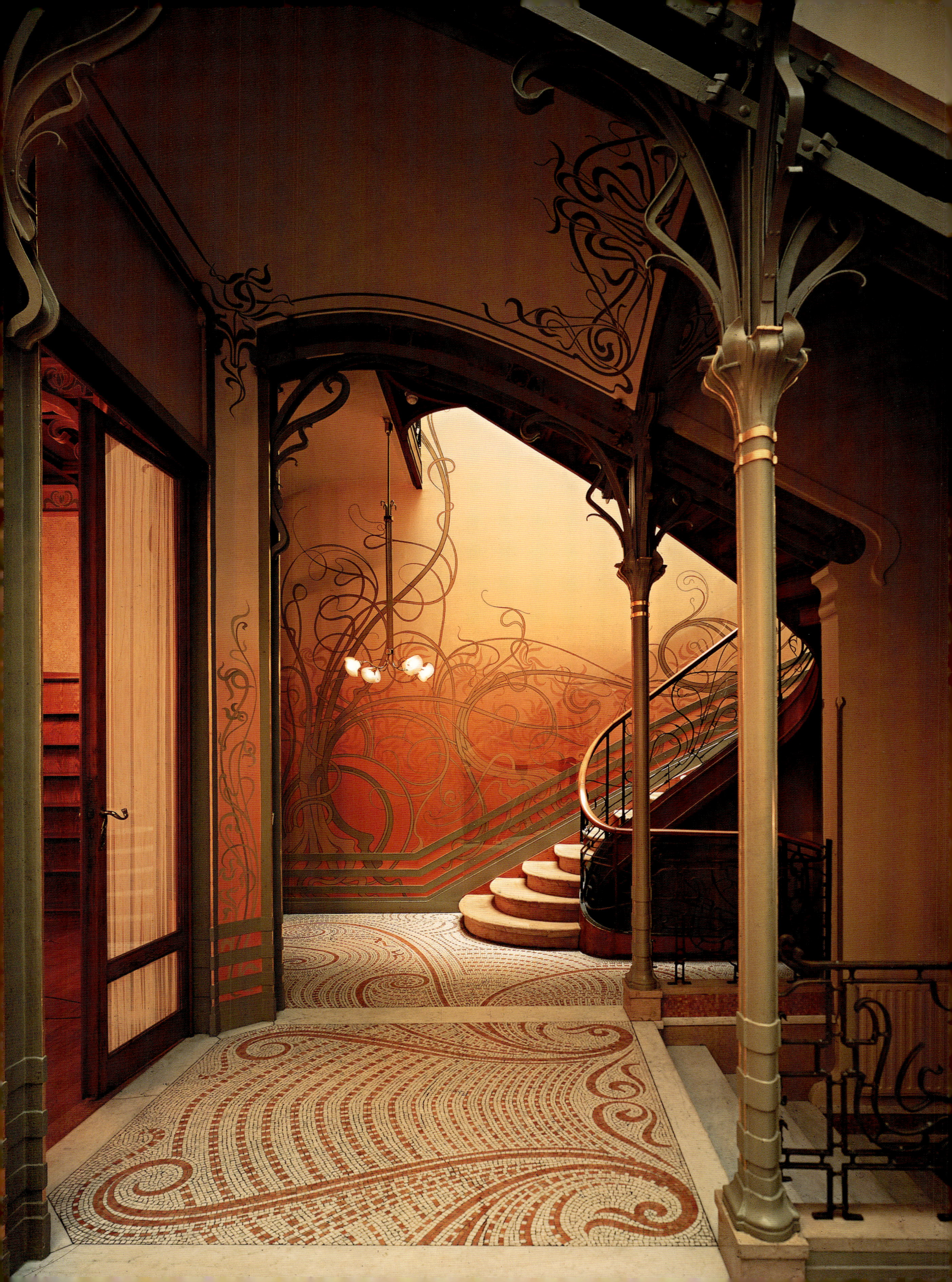

OPPOSITE
Victor Horta's house for the Tassel family in Brussels, built in 1892. In 2000 it was classified as a UNESCO World Heritage Site.

PREVIOUS PAGES
At the Ewha Women's University in Seoul, the French architect Dominique Perrault sliced an artificial valley through the centre of the campus, building two monumental staircases to provide access to the main communal facilities (2009).

The final chapter in this journey through the architectural history of the staircase covers the huge diversity of forms conceived and built during the modern era. From Art Nouveau to the present day, the twentieth and twenty-first centuries have embraced a wealth of rapidly changing styles. An exploration of twenty cultural trends will allow us to discover their particular aims and ambitions, which will be further illustrated by a selection of masterpieces in each style. The overall aim of this section, therefore, is to focus on fifty iconic designs in an attempt to decipher the key stages in the evolution of the modern staircase. A step-by-step exploration of these flights of the imagination will reveal the new relationships modern staircases have woven with their immediate surroundings.

ART NOUVEAU IN BRUSSELS The first revolution to bring about a radical change to our concept of domestic space – and to introduce a pioneering modernist style into the home – developed around a new interpretation of the staircase initiated in Brussels by the architect Victor Horta. The principal urban dwelling in Brussels at this time was the terraced house: three or four storeys high, it occupied a long, narrow plot 6 to 7 metres (20 to 23 feet) wide. Traditionally, this type of dwelling was served by a staircase enclosed in a stairwell that was relegated to the far side of the house, where it formed a dark, utilitarian area devoid of appeal.

In 1892 Victor Horta built a town house for the Tassel family in which this outmoded arrangement was replaced by a dignified, meaningful architecture that instantly seemed to signal the beginning of a new artistic era. Here, Horta opened up a new space, and dramatized it by introducing four innovations of crucial importance: a shaft let into the roof, which allows natural light to flood into the centre of the house; the graceful curvilinear decoration of the adjoining walls and floors, which echoes the rhythmic energy of the staircase, and which was to become one of the signatures of Art Nouveau; the voluptuous, sensual atmosphere generated by the warm palette used for the walls and floors, and by the floral inspiration of their decorative motifs; and, finally, the staircase's novel combination of materials, which linked tradition (represented by stone, mosaic and precious wood) with modernity, celebrated in the confident presence of exposed steel pillars, whose soaring elegance contributes a feeling of lightness to the complex spatial structure of this new and important space. Through this metamorphosis, the innovative potential of the staircase is revealed: not only structurally and spatially, on account of its luminosity and decorative character, but also symbolically and architecturally. A new focus of domestic life, it also proclaimed to visitors, as soon as they entered the house, the progressive social and intellectual credentials of those who lived there. The modern staircase had become an autonomous entity, liberated from its marginal status in the shadows. It was the fact that this house enshrines a radically new approach, both conceptually and artistically, that earned it its classification in 2000 as a UNESCO World Heritage Site.

In the house that he built for himself between 1898 and 1901 – now the Musée Horta – the master of Art Nouveau was even bolder. Two staircases animate this dwelling: one, intended for servants' use, is concealed, while the other is a spinal column around which Horta deployed a new and spectacular use of space. Here, the idea of the stairwell was abolished in favour of rearranging the circulation around the building. The house was no longer laid out as a series of different floors, hermetically sealed one from another but, rather, as an open, flexible and subtle sequence of half-floors, or even third- or quarter-floors, all distributed around each staircase landing, which becomes the focus of a rhythmical, theatrical design. Well before Le Corbusier, Horta invented the idea of the open plan and banished the time-honoured tradition of living spaces separated by walls. In so doing, he transformed the whole house, from ground floor to attic, into a series of spectacular spatial sequences of astonishing inventiveness, brought together by the staircase, which affirmed these strokes of boldness and was now elevated to the status of artistic fulcrum. A drawing by the British artist Paul Day captures this sculptural 'magic of place'. It depicts this rising space as lined with a sumptuous range of materials, colours and mirrors. The function of the mirrors is twofold: they reflect the warm light entering from the roof shaft into the heart of the house, and they create a magical kaleidoscope of the domestic space, fragmenting it into a collection of dreamlike images of its architecture.

Horta also adapted this skilful mastery of space to his numerous commercial buildings, such as the former Wauquiez shop building of 1906, now the Centre Belge de la Bande Dessinée, in Brussels. The comic book artist François Schuiten has himself immortalized its staircase.

OPPOSITE
The bright, airy staircase of the house Victor Horta built for himself in Brussels in 1898, now the Musée Horta. The building was classified as a UNESCO World Heritage Site in 2000.

LEFT
The theatrical space of the staircase in Horta's house, drawn in 1995 by the British sculptor Paul Day while working on Brussels, an Urban Comedy, *an exploration of the city's culture.*

OVERLEAF
The grand staircase built in 1900 by the architects Albert Louvet and Henri Deglane at the heart of the Grand Palais in Paris (restored in 2010).

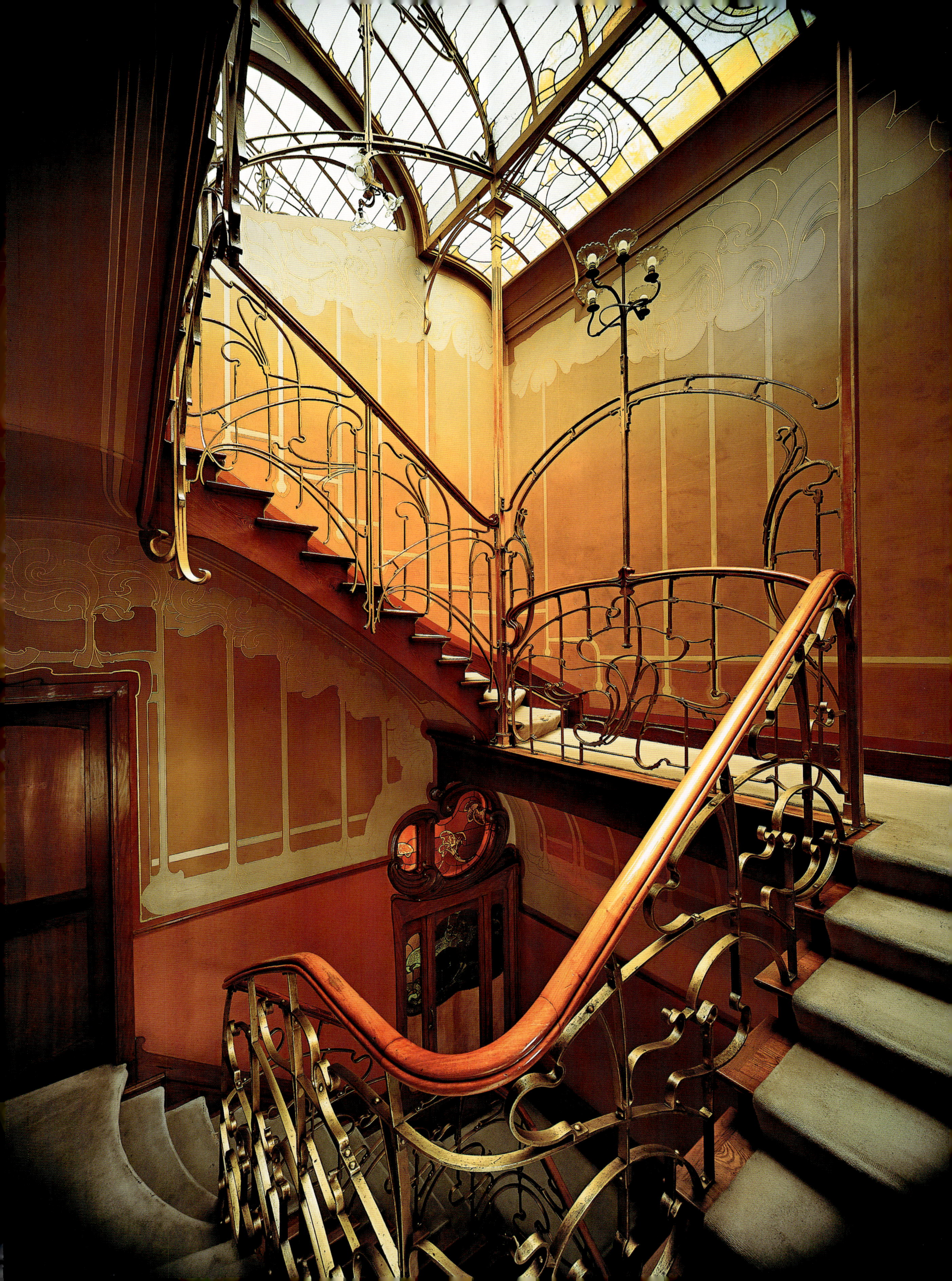

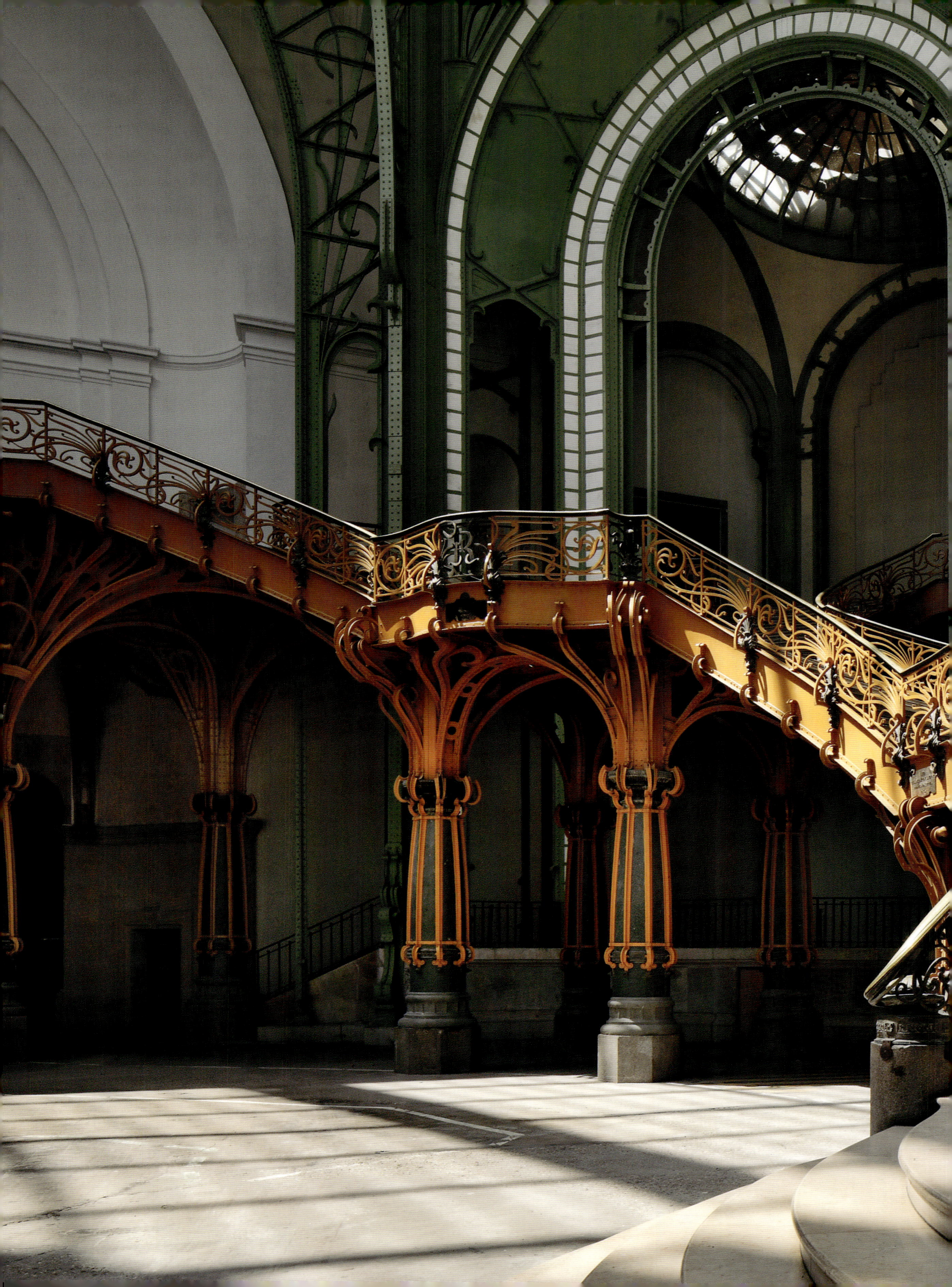

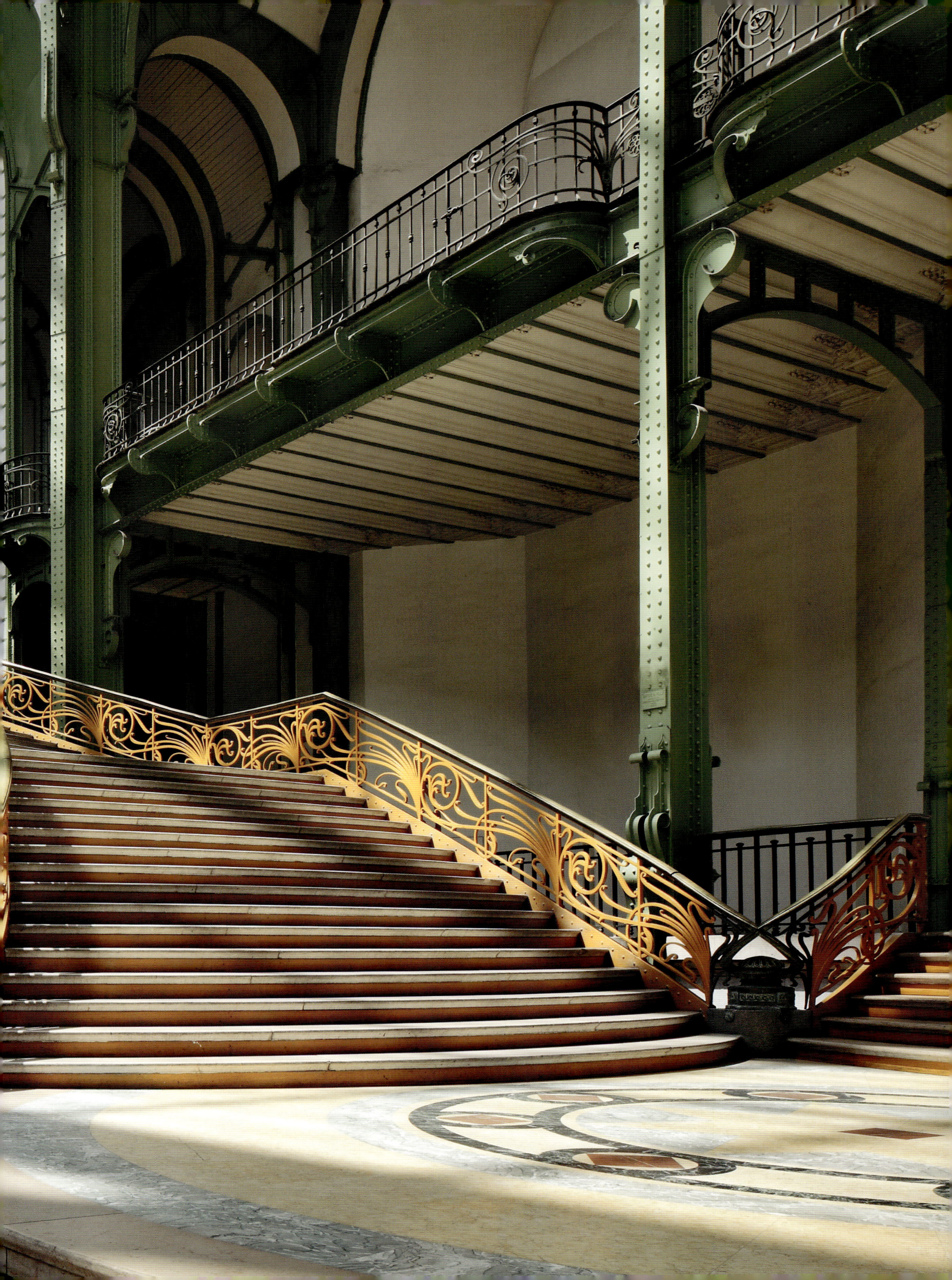

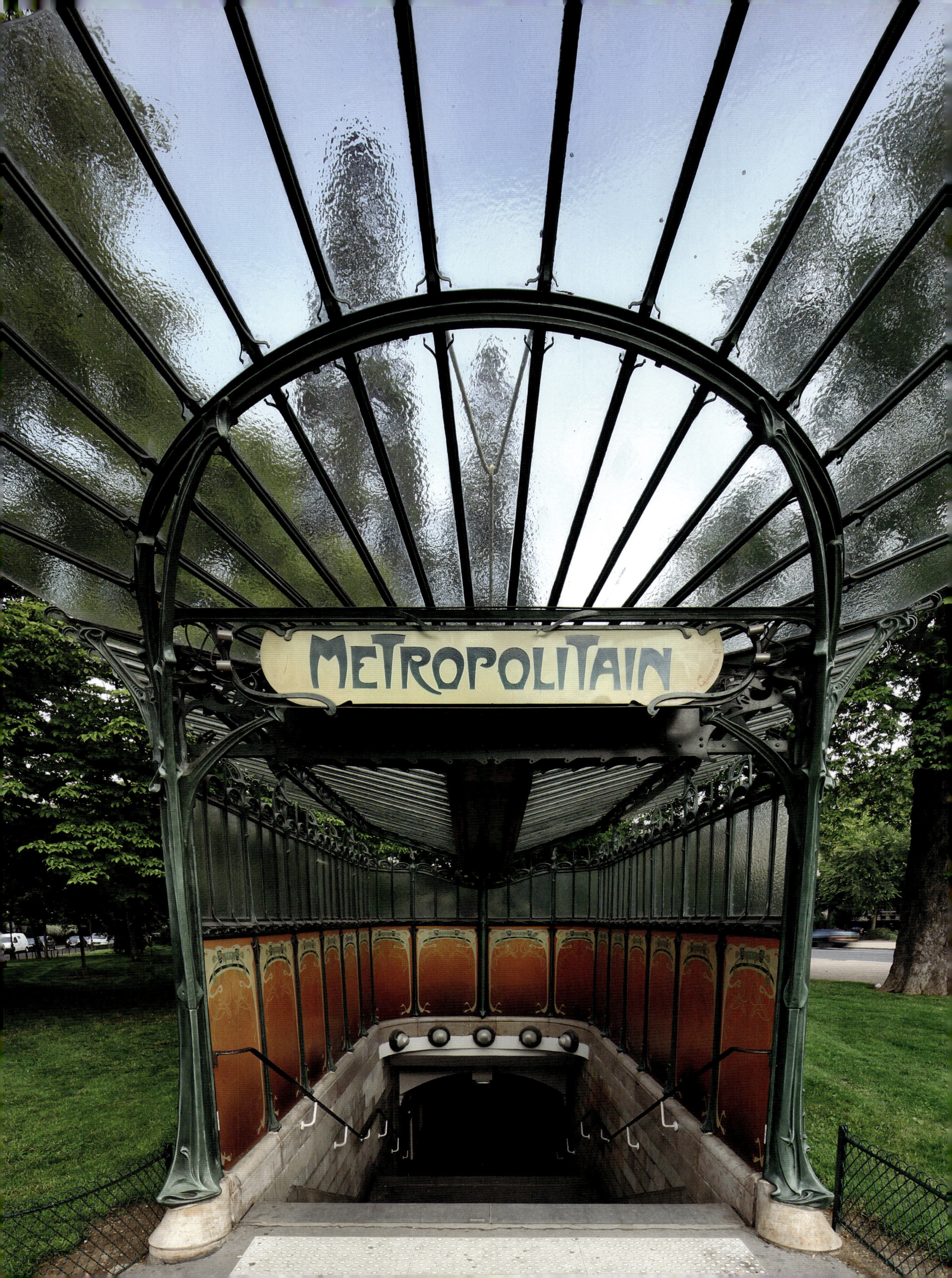
METROPOLITAIN

OPPOSITE

Entrance to Porte Dauphine metro station in Paris, built by Hector Guimard in 1900 and now a classified historic monument.

ART NOUVEAU IN PARIS With the opening of the first line of the Paris Métro in 1900, passengers had to plunge into the bowels of the earth to use this new form of public transport. Since the public viewed this descent underground with some anxiety, it seemed wise to allay their fears by introducing a different treatment for each metro station. It was decided that these abhorrent technological spaces should be transformed into attractive areas redolent of art and high culture. The railway company's president was attracted to the new Art Nouveau style, and settled on the choice of the architect Hector Guimard to effect this metamorphosis. Guimard accomplished his commission in bravura fashion by wrapping every entrance staircase in a work of art in cast iron, creating a poetic image that turned the act of descending underground into a celebration. Since many of the principal themes of Art Nouveau were inspired by the plant world, Guimard designed his structures to resemble so many trees in blossom, appearing to grow quite naturally from the fertile ground. In this transcendent form, the entrances to the Paris Métro would become an enduring symbol of the City of Light, and of its beauty and elegance.

In 1911 Guimard built the Hôtel Mezzara: here, the principal staircase in the entrance hall demonstrated Guimard's talent by bringing enchantment into the domestic life of Paul Mezzara, a textile magnate, just as the latter had inspired the daily lives of Parisians. While these creations have long been recognized as masterpieces of Parisian Art Nouveau, it was not until 2010 that the great monumental staircase Guimard designed for the central hall of the Grand Palais in 1900 was at last restored to its former glory (pp. 188–89). Its spectacular metal structure, unfolding over more than 500 square metres (5,400 square feet), was constructed by Albert Louvet and Henri Deglane.

RIGHT

The Hôtel Mezzara, built in Paris for Paul Mezzara in 1911 by Hector Guimard.

CATALAN MODERNISM In Barcelona, Art Nouveau's counterpart was known as Catalan Modernism. Since 2000 a number of works in the city by Antoni Gaudí – its most celebrated exponent – have been classified as UNESCO World Heritage Sites. Among them are audacious designs for stairs and steps. The staircase of the Casa Batlló (1900) bears witness to the sublime architectural fluidity that Gaudí ushered in. The space created by this staircase takes on a sculptural beauty: the balustrade and steps in red-toned wood establish a dialogue with the undulating walls and ceiling, which are lined with fragments of off-white ceramic and adiate a warm light, filling the space with a Mediterranean sensuality.

It was with a similar passion that in 1900 Gaudí laid out, at the entrance to his Parc Güell, eight flights of an open-air staircase that climbs the slope, employing polychrome ceramic tiles to reflect the sunlight and magnify its effect. The lyricism of this composition is a modern echo of the theatricality deployed in Rome by Francesco de' Sanctis for the Spanish Steps, which lead up to the church of Trinità dei Monti (1723–26), or by Michelangelo in the steps that form the approach to the Piazza del Campidoglio (1538; p. 45).

In his Casa Milà apartment building, also known as La Pedrera, completed in 1910, Gaudí gave full rein to his protean genius. The concept of the roof terrace here appears as a peerless synthesis of sculpture, architecture and urban landscape. In this remarkable roofscape, at once sumptuous and ethereal, the powerful verticality of the numerous monumental chimneys, transformed into so many characters from some celestial opera, alternates with the subtle curves and changes of level of the steps, which seem to multiply into a magical, theatrical illusion. Viewed by moonlight, this inspired play on different levels anticipates the epic power of Fritz Lang's *Metropolis* (1927) or Eisenstein's *Battleship Potemkin* (1925). Transcending Mediterranean Art Nouveau, Gaudí's visionary talent heralds the developments of Northern European Expressionism.

LEFT
The roof terrace of the Casa Milà in Barcelona, also known as La Pedrera, completed by Gaudí in 1910.

OPPOSITE
Main entrance to the Parc Güell in Barcelona, laid out from 1900 by Antoni Gaudí.

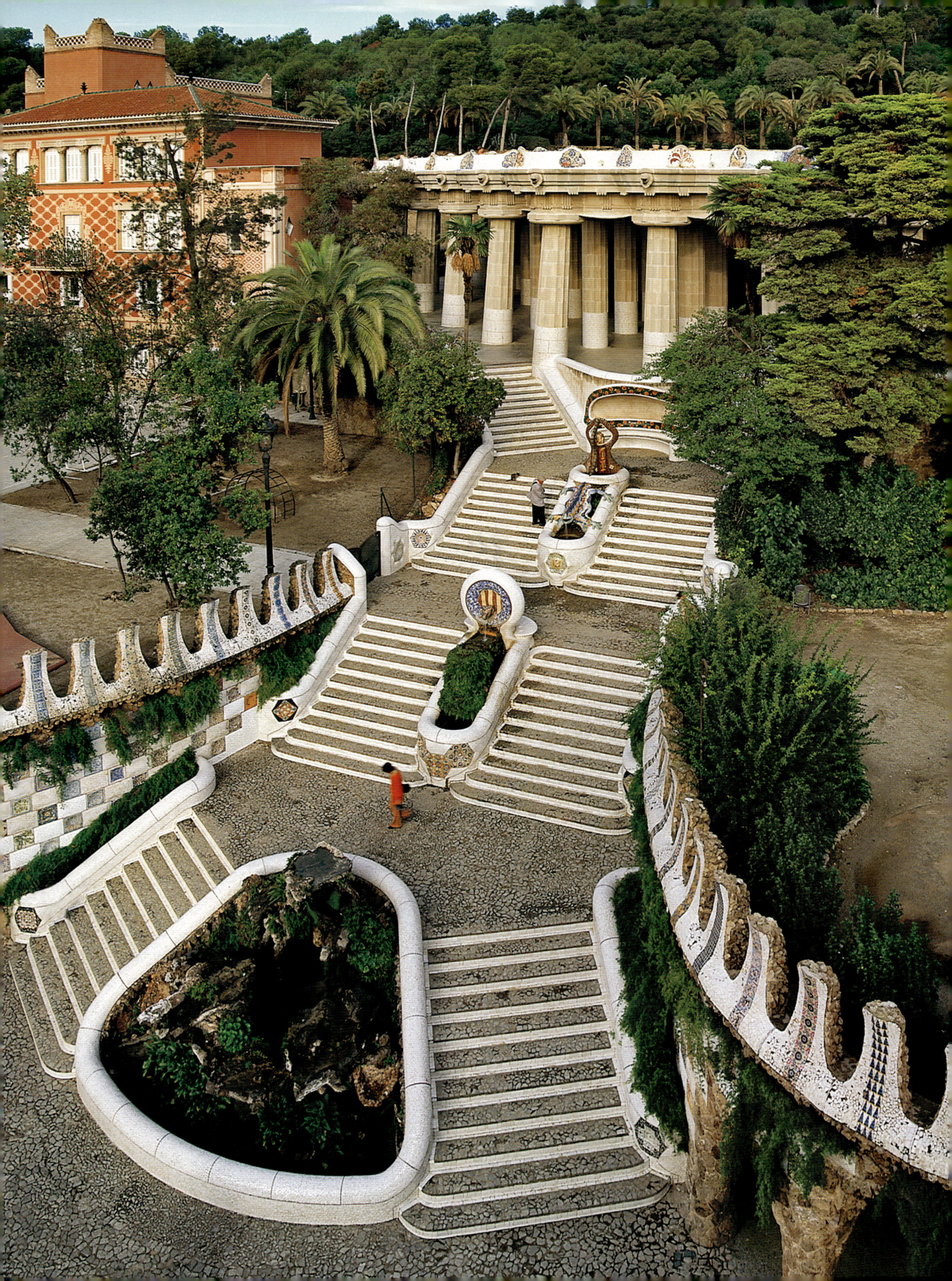

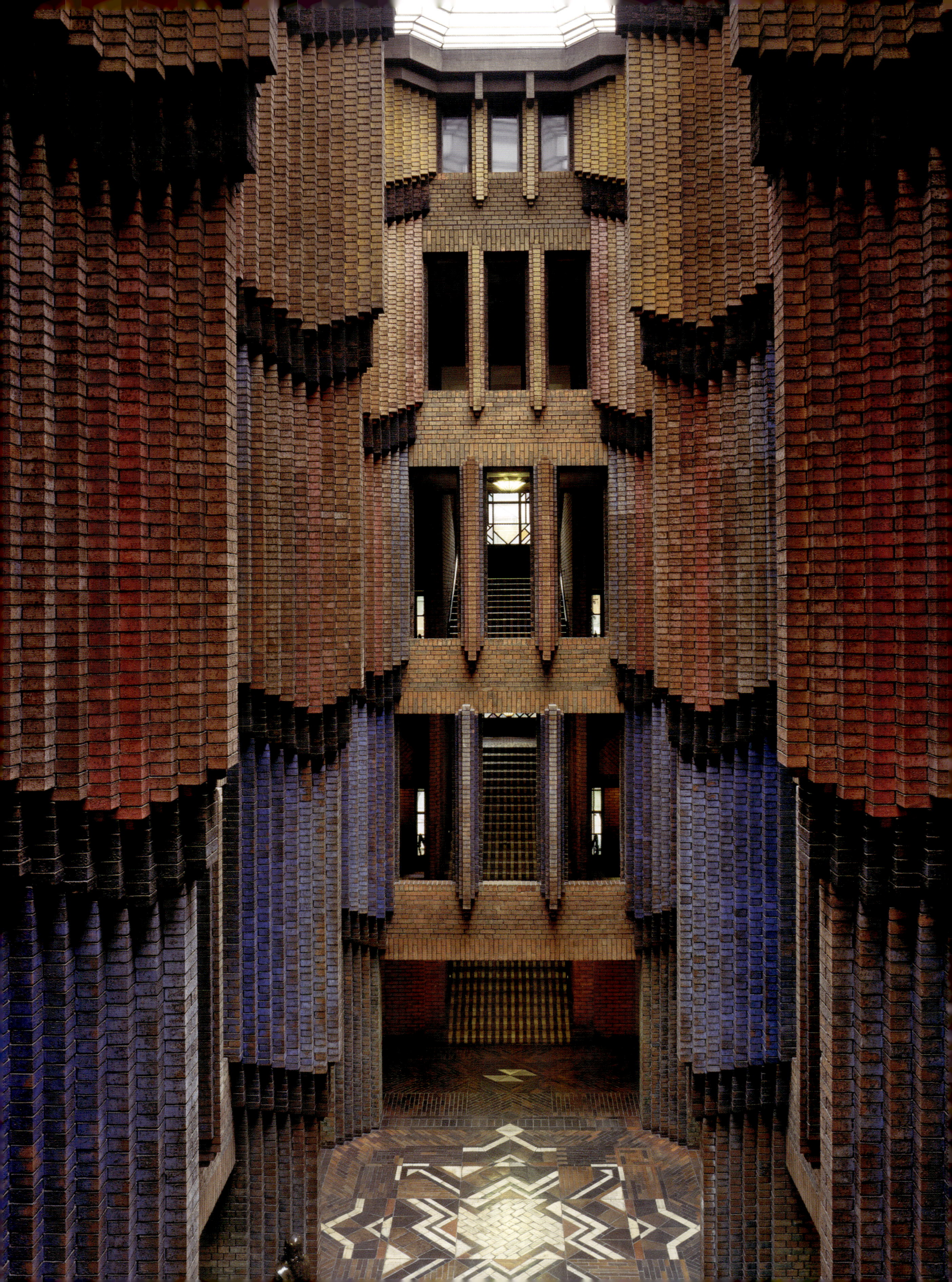

OPPOSITE
The main hall of the Frankfurt headquarters of the IG Farben company, an Expressionist masterpiece built by Peter Behrens from 1920.

RIGHT
The central hall of the Scheepvaarthuis (Shipping House) in Amsterdam, built from 1912 by the architects J. M. van der Meij, P. L. Kramer and Michel de Klerk. In 2005 this masterpiece of the Amsterdam School of Expressionist architecture was skilfully converted into a luxury hotel.

OVERLEAF
The Goetheanum, the headquarters of the General Anthroposophical Society. It was built at Dornach, near Basel, by the Austrian philosopher Rudolf Steiner and opened in 1928.

EXPRESSIONISM Of all European artistic movements of the twentieth century, Expressionism left the most powerful mark on the widest variety of disciplines, including painting and sculpture, literature and cinema, music, dance and architecture. But in its geographical scope its supremacy was limited to Germany and a few neighbouring countries. Having made its appearance in the 1910s, Expressionism flourished until 1933, when Nazism and the Third Reich denounced this great cultural movement as 'degenerate'. While Art Nouveau drew much of its inspiration from the world of plants, Expressionist architecture was more mineral in conception. But the ideal of fusing the arts and crafts remained common to both movements. Unlike the Rationalist movement that was to come after it, Expressionism viewed itself as the projection of subjectivity seeking a heightened expression of emotions. Under the influence of Sigmund Freud and Carl Jung, the exploration of the psychological effects of form and space was now taken up by a number of architects. It was an approach that would lead them to pay particular attention to the spatial, symbolic and aesthetic treatment of staircases, which essentially contributed to an emotional and poetic perception of the spirit of place.

In 1920 Peter Behrens built the headquarters of the IG Farben company (later refounded as Hoechst after the company's indictment in Nazi war crimes). His great central hall transforms the space into a cascading composition of stalactites and stalagmites in polychrome brick, their powerful rhythms echoing and enhancing its monumental staircase.

The Atlantis Haus, built in 1931 on Bremen's famous Böttcherstrasse, immediately became one of the most outstanding examples of Expressionist architecture. It is revealing that the man who designed it, Bernhard Hoetger, was not an architect by training, but was rather a painter and sculptor influenced by both Rodin and Gaudí. The stairwell of this building is his masterpiece (p. 198). Here, he created a space that was at once intimate and powerful, in which the manifold resources of art and craftsmanship were combined to celebrate dynamic beauty, a luminous verticality and dazzling lyricism.

The Austrian philosopher, social reformer and pedagogue Rudolf Steiner was the founder of the anthroposophical movement, which sought to 'restore the link between Man and the spiritual worlds'. At Dornach, near Basel in Switzerland, he built his 'Goetheanum' as the seat of the General Anthroposophical Society. The final version of this project, which opened in 1928, was one of the first major cultural buildings in Europe to be built of reinforced concrete, deliberately left in its raw state. The grand staircases of this temple to a new ethic are both massive and lyrical (pp. 196–97), evoking an organic Expressionism but using a deliberately puritanical and austere vocabulary that anticipates what would later be called Brutalism. The Goetheanum can thus be viewed as a bunker of faith.

From 1910 Expressionism also took root in the Dutch capital, where it became known as the Amsterdam School, setting in train a new architecture of exceptional creative zest and harmony. Although the Netherlands was historically a Protestant country – the place where in 1908 Adolf Loos had published his influential purist manifesto *Ornament*

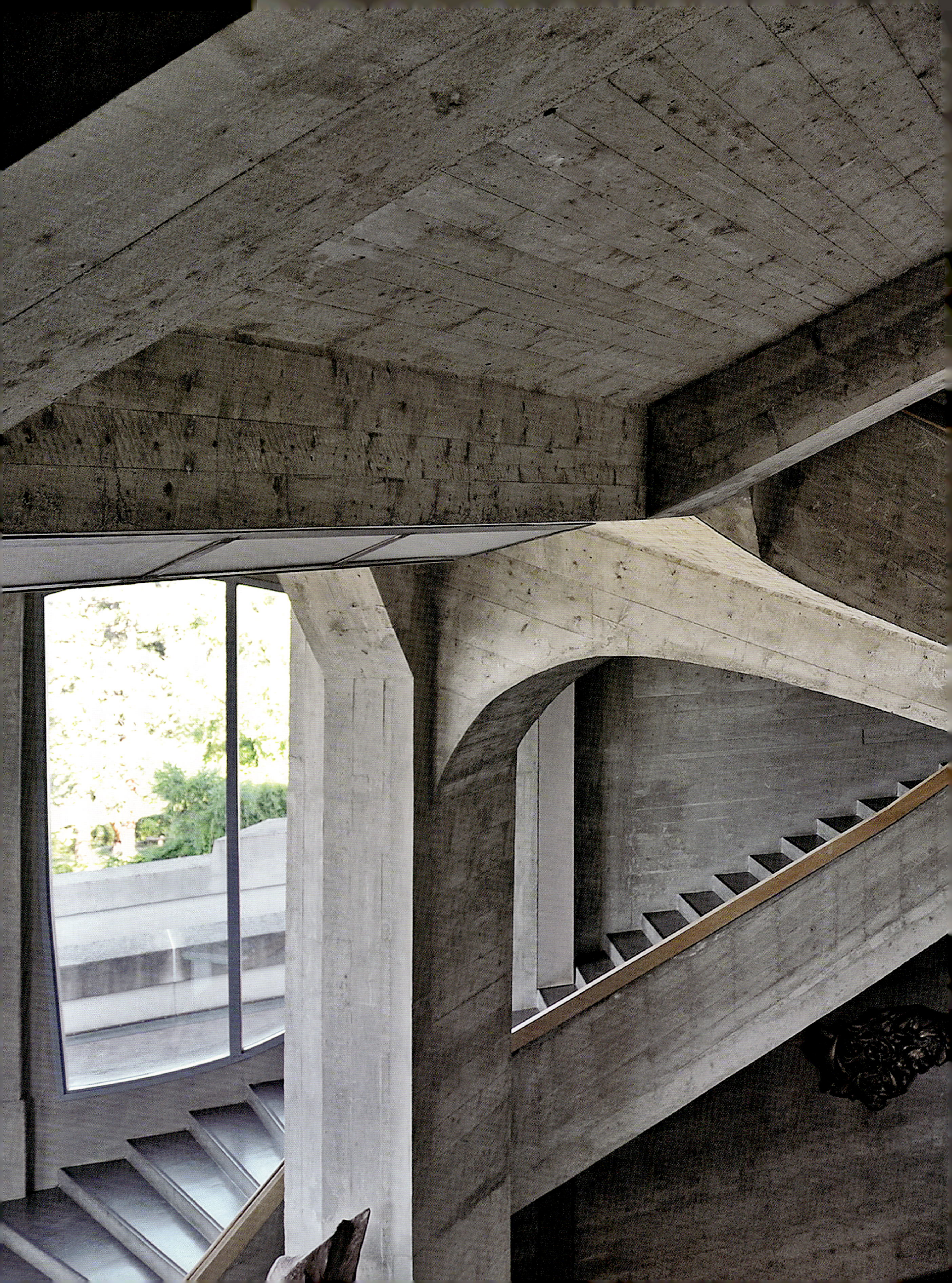

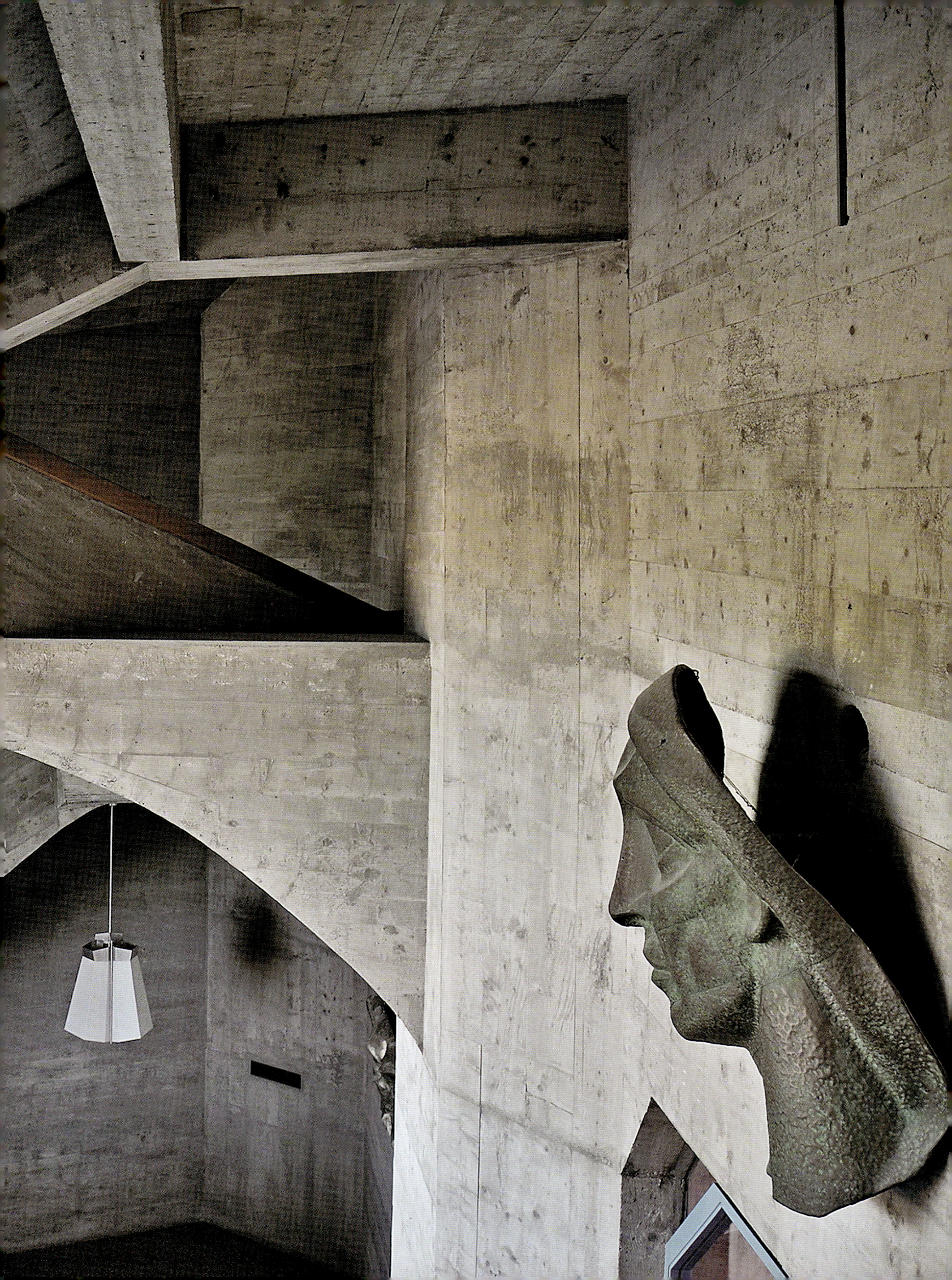

and Crime – architectonic decoration remained a favoured means of creating an exhilarating synthesis of architecture, art and craftsmanship. In 1912 work began on the sublime Scheepvaarthuis, designed by J. M van der Meij, P. L. Kramer and Michel de Klerk (p. 195). In 2005 this 'Shipping House' was skilfully converted into a luxury hotel. Even in its new guise, this maritime cathedral remains a major masterpiece of European Expressionism. On entering, the visitor is struck by the almost mystical atmosphere of an interior that reaches its artistic apotheosis in the staircase. The immense space in which this structure unfolds, over five floors, is conceived in the form of an inverted ship's hull and is flooded with warm and vibrant light, filtered through a vast glass roof studded with stained-glass windows in geometric patterns that herald the spirit of Art Deco.

LEFT
The stairwell of the Atlantis Haus, built in 1931 by Bernhard Hoetger on Böttcherstrasse in Bremen, Germany.

FUTURISM AND CONSTRUCTIVISM A number of modern cultural movements issued impassioned manifestos – sometimes lucid, sometimes violent – to declare their ambition of bringing about a revolution in the arts and architecture. Among them were the Futurists and the Constructivists. Futurism, born in Italy, rejected the heritage of history wholesale in order to focus its energies on celebrating the modern world: urban and industrial civilization, the machine, speed and the dynamic vitality of movement. Inspired by these values, the architect and set designer Virgilio Marchi designed curvilinear buildings of great forcefulness, traversed from top to bottom by soaring external staircases that shot off in all directions, as if looking for new civilizations to conquer. In his drawings of this Futurist utopia, people crowd eagerly onto these thrusting new stairways, the embodiment of progress.

In Russia, modernism initially followed the paths created by Cubism in France and by Futurism in Italy. The Cubo-Futurist movement flourished in Moscow between 1910 and 1917 in the hands of avant-garde artists such as Vladimir Tatlin. It was Tatlin who was called on by the new regime of the proletariat to draw up a manifesto for the culture of the Revolution. The style that emerged, known as Constructivism, also sought to bring together the arts and architecture. These disciplines were now at the service of the emancipated Russian people and were to be an expression of their new ambition. This movement was driven by Communist strategy and included a particular focus on the 'geometric reconstruction of space'. In 1919 Tatlin conceived a masterpiece, the most celebrated and iconic product

FAR LEFT
Unbuilt design for a Futurist housing project by the Italian architect Virgilio Marchi, c. 1919.

LEFT
Drawing for the Monument to the Third International, *designed by Vladimir Tatlin in 1919. Though never realized, it remains the masterwork of Russian Constructivist utopianism.*

of Constructivism: the *Monument to the Third International*. Consisting of an 'inhabited tower' in steel, the project was on a gigantic scale: it was intended to demonstrate the strength and vision of the Soviet Union and would have risen far higher than the Eiffel Tower. Tatlin's monument was designed to thrust into space three colossal geometrical symbols evoking the new power of the Komintern. Suspended within the central space were a cube (at the bottom, marked A on the drawing) to house a vast hall for political meetings; a central cone (B), dedicated to executive bodies; and at the top a cylinder (C) to accommodate the media and educational activities. These three giant volumes were strengthened by an external supporting structure in the form of a double helix, full of swooping, vital energy. Stairs would allow public access to the tallest observatory on the planet. These spiralling steps were accorded the status of a supreme symbol of social dynamism, stretching upwards toward progress. Though never built, this example of utopian architecture remains one of the icons of modernism.

THE BAUHAUS In the early twentieth century, Germany became the world centre for the development of teaching methods aimed at creating a new symbiosis between the arts, crafts and architecture. This initiative, which proved to be of universal significance, was started in Weimar in 1908 by the Belgian

RIGHT
The Sommerfeld House, Berlin, built in 1920 by an interdisciplinary team of professors and students from the Bauhaus School under the direction of Walter Gropius. Sadly, this seminal example of the Bauhaus ethic was destroyed during the Second World War.

artist Henry Van de Velde, who in 1919 appointed Walter Gropius as his successor. It was Gropius who published the *Bauhaus Manifesto*, proclaiming that 'the ultimate goal of all plastic activity is construction: together we must invent for the future a new art of building'. Convinced that the principle of working in interdisciplinary teams was the way forward, he was committed to the idea of bringing together teachers, researchers and students, 'to embrace architecture and sculpture and painting in one unity'.

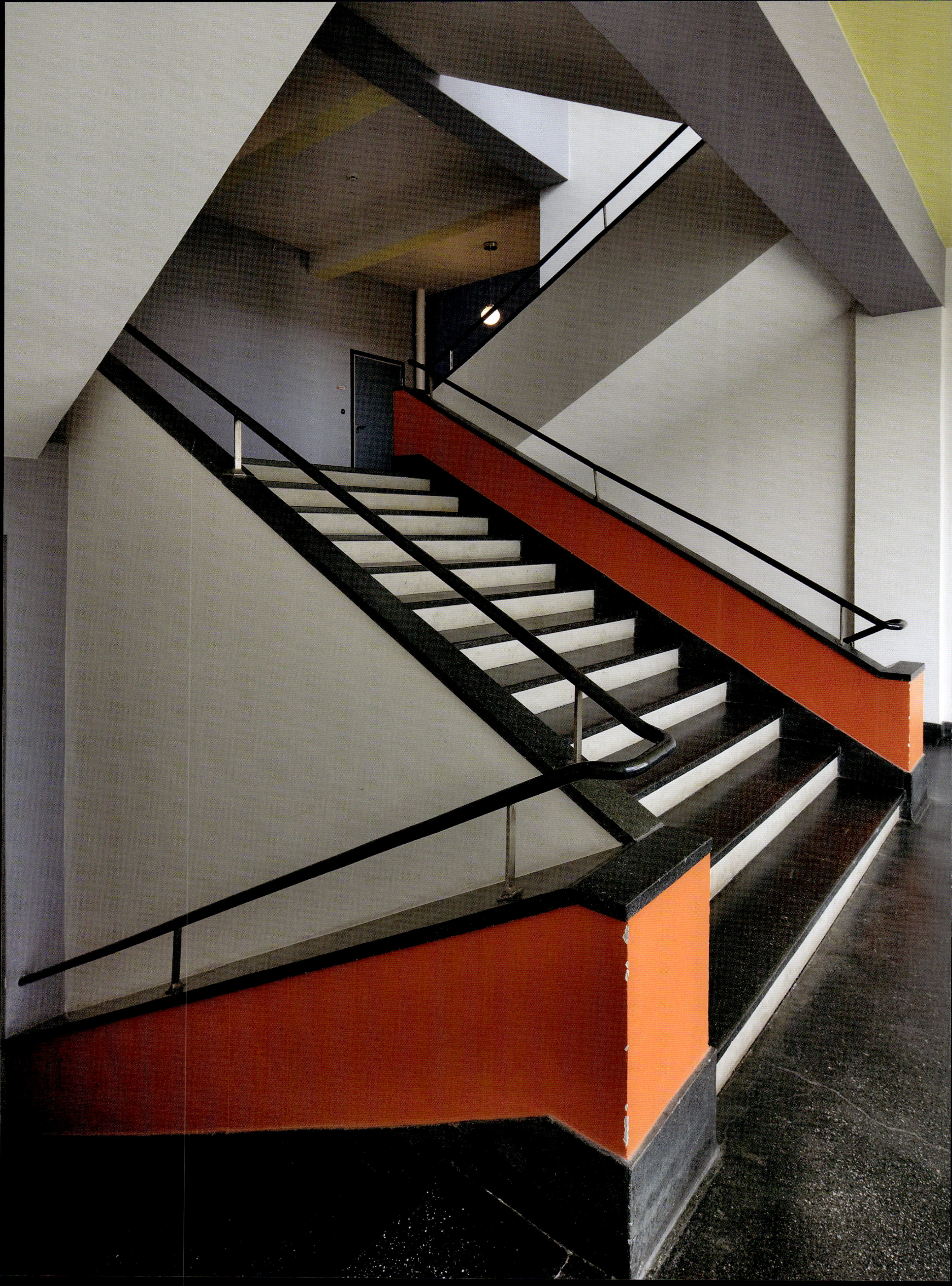

OPPOSITE
The principal staircase of the Bauhaus School in Dessau, by Walter Gropius (1925). This iconic building of German Functionalism, now restored, has been classified as a UNESCO World Heritage Site.

RIGHT
Two interior views of the houses built at Dessau by Walter Gropius in 1925 to house teachers from the Bauhaus School, including, notably, the artist Paul Klee.

OVERLEAF
Vitebsky railway station in St Petersburg, built in 1904 by the architects Brzozowski and Minash.

In 1920 Gropius began work on the experimental timber construction of the Sommerfeld House in Berlin (p. 199). Although this built manifesto was still of Expressionist inspiration and displayed the early American influence of Frank Lloyd Wright, it offered the first three-dimensional expression of the Bauhaus ideal: the creation of a total work of art. At its heart, Joost Schmidt created a skilful and dynamic staircase to link the drawing room with the first floor. This legendary building exemplified the quest for a new type of middle-class dwelling that would be both modern and cosy.

In 1925 the Bauhaus moved to the industrial city of Dessau, where it made an ideological change of direction in favour of the industrialization of the building process. It was in this avant-garde spirit – now stripped of the emotional connotations of Expressionism – that Gropius designed the school's buildings. His most important work, the new Bauhaus was emblematic of the Functionalist movement that would soon to give birth to the International Style in architecture. And at the school's heart was a staircase that would also acquire iconic status.

That same year Gropius built a number of houses for the Bauhaus teachers. These were effectively experimental prototypes of the new dwelling space, in which Gropius's use of geometric volumes and bright colours – blue, white, red and yellow – transformed the internal staircase into a work of chromatic sculpture. When the Nazi party came to power in 1933 it demonstrated its violent opposition to the doctrines of the Bauhaus by immediately shutting the school down. The buildings, damaged during the war, were eventually restored and in 1996 were classified as a UNESCO World Heritage Site.

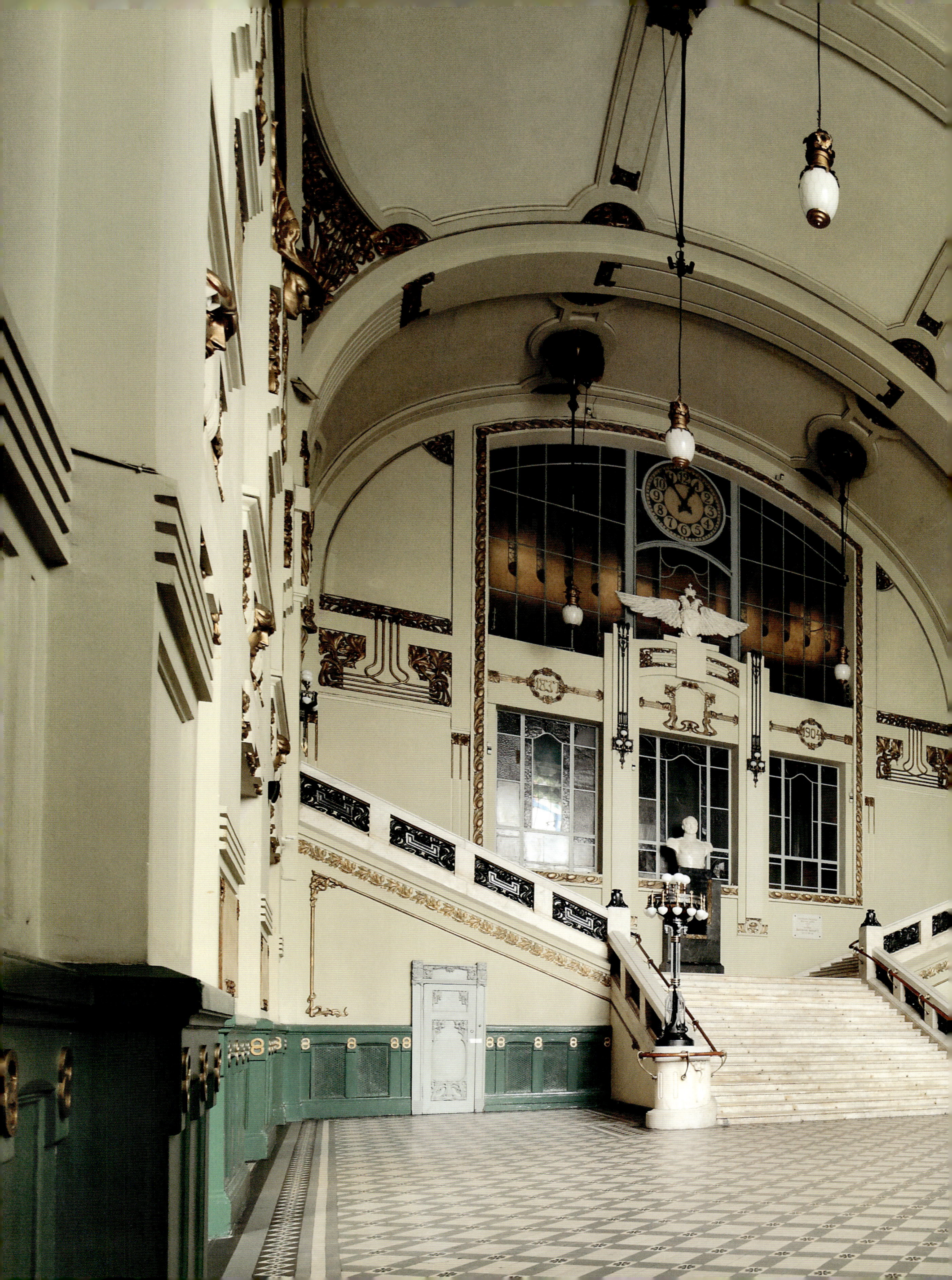
1904

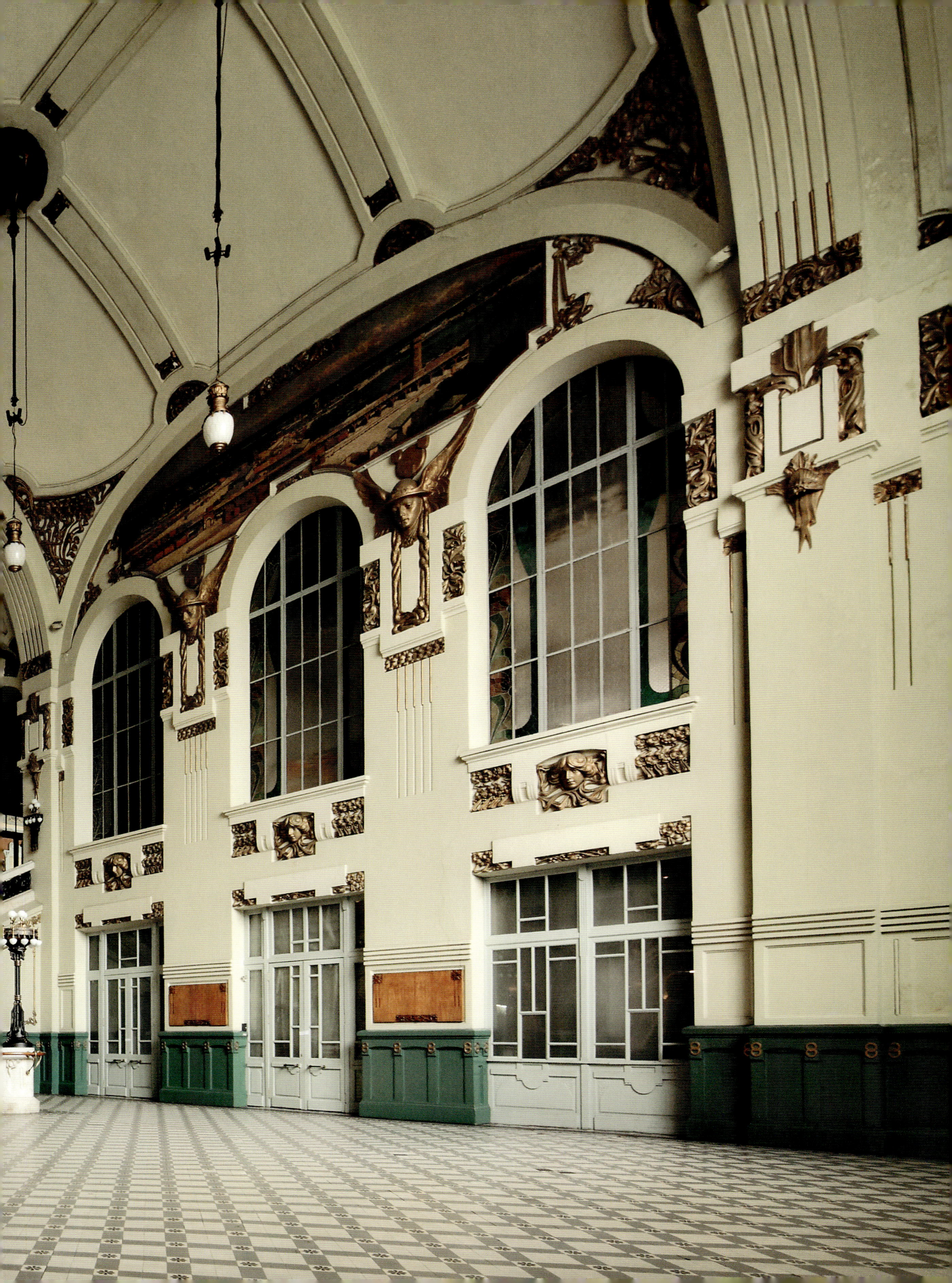

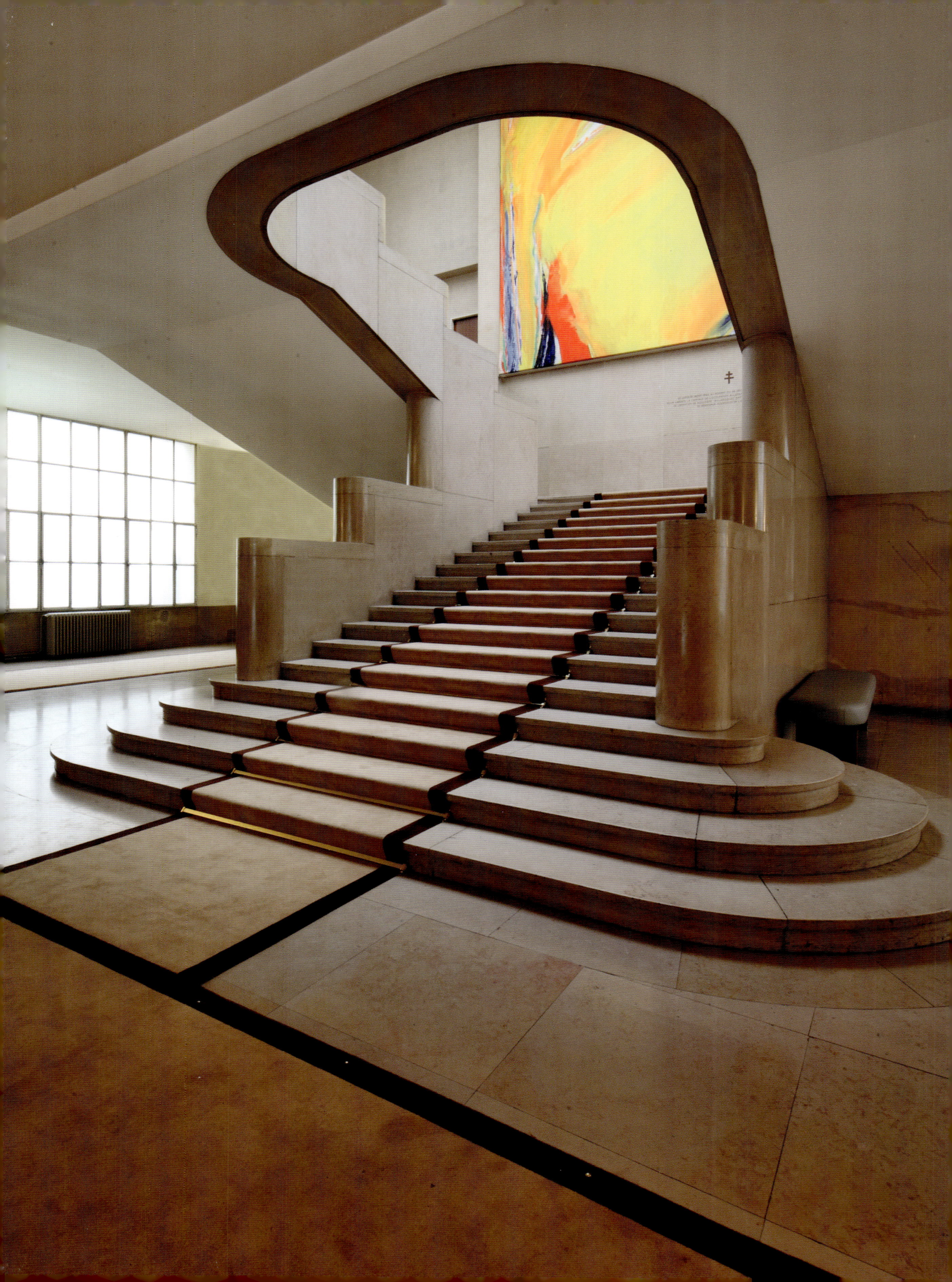

OPPOSITE
The vestibule of the town hall at Boulogne-Billancourt, Paris, built in 1934 by Tony Garnier.

RIGHT
The Custom House in Philadelphia, built in 1932 by Ritter & Shay.

RIGHT
The grand helical staircase in the Vatican Museums, Rome. Rising the full height of the building, it was designed in 1932 by Giuseppe Momo.

OVERLEAF
Auguste Perret's staircase in reinforced concrete built in 1937 for the Musée National des Travaux Publics on Place d'Iéna, Paris.

THE ÉCOLE DES BEAUX-ARTS In the face the wildly different avant-garde movements flooding Europe with a constant stream of innovation, the famed École des Beaux-Arts in Paris remained an unassailable bastion of orthodox, traditionalist teaching, both in architecture and in other disciplines. (The teaching of architecture was hived off in 1968.) The students who flocked here from all over the world were therefore responsible for exporting a historicist approach to architecture. This was particularly visible in a number of monumental staircases from the first half of the twentieth century.

In Rome, there was Giuseppe Momo's elegant spiralling staircase rising the full height of the Vatican Museums, built in 1932. The architects of the US Custom House in Philadelphia, Ritter & Shay, flanked their helicoidal staircase – constructed in buff-coloured travertine, with an aluminium guardrail punctuated by gilt mascarons – with fluted black marble columns of impeccably classical pedigree. And in Russia, the grand staircase of the Vitebsky railway station (pp. 202–3), built in St Petersburg in 1904 by Stanislaw Brzozowski and Sima Minash, is a joyous combination of Neoclassical regularity and symmetry, lightened with decorative Art Nouveau flourishes.

Paris – home to the École des Beaux-Arts, just across the river from the Louvre, since 1692 – was not short of staircases that bore witness to this academic institution's long and powerful influence, and to the monumental, grandiose styles it favoured. Charles Garnier's tour de force at the Paris Opéra (1875), which provided a theatrical, stylish backdrop to high society in all its finery, was a bravura example of the type (pp. 128–29, 132–33). Tony Garnier's staircase for the town hall of Boulogne-Billancourt near Paris, built in 1934, attempted to combine Neoclassicism and Art Deco. By contrast, Auguste Perret – also a graduate of the Beaux-Arts – managed to create a harmonious combination of Neoclassicism and Functionalism in the exposed reinforced-concrete staircase he designed in 1937 for the Palais d'Iéna in Paris, now an icon of modernism (pp. 206–7). Its elegant curves are an apposite illustration of one of Perret's sayings: 'Architecture takes possession of space and structure; it therefore enjoys the privilege of creating a work that is of fundamental importance for the magic of a place.'

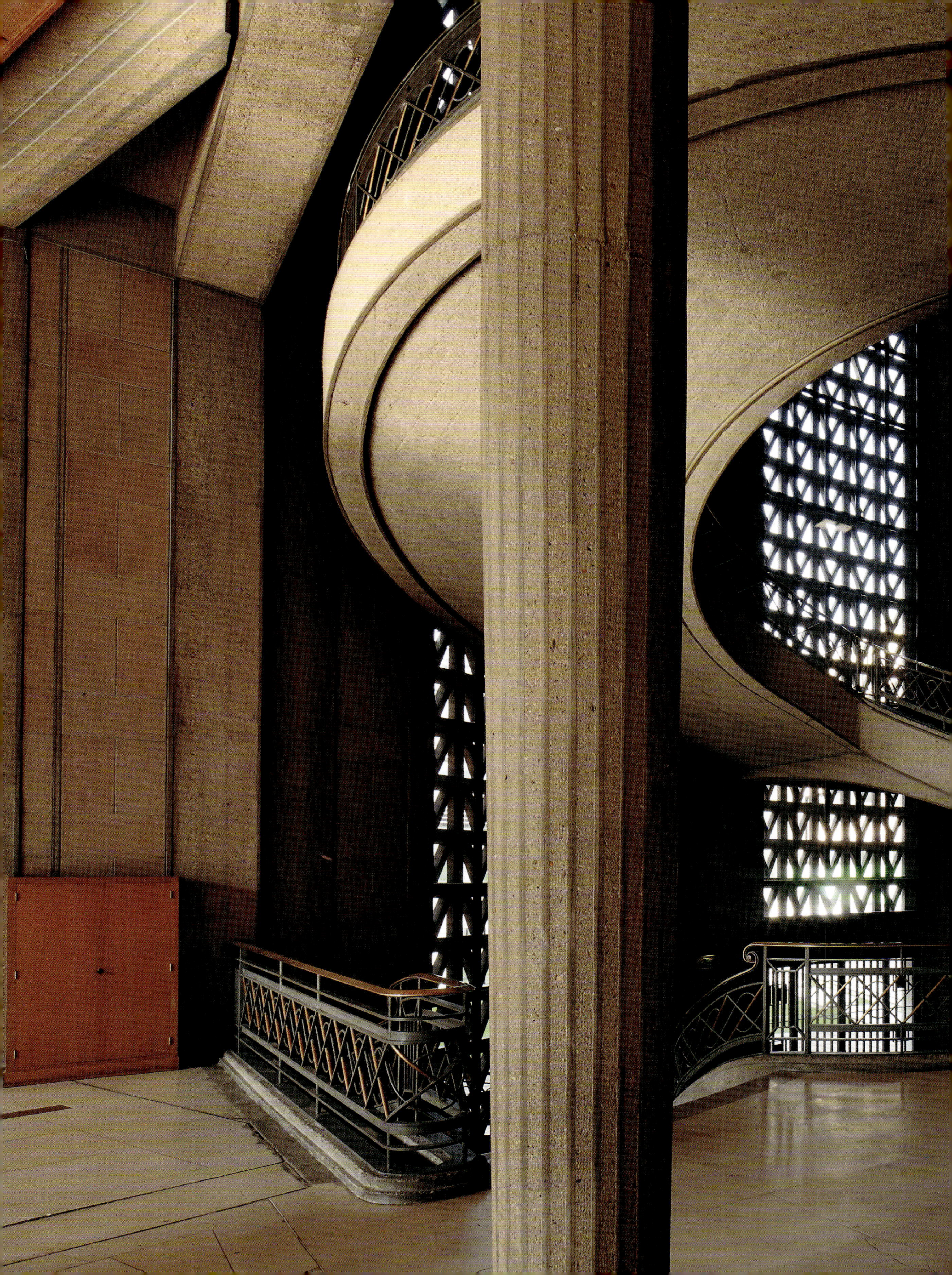

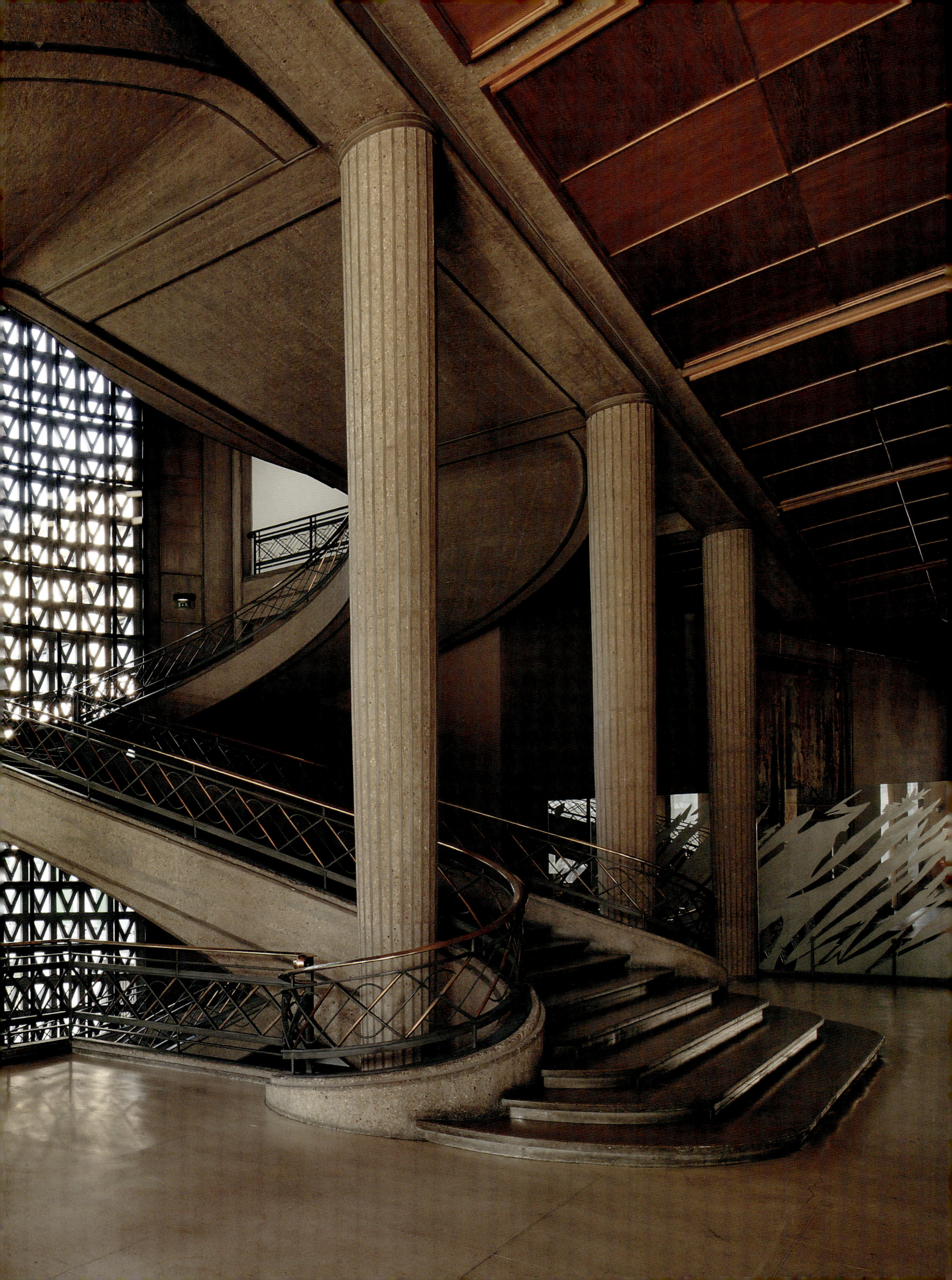

FUNCTIONALISM After the innumerable battles between the 'ancients' and the 'moderns' that punctuated the first part of the twentieth century, architecture inspired by the ideology of Functionalism began to achieve universal dominance in the 1920s and 1930s. Dubbed the 'International Style', its name pointed to the global reach of cultural movements that would soon sweep the world. Even within the context of 'orthodox' modernity, the staircases designed for these avant-garde buildings displayed a great diversity of form and construction.

For the Deutscher Werkbund exhibition in Cologne in 1914, Bruno Taut built his Glass Pavilion, which was conceived as a prototype for an 'art-lover's house' and can be seen as transitional between Expressionism and Rationalism. Three types of stair served this glass-domed structure. Outside, steps led up to the plinth on which the structure stood, in classic fashion. Inside, the first floor was reached via stairs made from glass tiles, which hugged a curved wall, also of glass (Taut thus invented the first 'staircase of light', which radiates the spirit of modernity). Finally, the studio space at the top of the house was crossed by three parallel stepped descents lined with polychrome ceramic tiles, the central one forming a magical 'waterfall staircase'.

The same year Le Corbusier produced his prophetic design encapsulating the essence of the modern dwelling. The Domino House consisted of a reinforced-concrete structure composed simply of three horizontal slabs and six supporting pillars, the only 'event' punctuating this domestic space of the future being its four flights of stairs. Reduced to its essentials, the 'machine for living' heralded the implacable logic of an architecture for a new era. In 1924 Le Corbusier proposed a project for an 'artisan's house'. Here, the spacious living room was split over two levels. Occupying the centre of the space was a sculptural concrete staircase, its single, straight flight – slim, linear and diagonal – providing the composition with a strong visual dynamic.

The following year, Konstantin Melnikov designed the Soviet Pavilion for the Exposition Internationale des Arts Décoratifs in Paris. Here, initiating a symbiosis between Russian Constructivism and French Rationalism, he proposed a similar concept, but this time on a monumental scale. Spanning the building diagonally, his immense staircase helped to create the powerful dynamic of this architectural space.

In 1926 the Swiss architect Hannes Meyer was unsuccessful with his design for a competition to build a large school in Basel, the Petersschule. His bold idea was well ahead of its time, featuring an immense strip of staircases suspended in space and running the full length of the main façade. This considered externalization of the stair system displayed the ideals of the Neue Sachlichkeit ('new objectivity') movement. It was to be another fifty years before Meyer's visionary concept was transformed into 'objective' reality, on the façade of the Pompidou Centre in Paris (p. 213).

During the 1920s and 1930s Le Corbusier emerged as one of the most influential pioneers of the twentieth century. His Villa Savoye – a weekend house for a well-to-do middle-class family, completed in 1931 at Poissy, near Paris – was one of the most elegant, seductive and polished manifestos of his style. It illustrates the vocabulary that he defined as the 'five points of architecture': pilotis, a flat roof terrace, ribbon windows, an open plan and a façade free of structural members. To impose unity on these different elements he deployed a varied range of staircases and inclined planes, creating a spatial dynamic of great power. The villa that Marcel and Henri Leborgne built between 1929 and 1933 for the industrialist H. Dirickz on the outskirts of Brussels follows the same 'radiant' logic of eloquent architectural purism. But here a spectacular spiral staircase, erected in reinforced concrete on the outside of one of the façades, claims a sculptural autonomy.

FROM ORGANIC TO HIGH TECH After the violence and brutality of the Second World War, it might have been hoped that an architecture would appear that would inspire a new humanism in survivors and restore their faith in life. But the opposite was the case. Never in European history has the construction

LEFT
The Glass Pavilion, by Bruno Taut for the Deutscher Werkbund exhibition in Cologne in 1914 (since demolished).

OPPOSITE
The graceful staircase of the Villa Savoye at Poissy, built by Le Corbusier between 1929 and 1931. Acquired by the French Ministry of Culture and classified as a historic monument in 1965, it is now open to the public.

OVERLEAF
The staircase in Le Corbusier's Paris apartment and studio, which he designed himself in collaboration with his cousin Pierre Jeanneret.

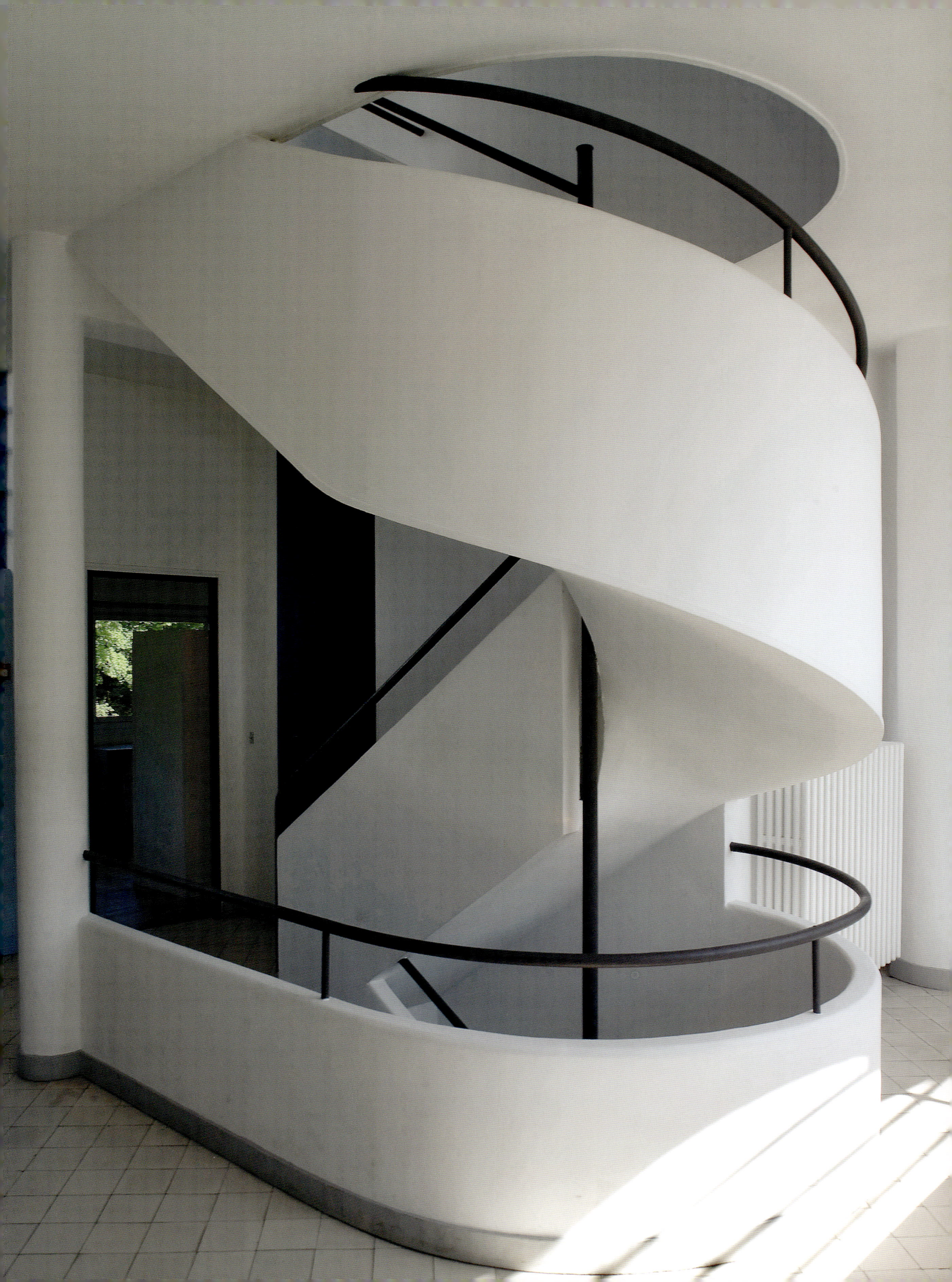

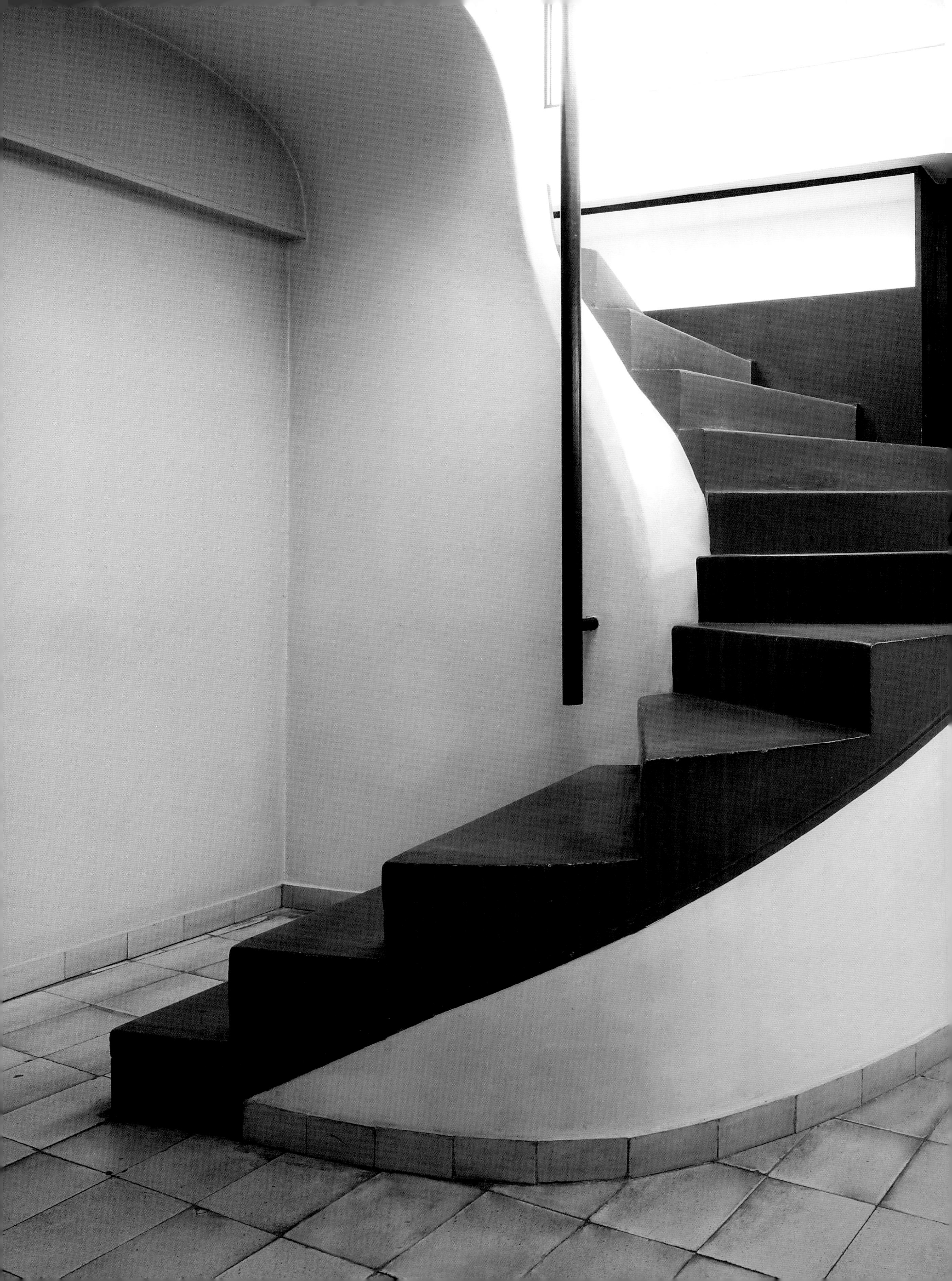

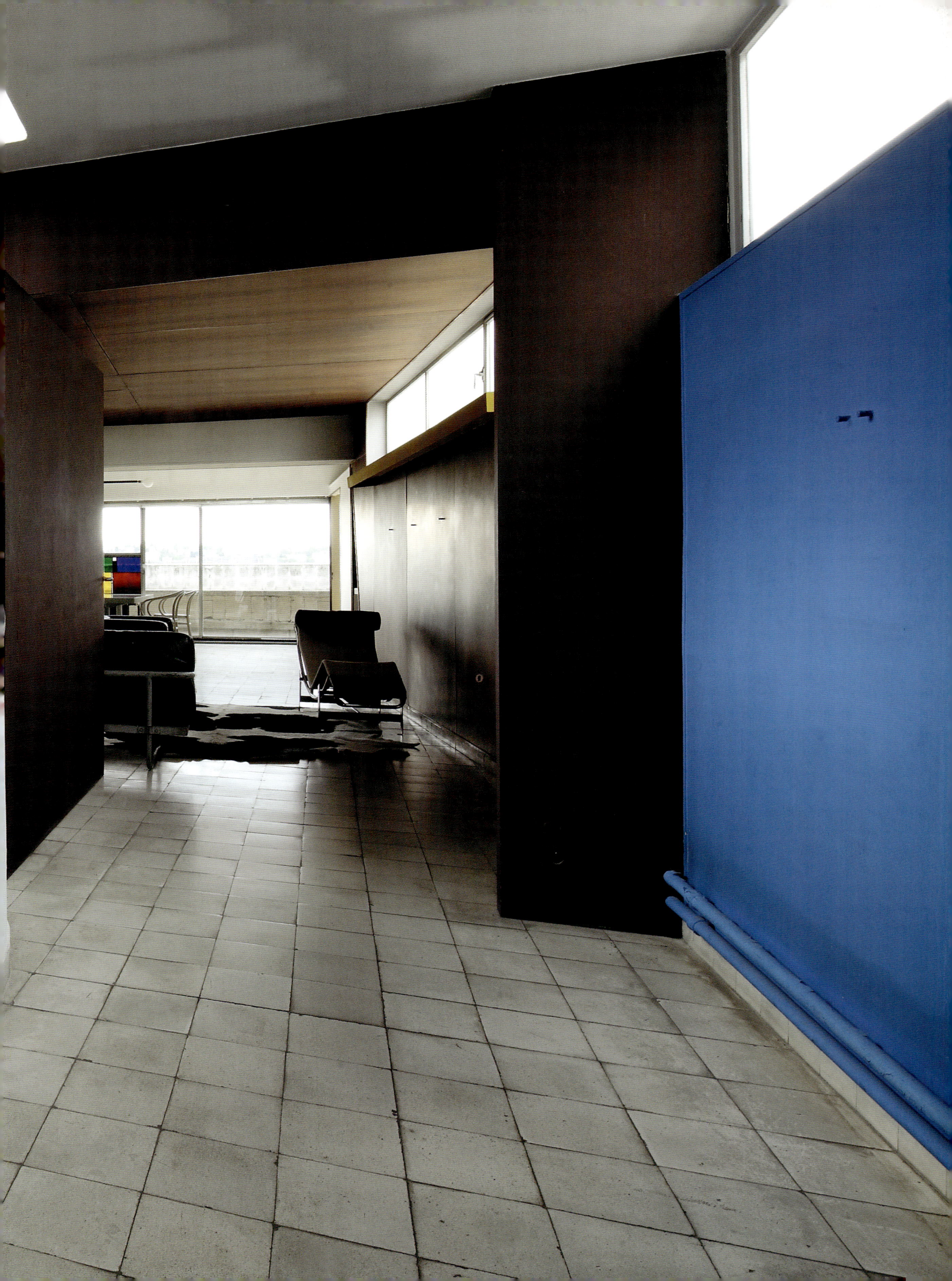

of towns and dwellings been so stereotyped, technocratic and uninviting. The building sector started on a course of massive industrialization from 1946, adopting the rationale underpinning Henry Ford's automobile production lines in America. Thus 'Fordism' joined forces with Functionalism to produce a culturally nihilistic architecture devoid of any vital élan. It was from the forces of nature, by contrast, that Frank Lloyd Wright drew inspiration for his doctrine of organic architecture, which he developed in America from 1939. It was a philosophy that revived a lost harmony between man and his environment, and that celebrated life, its rhythms and its dynamic. And it was a choice that led Wright to favour the vigorously expressive nature of architectonic features dedicated to human motion.

In Wright's final masterpiece – the Solomon R. Guggenheim Museum in New York, which opened in 1959 – the building's overall form, both internally and externally, is dictated by a desire to celebrate the movement of visitors through the museum's six floors. Rather than slice the space into self-contained

FAR LEFT AND LEFT
The iconic quality of the Guggenheim Museum in New York – Frank Lloyd Wright's final work, completed in 1959 – derives from his decision to use the helical ramp surrounding the circular atrium as a unifying theme.

levels, and allow conventional access arrangements between them, Wright adopted the novel approach of an immense central atrium – circular and roofed with a glazed dome – around which spirals a broad ramp, allowing visitors to amble up and down, and to move into the many different exhibition spaces on the way. Here, the magic of place is twofold: inside, it creates a warm and lively intimacy; outside, facing the natural landscape of Central Park, it highlights – with unrivalled sculptural power – the museum's internal logic and the dynamic flow of movement within. Never since has a gentle slope been used to replace stairs with such grace and power.

During the 1970s, as a counterpoint to the nature-based, humanist ethic of this organic architecture, there appeared – particularly in Europe – a new fascination with cutting-edge technology, dubbed 'High Tech'. Ushering in a new phase in the evolution of modernism, it was championed in opposition to the historicist and neo-vernacular approaches espoused by Post-modernism. Welcoming of scientific progress – and especially the conquest of space, culminating in the Moon landing of 1969 – and allergic to all forms of cultural nostalgia, High Tech architects incorporated a variety of industrial elements in their architectural concepts.

A telling example, which opened in the Beaubourg district of Paris in 1977, and which was immediately nicknamed the 'gasworks' or 'culture refinery', was the Pompidou Centre. In effect, this building invented a vocabulary with which to celebrate technological progress. In a grandiose theatrical gesture, Richard Rogers and Renzo Piano, the architects, strung a multitude of stairways across the full width of the

RIGHT
Richard Rogers's Lloyds Building in the City of London, completed in 1986.

main façade. Innovative in terms of both architecture and urban design, the stairway stretched across all six floors, obeying two complementary rationales: the functional and the geometric. On the one hand, two sets of emergency stairs on a vertical axis permit the evacuation of visitors in case of danger. On the other, the constant movement of the public in both directions is assured by two immensely long escalators – one up, one down – on the outside of the façade. In a spectacular *coup de théâtre*, the escalators are suspended up to 50 metres (164 feet) in the air. They form the major unifying feature of the composition: a powerful diagonal, brought alive by the movement of visitors, that transforms this inspired building into a work that is both kinetic and dynamic. It is this inventiveness that has made the Pompidou Centre a major icon of modern times. Its logo, designed in 1977 by the graphic artist Jean Widmer, is moreover reduced to this single unique feature, conveyed in a few forceful strokes: six horizontal lines signify the floors, bisected by two parallel diagonals rising level by level. So it was that the great Piano and Rogers escalator also became one of the most memorable symbols of visual communication.

The Lloyds Building in London, designed by Richard Rogers and completed in 1986, also wore its High Tech credentials on its sleeve. This high-rise office building avoided the genre's usual banality by once again pushing a multitude of emergency stairs beyond the envelope of the building. All are sheathed in aluminium – a generous gesture that endows them with a sense of movement and a sculptural dimension.

The emergence of High Tech architecture was itself a form of radical opposition to what has sometimes been dubbed – be it ironically or patronizingly – 'low tech': a portmanteau term for traditional buildings not designed by architects. These structures are generally the result of a modest and appropriate use of the natural materials available within the proximity of a building site, which require no energy-inefficient industrial processes. Unlike High Tech architecture, low-tech buildings are by their nature ecologically friendly. This is particularly the case in Africa and Asia, which boast an abundance of traditional architecture, sometimes as recent as the twentieth century. In these examples, the sculptural expressiveness of the staircase is above all a sign of creative energy: here, it signifies an architecture whose performance is measured in terms not of technology, but of cultural and human value.

RIGHT
The Pompidou Centre in Paris, which opened in 1977, was designed by Renzo Piano and Richard Rogers. Theirs was the winning entry in an international competition presided over by Jean Prouvé in 1971.

OVERLEAF
The steps leading up to the Grande Arche de la Défense, Paris, by the Danish architect Johann Otto von Spreckelsen (1985). The building now houses the French Ministry of Ecology.

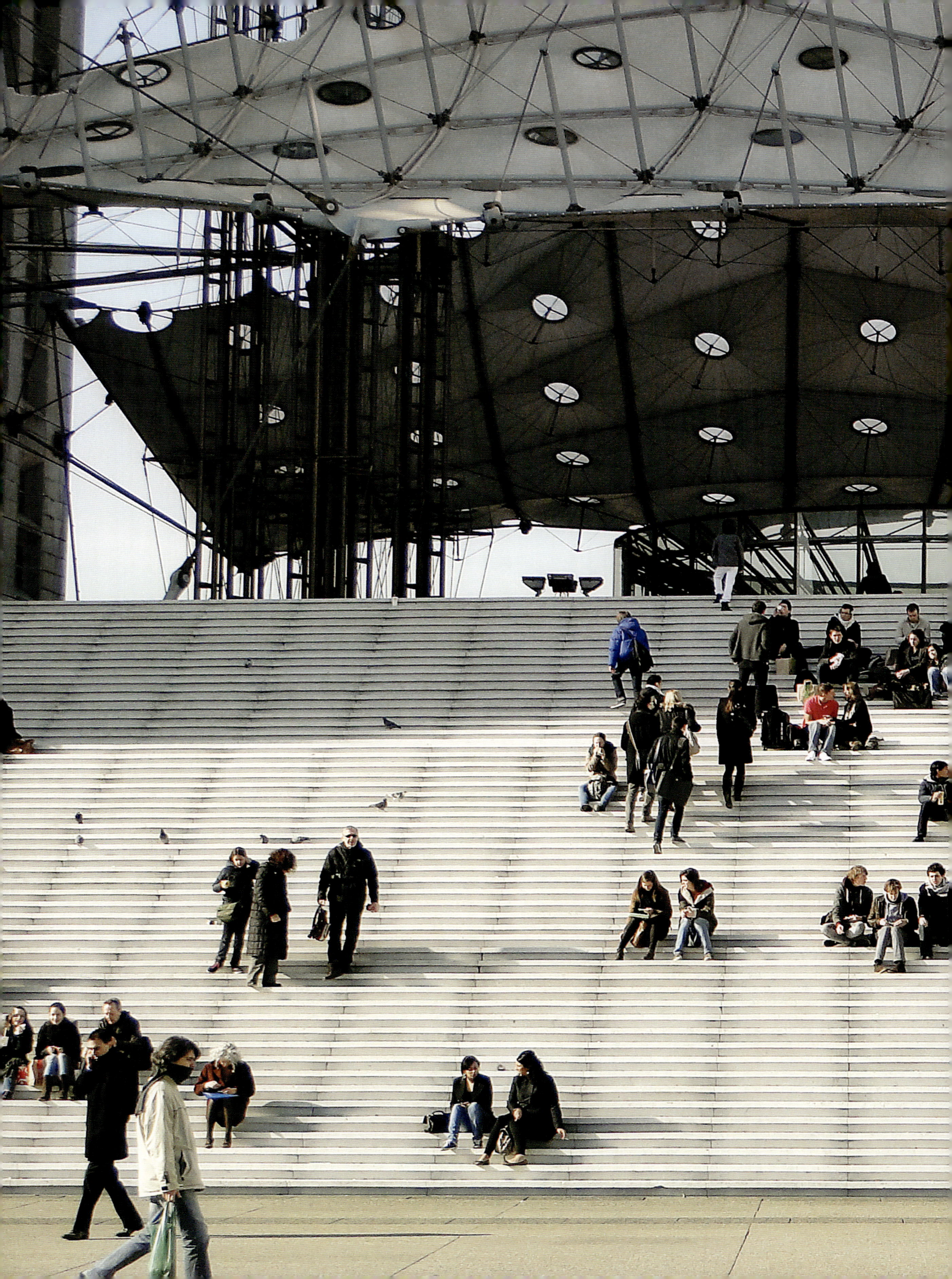

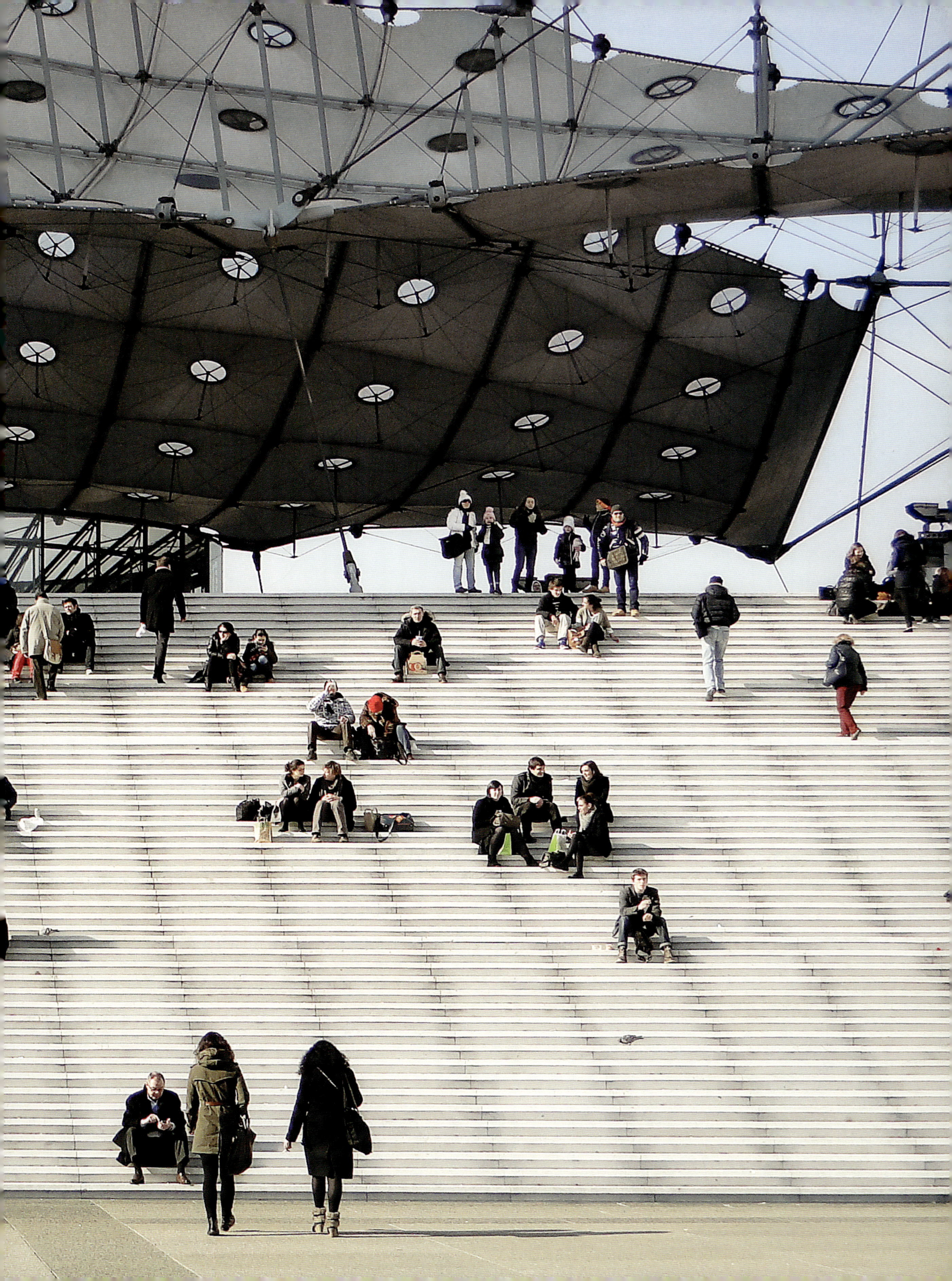

THE 'GRANDS PROJETS' IN PARIS The signs of a renewal in contemporary architecture became visible in Paris in the years between 1975 and 1995, as four successive French presidents adopted the strategy of the 'Grand Projets'. This was a programme of urban planning and construction intended to endow the city with a string of prestigious buildings devoted to cultural activities. Despite their avowedly modern nature, it is striking to notice that several of these buildings retained one ancient principle common to all grand civic architecture: they are lifted upwards, both visually and symbolically, by means of their imposing external stairs, which serve as a plinth. This time-honoured technique dates back to the Greeks and the Romans, who used it when constructing their temples, thus ensuring that places connected with the gods were treated with due solemnity and decorum.

The four towers of the new Bibliothèque Nationale de France, completed by Dominique Perrault in 1995, rest on an immense platform that overlooks the Seine from the top of a vertiginous flight of steps. The approach to this modern temple of knowledge is via a daunting sea of steps that the visitor is obliged to scale. Furthermore, they are made from an exotic wood that becomes dangerously slippery in wet weather. As many unfortunate victims have discovered, there are times when you climb these steps at your peril.

The Grande Arche de la Défense, built by Johann Otto von Spreckelsen in 1985, displays a similar trick: the great 'hollow cube', whose sides measure 112 metres (367 feet), stands on a plinth consisting of a particularly imposing flight of steps (pp. 214–15). With a little effort, the visitor can climb up to the entrance of the Ministry of Ecology, which appears to be elevated among the clouds, on a par with the gods of Olympus.

Among the Grands Projets that have eschewed this rather lofty approach is I. M. Pei's glass pyramid in the main courtyard of the Louvre, at the heart of this august institution. Since 1988 it has provided a logical means of accessing every wing of the museum. To reach the collections, instead of climbing up towards the heights of artistic and cultural achievement the visitor first goes down, following a system of accessibility that appears quite democratic. The descent is handled with grace: around a hydraulic lift of ethereal lightness (it does not require a safety cage) spirals one of the most elegant and playful staircases in Paris.

THE POETICS OF SPACE Modern museums and galleries – high points of creativity since the 1970s – can be seen as experimental spaces, in the sense that architects are constantly trying to create the best possible conditions in which visitors can appreciate the masterpieces they have come to see. This quest has necessitated the invention of a new poetics of space – to use a phrase coined in 1957 by Gaston Bachelard – that has also influenced the staircase. Indeed, museum staircases are sometimes treated as works of art in their own right.

In Paris, Jean Nouvel and Architecture Studio succeeded in bestowing a 'magic of place' on the Institut du Monde Arabe, which opened in 1987. Behind a glazed façade that lets in a filtered, rippling light lie eight spacious floors dedicated to vertical circulation. The flow of visitors, passing each other as they go up and down in the transparent lifts and on stairways that seem to hang in the void, creates a never-ending, vertiginous ballet. This masterly composition generates a sensuous feeling of insubstantiality.

The British Museum in London unveiled a striking transformation of its Great Court in the year 2000, undertaken by Norman Foster (overleaf). A gracefully curved glass and steel roof surrounds the circular Reading Room, which used to form

LEFT
The space dedicated to public circulation at the heart of the Institut du Monde Arabe, Paris. Completed in 1987, it was designed by Jean Nouvel and Architecture Studio.

OPPOSITE
The glass pyramid in the courtyard of the Louvre, Paris, designed by the Chinese–American architect I. M. Pei and completed in 1989.

OVERLEAF
The Great Court of the British Museum, London, as transformed by Norman Foster in 2000.

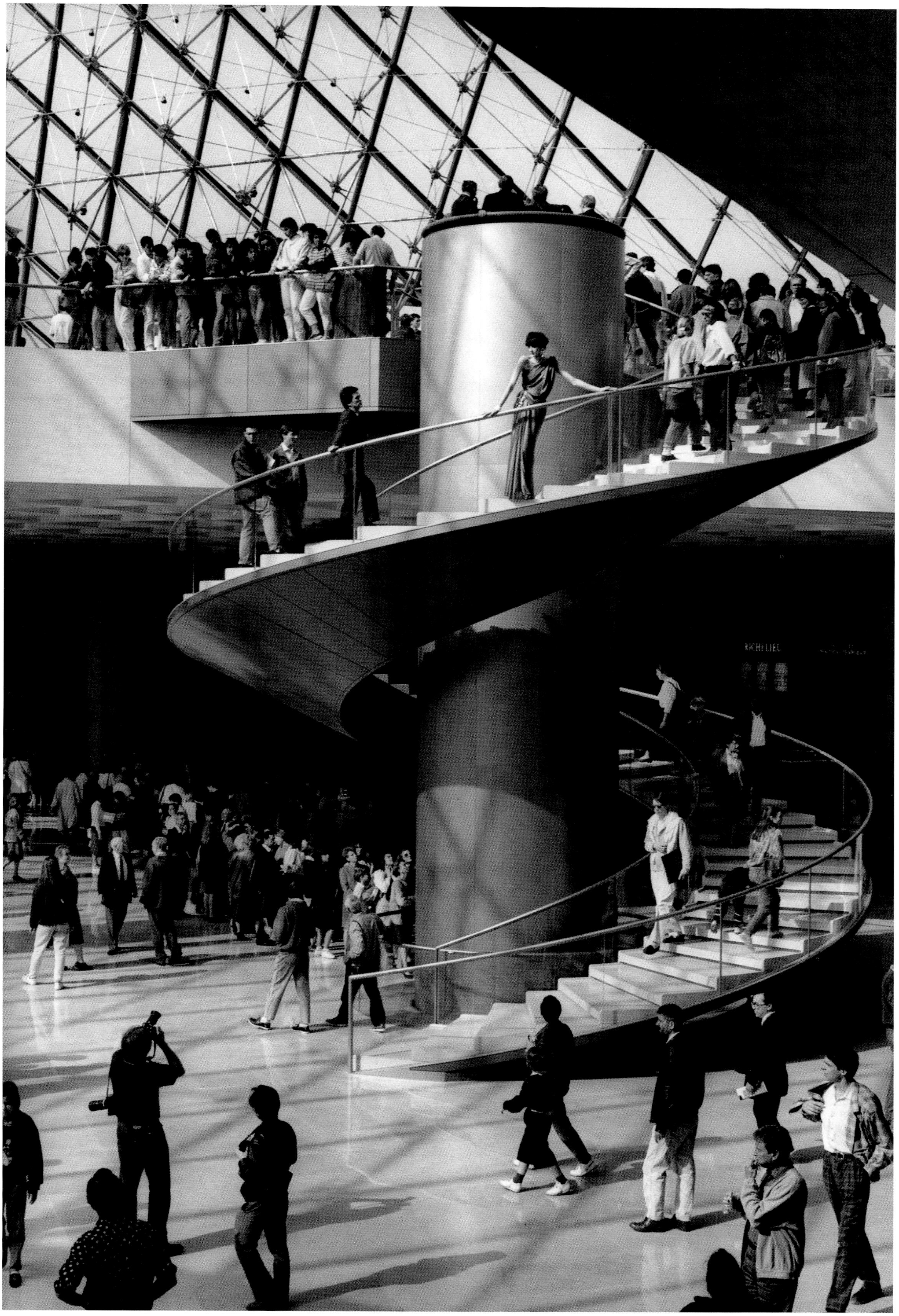
RICHELIEU

Grayson Perry
The Tomb of the
Unknown Craftsman

Until 26 February 2012

Open late Fridays
Members free
Book now

Exhibition entrance

Lower floor
Ground floor
Upper floor

Eating
Shopping

THIS GREAT COURT
Hajj
journey to the
heart of Islam
26 January –
15 April 2012
Open late Fridays
Members free
Book now
Exhibition entrance
opposite the Ticket Desk
Eating
Shopping
Lower floor
Ground floor
Upper floor
and let thy

the nucleus of the British Library (now moved to St Pancras). This room in turn is set within a monumental double staircase of great elegance. The overall effect is of a beautiful urban oasis.

In California, the Swiss architect Mario Botta has endowed the central atrium of the San Francisco Museum of Modern Art (1989–95) with an atmosphere of such serenity and ethereal beauty that the visitor feels as though he or she is entering a place of spiritual vocation. Echoing the vertical lines of the atrium's elegant columns, a sculptural, pure-white staircase rises up to the galleries.

So striking was these projects' success with both the public and the media that the search for a new poetics of space now moved beyond the confines of pioneering museums and galleries. Recent temples of winemaking are a notable example. The panache with which Louis Combe designed Châteaux Margaux in Bordeaux between 1810 and 1816 had long since vanished, but Michael Graves's work in 1987 for the winery of Clos Pegase in Calistoga, California – a high point of Post-modernism – signalled its spectacular revival. Others soon followed, affirming the winery as an architectural genre worthy of attention. In France, in the wake of the *Châteaux Bordeaux* exhibition at the Pompidou Centre in 1988, Jean de Gastines built the elegant warehouse at Château Pichon-Longueville (1993); and in Italy, the principal building of the Petra vineyard at Suvereto, Tuscany, was completed in 2003.

The Petra winery was designed for the Moretti family – who are active in both the construction industry and winemaking – by Mario Botta. This major work celebrates their twofold activity with remarkable success, and has even been compared to a 'cathedral of wine'. Indeed, this dreamlike building recalls Botta's design for the cathedral of Evry, near Paris, the only Catholic cathedral built in France in the twentieth century (it was consecrated in 1995). In that sacred context, Botta developed some of his fantasies and projected them skywards: the powerful cylindrical structure is canted so as to greet visitors at an angle, like a visual link between heaven and earth. The stepped glass roof is encircled by an airy ring of trees (twenty-four silver limes), which are 'suspended' over 17 metres (56 feet) above the ground, reminding worshippers of St Augustine's description of God's nature as a circle whose centre was everywhere and circumference nowhere.

It was this architectural symbolism that Mario Botta chose to revisit at the Petra winery, in order to celebrate the more pagan religion of wine. But Petra has another metaphorical dimension. The sloping roof of the vineyard's central, cylindrical building is topped with two flights of steps: one is centrally positioned and offers visitors commanding views over the Tuscan landscape of vineyards, olive groves and woods; the other, occupying the rest of the circular space, takes the form of a stepped roof with glass panels that shed light from above onto the holy of holies: the warehouse where the great vintages are created. Dominated from above by a ring of olive trees planted around the edge of the cylindrical roof, this spectacular project celebrates the contemporary nature of an operation that relies on a synthesis between the science of winemaking and the new demands of marketing and communications. And, less prosaically, it also pays subtle and skilful homage to the area's many-stranded cultural heritage: Roman and Byzantine art, vernacular architecture and the glorious houses of the Tuscan countryside. We may even detect poetic allusions to the stepped observatories of eighteenth-century India (p. 29), or to the immense ziggurats of Mesopotamia, rising from earth to heaven and imbued with mystical, religious

LEFT
The grand atrium of the San Francisco Museum of Modern Art, built between 1989 and 1995 by the Swiss architect Mario Botta.

RIGHT
The Petra winery, Suvereto, Tuscany (2003). The Moretti family commissioned the complex from Mario Botta in order to give their winery a monumental and memorable character, following the example of historic French vineyards.

significance. The Petra winery transcends this sacred symbolism, reminding us through its architecture that, while wine was traditionally viewed as a privilege of the gods, nowadays its makers know how to respond to the global expectations of a new market.

LANDSCAPES URBAN AND RURAL Steps and stairs fulfil specific functions – material or spiritual – in cityscapes just as they do in rural settings (as Mario Botta's work in Tuscany demonstrates). Sometimes this approach to urban staircases is metaphorical in nature, as in Hugh Ferriss's drawings produced in 1922 for the skyscrapers of Manhattan, or the designs conceived by Henri Sauvage in 1928 for new social dwellings in Paris. Both cases offered a new model of urban architecture that featured stepped silhouettes, and by reaching into the skies above the city represented the new vogue for bringing sunlight into the lives of its citizens. The potent image of these celestial steps proclaimed the emergence of a new *art de vivre*.

The countless metal fire escapes required by New York fire regulations are a familiar feature of the streets of Manhattan. In 1961 they were raised to iconic status by the film *West Side Story*, which transposed the tragedy of *Romeo and Juliet* to the gang culture of New York (p. 35). Here, these unpretentious ladders and gangways contrive simultaneously to fulfil the functions of safety apparatus, urban landscape design and film set.

In Rio de Janeiro, the steps of the Rua Regadas serve a radically different cultural purpose. Starting in 1983, the Chilean artist Jorge Selarón transformed the ordinary but hilly working-class area in which he lived through a lengthy collective art project that involved local people in the improvement of their neighbourhood. Inspired by Gaudí's Parc Güell (p. 193; he had lived for a long time in Barcelona), Selarón coordinated the decoration of the area's thousands of steps with fragments of ceramic tiles salvaged from municipal dumps. This people's art initiative created a raw, immediate artwork and an exhilarating kaleidoscope of colour in the heart of the city.

In Seoul, Dominique Perrault's work represents the outcome of a rational approach to planning. Commissioned to build the new campus for the Ewha Women's University, he set out to give it a strongly civic character. He designed a double monumental staircase that is unique, slicing into the landscape so as to create a man-made valley in the city's centre (pp. 182–83). Its two sides, which mirror each other on four levels, give access to the main student amenities. Since 2009 this remarkable site has been the heart and soul of the university campus.

In the new business area of La Défense, in Paris, one of the aims of the landscape architects was to create from scratch an attractive urban environment that would soften the harshness of the surrounding skyscrapers. To this end, the Allée de l'Arche, laid out in 2008,

RIGHT
The urban steps of the Rua Regadas: a raw and energetic work of art created in a working-class district of Rio de Janeiro by the Chilean artist Jorge Selarón.

OVERLEAF
Laid out in 2000 on the Japanese island of Awaji by the architect Tadao Ando, this garden is a national memorial to the powerful earthquake that shook the country in 1995.

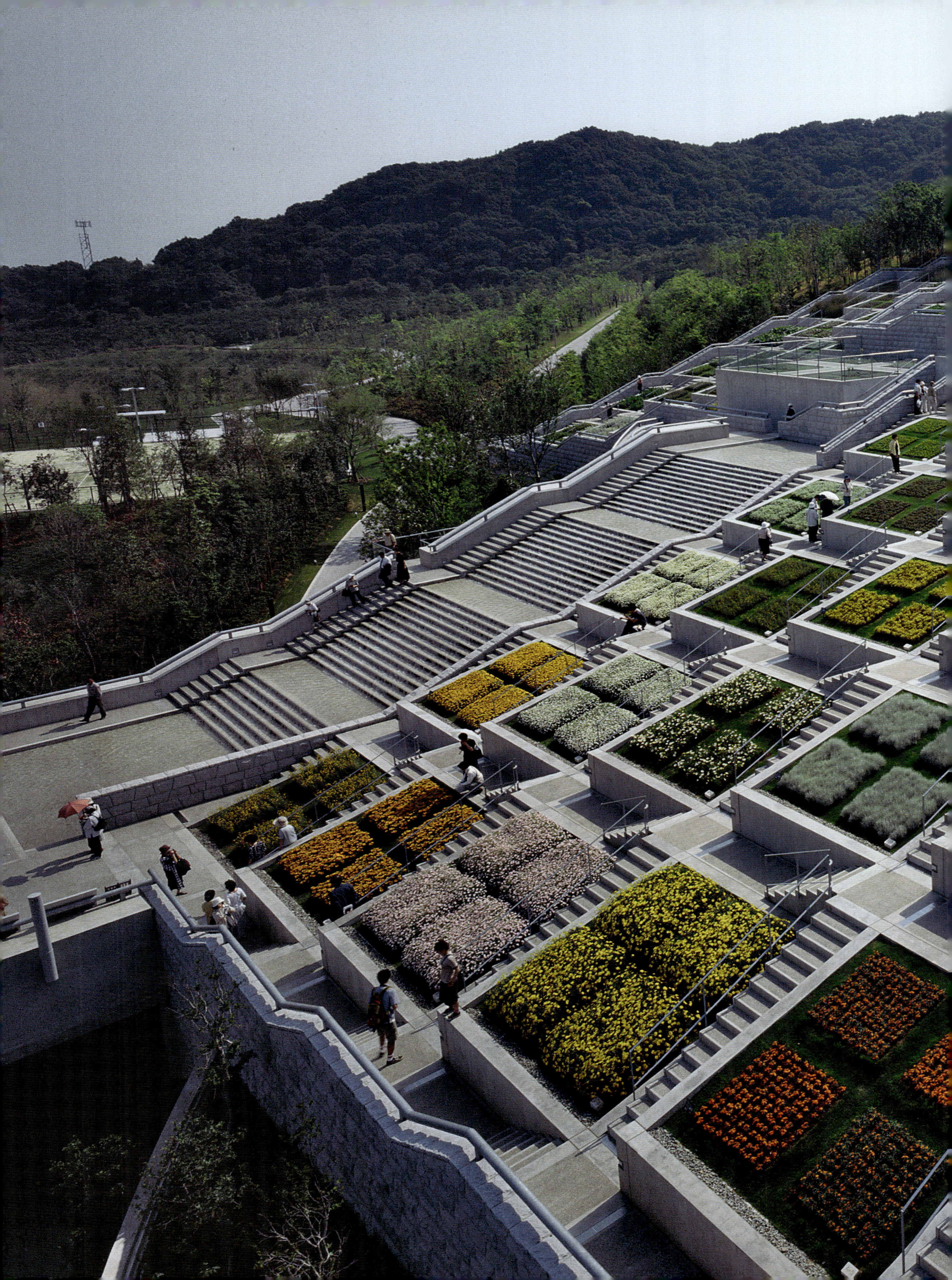

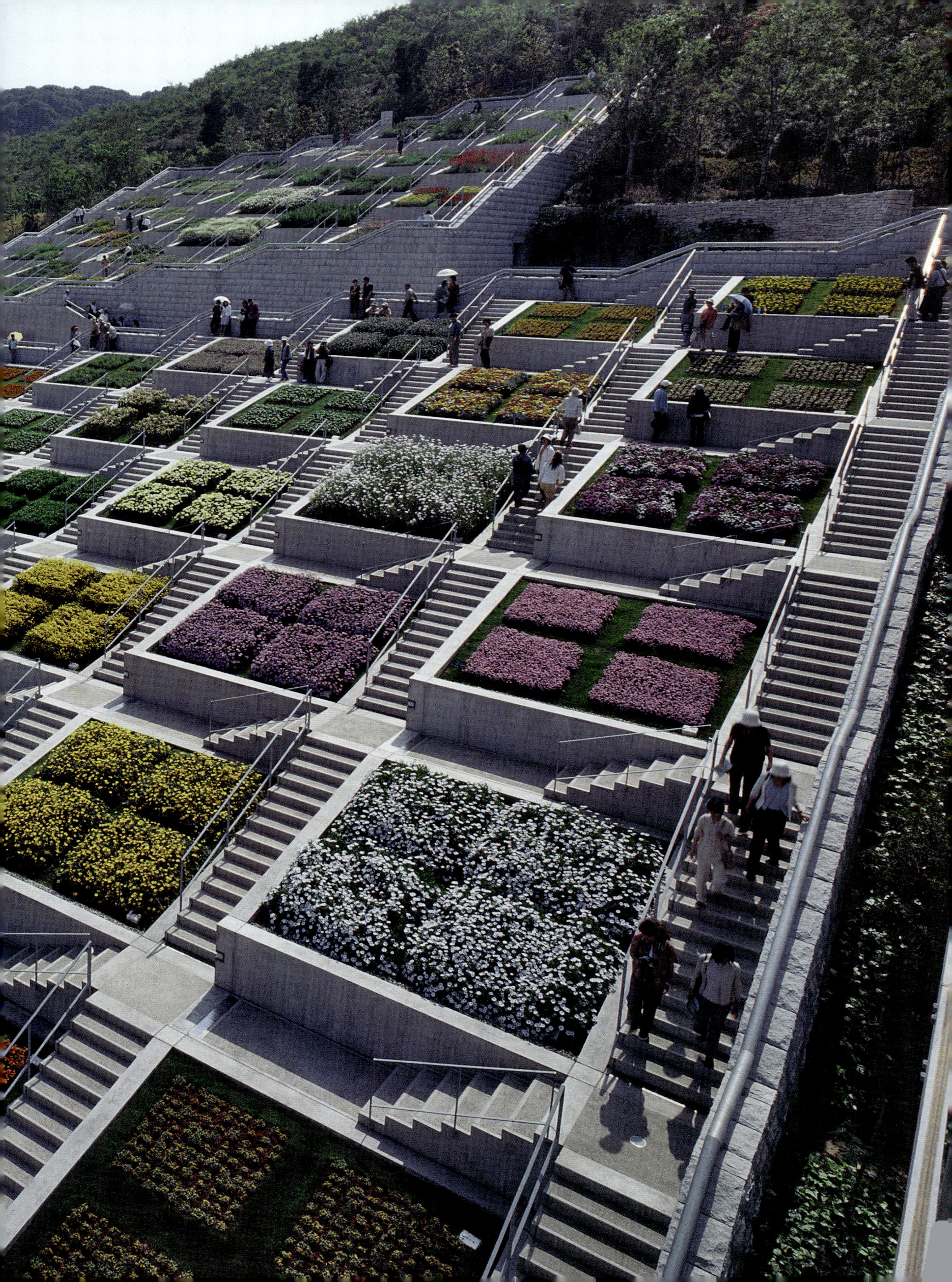

adopted three different ways of managing the artificial changes in ground level: an open-air escalator, a slope for cyclists and – most importantly, since they formed the centrepiece of this new landscape – attractive flights of monumental steps.

To commemorate the Japanese earthquake of 1995, Tadao Ando was commissioned to erect a memorial on the island of Awaji. Completed in 2000, this monument takes the unexpected form of an immense botanical garden, laid out over two hectares of steeply sloping ground on the flank of a hill (pp. 222–23). On this virgin rural site, a hundred or so terraces, filled with every known variety of chrysanthemum, are linked by a corresponding number of flights of steps, resulting in one of the most spectacular creations of contemporary landscape architecture.

FROM THE NEW RATIONALISM TO CONCEPTUAL ART The new Rationalist practices introduced in 1919 by the Bauhaus fostered the skills of designers whose brief was to invest everyday objects with a functional beauty. It was in this spirit of harmonious simplicity that, in 1974, the French designer Roger Tallon sketched out the elements of an elegant spiral staircase destined principally for domestic use. Slotted into each other around a vertical axis in cast aluminium were steps of airy lightness, available in either cast aluminium or precious wood. Once assembled, the stairs had the appearance of a piece of sculpture, introducing a flowing dynamic into the domestic interior.

In the 1960s and 1970s, architects set out to explore new interpretations of the principles of Rationalism, which had gradually shrivelled into an arid field dealing in stereotypes, mechanistic and lacking in eloquence. In 1968 the architect Ricardo Bofill produced his first major design. The housing project of La Muralla Roja, on a clifftop overlooking the Mediterranean at Calp, near Alicante, had two sources of inspiration: the southern vernacular heritage of the Berber kasbahs, built in the red earth of Morocco; and, from the north, the avant-garde Russian Constructivist movement. This unprecedented combination produced a fresh interpretation – less inhibited and more festive – of the austere puritanism that had dominated Rationalism for many years. In Bofill's hands it now possessed a sensual *joie de vivre*. In this compact and intimate labyrinth of holiday apartments, Bofill seems to promote the notion of architecture as a dreamscape.

At the same time, the New Rationalism of the 1970s could still be severely minimalist. Richard Meier's work in America – invariably of crystalline whiteness – is a case in point. His Atheneum, a tourist information centre in New Harmony, Indiana, of 1975, testifies to Meier's quest for a new purist aesthetic that, without repudiating the Functionalist lessons of the Bauhaus, would express an architectural vocabulary that was more complex in its articulation of space, and be more varied and vivid. He expressed this poetic Constructivism in a sophisticated arrangement of projecting staircases, designed to produce – as in Le Corbusier's definition of architecture – 'the skilful, accurate and magnificent play of volumes seen in light'. They cast slender, tapering shadows, a monochrome projection of their own forms.

The *raison d'être* of the monumental staircase often results in it becoming an autonomous object, freed from any architectural context and sometimes from all Rationalist restraint. In this case it acquires the status of a work of art in its own right. One example is the installation at Senftenberg in Germany by the Architektur & Landschaft group (2008; pp. 226–27). Over the course of a dozen flights of steps, this giant steel staircase, weighing 100 tons, rises to a height of 30 metres (98 feet). From the top, visitors can gaze out over the results of an extraordinary transformation: during the last few decades, the vast industrial wasteland of Lausitzer Seenland, between Berlin and Dresden, has been turned into a harmonious landscape set to become a new regional centre for ecotourism. Here, amid its natural setting, the staircase assumes the novel roles of observatory and foil for a pioneering large-scale ecological project.

TOWARDS A MAGICAL LIGHTNESS Following a long period of evolution during the twentieth century, architecture has adapted itself to a multitude of doctrines and methods. Architects dedicated to Functionalism have too often promoted an overwhelmingly generalized built environment, devoid of meaning, character or conviviality. But is a cause for celebration that the early years of the twenty-first

OPPOSITE ABOVE
The Atheneum at New Harmony, Indiana, by Richard Meier (1975). It was built as a tourist information centre for the region.

OPPOSITE BELOW
La Muralla Roja is a compact development of holiday apartments on a clifftop overlooking the Mediterranean (1968–73). Its design, by Ricardo Bofill, derives much of its inspiration from Moroccan vernacular architecture.

OPPOSITE RIGHT
A spiral staircase in cast aluminium for domestic use, created in 1974 by the French designer Roger Tallon.

OVERLEAF
The access steps to the observatory overlooking the former industrial wasteland of Lausitzer Seenland, Senftenberg, Germany. This monumental work, completed in 2008, is by the Architektur & Landschaft group.

1900–NOW | 225

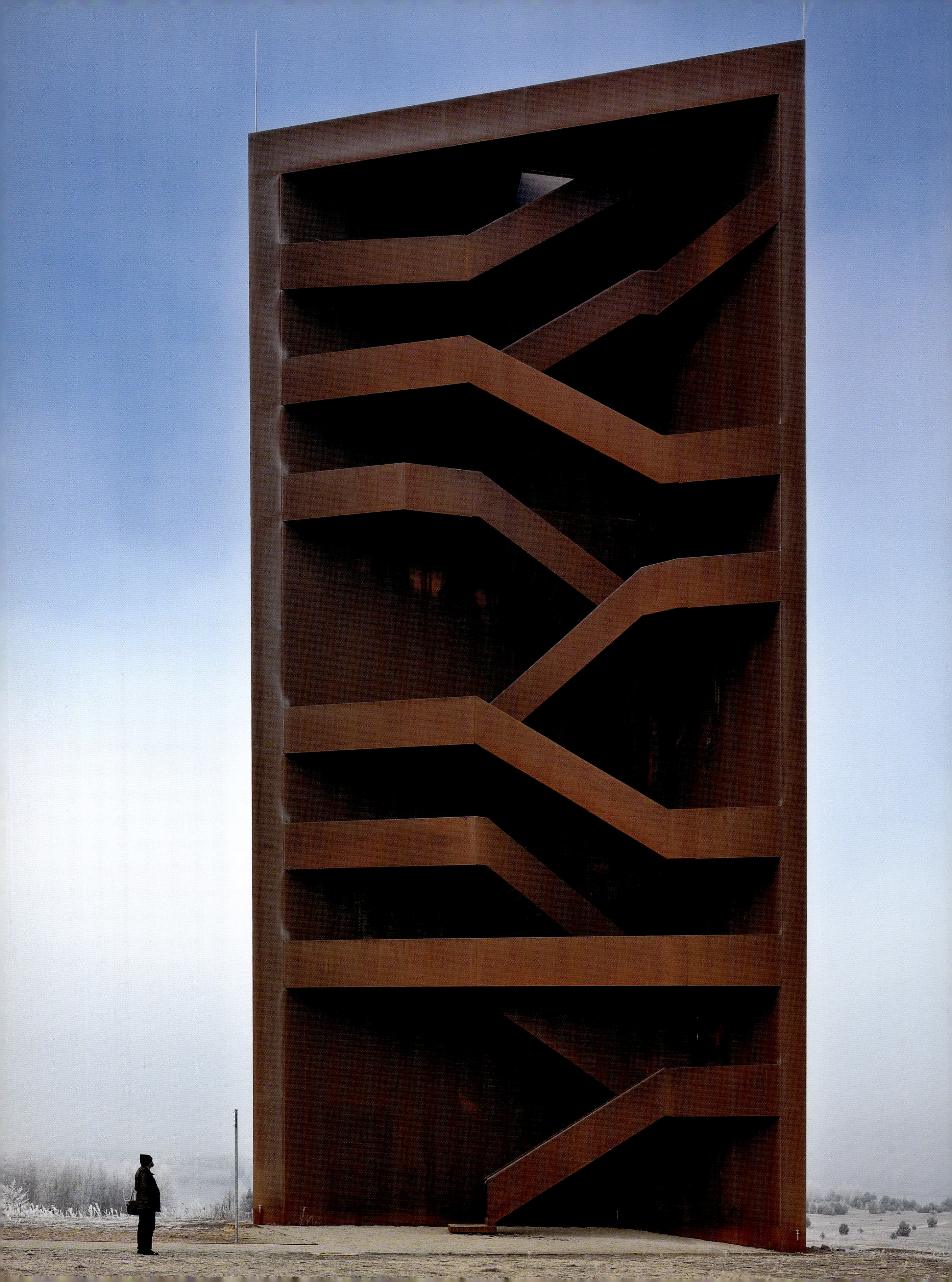

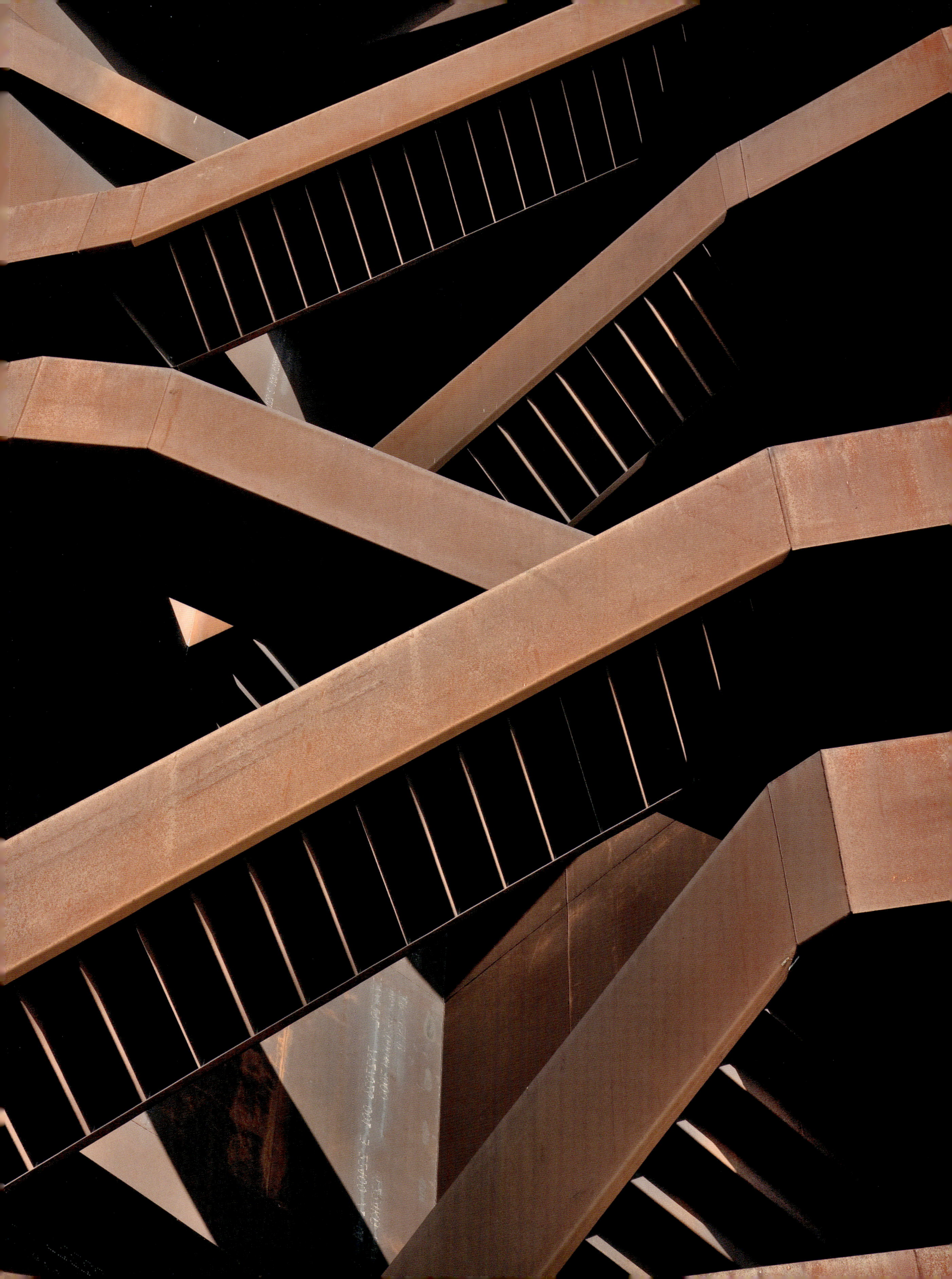

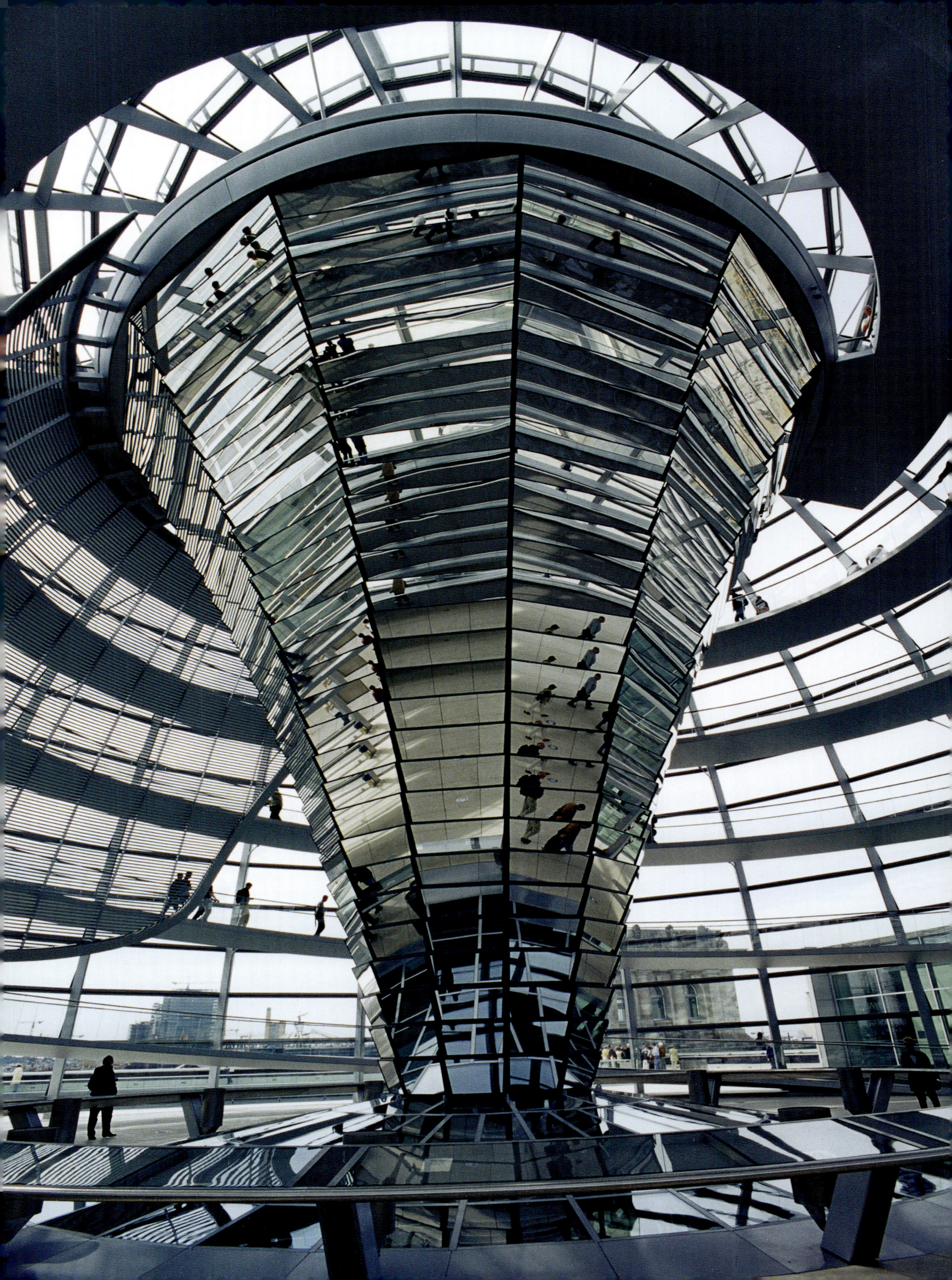

The glass dome of the Bundestag in Berlin (1999), with its helical ramp. Designed by Norman Foster, the building is open to the public, and its ramp offers views down into the parliamentary debating chamber.

century have seen a resurgence in architectural projects that are richer in political, social, symbolic and poetic connotations. This emancipation has given rise to a new generation of staircases, which sometimes display a magical aura of insubstantiality.

The Reichstag building in Berlin bears a heavy burden of historical and political significance. Originally built in 1894 to house the German parliament, it was severely damaged by fire in 1933. The Nazis attributed this misfortune to a Communist plot in order to justify their first campaign of terror and repression. During the Second World War, the building – including its cupola, some 75 metres (246 feet) in height – was further damaged by air raids. After the war the cupola was demolished, and rest of the building was left standing as a shell. In 1991, after German reunification, the government decided to transfer the country's capital from Bonn to Berlin and to house the new Bundestag in the Reichstag building. Entrusted with carrying out this delicate metamorphosis, Norman Foster raised a new glass cupola over the refurbished structure. It is unique among parliaments in that it contains a spiralling ramp, from which the public can observe the proceedings going on below them. This gently sloping staircase thus becomes a potent symbol of the transparency of democratic debate, carried out under the scrutiny of ordinary citizens.

Foster employed a similar symbolism in the new home he designed for the Greater London Authority, which opened on the South Bank of the Thames in 2002. Through the ten floors of City Hall rises a broad spiral staircase, which along its length of 500 metres (1,640 feet) either passes or looks down into the transparent debating chamber, meeting rooms and administrative offices (p. 234). While the similar helicoidal ramp at the Guggenheim Museum in New York expresses the space's cultural dynamic, this more recent version in London, conceived as a staircase, with multiple landings of breathtaking elegance and lightness, celebrates the political energy and transparency of local democracy.

The new cultural centre of Matadero Madrid, which opened in 2007, is skilfully integrated into the former municipal abattoir, which has converted into pavilions welcoming many different artistic disciplines. One of these pavilions has been designed by the architects of the CH+QS group to accommodate a film institute (pp. 230–31). The centre's various levels are linked by staircases that are relatively small in scale but treated with a poetic sensibility. Thanks to the subtle woven appearance of the wall materials and the equally inventive low-angle lighting, this space devoted to the celebration of film has its own distinctive visual magic. The grandeur of the effect produced by these steps is a reminder that, when approached with genuine creativity, architecture will happily accommodate itself to the most modest of circumstances.

At Lommel in Belgium, another small art institution provided an opportunity for the architect and engineer Philippe Samyn to demonstrate his skills. He crowned the galleries of the Flemish Centre for Contemporary Glass Art, which is dedicated to promoting the aesthetic potential of glass and spreads over two levels, with a conical steel and glass tower. The steel elements of the structure, which measures 8 metres (26 feet) in diameter at the base and 30 metres (98 feet) in height, decrease in size as it rises, and the ensemble houses a floating circular double stair of choreographic elegance (pp. 236–37). The tower soars upwards with a grace and harmony that are as insubstantial as they are magical. After dark, the steps radiate a serene beauty thanks to the light emitted by rows of LEDs, and the staircase seems to lifts this ethereal masterpiece up into the heavens.

FLASHBACK TO THE FUTURE As this journey through the architecture of modernism reaches its end, we should perhaps pause to consider the revival of the staircase in its proper historical context. Some concepts are far older than they may seem. As he worked on his last inventions in early sixteenth-century France, Leonardo da Vinci produced a drawing of a tall cylinder-shaped building, its outer wall encrusted with parallel curving staircases that lend the architecture a powerful kinetic energy, thus transcending the intrinsically static quality of all buildings. The notion of externalizing staircases in spectacular and artistic ways had already made an occasional appearance during the Renaissance, for example at the Palazzo Contarini del Bovolo in Venice (p. 58), and in the Italian-inspired François I wing at the château of Blois (pp. 60–61). But Leonardo's drawing went further, pushing the idea to its logical conclusion with eloquent clarity. It not only transformed our perception of external architecture, but also

230 | FROM ART NOUVEAU TO THE PRESENT DAY

ABOVE AND RIGHT
The entrance to the film institute created in 2007 as part of the Matadero Madrid cultural centre. This new institution was developed in the former municipal abattoirs by the CH+QS group.

OVERLEAF
I. M. Pei's staircase at the Museum of Islamic Art in Doha, Qatar (2008).

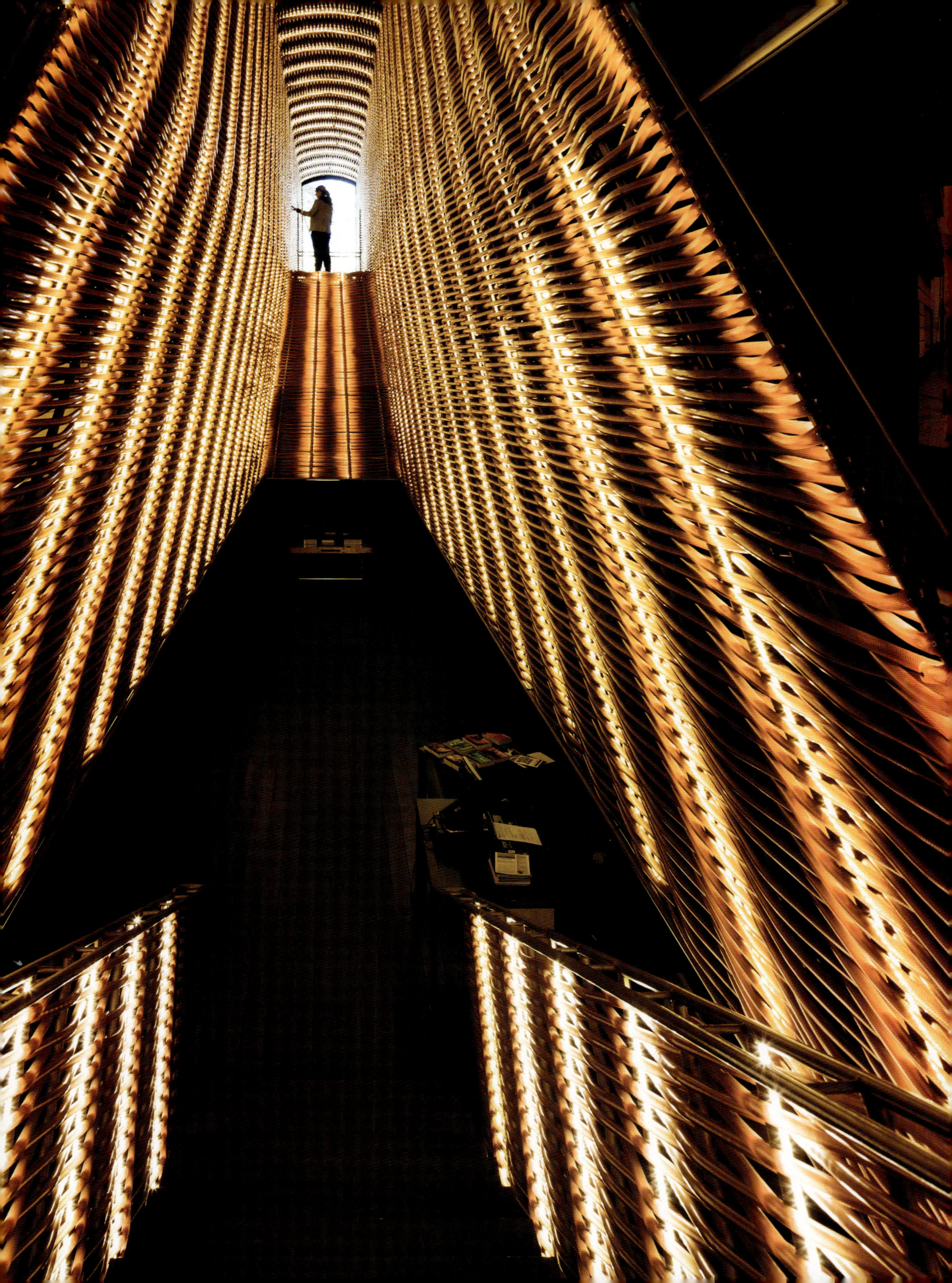

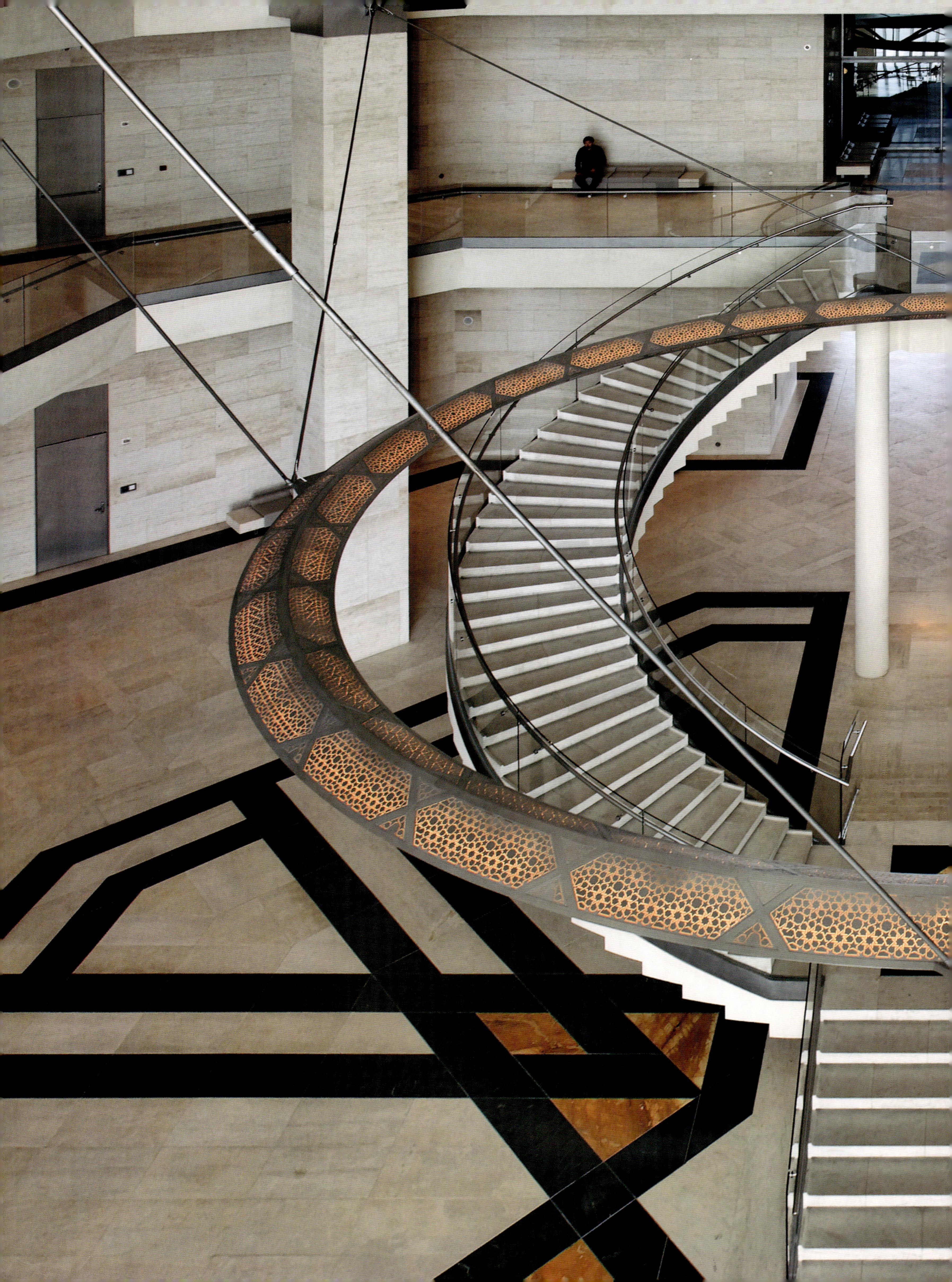

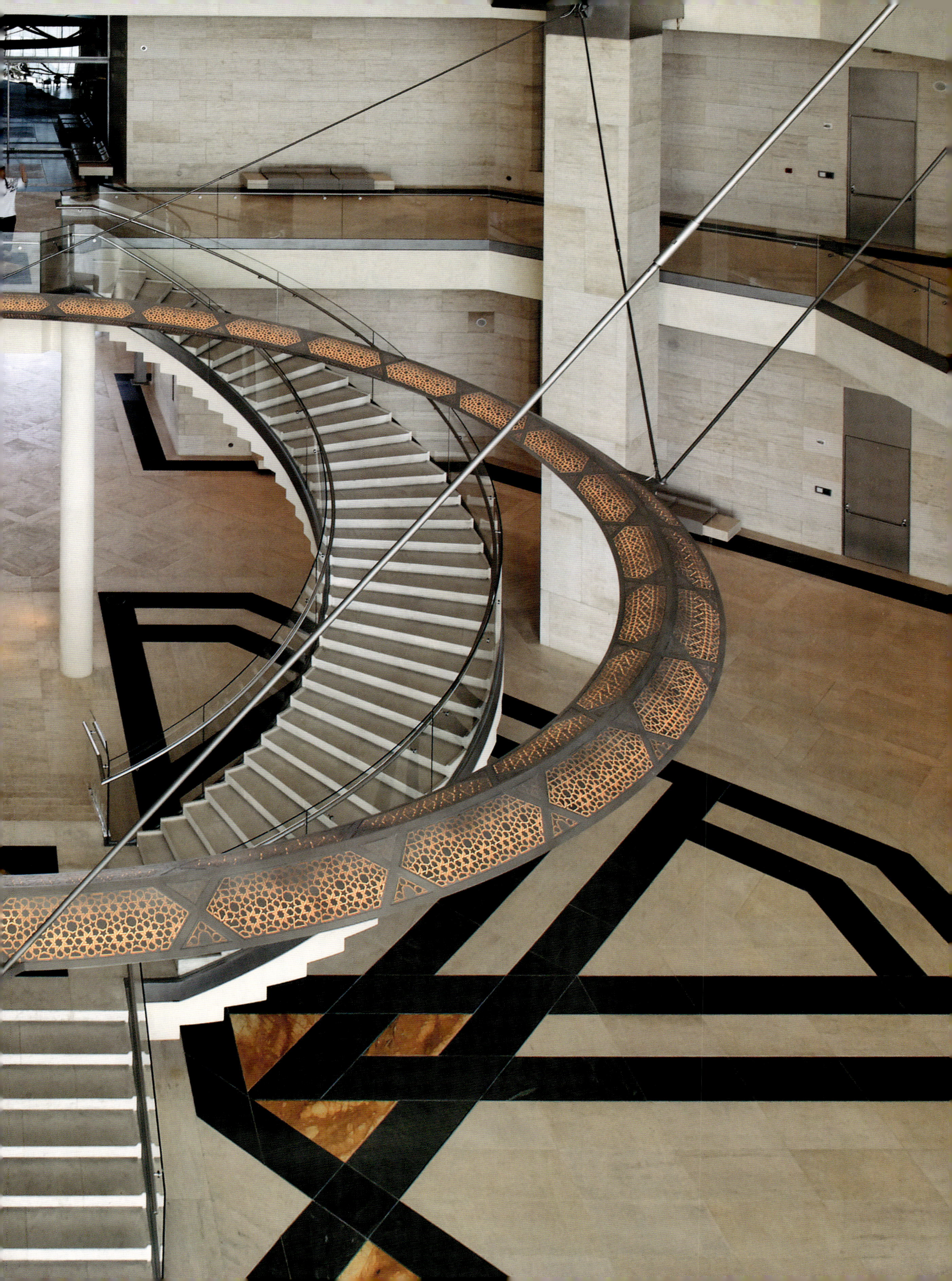

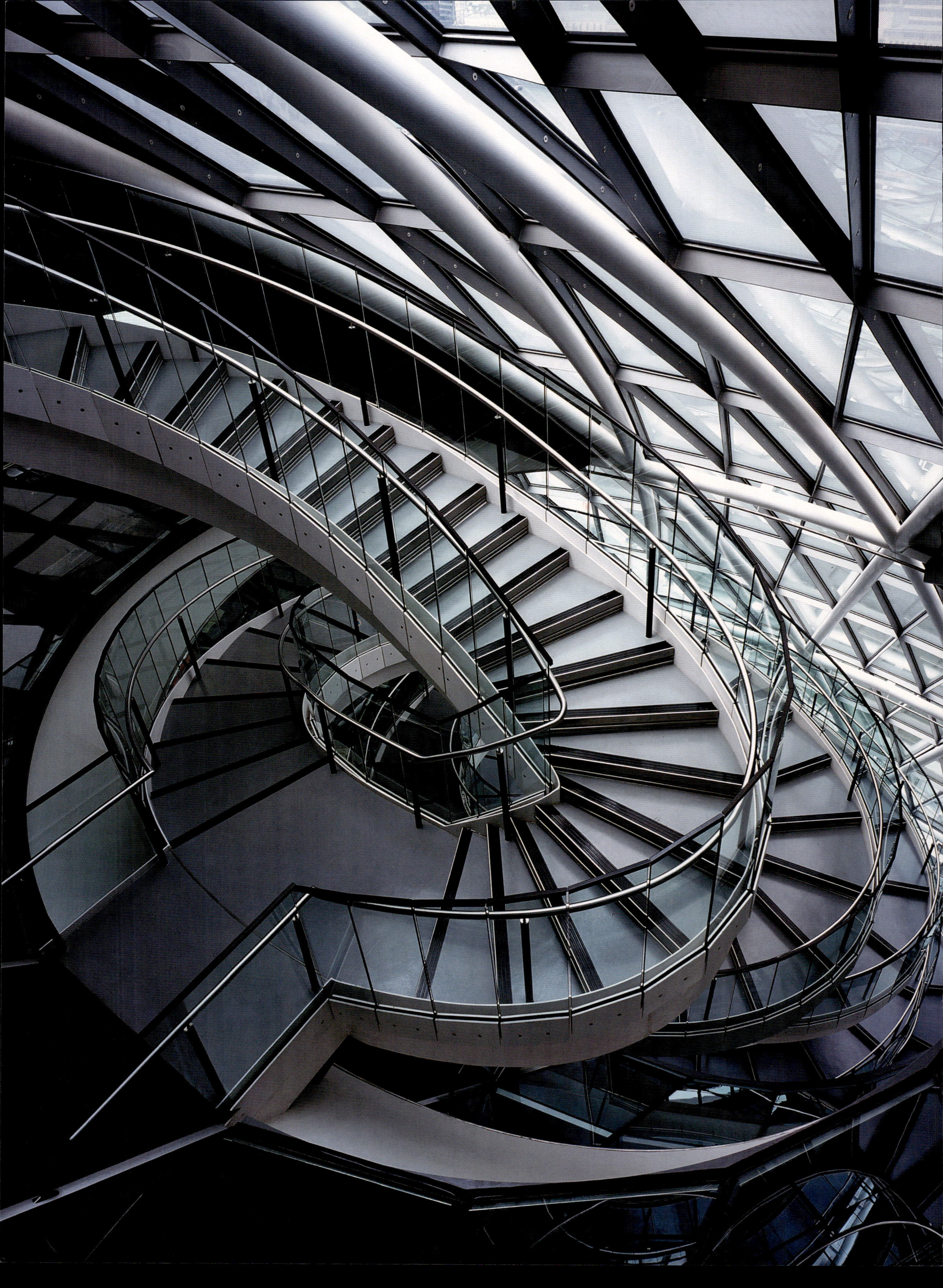

OPPOSITE
The new City Hall, the headquarters of the Greater London Authority, built beside the Thames by Norman Foster (2002).

RIGHT
Two striking circular plans – both unbuilt – with external staircases. They were designed by Leonardo da Vinci in the sixteenth century (left) and by the Belgian architect and engineer Philippe Samyn in 2007 (right).

gave it an added dimension: an expression of energy in time and space that anticipated the architecture of modernism.

It was to be nearly five centuries before another talented builder, Philippe Samyn, created a modern design of comparable creativity and eloquence. The circular office tower he proposed for the centre of Brussels, twenty-five storeys high and of wooden construction, is sheathed in a double skin of glass and gracefully encircled by two circular ramps designed to serve as fire escapes. These, in turn, are connected to a further set of spiralling staircases, also external. This is architecture conceived as an aerial symphony of movement.

These two projects, both sadly unbuilt, display the same Expressionist approach and celebrate the place of the staircase at the heart of modern society, both as a statement of its vitality and dynamism, and as a tribute to the cult of mobility with which contemporary society is so preoccupied. Today, notwithstanding the many constraints with which architects have to contend, at the risk of having their creative wings clipped – building regulations, health and safety considerations and general bureaucracy – the staircase remains an iconic expression of the technological and artistic innovation of modern times.

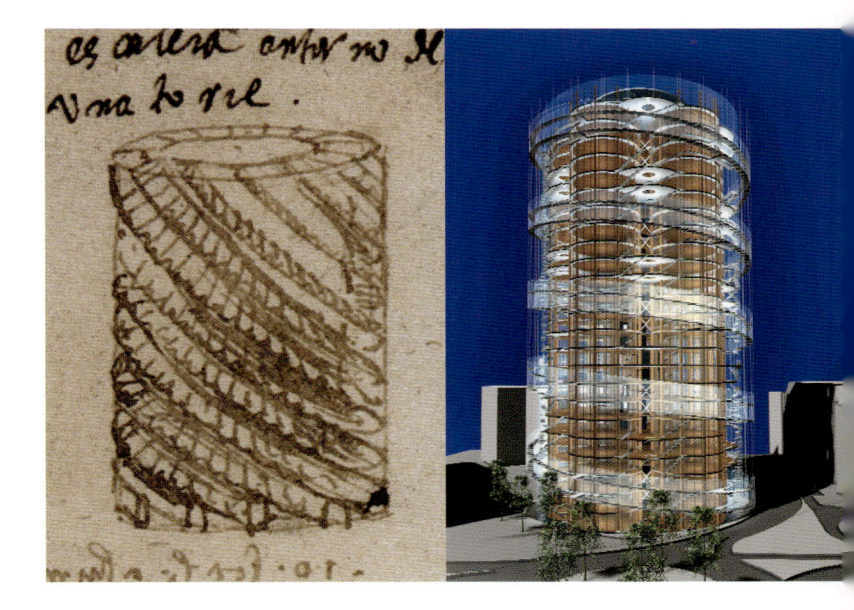

236 | FROM ART NOUVEAU TO THE PRESENT DAY

ABOVE AND RIGHT
Three views of the ethereally delicate Glass Centre at the Flemish Centre for Contemporary Glass Art in Lommel, Belgium, built in 2007 by Philippe Samyn.

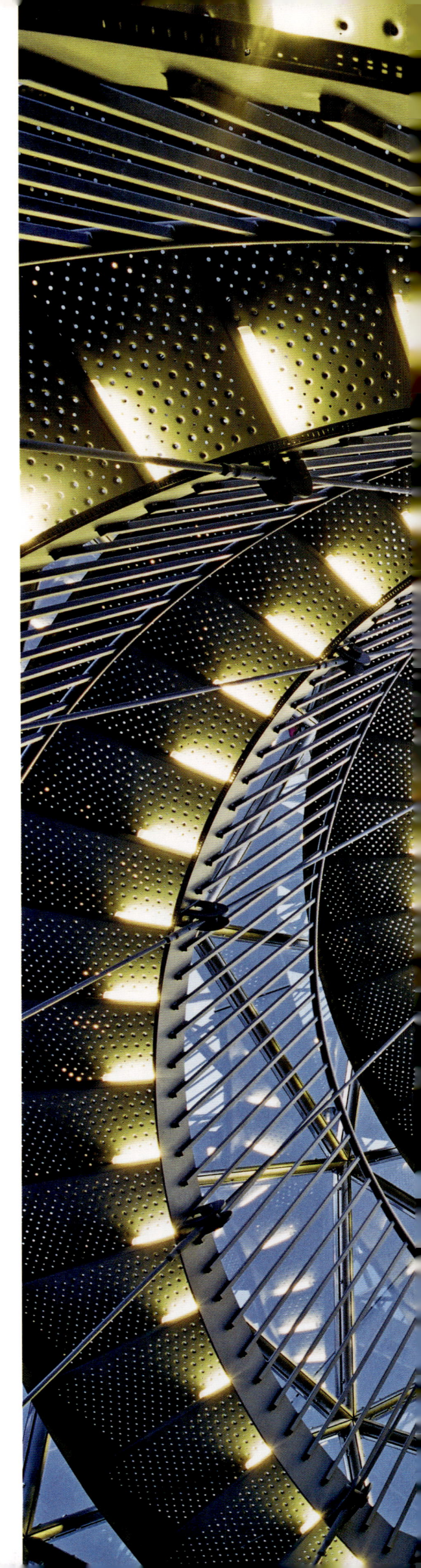

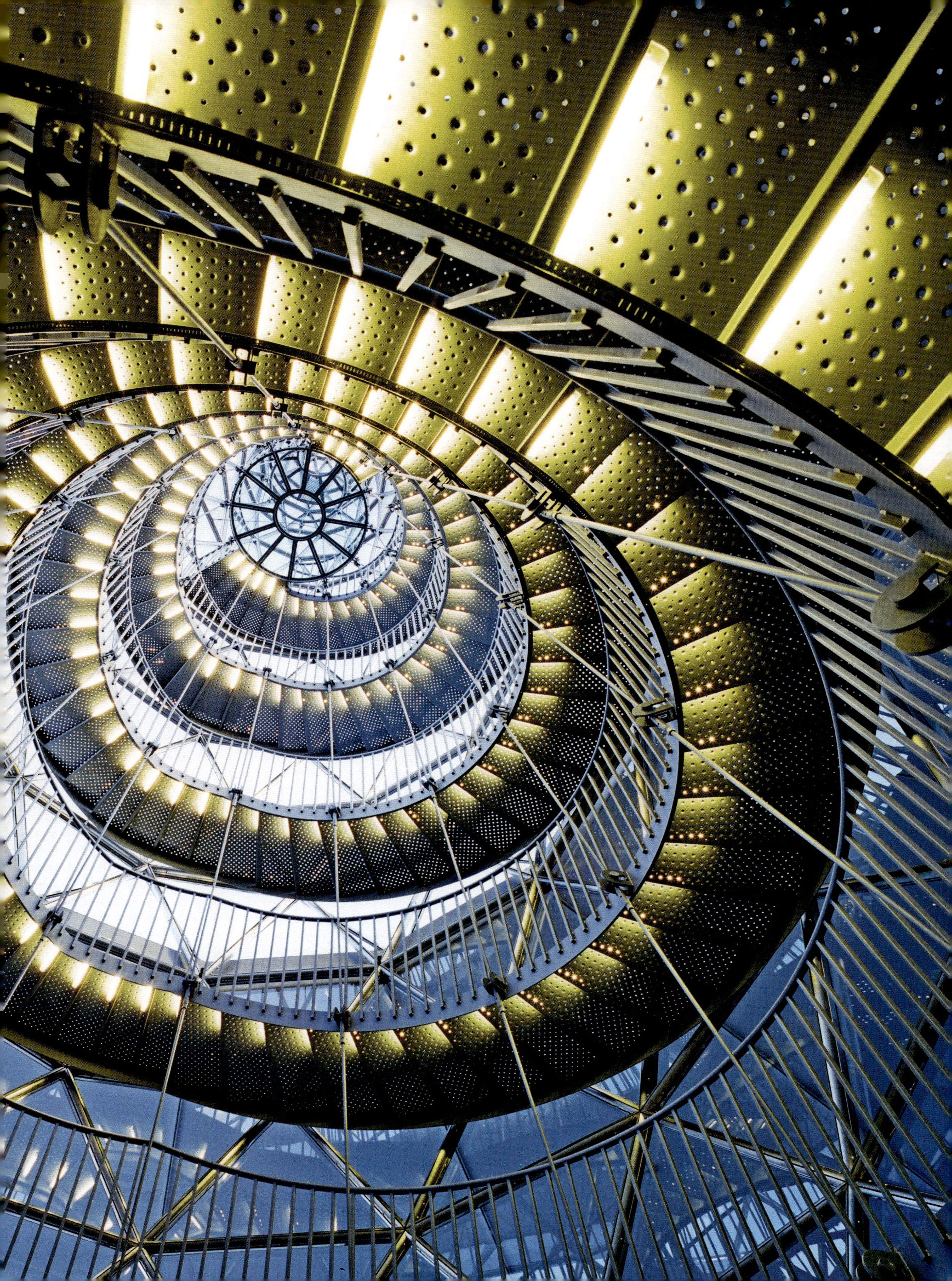

Further Reading

Leon Battista Alberti, *De re aedificatoria* (Florence, 1485); Eng. trans. by J. Rykwert, N. Leach and R. Tavernor as *On the Art of Building in Ten Books* (Cambridge, MA, and London, 1988)

Elizabeth Mary André, *Fire Escapes in Urban America: History and Preservation*, PhD thesis (University of Vermont, 2006)

Jean-Pierre Babelon, *Châteaux de France au siècle de la Renaissance* (Paris, 1989)

Germain Bazin, *Baroque and Rococo* (London and New York, 1974)

Anthony Blunt, *Art and Architecture in France, 1500–1700* (Harmondsworth, 1953; rev. edn 1980)

Anthony Blunt (ed.), *Baroque and Rococo: Architecture and Decoration* (London and New York, 1982)

C. Brothers, *Michelangelo, Drawing and the Invention of Architecture* (New Haven, 2008)

Stephen J. Campbell and Michael W. Cole, *A New History of Italian Renaissance Art* (London, 2012)

J. Cracraft, *The Petrine Revolution in Russian Architecture* (Chicago and London, 1988)

W. J. R. Curtis, *Modern Architecture since 1900* (Oxford, 2nd edn 1987)

D. Davis, *The Museum Transformed: Design and Culture in the Post-Pompidou Age* (New York, 1991)

M. Dennis, *Court & Garden: From the French Hôtel to the City of Modern Architecture* (Cambridge, MA, 1986)

Emmanuel Ducamp (ed.), *Tsarskoïe Selo. De Catherine II à Nicolas II: trois siècles de splendeur impériale* (Paris, 2010)

Emmanuel Ducamp (ed.), *The Summer Palaces of the Romanovs: Treasures from Tsarskoye Selo* (London and New York, 2012)

Kenneth Frampton, *Modern Architecture: A Critical History* (London, 4th edn 2007)

P. Frankl, *Gothic Architecture* (Harmondsworth, 1962)

Christoph Luitpold Frommel, *The Architecture of the Italian Renaissance* (London, 2007)

P. Galluzzi, *The Renaissance Engineers from Brunelleschi to Leonardo da Vinci* (Florence, 1996)

Charles Garnier, *Le Nouvel Opéra de Paris*, vol. 1 (Paris, 1878)

Diane Ghirardo, *Architecture after Modernism* (London, 1996)

Mark Girouard, *The Victorian Country House* (New Haven and London, 1979)

R. J. Goy, *Venice: The City and its Architecture* (London, 1997)

Francesco Gurrieri, *Palaces of Florence* (New York, 1996)

H. R. Hitchcock Jr, *German Renaissance Architecture* (Princeton, 1981)

W. G. Kalnein and M. Levey, *Art and Architecture of the Eighteenth Century in France* (Harmondsworth, 1972)

E. Kaufmann, *Architecture in the Age of Reason* (Cambridge, MA, 1955)

Robert Kerr, *The Gentleman's House, or How to Plan the English Residences, from the Parsonage to the Palace* (London, 2nd edn 1865)

M. Kitson, *The Age of Baroque* (London, 1966)

George Kubler and Martin Soria, *Art and Architecture in Spain and Portugal and their American Dominions, 1500 to 1800* (Harmondsworth, 1959)

Adolberto Dal Lago, *Villas and Palaces of Europe* (London, 1988)

James Lees-Milne, *English Country Houses: Baroque, 1685–1715* (Woodbridge, 1986)

Michael J. Lewis, *The Gothic Revival* (London and New York, 2002)

Nathaniel Lloyd, *A History of the English House* (London, 1975)

T. A. Marder, *Bernini's Scala Regia at the Vatican Palace* (Cambridge, 1997)

Bernard Marrey, *Les Grands Magasins, des origines à 1939* (Paris, 1979)

R. Middleton (ed.), *The Beaux-Arts and Nineteenth-Century French Architecture* (Cambridge, MA, 1982)

Linda Murray, *The High Renaissance and Mannerism: Italy, the North and Spain 1500–1600* (London, 1977)

Peter Murray, *The Architecture of the Italian Renaissance* (London, 3rd edn 1986)

Andrea Palladio, *I quattro libri dell'architettura* (Venice, 1570; Eng. trans. by I. Ware (London, 1738; repr. New York, 1965)

André Parreaux, *L'Architecture en Grande-Bretagne* (Paris, 1969)

Nikolaus Pevsner, *A History of Building Types* (London, 1976)

Jean-François Pinchon, *Les Palais d'argent: l'architecture bancaire en France de 1850 à 1930* (Paris, 1992)

Kenneth Powell (ed.), *The Great Builders* (London, 2011)

E. Graeme Robertson and Joan Robertson, *Cast Iron Decoration: A World Survey* (London, 1977)

F. Russell (ed.), *Art Nouveau Architecture* (London, 1979)

R. W. Sexton, *American Theatres of Today* (New York, 1927)

D. Sharp, *Twentieth Century Architecture: A Visual History* (London, 1991)

Ian Sutton, *Western Architecture: A Survey from Ancient Greece to the Present* (London and New York, 2000)

John Templer, *The Staircase: History and Theories* (Cambridge, MA, 1992)

Oscar Tusquets Blanca (ed.), *Réquiem por la escalera / Requiem for the Staircase* (Barcelona, 2004)

Eugène-Emmanuel Viollet-le-Duc, *Dictionnaire raisonné de l'architecture française du XIe au XVIe siècle*, 10 vols (Paris, 1854–68)

D. Watkin, *A History of Western Architecture* (London, 1986)

Frank Whitford, *Bauhaus* (London, 1984)

Picture Credits and Acknowledgments

AKG-images/Schuetze/Rodemann: p. 56; Alimdi/Martin Engelmann: pp. 5–6; Arxiu Fotografic/Centre Excursionista de Catalunya: p. 192; Bastin & Evrard/Brussels: pp. 148, 170, 184, 187, 191, 196–97; Bibliothèque Nationale de France: p. 174 right; Bildarchiv Monheim: pp. 4 (Florian Monheim/Roman von Goetz), 36 (Schuetze/Rodemann), 96–97 (Lisa Hammel/Annet van der Voort), 105 (Florian Monheim), 112 (Florian Monheim), 113 (Florian Monheim), 125 (Florian Monheim), 194 (Achim Bednorz), 200 (Schuetze/Rodemann), 209 (Schuetze/Rodemann/© Adagp-Fondation Le Corbusier), 218–19 (Florian Monheim), 226–27 (Schuetze/Rodemann), 232–33 (Jochen Helle); Mario Botta Architetto: pp. 220, 221 above (Enrico Cano); Jacques Boulay: pp. 42–43, 58; Bridgeman/Giraudon: pp. 24 below (Frederick Henry Evans/Private Collection/The Stapleton Collection/The Bridgeman Art Library), 33 (Philadelphia Museum of Art, PA/The Louise and Walter Arensberg Collection, 1950), 120 (bridgemanart.com), 122 (bridgemanart.com), 145 above (bridgemanart.com); Churtichaga + Quadra-Salcedo Arquitectos/photo: Sergio Guerra: pp. 230, 231; Private Collection: pp. 18 below, 22, 28 left, 30 above and left, 35, 48, 52 below, 66, 110–11, 134 below, 142 below, 195, 198, 199, 208, 210, 211, 225; © Constantinos Hinis 2011: pp. 172–73; Corbis: pp. 90–91 (© Massimo Listri), 228 (Morton Beebe), 234 (Peter Durant/Arcaid); Paul Day: p. 186; Eloïse Dethier: p. 213; Catherine Donzel: p. 25; Emmanuel Ducamp: pp. 99, 149; École Nationale Supérieure des Beaux-Arts de Paris: p. 82; © FAI-Fondo Ambiente Italiano/photo Matthias Wolff: p. 31; Fotolia.com: pp. 17 (David Davis), 21 (Kippis), 29 (Angelo Giampiccolo), 34 above (Yves Roland), 57 (Giupax); Harlaxton College/photo: Andrew Midgley: pp. 164–65; Frédéric Kister: pp. 102, 103 below; The Kobal Collection: pp. 20 (Paramount), 32 (Tri-Star/American Zoetrope); Leemage © Jemolo: p. 77; Library of Congress, Washington DC: pp. 10, 16, 24 above, 142 above, 167, 171, 174 left, 205 above; Pierre Louis: pp. 5, 9, 23, 26, 27, 28 above (All Rights Reserved/Hannsjörg Voth), 28 right, 30 below right, 37 above, 44, 45, 92, 94, 157, 177 above, 201, 205 below, 214, 221 below; Musée de Morlaix/All Rights Reserved: p. 52; © National Trust Images: pp. 86 (Andreas von Einsiedel), 87 (Horst Kolo), 88 (John Hammond), 89 (Dennis Gilbert), 98 (John Miller), 121 (Dennis Gilbert), 123 (Andreas von Einsiedel), 145 below (National Trust Images), 146 (Andreas von Einsiedel), 147 (Andreas von Einsiedel); Jon Ortner: p. 175; Pere Vivas/Triangle Postals/Caixa Catalunya: p. 193; Dominique Perrault Architecture/Ewha Womans University/© André Morin/DPA: pp. 182–83; Allison Phliponeau: pp. 100–1; RMN: pp. 12 (Musée du Louvre/Hervé Lewandowski), 46 below (© Ministère de la Culture–Médiathèque du Patrimoine), 50–51 (© Ministère de la Culture–Médiathèque du Patrimoine/Georges Estève), 52 above (© Ministère de la Culture–Médiathèque du Patrimoine/image Médiathèque du Patrimoine), 53 (© Ministère de la Culture–Médiathèque du Patrimoine/image Médiathèque du Patrimoine), 55 (Musée du Louvre/Thierry Le Mage), 67 (Institut de France/Gérard Blot), 78–79 (Musée d'Orsay/Hervé Lewandowski), 138 (Musée du Louvre/Gérard Blot), 139 (Musée d'Orsay/Hervé Lewandowski), 166 above (Château de Versailles), 235 left (Institut de France/Gérard Blot); Roger-Viollet/Archives Alinari: pp. 59, 74–75, 93 (Gian Lorenzo Bernini), 176, 217 (Jean Mounicq); Rue des Archives: p. 168; Philippe Samyn & Partners architects and engineers: pp. 235 right (Marie-Françoise Plissart), 236, 237 (Rendering); Galerie Sentou/Roger Tallon: p. 225; Shutterstock: pp. 95, 130 (Worldpics); St Pancras Renaissance Hotel, London/photo: Edmund Sumner: pp. 180, 181; Tadao Ando Architects & Associates: pp. 222–23 (Awaji Yumebutai); Oscar Tusquets Blanca/Escola Arquitectura la Salle Barcelona/Rafael Vargas: pp. 14–15; Erica Van Horn/Beinecke Library, Yale University: p. 45 below; Louis Volant: p. 49; Gaspard Walter: p. 124; Marc Walter: pp. 1, 2–3, 8, 13, 19, 34, 38–39, 40, 46 above, 47, 53, 60, 61, 62–63, 64–65, 68, 69, 70, 71, 72, 73, 80, 83, 84–85, 94, 103 above, 104, 106–7, 108–9, 115, 116–17, 118, 119, 126–27, 128–29, 132–33, 134 above, 135, 136–37, 140, 141, 143, 144, 150, 151, 152, 153, 154–55, 156, 158, 159, 160–61, 162, 163, 166 below, 169, 177 below, 178, 179, 188–89, 190, 202–3, 204, 206–7, 210–11 (© Adagp-Fondation Le Corbusier); Philip Watson/All rights reserved: p. 22 below.

Studio Chine would like to thank François and Matthieu de Waresquiel and Agnès de Gorter for their support.

The publishers and Studio Chine would like to thank all those who helped make this project a success. We are very grateful to all the museums, institutions and collections that opened their doors to our photographer, especially the following:
The Réunion des Musées Nationaux et du Grand Palais (Florence Le Moing, Caroline Prual, Pauline Hespel)
Éditions du Patrimoine, Centre des Monuments Nationaux (Eva Grangier-Menu, Jocelyn Bouraly, Daniel Reythier) and Château d'Azay-le-Rideau (Jérôme Raffault)
Tour Jean sans Peur (Agnès Lavoye)
Fondation Le Corbusier (Paula de Sa Couto)
The Mairie de Boulogne-Billancourt (Emeric Pinkowicz)
Musée Jacquemart-André (Romane Dargent, Aude Durand)
Opéra National de Paris/Palais Garnier (Christophe Ghristi, Catherine Plichon)
The Domaine de Chambord (Luc Forlivesi)
The City of Blois (Pierre-Gilles Girault)
Château de Chenonceau (Nathalie Renou, Laure Menier, Caroline Darrasse)
The Romanian Embassy (Yvette Fulicea, Laria Stoian, Alexandra Brasat)
Centre des Monuments Nationaux (Isabelle de Gourcuff) and the Conciergerie (Christopher Wride)
The Travellers Club/Hôtel de la Païva (Mr Duplessis)
Crédit Lyonnais (Cynthia Cabuil, Laurence Michel)
Musée de l'Oeuvre de Notre-Dame, Strasbourg (Cécile Dupeux)
The City Hall of Nancy (Sophie Maurand, Serge Martinez)
Conseil Économique et Social/Palais d'Iéna (Melvyn Beaumont, Christine Tendel)
Bibliothèque Mazarine/Institut de France (Mireille Pastoureau, Yann Sordet)
Cour Administrative d'Appel de Paris/Hôtel de Beauvais (Romain Praquin)
The Vice President of the Tribunal de Commerce de Paris and Sylvie Freulon
The Palais de Justice, Paris (Ms Beauvillain)

We would also like to thank the Prensa Obra Social de Catalunya Caixa (Goretti Palau); Triangle Postals (Paz Marrodan); the Arxiu Fotografic del Centre Excursionista de Catalunya (Berenguer Vidal); Robert Terradas i Muntañola, director of La Salle School of Architecture, Barcelona; the St Pancras Renaissance Hotel, London (Caroline Drayton); the FAI-Fondo Ambiente Italiano; Galerie Sentou (Marielle Dhuicque-Hénon); Harlaxton College, Oxford (Linda Dawes); and Paul Day.

Thanks to all those who have kindly allowed us to publish their photographs: Jacques Boulay, Eloïse Dethier, Sergio Guerra, Constantinos Hinis and Frédéric Kister.

Jean Dethier, author of the chapter on the modern period, would like to thank his fellow architects who have generously provided photographs of their works: in Belgium, Philippe Samyn & Partners; in Switzerland, Mario Botta Architetto; in France, Dominique Perrault Architecture; in Japan, Tadao Ando Architect & Associates; and in Spain, Churtichaga + Quadra-Salcedo Arquitectos.

Jérôme Coignard would like to thank Peter Howell not only for sharing his extensive knowledge of nineteenth-century British and European architecture, and his no less extensive library, but also for making him feel so welcome in Oxford. Jérôme is also indebted to the following for their help and advice: Edward Diestelkamp, Marie-Cécile Forest, Marike Gautier and Claude Mignot.

Marc Walter and Sabine Arqué would like to give their personal thanks to Jean Dethier, Pilar Pardal, Emmanuel Ducamp, Étienne Martin, Gabriel Badea-Paun, Catherine Donzel, Pauline Hespel, Suzanne Madon and Florence Cailly.

Index

Page numbers in *italic* refer to illustrations.

Abbaye aux Hommes, Caen 102, *102-3*
Adam, Robert 120, *120*
Aldermaston Manor, Berkshire 145
Ambassadors' Staircase, Versailles 82, 92, 111, 166, *166*
Ando, Tadao *222-23*, 224
Art Gallery of Ontario 27
Atget, Eugène 82
Atlantis House, Bremen 195, *198*
Awaji, Japan *222-23*, 224
Azay-le-Rideau, château of 71, 72, *72*, *73*

Bargello, Florence *38-39*, 45
Bass, Saul 35
Bauhaus School, Dessau *200*, 201
Behrens, Peter *194*, 195
Bénouville, château of 103, *103*
Bernini, Giovanni Lorenzo 92-93, *93*
Biblioteca Laurenziana, Florence 12, 22, *74-75*, 76
Bibliothèque Mazarine, Paris *136-37*, 138
Biet, Léon *136-37*, 138
Blanca, Oscar Tusquets *14-15*
Blois, château of *60*, 61, 82, 152, 229
Bom Jesus do Monte (sanctuary), Braga 21, *95*, 99
Botta, Mario 220, *220*, 221
British Museum, London 216, *218-19*, 220
Bukovich, August von *178*
Bundestag, Berlin *228*, 229
Burgos Cathedral 23
Buron, Jean-Baptiste 179

Cameron, Charles 114, *118*, 119
Capitol, Washington, DC 167, *168*
Carito, Raffele *178*
Carlone, Carlo *110*, 111
Casa Batlló, Barcelona 192, *193*
Casa Milà, Barcelona 192, *192*
Casey, Edward Pierce *171*
Castle Drogo 22, *22*
Cedar Staircase, Harlaxton Manor, Lincolnshire 163, *164-65*, 166
Censerie, Louis de la *157*, 163
Cent Marches, Versailles 123, *126-27*
Centraal Station, Antwerp *157*, 163
Chambers, William 120, *122*
Chambord, château of 27, *40*, 61, *62-65*, 66, 68, 69, 94, 152
Châteaudun, château of 49, *49*, 72
Chenonceau, château of *70*, 71
Chivers, Herbert C. *142*
City Hall, London 229, *234*
Clandon Park, Surrey *98*, 99
Claydon House, Buckinghamshire 120, *123*
Cloister of John III, Tomar 56, *56*
Coeur, Jacques *48*, 49
Cour du Cheval Blanc, Fontainebleau *99*, 99
Crédit Lyonnais head offices, Paris 152, *152*, *153*
Curtis, Edward *16*
Custom House, Philadelphia 205

Day, Paul *186*, 186
Deglane, Henri *188-89*, 191
Destailleur, William *157*, 163
Dollmann, Georg *144*, 166
Domabahçe Palace, Istanbul *130*
Dommey, Théodore *135*
Duc, Joseph-Louis *135*, 138
Duchamp, Marcel 33
Durand-Gosselin, Hippolyte 179

Eiffel Tower, Paris 174, *176*, 199
Eliasson, Olafur *30*
Empire State Building, New York 174
Escalier des Minimes, Palais de Justice, Brussels 168, *170*
Escher, M.C. 28, *30*, 31
Esteves, Francisco Xavier *142*
Evans, Frederick H. *24*
Ewha Women's University, Seoul *182-83*, 221

Ferrières, château of *134*
Fiorivanti, Neri di *38-39*
Flemish Centre for Contemporary Glass Art, Lommel 229, *236-37*
Foster, Norman *218-19*, *228*, 229, *234*
Frombork Cathedral *36*

Garnier, Tony *204*
Garnsey, Elmer Ellsworth *171*
Gehry, Frank 27, *27*
Gengenbach, Heinrich von *46*
Gérôme, Jean-Léon *78-79*, 82
Giant's Staircase, Palazzo Ducale, Venice *42-43*, 45
Giraudet, Jean *80*
Glass Pavilion, Cologne 208, *208*
Goetheanum, Dornach 195, *196-97*
Grand Palais, Paris *188-89*, 191
Grande Arche de la Défense, Paris 18, *214-15*, 216, 221
Graz Castle 24, 56, *57*
Greene Street, New York *175*

Gropius, Walter 199, *200*, 201
Guggenheim Museum, New York 212, *212*, 229
Guimard, Hector *190*, 191, *191*

Hanbury Hall, Worcestershire 86, *88*, 89
Hawkins, G. 145
Hildebrandt, Johann Lukas von 104, *105*
Hoetger, Bernhard 195, *198*
Hofmann, Julius *144*
Home House, London 120, *120*
Hopper, Thomas 145, *146*, *147*
Horta, Victor *184*, 185-86
Hôtel André, Paris *142-43*
Hôtel Binet, Tours *50-51*
Hôtel d'Artois (Hôtel de Bourgogne), Paris 46, *46*
Hotel Danieli, Venice 59
Hôtel de Beauvais, Paris 82, *83*
Hôtel de Béhague, Paris *163*, 166
Hôtel de Ville, Nancy *80*
Hôtel du Maréchal de Tallard, Paris 82
Hôtel Mezzara, Paris 191, *191*

IG Farben company headquarters *194*, 195
Institut du Monde Arabe, Paris 216, *216*

Jantar Mantar observatory, Jaipur 27, *28*
Jones, Inigo 86, 119
Jordan Staircase, Winter Palace, St Petersburg 114, *116-17*

Kircher, Athanasius *28*
Klerk, Michel de 195, *198*
Knole, Sevenoaks 86, *87*
Kramer, P. L. 195, *198*

Lami, Eugène *134*
Lamour, Jean *80*
Lausitzer Seenland 224, *226-27*
Le Bon Marché, Paris 174, *174*
Le Brun, Charles *78-79*, 82, 86, 166
Le Corbusier 16, 31, 37, 186, 208, *209*, *210-11*, 224
Lello & Irmão bookshop, Oporto *142*
LeRoy, Mervyn *30*
Les Granges-Cathus, château of, Talmont-Saint-Hilaire *66*, 66
Library of Congress, Washington, DC *171*
Liman, Karel *157*, *158*, 159
Lloyds Building, London 213, *213*
Louvet, Albert *188-89*, 191
Louvre, Paris 24, 46, 138; glass pyramid 216, *217*
Lutyens, Edwin 22, *22*

McKim, Mead & White 174, *174*
Maison de la Reine Berthe, Chartres *52*
Marchi, Virgilio *198*
Matadero Madrid 229, *230-31*
Mathey, Jean-Baptiste *96-97*, 99
Medenine, Ksar of *21*
Mej, J. M. van der *195*, 198
Michelangelo 12, 21, 44, 45, *45*, *74-75*, 76, 192
Midland Grand Hotel, London 177, *180-81*
'Million Dollar Staircase', Capitol Building, Albany 167, *167*
Mirabell Palace, Salzburg 104, *105*
Momo, Giuseppe 205, *205*
Morlaix *52*, 52
Musée de l'Oeuvre Notre-Dame, Strasbourg *54*, 56
Musée Gustave Moreau, Paris *177*
Musée Horta, Brussels 186, *186*, *187*
Musée National des Travaux Publics, Paris *206-7*
Museum of Islamic Art, Doha *232-33*

Nash, Joseph *145*
Natural History Museum, London *172-73*, 178
Navy Staircase, Somerset House, London 120, *122*
Neumann, Johann Balthasar 22, 104, *104*, 111, *112*
Neuschwanstein *144*, 145
Nikolaievsky Palace, St Petersburg *154-55*
Nouvel, Jean 216, *216*
Nuremberg Castle, Sinnwell tower *52*

Odessa Steps 16, *18*, 27, 168
Olivetti showroom, Venice *31*, 32
Olympic *134*
Onyx Staircase, Hôtel de Paiva, Paris *162*, 163
Orbay, François d' *78-79*, 82, 166

Palace of the Marquesses, Fronteira *94*, 94
Palais de Justice, Paris *135*, 138
Palazzi dei Senatori, Rome *44*, 45, *45*
Palazzo Canossa, Mantua 89, *90-91*
Palazzo Contarini del Bovolo, Venice *58*, *58*, 229
Palazzo Dandolo, Venice *59*
Palazzo Reale, Naples *92*, 92
Panier Fleury inn, Tours *52*, *53*
Parent, Henri *142-43*, 166
Paris Opéra 22, *34*, 35, *128-29*, 131, *132-33*, *134*, 166, *178*
Passage Pommeray, Nantes *179*
Paxton, Sir Joseph *134*
Pei, I. M. 24, 216, *217*, *232-33*
Peles Castle, Romania *157*, *158*, *159*
Pennsylvania Station, New York 174, *174*

Penrhyn Castle, Caernarvonshire 145, *145*, *146*, *147*
Pera Palace Hotel *37*
Perrault, Dominique *182-83*, 216, 221
Perret, Auguste *206-7*
Peterhof Palace, St Petersburg 114, *115*
Petit Trianon, Versailles 103, *103*
Petra winery, Suvereto *220-21*, *221*
Piano, Renzo 212, *213*
Piazza del Campidoglio, Rome *44*, 45, *45*, 192
Pierrefonds, château of *151*, 163
Piranesi, Giovanni Battista 22, *22*, 31
Polaert, Joseph 168, *170*
Pompidou Centre, Paris 208, 212-13, *213*, 220
Porte Dauphine metro station, Paris *190*
Powis Castle 86, *86*
Pozzo, Andrea 111, *111*
Prémontré, abbey of, Aisne *100-1*, 102

Queen's Staircase, Versailles 82, *84-85*, 166
Quinta da Regaleira *13*

Rastrelli, Bartolomeo 114, *114*, 119
Rathaus, Bern *46*
Rezanov, Aleksandr *160-61*
Richardson, Henry Hobson *167*
Riedel, Edward *144*
Rizzio, Antonio *42-43*
Rogers, Richard 212, 213, *213*
Rua Regadas, Rio de Janeiro 221, *221*

Saint-Cloud, Parc de *124*, 124
Salle des Gens d'Armes, Conciergerie, Paris *150*, 151
Salles, Adolphe *176*
Salvador Dalí Museum *26*
Samarra, Great Mosque of 27, *28*
Samyn, Philippe 229, *235*, *236-37*
San Francisco Museum of Modern Art 220, *220*
Sansovino, Jacopo *42-43*, 45
Sanssouci, palace of, Potsdam 123, *125*
Scala Regia, Vatican 92-93, *93*
Scarpa, Carlo 22, *31*, 32
Scheepvaarthuis, Amsterdam 195, *198*
Schloss Augustusburg, Brühl 104, 111, *112-13*
Schloss Bruchsal, Baden-Württemberg 104, *104*, *106-9*, 111
Schloss Herrenchiemsee, Bavaria 166, *166*
Scott, Sir George Gilbert 135, 151, 166, 177, *180-81*
Seaton Deleval Hall, Northumberland 120, *121*
Selarón, Jorge 221, *221*
Sigiriya, fortress of *25*
Siloé, Diego de *23*
Sommerfeld House, Berlin *199*, 201
Spanish Steps, Rome 21, 124, 192
Stackenschneider, Andrei *154-55*
Stasov, Vassili P. 114, *149*
State Law Library of Iowa, Des Moines *177*

Tassel family house, Brussels *184*, 185-86
Tatlin, Vladimir *198*, 198
Taut, Bruno 208, *208*
Thornhill, Sir James 86, *89*
Tiepolo, Giambattista 22, 111, *112*
Torralva, Diogo de 56
Tour Jean sans Peur, Paris 46, *46*, *47*
Tribunal de Commerce, Paris 152, *156*
Troja Palace, Prague *96-97*, 99
Tsarskoye Selo 114, *118*, 119, *119*, *149*, 177
Tuileries, Paris 76, *138*, *139*, *178*

Ulberger, Hans Thomann *54*, 56

Van Horn, Erica *37*
Vatican Museums, Rome 16, 205, *205*
Verney, Ralph 123, *123*
Vernon, Thomas 86, 89
Verrio, Antonio 86, *86*
Versailles, château of 138, *141*
Villa Achilleion, Corfu *178*
Villa Farnese, Caprarola 76, *77*
Villa Lecchi, Montirone *110*, 111
Villa Malaparte, Capri 16, *18*, *19*
Villa Savoye, Poissy 208, *209*
Viollet-le-Duc, Eugène 22, 41, 138, *138*, *139*, 151, *151*, 163, 178
Vitebsky railway station, St Petersburg *202-3*
Vittorio Emanuele II, monument to, Rome 167, *169*
Vladimir Palace, St Petersburg *160-61*
Voth, Hannsjörg 27, *28*

Warsberg, Alexander von *178*
Weinert, Albert *171*
Wells Cathedral 24, *24*
Weymouth, Yann *26*
Woman's Magazine Building, University City, Missouri *142*
Wright, Frank Lloyd 24, 201, 212, *212*
Würzburg Residenz 22, 111, *112*